Fanatical Schemes

Fanatical Schemes

Proslavery Rhetoric and the Tragedy of Consensus

Patricia Roberts-Miller

THE UNIVERSITY OF ALABAMA PRESS
Tuscaloosa

Typeface: Caslon

∞

The paper on which this book is printed meets the minimum requirements of American National Standard for Information Sciences-Permanence of Paper for Printed Library Materials, ANSI Z39.48-1984.

Paperback edition/2010 ISBN: 978-0-8173-5653-8
Electronic edition/2010 ISBN: 978-0-8173-8125-7

A previous edition of this book has been catalogued by the Library of Congress.

Library of Congress Cataloging-in-Publication Data
Roberts-Miller, Patricia, 1959–
Fanatical schemes : proslavery rhetoric and the tragedy of consensus / Patricia Roberts-Miller.
p. cm.
Includes bibliographical references and index.
ISBN 978-0-8173-1642-6 (cloth : alk. paper) — ISBN 978-0-8173-8125-7 (electronic)
1. Slavery—United States—Justification—History—19th century. 2. Slavery—Political aspects—United States—History—19th century. 3. Consensus (Social sciences)—United States—History—19th century. 4. Rhetoric—Political aspects—United States—History—19th century. 5. Fanaticism—United States—History—19th century. 6. Politicians—United States—History—19th century. 7. Antislavery movements—United States—History—19th century. 8. Abolitionists—United States—Political activity—History—19th century. 9. United States—Politics and government—1829–1837. 10. United States—Politics and government—1837–1841. I. Title.
E449.R635 2009
973.7'1—dc22

2008029613

If there is no struggle there is no progress. Those who profess to favor freedom, and yet depreciate agitation, are men who want crops without plowing up the ground. They want rain without thunder and lightning. They want the ocean without the awful roar of its many waters. This struggle may be a moral one; or it may be a physical one; or it may be both moral and physical; but it must be a struggle. Power concedes nothing without a demand. It never did and it never will.

—Frederick Douglass

We cannot be expected to march and have our heads broken in order to say to whites: come on, you're nice guys. For you are not nice guys. We have found you out.

—Stokely Carmichael

Contents

Acknowledgments

Ah, come on, you ain't got nuthin' to do but count it off.

—Chester Burnett

This project has been very difficult, and its completion has only been accomplished because of help given along the way. I am grateful to The University of Alabama Press for support throughout the process, especially from the two outside readers. My colleagues Erin Boade, Eric Dieter, Zachary Dobbins, Douglas Eskew, Janice Fernheimer, Sylvia Gale, Jacqueline Henkel, Rodney Herring, Mark Longaker, Judith Rosenberg, Sara Sliter-Hays, and Jeff Walker have read and usefully criticized large portions of the manuscript. Erin Boade also copyedited the penultimate version. My department chairs, Lester Faigley, Linda Ferreira-Buckley, and John Ruskiewicsz, have been tremendously supportive, tireless at getting leaves, grants, and resources for the Faculty in Rhetoric and Writing. Janet Atwill, Jacqueline Bacon, Gregory Clark, Mike Bernard-Donals, Sally Greene, Susan Jarratt, Steve Mailloux, and Pat Okker have read sections, asked hard questions, and been encouraging at just the right moments. Coleman Hutchison, Lisa Moore, and Michael Winship have helped me with obscure points of nineteenth-century culture and publishing. Janet Davis and Todd Onderdonk pointed me toward useful texts on masculinity, and Eric Mallin and David Read helped me think through Shakespearean hyperbole. Timothy Lincoln answered questions about the history of American Protestantism and slavery, sending me references, and explaining terms. Ann Fabian, William Freehling, and Matthew Mason graciously answered time-consuming email queries from a complete stranger. While all of the reference librarians at the University of Texas are extraordinary, and have been tireless in helping me find sources, I am especially indebted to Lindsey Schell. The College of Liberal Arts has twice given me a Dean's Fellowship, enabling me to start this project in the fall of 2001 and finish it in the fall of 2007. The Big XII Fellowship allowed me to travel to the University of Missouri to research Missouri legislation, and the dean's office has been generous with providing funds for a research assistant. Arnold Cantu has spent far more time checking quotes than he was paid for; his diligence and intelligence have saved me from much embarrassment. Kirsten Holliday and Rodney Herring's last-minute help with panics and crises was much appreciated. I am grateful to Peter Caster, Evelyn Westbrook, and Laura Wilder for drawing my attention to the conflict between my rosy view of agonism and the historical record of debate over slavery. I am particularly grateful to the University of Texas Cooperative Society for a generous subvention grant.

I have benefited to an extraordinary degree from the mailing lists of H-Slavery, H-Rhetor, Rhetoricians for Peace, and the Society of Early Americanists; I cannot imagine what it must have been like to have had to work without instantaneous access to that kind of expertise. I am deeply obliged to Michigan State University for its support of H-Net; it has changed the nature of academic communication in invaluable ways. My research at the State Historical Society of Missouri was greatly assisted by Kimberly Harper and Gary Kremer. I am also thankful for comments on a talk given at the University of Missouri; the English department there was tremendously supportive when I was a faculty member, and I am still benefiting from their professionalism, intelligence, and kindness. Mary Teague's assistance has been directly and indirectly helpful in too many ways to list. Jacob and Jim Roberts-Miller have been loving and tolerant, even when the papers and books spilled far past my desk (and even past the study). My dogs have been helpfully attentive as I talked through the argument (my cats, as much as I love them, have not). Unhappily, Chester Burnette died as I was working on this project, so I have had to complete it without his considerable assistance.

Portions of this project have been published in "Agonism, Wrangling, and John Quincy Adams" (*Rhetoric Review*) and "Robert Montgomery Bird and the Rhetoric of the Improbable Cause" and "John Quincy Adams' *Amistad* Argument: The Problem of Outrage; Or, the Constraints of Decorum" (*Rhetoric Society Quarterly*). I am indebted to the editors of those journals for permission to use that material in this book.

Finally, Eric Dieter's last-minute compilation of an intelligent and helpful index contributed significantly to the project.

Introduction

"Industrious in scattering the seeds of insurrection"

> A society reveals its deepest anxieties when it responds hysterically to a harmless attack.
>
> —William Freehling

In late July 1835, the New York–based American Anti-Slavery Society (AAS) mailed, or, more accurately, tried to mail, the first number of a new publication, *Human Rights,* to citizens in South Carolina. The pamphlets were never delivered. Seized in the Charleston post office by the postmaster, they were destroyed by a self-appointed vigilante group. There was a flurry of correspondence among the Charleston postmaster (Alfred Huger), the postmaster of New York City (Samuel Gouverneur), John Calhoun (then senator for South Carolina and a presidential hopeful), and the U.S. postmaster (Amos Kendall). There were alarmist articles in newspapers, meetings of Vigilance groups, and, in the next congressional and Senate session, multiple proposals for censoring the mails. That same session was the beginning of the infamous "gag" rule (discussed in chapter 6), a response to James Henry Hammond's and John Calhoun's insistence that the House and the Senate not simply table, but explicitly reject, all abolitionist petitions. Rioting, much of it anti-abolitionist, peaked in the mid-1830s (Grimsted 4), with anti-abolitionist mobs "clustered in the years 1834–38" (Grimsted x, see also Richards, *Gentlemen of Property and Standing*). And 1835 was the beginning of a mid-decade peak in publication of extended defenses of slavery.

Many scholars assume a causal relationship between the mailing of the pamphlets and the increased rhetorical and political bellicosity of anti-abolitionism. They tend to describe, not a targeted mailing to South Carolina, but a "flood" of pamphlets sent through the federal mails to people throughout the South: "bags loaded with papers such as *Human Rights* and Arthur Tappan's *Emancipator* were mailed to community leaders everywhere" (Fuller, *Morality and the Mail* 39–40).[1] Larry Tise refers to "the drenching of every part of the nation with propagandistic literature bearing the name of the American Anti-Slavery Society" (275). Bertram Wyatt-Brown refers to the actions of "other cities of the South [. . .] as the antislavery material arrived in their midst" ("The Abolitionists' Postal Campaign" 230).

Proslavery rhetors made this accusation at the time. The August 8, 1835, article, "Destestable Villainy" (reprinted from the *National Intelligencer*), begins: "Concurrent testimony, from different parts of the southern states, satisfy us that the miserable fanatics, few in number, as they are, who manufacture the abolition journals, have flooded the mails with them, to the just exasperation of the south, and to the great peril of the whole slave population of their country" (402).

This mailing is often supposed to have provoked increased conflict over slavery. Wyatt-Brown argues that "the postal effort and the uproar it caused quickened the anti-slavery pace and aroused the nation to the slavery question" ("The Abolitionists' Postal Campaign" 227–28). Susan Wyly-Jones says, "Like Jefferson's famed firebell in the night, the abolitionists' postal campaign of 1835 re-ignited the slavery controversy in the South" (290). Mitchell Snay claims that the postal campaign was "an assault on the morality of slavery [that] created a political crisis that drew Southern ministers into sectional politics" (19–20). According to Drew Gilpin Faust, "*Only when northern abolitionists in 1835 inundated the South with antislavery propaganda sent through the federal mails* did southerners respond in force, exhibiting a new vehemence in their defenses of their way of life. The attack from the North made southern mobilization an immediate necessity, and latent proslavery feeling was quickly translated into action" ("Introduction," *The Ideology of Slavery*, 9–10, emphasis added).[2] Faust's military metaphors make proslavery rhetors the defenders: abolitionists (from the North) attacked first, and the South needed to reply—they were, so to speak, forced into it. This version rationalizes (in several senses of the word) the political and rhetorical practices of proslavery rhetors. If abolitionists were "flooding" the slave states with material that inspired slave insurrection, it was rational for proslavery politicians to try to stop them. Faust's version typifies a line of argument scholars have traced back to Reconstruction, which is often part of a larger attempt to present the Civil War as having been forced on a chivalric and unwilling South by fanatical and irrational northerners.[3] This way of describing cause and effect in antebellum slavery politics makes (or implies) three claims: first, that the AAS flooded the South; second, that proslavery rhetors *then* became more aggressive; third, the first *caused* the second. If that narrative claim is correct, then, if the AAS hadn't sent the pamphlets, proslavery rhetors would not have become more aggressive.

Sometimes, the pamphlet mailing is not the specific act that catalyzed proslavery agitation, but it typifies a shift in abolitionist strategy toward a more aggressive ("strident" is a common word) rhetoric. Fehrenbacher refers to the "vast quantities of abolitionist literature" sent through the mails (Fehrenbacher 74) and argues that southern members of Congress "were already fed up to the point of fury with the badgering of anti-slavery petitioners" (74), thereby making them willing to support more extreme measures against abolitionists such as the gag rule (discussed later). As Eric Foner and Olivia Mahoney say, "The abolitionist movement that arose in the 1830s differed profoundly from its genteel, conserving predecessor [. . .] They directed strident, explosive language against slavery and slaveholders" (42–43). In the words of Richard Ellis and Aaron Wildavsky, "The abolitionists' role in the coming of the Civil War was that of a spark and bellows—igniting and then fanning a dynamic process of cultural escalation. While slavery gave the South a distinctive pattern of social relations, this had divisive implications for the Union *only* when abolitionist agitation forced the slaveholders to defend their practices" (116). Margaret Coit goes so far as to argue that, had the abolitionists not been so offensive, slavers might have emancipated their slaves without a war: "The abolitionists' own zeal ripped the problem right out of practical politics [. . .] It is undoubtedly true that Southerners talked about emancipating more than they emancipated. Yet so eminent a historian as Albert J. Beveridge has argued that, had it not been for the anger and fear aroused by the abolitionist onslaught, 'it is not altogether impossible that there would have been no war, and that slavery would in time have given way to the pressure of economic forces'" (296). Yet, Coit's next sentence says that Allan Nevins, "conceding that abolition, gradual or otherwise, was impossible in the Deep South" (296), blamed abolitionists for making it impossible in the Border States.

Coit's use of Nevins and Beveridge is puzzling. Beveridge's blame of abolitionists presumes that abolition might have happened in the South, whereas Nevins says that was impossible. Coit's use of the word "conceding" suggests she agrees with Nevins. By her argument, abolitionists are to blame for making something impossible that she thinks was impossible anyway. William Hobby, in his 1835 attack on abolitionists, says that slavery will probably never be abolished in the South; two sentences later, he says that the "imprudent course" of abolitionists "will tend rather to retard than advance the object at which they run" (30), thereby making the same argument as Coit.

Abolitionists were similarly blamed (I will argue scapegoated) at the time, as when the 1836 anonymous *Remarks on "Slavery by William E. Channing"* insists that defenders of slavery "have said little, and done less, until abolitionists created such a ferment in the South" (7). In his 1836 proslavery book, William Drayton explains the necessity of repressive slave codes: "We may be permitted to remark, that, but for the intrusive and intriguing interference of pragmatical fanatics, such precautionary enactments would never have been necessary. When such foes are abroad, industrious in scattering the seeds of insurrection, it becomes necessary to close every avenue by which they may operate upon the slaves" (68, see also "Abolitionism" 286, *Baltimore Literary and Religious Magazine,* September 1835). And in regard to the laws about slaves generally, which Drayton grants are "rigid," "When abolitionists make the application of these laws necessary, it is they, and they alone, who are the authors of the restraint placed upon the slaves" (72). Even fellow antislavery rhetors sometimes condemned abolitionists for the vehemence of their rhetoric. William Ellery Channing, in his 1835 *Slavery,* bemoans the culture's inability to discuss slavery, and he blames abolitionists for that inability: "There was never such an obligation to discuss slavery as at this moment, when recent events have done much to unsettle and obscure men's minds in regard to it. This result is to be ascribed in part to the injudicious vehemence of those who have taken into their hands the cause of the slave" (iv). Benjamin Ober's antislavery *Slavery a Lecture Delivered before the Lyceum* condemns abolitionist petitions for the gag rule: "Abolitionists have driven our Senators to a violation of the Constitution" (24). Tise refers to "the crisis that abolitionism created for America in the 1830s and beyond" (260), rather than the crisis slavery created, and he regularly refers to "the crisis of 1835" (see especially 291, 308).[4]

This understanding of the origins of the Civil War typifies one conventional way of understanding conflict, exemplified in the saying that "it takes two to make a fight." According to this view, if there is a violent conflict, it is the result of at least two parties who have refused to compromise, so both parties are to be equally blamed for their intransigence. This sense of a public sphere of compromise and concession is often connected to privileging civility, a powerful, but very vague, concept. "Civility" tends to be defined through negation: it is not emotional or abusive; it does not involve personal attack; it is not offensive. Offending one's audience, it is argued, alienates them, and persuading them necessitates moving them to one's side, not pushing them away: "When the ebullitions of passion burst in peevish crimination of the audience themselves, when a speaker sallies forth, armed with insult and outrage for his instruments of persuasion, you may be assured, that this Quixotism of rhetoric must eventually terminate like all other modern knight errantry and that the fury must always be succeeded by the impotence of the passions" (John Quincy Adams, *Lectures on Rhetoric and Oratory* I: 365). The hope is that a rhetor can find a civil way to make any argument—including dissent. Yet, dissent is inherently disruptive and necessarily upsetting to anyone who identifies with the current system. Hence, as various scholars have noted, privileging discourse that is not upsetting necessarily furthers the disenfranchisement of the already marginalized (see especially Darsey).

This notion of the power of civil discourse is wonderfully optimistic, as it suggests that there might be a discursive solution to every conflict, that violence happens when only rhetors make their arguments badly. In its most extreme form, this theory of rhetoric makes an absolute distinction between the content and form of an argument, so that abolitionists were not wrong to want slavery abolished, but in how they made their case. Had abolitionists tempered their rhetoric, had they not armed themselves with insult and outrage, they might have persuaded slavers to free their slaves; this was the argument that Channing made in *Slavery*. Condemning abolitionists for their vehemence, Channing promises a different kind of criticism of slavery: "I propose to show that slavery is a great wrong, but I do not intend to pass sentence on the character of the slave-holder" (16). As demonstrated by the reaction to Channing's book, his readers did not see the distinction; his book was characterized as "pouring oil on a conflagration" (Austin 11), and, despite Channing's claims to reject violence, "it is insurrection that he preaches" (Austin 14). The 1836 anonymous response insists that, although Channing may not have intended "to excite the blacks to take 'vengeance,' and free themselves," "no work has appeared (so far as I know) so well adapted to produce precisely that attempt" (11). Proslavery readers saw no difference between his rhetoric and the rhetoric of the people he condemned.

As will be discussed in chapter 7, the issue of civil language came up continually in regard to the antislavery petitions presented to Congress. When a representative from Massachusetts, George Briggs, pointed out that the language was respectful, James Bouldin (from Virginia) responded that the very nature of the petitions—their criticizing slave owners—meant that they were inherently disrespectful (49). If "civility" and "respectful" are seen as synonymous, there is no such thing as civil criticism of people higher in any hierarchy. Criticism is only permitted when it is superiors criticizing inferiors, which means, necessarily, the hierarchy itself cannot be criticized; substantive social change is impossible. It is equally impossible if "civility" is defined by the reaction of the audience—that is, if it is assumed that "uncivil" and "upsetting" are synonymous, then civil disagreement on central issues is impossible. Under such limitations, rhetoric cannot solve political conflicts.

I do not mean to suggest that the narrative of proslavery forces provoked by abolitionists is obviously false; it is clear that anti-abolitionism significantly increased in the mid-1830s, and proslavery rhetors certainly blamed abolitionists for their actions. Although I will argue that seeing abolitionist rhetorical stridency as the catalyst for anti-abolitionism is a mistake, it occurs naturally from the sensible project of looking at what participants in a debate say about their motives in getting uglier. In addition, our habit of imagining issues as binaries, coupled with how difficult it is to articulate the relation between rhetoric and reality, means that there is a tendency to assume that discourse either really is or really is not about the purported issue. To suggest that proslavery rhetors were not really provoked by abolitionist rhetoric seems to imply that that rhetoric did not really bother them, and that's an absurd proposition. People argued about slavery because they genuinely (and vehemently) disagreed about it.

They did not, however, disagree about it in a way that is usefully captured by a pro- or anti-slavery binary, or even continuum. A traditional way for rhetoricians to describe points of agreement is in terms of the "stases": event, definition, causation (including consequences), evaluation, policy. All the participants in the debate agreed that the slave states had slavery, and they almost all shared the same explicit definition of slavery (although I will argue that proslavery rhetors appealed to contradictory implicit definitions). They disagreed as to what caused slavery (with most proslavery rhetors putting the causation in England, and antislavery rhetors putting it in the act of failing to free one's slaves). In the 1830s they came to disagree profoundly about its consequences (with as much disagreement among proslavery rhetors as between defenders and attackers of slavery). The most severe disagreement was, as it often is, about policy. Some argued that the United States should increase its commitment to, and protection of, the practices specific to slavery as practiced in what are commonly called "the slave states"; some argued for transporting African Americans to other areas (colonization); some argued for gradual emancipation with compensation to owners; some argued for immediate, but voluntary, noncompensated emancipation (the position taken by the most famous "abolitionists" of this time); a very small number argued for forced, immediate noncompensated emancipation (the view conventionally attributed to Garrison and Tappan, but not what they were advocating at this time); some argued against the expansion of slavery (called "abolitionist" or "restrictionist" by proslavery rhetors, but what would eventually be called the "free-soil" position). I will use "proslavery" to mean the first category, but that does not mean that the other positions are antislavery. Some colonizationists and gradualists wrote defenses of slavery, and they (as well as some free-soil advocates) could be vehemently critical of abolitionists; Channing, for instance, was anti-abolitionist and antislavery. So, my use of the terms "anti-abolitionist" and "proslavery" should not be taken to mean that I think those terms are synonymous, nor that the categories of pro- and anti-slavery exhaust the political landscape. If the question is whether abolitionists provoked proslavery politics, then it seems most sensible to focus on anti-abolitionist and proslavery rhetors: the important data is when (and how) proslavery rhetors began actively defending slavery.

In this next section, I will cursorily review the publication of such texts between 1800 and 1840. George Orwell, in *Homage to Catalonia,* tells readers that they may well wish to skip a chapter that goes into more detail than most people might find interesting. I should preface this section the same way; it is primarily of interest to scholars of the slavery debate, and most readers may want to skip to the conclusion of this section. This cursory history shows three things. First, proslavery rhetors began publishing defenses of slavery long before abolitionists are supposed to have become more strident. Second, those rhetors blamed criticism of slavery for slave insurrection; as early as 1802, proslavery rhetors called for silencing dissent on the expansion of slavery. They did not object to vehement criticism of slavery: they objected to any criticism at all. Third, defenses of slavery were disproportionately published in South Carolina or by South Carolina authors.[5]

From 1800 until 1822, proslavery texts were primarily concerned with slavery in the West Indies and the slave trade, or a controversy instigated by hostile responses to Charles Ingersoll's *Inchiquin.* An exception to that trend is John Drayton's *A View of South Carolina* (1802), a description of South Carolina's geography, population, and so on. After insisting that slavers' rights in slaves are "indefeasible," Drayton protests that "*those of the Northern States*" have been agitating:[6] "Notwithstanding, however, this barrier, which has been, and will continue to be placed against any innovations respecting this property; many are the efforts, which are not only tried individually, but collectively, to weaken this right of property, and, ultimately, to change its very nature" (144). Southerners might as well "request them to dismiss their horses from the plough; as for us to dismiss these people from labour. For in both cases, lands of excellent quality, which are cultivated by them, would revert to a state of nature" (144, an argument expanded on 146–47). The swamps, he says, cannot be worked by whites because "these situations are particularly unhealthy, and unsuitable to the constitution of white persons; whilst that of a negro, is perfectly adapted to its cultivation [. . .] He can work for hours in mud and water (which he is obliged to do in the rice culture, in ditching and draining,) without injury to himself; whilst to a white this kind of labour would be almost certain death" (147). This argument was commonly made, especially by South Carolinians, as when Edwin Holland says, "The climate [. . .] is inconceivably hostile to the white constitution, and the experience of more than a century has shown that this opinion is a correct one [. . .] In breathing this pestilential atmosphere, the negro, whose constitution seems better adapted to it, subjects himself to the introduction of none of those fatal distempers, to which the white man falls a sure and certain victim" (430). Whereas these conditions are deadly to whites, slaves thrive in them: "the same season of the year which carries on its wings the blessings of health to the negro, gives an early warning to the Planter to quit his estates and flee from the destruction that awaits him" (44). Frederick Dalcho similarly insists on the swamps' healthfulness for African Americans: "The constitutions of the Negroes appear to be perfectly adapted to the climate; and they thrive and increase, under our burning sun and humid atmosphere" (7).[7]

What makes this such a puzzling, albeit common, assertion is that it was false—the mortality rates for slaves in swamp areas were "appallingly high," and the contrast between mortality rates in healthier climates and those in tidewater were "dramatic and disturbing" (Young, "Ideology and Death," 681, 689). After noting that extreme mortality rates in the Upper South and Southwest were not the norm, William Scarborough says, "Beyond question, however, the slave mortality rate was highest along the Georgia-South Carolina rice coast" (186). Scarborough cites William Dusinberre, who "has estimated that two-thirds of the slaves on nineteenth-century rice plantations died before they reached the age of fifteen" (186). Unless we are to believe that slavers didn't notice their slaves were dying, or didn't notice a difference between plantations in the tidewater and other regions (a hypothesis not confirmed by slavers' diaries), we have to infer that Drayton, Holland, and the others who made that argument were grounding their argument on an assertion that was false, that the rhetors knew to be false, and that a large number of their readers would know to be false.

Drayton's text contains another puzzle that reappears throughout proslavery writings: having argued that slavery is absolutely necessary given the conditions of the state, he expresses a vague hope that it will disappear on its own. After complaining about societies that send "addresses to the different branches of our legislature" with "modes, which they deem most eligible for us to pursue in this respect; and all this for the good of the whole family of mankind!" Drayton concludes that, "This much, however, may be said; that, if it be an evil, it will sooner, or later, effect its own cure" (145). One point he makes that is not present in later proslavery writings is that slaves have economic autonomy: slaves "are encouraged to plant for their own emolument [. . .] and are protected in the property which they thus acquire" (145, something that would change over time; see also his description of their having their dances, holidays, and so on, 148).

In 1810, Charles Ingersoll published *Inchiquin, the Jesuit's Letters, during a Late Residence in the United States of America,* a fictional account of a Jesuit's travels (and travails) mostly in the Washington, D.C., area. While critical of slavery, the book is largely a paean to the wonders of a republican system. As had happened during the Revolution, British authors attacked the self-congratulation, pointing out that it was odd for slave owners to boast about their republican principles. Timothy Dwight (*Remarks on the Review,* 1815), "An American" (*Letter to the Edinburgh Reviewers,* 1819), and Robert Walsh (*An Appeal from the Judgments of Great Britain,* 1819) responded. Dwight and Walsh defended the claims of the United States to republicanism despite the presence of slavery; they insisted that it had been imposed on the United States by Britain, was worse in British colonies, and was compatible with democracy. While Dwight explicitly says that slavery will disappear, Walsh (who praises the free states for having abolished slavery) typifies a fatalist view of southern slavery (what is generally called "the necessary evil" topos):[8]

> We do not deny, in America, that great abuses and evils accompany our negro slavery. The plurality of the leading men of the southern states, are so well aware of its pestilent genius, that they would be glad to see it abolished, if this were feasible with benefit to the slaves, and without inflicting on the country, injury of such magnitude as no community has ever voluntarily incurred. While a really practicable plan of abolition remains undiscovered, or undetermined; and

while the general conduct of the Americans is such only as necessarily results from their situation, they are not to be arraigned for this institution. (421)[9]

Walsh's 1819 *Free Remarks on the Spirit of the Federal Constitution, the Practice of the Federal Government, and the Obligations of the Union, Respecting the Exclusion of Slavery from the Territories and New States* compares slavery to leprosy (14, see also 9) and calls the establishment of slavery in Missouri "a catastrophe" (103), so he was what proslavery rhetors would call "restrictionist" (keep slavery restricted, and it may die out on its own). Of these texts, only "An American's Letter" actively defends slavery, relying on several of the themes that would be important later: that England had imposed slavery on the United States, scripture does not condemn slavery (citing the "Bishop," presumably Thomas Newton, on this point), slaves are happy (see especially 53), abolition may result in "the extirpation of the very people who are the object of all this indignant eloquence" (54), and southerners are just as virtuous and wise as northerners (45). Slavers have their hearts in the right place, and would do the right thing if they could, but "no scheme of emancipation can, in the present state of things be realized" (40); they are forced by circumstances to remain slave owners, another line of argument common in 1830s proslavery rhetoric. This rhetor says that slavers will free slaves voluntarily "whenever the white people are convinced that the scheme is practicable" (29) and, in answer to the question of whether slavery can be abolished, answers, "I have already said that it cannot. I repeat that it cannot" (59), so, again, he argues it will die out *and* it is eternal.

Edwin Holland's 1822 *A Refutation of the Calumnies Circulated against the Southern and Western States* primarily concerns the Denmark Vesey rebellion. Some antislavery rhetors had, apparently, said that Vesey's plot showed the danger of slavery: insurrection (and it may be that argument that Holland means by "calumnies"). Several South Carolinians responded with explanations of the rebellion that tried to refute any inherent connection between slavery and slave insurrection: in addition to the Holland text, there was Henry de Saussure's 1822 *A Series of Numbers Addressed to the Public* (which complains about northern papers "throwing around fire brands," 3), the anonymously written *Negro Plot,* which blames the insurrection on the Congressional Debate over Missouri (as would the South Carolinian Whitemarsh Seabrook, see especially *Essay* 24), Thomas Pinckney's 1823 *Reflections, Occasioned by the Late Disturbances in Charleston,* which also blames "The indiscreet zeal in favor of universal liberty, expressed by many of our fellow-citizens in the States north and east of Maryland" (6) and "incendiary publications"(8). It is also interesting, in light of the historical context for their texts, that the authors insist that emancipation is impossible because it *would* result in insurrection (de Saussure 18–19), an argument that fails to take into account that they are writing these accounts *because* insurrection just happened in Charleston.

Richard Furman's *Exposition of the Views of the Baptists* and Frederick Dalcho's *Practical Considerations Founded on the Scriptures* were both published in 1823 by the Charleston publisher A. E. Miller. Furman's *Exposition* blamed the Vesey insurrection on "sentiments, very unfriendly to the principle and practice of holding slaves" have "been advanced among us, tending in their nature, *directly* to disturb the domestic peace of the State, to produce insubordination and rebellion among the slaves, and *indirectly,* to deprive the slaves of religious privileges, by awakening in the minds of their masters a fear, that acquaintance with the Scriptures" (7). Miller also published the nullifier Whitemarsh Seabrook's *A Concise View of the Critical Situation, and Future Prospects of the Slave-holding States* in 1825 which poses the rhetorical question: "Did not the unreflecting zeal of the North and East, and the injudicious speeches on the Missouri question animate Vesey in his hellish efforts?" (14). Seabrook is insistent that no discussion of slavery is possible: "no subject, in which the question of slavery may be directly or incidentally introduced, can be canvassed, without the most malevolent and serious excitement" (12). These texts call for the end of discussion of slavery (even in Congress), and condemn abolitionists (using the same clichés that would figure later) several years before abolition is supposed to have become more strident. Their explicit grievance was that people were criticizing slavery, but their persistent problem was that such criticism was aired every time proslavery rhetors tried to change Federal policy to expand slavery.

The South Carolina publisher, D&J Faust, published *Two Essays* by Thomas Cooper, president of South Carolina College, and a "leading Columbia nullifier" (Freehling, *Prelude*) in 1826. The only 1827 proslavery text I have found, and its inclusion is problematic, is Thomas Jones's *An Address on the Progress of Manufactures* (Philadelphia, not a defense of slavery, per se, as much as an argument that manufacturing and slavery are not incompatible). The seventeen-year-old Charles Cotesworth Pinckney's *An Address Delivered in Charleston, before the Agricultural Society of South Carolina* was published by A. E. Miller in 1829. In that year, the first edition of Zephaniah Kingsley's pro-amalgamation *A Treatise on the Patriarchal, or*

Co-operative System of Society as It Exists in Some Governments, and Colonies in America, and in the United States, under the Name of Slavery, with Its Necessity and Advantages was self-published, which was intended "to destroy the prejudice existing against slavery" (4).[10]

In 1830, Seth Lewis produced two texts, *A Review of Abolitionism, or, The Question of Slavery, as It Exists in the United States* and *Abolition Reviewed, Being a Further Exposure of the False, and Most Dangerous and Mischevious [sic] Doctrines and* Proceedings *of the Abolitionists,* both in Louisiana. That same year, John Steele's *The Substance of an Address* was published in Ohio, a text on the edge of defending slavery (it could be categorized as a defense or not). His argument is that owning slaves should not preclude membership in the church, and he argues that slave owning and church membership are compatible—that scripture does not forbid slave owning. In that sense, it is a defense of slavery. But, he does condemn slavery: his second sentence is, "Few, we apprehend, are to be found in the present day who will candidly justify the abstract principle of involuntary slavery" (3). Steele's address is unusual in several other ways. It begins by saying that there is disagreement regarding the origins of slavery, and goes on to note the disagreement regarding whether all or some servants were freed in Jubilee. Steele does not rely on Noah's curse, and he goes into more detail on the New Testament discussions of servitude than any other proslavery rhetor I've read.

I find no record of separately published American proslavery texts in 1831, although that was the year that the Virginian legislature debated whether or not to debate emancipation. That debate led to two defenses of slavery: "Appomattox's" attack on Virginians who petitioned the state legislature to abolish slavery; and Thomas Dew's *Review of the Debate in the Virginia Legislature,* both published by T. W. White in 1832. (*Review of the Debate* was also published in 1833 in Washington; Dew, although not a South Carolinian, was an advocate of the nullifying theory of the Constitution.) Appomattox says that, if there is another Turner-like rebellion, "It will be owing, not to the hallucinations or imposture of another Nat Turner, nor to the seditious practices of negro preachers, nor to the machinations of the organized convention of free blacks in Philadelphia, nor to the dissemination of the incendiary writings of *The Liberator,* or *The African Sentinel,* or *The Genius of Universal Emancipation*—but to measures proposed, and to speeches delivered, in our own legislature, published and disseminated by our own public journals" (21). Like the South Carolina rhetors who condemned the congressional debate, Appomattox is arguing that even legislatures should not be allowed to criticize slavery. It is not, then, that strident abolitionism is a problem—*any* abolitionism is a problem (see also 29).[11]

In 1833, John Vaughan's *Negro Slavery* was self-published in Philadelphia (it had been published in the *American Quarterly Review*). In 1834, A. E. Miller published the nullifier Alexander Sims's *A View of Slavery*, which was, Sims says, a response to an article the previous summer in the New York *Christian Advocate and Journal*, which "denounced Slavery as immoral and anti-Christian, and by consequence, inferred the immorality and impiety of all slave-holders" ("Preface"). Sims says, "The fact is, the slave-holders have been too long silent under the sneers and fanatic ebullitions of ignorant and wicked pretenders to philanthropy" ("Preface"). Simon Clough's *A Candid Appeal to the Citizens of the United States* (which predicted a civil war over slavery if abolitionists persist, see especially 38) was published in New York.[12] Another New York publisher put out Richard Colfax's *Evidence against the Views of the Abolitionists: Consisting of Physical and Moral Proofs, of the Natural Inferiority of the Negroes*, which relied heavily on the polygenist Samuel von Soemmering (who would be translated and published in 1837) and other racialist scientists in order to argue that "it is more an act of piety to keep [African Americans] in slavery" (38). Colfax uses the term "amalgamationist" (usually in italics) interchangeably with abolitionist, only acknowledging toward the end of his pamphlet that this is an inference on his part, that abolitionists do not explicitly advocate amalgamation. He infers that they are amalgamationist because freedom and citizenship for African Americans is impossible given the inherent conditions of the African race (or species, his other term), so abolitionists must intend to intermingle; he dismisses the counterexamples of various scientists and philosophers of African descent, demonstrating a tight logical circle that would typify racist discourse for the next hundred and ninety years.

That same year, the nullifier Whitemarsh Seabrook self-published *An Appeal to the People of the Northern and Eastern States, on the Subject of Negro Slavery in South Carolina*, and his *An Essay on the Management of Slaves and Especially, on Their Religious Instruction: Read before the Agricultucal [sic] Society of St. John's Colleton* was published by A. E. Miller. Although the latter text is primarily advice on slave mastering, it does defend slavery, and does insist that slaves are happy until abolitionists get to them (with the help of strong drink, see especially 6–8).

In 1835, there were fifteen extended arguments for slavery, six of which were published in South Carolina. Edward Laurens, a notorious fire-eater (see Freehling, *Prelude* 335), had his *A Letter to the Honorable Whitemarsh*

B. Seabrook published in Charleston by the Observer Office Press; it was a defense of Laurens's position on the antiliteracy law passed in the state's 1834–35 legislative session (which had not been extreme enough for him or Seabrook). *Vindex on the Liability of the Abolitionists to Criminal Punishment* was published by A. E. Miller (Tise says that the author was the nullifier William Rice, 320). Richard Yeadon (the unionist publisher of the *Charleston Courier*) wrote *The Amenability of Northern Incendiaries as Well to Southern as to Northern Laws.* The anonymous *An Appeal to the People of the United States* (attributed to Thomas Hayden), and the nullifier Edmund Bellinger's *Speech on the Subject of Slavery* were also published in South Carolina. The nullifier William Harper gave a speech that inspired Daniel Whitaker's *Reflections on Domestic Slavery,* published in Charleston.

Anti-abolitionism outside of South Carolina was also active. Simeon Doggett's *Two Discourses on the Subject of Slavery,* which argued that slavery was evil, but emancipation worse (see especially 17), was published in Boston. T. R. Sullivan's *Letters against the Immediate Abolition of Slavery, Addressed to the Free Blacks of the Non-Slave-Holding States* was published in Boston. Both Doggett and Sullivan are difficult to characterize. Vehemently opposed to immediate abolition (and, in Doggett's case, advocating colonization), neither piece spends any time defending slavery, arguing that it will go away by itself. Sullivan's pamphlet (originally published in the Whig paper, the *Boston Courier*) ends with: "What then is to be done with the great moral evil of slavery, (for so all intelligent slave owners consider it to be?) NOTHING, NOTHING, *out of slave-holding states.* He, by whose providence slavery was permitted to begin in this land three hundred years ago, will, in his own due time end it, if such be his will. His instruments will be those who have inherited slaves, and those who dwell in slave-holding countries" (45). James Trecothick Austin's *Remarks on Dr. Channing's "Slavery"* was published in Boston. This hostile response to Channing begins by insisting "That Domestic Slavery is a deep and dreadful evil" is a truism that "has been so long acknowledged and so recently repeated that it needs no additional enforcement" (5), yet it also argues that slave owners think slavery is right. Joseph Williams's *An Oration Delivered before the Citizens of the Town of New-Bedford* was published in Massachusetts; Thomas Man, a professor of eloquence, self-published *A Picture of Woonsocket* in Rhode Island; Charles Farley's *A Discourse Delivered in the Unitarian Church* was published in Virginia; William Hobby's *Remarks upon Slavery* was published in Georgia; and the anonymous *Big-*

otry Exposed and William Thomas's *The Enemies of the Constitution Discovered* were published in New York.

In 1836, while the number of texts increases, South Carolina is still heavily represented. George McDuffie, the nullifier governor of South Carolina, had his *The Communication from His Excellency, Governor McDuffie [. . .] Relative to Incendiary Abolitionists* published in Maryland. Henry Laurens Pinckney, another nullifier, had weakened his political base in South Carolina by his pragmatic response to the abolitionist petitions, and he had been excoriated in the press (see Niven, *John C. Calhoun* 205). He published *An Address to the Electors of Charleston District, South Carolina* in defense of his actions and *Remarks of the Hon. H. L. Pinckney, of South Carolina, on the Resolution Offered by Him Relative to the Abolition of Slavery: Delivered in the House of Representatives, Monday, February 8, 1836* (the speech he had made in Congress). Duff Green, John Calhoun's loyal publisher of the *U.S. Telegraph,* published John Calhoun's *Speech concerning the Abolition Petitions* and the nullifier William Harper's *Anniversary Oration.* William Drayton, a Unionist (but who advocated what seems to me a nullifier interpretation of the Constitution, see especially 208–10) had *The South Vindicated from the Treason and Fanaticism of Northern Abolitionists* published in Philadelphia. Theophilus Fisk's *The Bulwark of Freedom* was published in Charleston. The governor of Georgia had published his *Communication from the Governor of Georgia, Relative to the Abolitionists of the South,* and James Smylie's *A Review of a Letter from the Presbytery of Chillicothe* was published in Mississippi. The anonymous *Remarks on "Slavery by William E. Channing"* was published in Boston. The Jacksonian publishers Blair & Rives published Martin Van Buren's rebuttal of charges of being antislavery, *Opinions of Martin Van Buren, Vice President of the United States, upon the Powers and Duties of Congress in Reference to the Abolition of Slavery Either in the Slaveholding States or in the District of Columbia.* James Kirk Paulding's *Slavery in the United States* was published in New York, and George Baxter's *An Essay on the Abolition of Slavery* was published in Virginia (by T. W. White), and Charles Hodge's *View of the Subject of Slavery* was published in Pittsburgh. George Freeman's two-part sermon, *The Rights and Duties of Slaveholders,* was published in North Carolina.

In 1837, although the number of texts dropped significantly, a number of ministers entered the fray, such as Samuel Dunwoody (*A Sermon,* Columbia, SC), Gabriel Caper (*Bondage, a Moral Institution,* Georgia), George Blagden (*The Principles on which a Preacher of the Gospel Should Condemn Sin,* Boston), and Rufus Bailey. Also published in New York was D. Lambert's *An Essay in Defence of Slave Holding.* Bailey, who had been living in the South since 1828, had two pieces published, both in New York, *The Family Preacher* and *The Issue, Presented in a Series of Letters on Slavery.* While on the edge of proslavery (see especially his twelfth letter, which is entitled "Grant that the slaves ought to be free"), Bailey has the standard defenses of slavery (such as that slaves are better off than free Africans, free African Americans, or the Irish), and condemnations of abolitionists (such as that they make things worse for slaves). D. J. Dowling, of Charleston, South Carolina, published the treatise *Natural History of the Negro Race,* which was a compilation of various European ethnologists' writings.

Theodore Clapp (*Slavery: A Sermon,* New Orleans), Edward Kingsford (*The Claims of Abolitionism upon the Church of Christ,* Pennsylvania), and Joshua Wilson (*Relation and Duties of Servants and Masters,* Ohio) were ministers who published in 1838 concerning the relation of scripture and slavery. In 1838, the office of the *Union Herald* published the multiply authored *The Problem Solved.* W. W. Sleigh had his *Abolitionism Exposed!* published in Philadelphia, and the nullifier Robert Barnwell Rhett had his *Address to the People* self-published in Washington. The South Carolina author William Gilmore Simms had his *Slavery in America* published in Richmond, Virginia, by T. W. White, and William Harper's *Memoir on Slavery* was published in Charleston.

In 1839, Clay had another speech published (by the Whig publisher Gales and Seaton), and Edward Stanley (the Whig North Carolina representative) self-published one of his congressional speeches. Joseph Prince's *An Address* was published in Massachusetts, and J. Davenport's *A Chapter in the History of Abolitionism* was published in Syracuse. Francis Philpot's *Facts for White Americans with a Plain Hint for Dupes, and a Bone to Pick for White Nigger Demagogues and Amalgamation Abolitionists, including the Parentage, Brief Career, and Execution, of Amalgamation Abolitionism, Whose Funeral Sermon Was Preached at Washington on the 7th of February, 1839* was self-published in Philadelphia.

Although there are striking trends in the history of proslavery defenses, it is difficult to narrate the history of such defenses accurately, and especially difficult to use such a narration to infer cause and effect. On the one hand, it is clear that something happened in the mid-1830s to make proslavery rhetors want to publish defenses of slavery, particularly rhetors in (or politically allied with) South Carolina; South Carolina authors and publishers (especially A. E. Miller) are distinctly overrepresented.[13] On the other hand, there is little if any textual evidence to cast the American abolitionists like Garrison and Tappan, let alone the summer of 1835 mailings, as the catalyst. Only William Drayton's book quotes from those pamphlets, although Hobby claims to have seen them (and then returned them to the person from whom they were borrowed). Many of the texts explicitly refer to other threats: *southern* antislavery (the impetus for the Dew, Appomattox, and the Georgia governor's "Communication"), insurrection plots (Dew, again, and the various texts written after the Vesey rebellion), British antislavery (Harper only discusses English abolitionists, and Simms was explicitly writing in response to Harriet Martineau), and resistance to the expansion of slavery (as in the post–Missouri Compromise texts).

It is equally striking how little proslavery rhetoric changed before and after 1831. Although there were more texts published, and they tended to be longer, most of the topoi used by later proslavery rhetors are also used by John Drayton (1802), St. George Tucker (1803), Edwin Holland (1822), and Thomas Pinckney (1822). Slaves are happy, slavery was forced on the South by the British, it will go away by itself *and* it will remain eternally, slavery is universal, slaves thrive under slavery (especially in regions deadly to whites), and so on.[14] The scriptural argument varied little from the one made in Thomas Newton's 1754 *A Dissertation on the Prophecies.* The most significant constant between earlier and later proslavery texts is the explanation of insurrections: proslavery rhetors insisted, as early as 1802, that they were caused by criticism of slavery. Proslavery rhetors did not object to the stridency with which abolitionists criticized slavery; they objected to the criticism, and they wanted it silenced.

I "Slavery shall not be discussed"

The Political Power of the Irrational Rhetor

> If we are to take it seriously, hyperbole must elicit some sort of belief or assent: that is to say that it demands of us the simultaneous perception of its literal falsehood and its imaginative relevance.
>
> —Janet Adelman

Slavery was an economic and political institution. It was also, however, a rhetorical construct. People argued for and against it, and, in the course of doing so, implicitly or explicitly defined it. For instance, while various speakers in the gag rule debate disagreed about the identity, motives, and rights of abolitionists, every speaker agreed that "the South" was proslavery. This fantastical synecdoche was created rhetorically, by the constant and cunning equation of "southern" identity with the experience and politics of a minority of people living south of the Mason-Dixon, by the erasure from public argument the fact that slavery had only recently been abolished in states like Pennsylvania and New York, and by the removal from public discourse of the views of slaves and southern abolitionists. Slavery was a real, physical fact, but also an imagined institution. Proslavery rhetors like William Gilmore Simms relied on abstractions about slavery: "the slave," "the woman," "the man," and "the slaveowner." These abstractions had more rhetorical power in the discourse than specifics, so the fact that some slave owners abused and exploited their slaves did not, for these rhetors, change the essentially loving and patriarchal nature of slavery. In proslavery ideology, the data exemplifies, but neither tests nor supports, the propositions; if a specific piece of data contradicts the abstraction, it is discarded in favor of another, or in favor of the abstraction.

Rhetoric affected the policy of slavery in yet another way. If the country were to have found a political solution to slavery, it would have had to have been done rhetorically: rhetors would have had to argue for abolition, or against slavery, persuasively. That persuasion might have been what abolitionists termed "moral suasion"—many abolitionists appear to have hoped that pamphlets and newspapers directed at slave owners would persuade them to free their slaves individually. Much rhetoric (meaning simply suasory discourse) was directed at political institutions; by the 1830s, many abolitionists were working to cease the expansion of slavery (which all agreed would ring the death knell for southern slavery), some were trying to persuade state legislatures to consider abolition, and some were trying to persuade Congress to abolish slavery in the District of Columbia. Thus, one might, as have many scholars, look at how abolitionists tried to persuade their readers and listeners. One might, as have fewer scholars, look at how proslavery rhetors argued for slavery. Of more interest to me is a question about public discourse itself: how did contemporary rules about political discussion (what are generally called rhetorical theories) constrain the political outcome?[1]

Rhetoric, the Greek word for "oratory," has long claimed to be the art of public discourse. Teachers of rhetoric claimed that it benefited not only the individual who could use rhetorical skill to achieve political power (the argument made by Callicles in Plato's dialogue *Gorgias*), but also to deliberate on issues of common concern. Aristotle and Cicero each present rhetoric as a skill of thinking from both sides; this ability to see the issue from a different side not only enables one to refute opposition arguments, but is actually a useful way for individuals and communities to come to decisions. By presenting arguments effectively, well-trained rhetors put forward the best possible case for the various options available to a community. By listening critically, audiences well trained in rhetoric discern the best option. For people like Aristotle and Cicero, rhetoric is not merely a way to dress up one's argument to make it more attractive, but an art of community deliberation on matters about which certainty is not possible.

Rhetoric is not always deliberation; the word "rhetoric" has a nasty connotation largely because people have experienced public discourse as manipulative, dishonest, and self-serving, what Wayne Booth calls "rhetrickery." But, as people ranging from Aristotle to Arendt have argued, the study of public discourse, or rhetoric, can also be used to disable rhetrickery. Rhetoric can be manipulative, and rhetoric can enable people to perceive the manipulation; rhetoric can be used to slide bad policies past an unquestioning public, and it can be the art of coming to better policies; rhetoric can be used for scapegoating marginalized groups, and rhetoric can be the way that those groups make themselves heard. Obviously, public discourse can be all sorts of different things; the question for people interested in representative government is what approach to public discourse promotes inclusive deliberation.

Perhaps the most popular model for public discourse now is the "marketplace of ideas," so that public discourse about products for sale is no different from that concerning policies to be considered. Both are considered products that someone presents as attractively as possible to as many markets as possible. Voters are seen as nothing more than consumers of ideologies (and products are often marketed as ideologies—ranging from clothes that look expensive to "fair trade" coffee). I've written elsewhere about the problems with this model (see *Deliberate Conflict* 98–120), but the main point here is that this model does not require, and sometimes does not even permit, deliberation. Consumers/voters choose from among the products made available to them by people who are precommitted (generally for economic reasons) to one product/political agenda. Like picking products off a store shelf, voters pick prepackaged politicians or ideologies.

Deliberation, or argumentation, is not the same as public argument. If one accepts the definition of "argument" as an assertion with a related reason, then much public discourse is not argument at all. Argumentation and deliberation are further distinguished by being dialectical—under those conditions, an argument is engaged with the discourse prior to it, and influences the outcome. Public discourse may involve arguments (assertions with reasons) that have nothing to do with the outcome because it is predetermined (as in the factionalized media of the 1830s or the 1835 Democratic convention), or shifting of positions may be forbidden (either explicitly, as in the kind of internal censorship in which the antebellum media engaged, or through cultural control, as in the equation of changing positions with unmanly vacillating) or the discourse can simply be the expression of opinion with no acknowledgment of other positions (as in the gag rule debate, in which many rhetors asserted unanimity in the face of disagreement). In contrast, while people participating in deliberation come to it with preferences, ideologies, and assumptions, these are not predetermined and protected commitments; they can be examined, modified, or abandoned. In the ideal speech situation (ideal not simply in the sense of being perfect, but also in the sense of being possible only as an idea and not a reality), individuals are willing to examine, explain, modify, and even abandon any belief disputed by another individual in the discussion. The more that interlocutors are willing to behave that way, the more that it is what some rhetoricians call "good faith" argumentation, Jürgen Habermas calls "communicative action," argumentation theorists like Frans Van Eemeren and Rob Grootendorst call "critical discussion," and political theorists call deliberation.

Deliberation is different from bargaining (which is not the same as "bad faith" argumentation). In a bargaining situation, everyone is presumed to have immovable precommitments, and no one is really trying to change anyone's beliefs; people are simply trying to get the best outcome for themselves and/or their constituents. One achieves the most advantageous outcome through making more credible threats and offering more attractive incentives. Because the outcomes depend on threats and incentives, those who enter the discourse with more power can get the most favorable outcome; it is about neither fairness nor reasons.

What is generally called "epideictic" rhetoric among historians of rhetoric is not really any of the above, although closest to the marketplace model. The term that Aristotle used for the "praise or blame" speeches common in Athenian culture (such as a funeral oration), this kind of public discourse functions rhetorically in very complicated ways. A funeral oration like Pericles's famous one during the plague that hit Athens in the early years of the Peloponnesian Wars does not look like what Aristotle calls a "deliberative" oration: it was not given in the Assembly, and Pericles was not advocating or attacking a proposal on which the listeners were about to vote (in fact, a large part of the speech is directed to women, who had no vote). But, he was clearly trying to persuade listeners to remain committed to a war that had already lasted longer than people had predicted and cost far more in lives and property than had been expected. Confirming Athenians' sense of themselves as intellectual and brave, Pericles was trying to connect that sense of self to the course of action he was advocating: do not lose hope. Epideictic does not look like deliberative rhetoric because it appears to be entirely based on confirming what people already believe; it appears to tell them nothing new. But, as in the case of Pericles's speech, it does have an impact with policy consequences.

In addition, it does persuade listeners about the speaker. Kenneth Greenberg (using the term "oration" for what rhetoricians call epideictic) says that both orations and speeches can be used to persuade or malign, but they are different in impact: "What was different about an oration was that one of its primary functions was to inspire rhetoric, even awe for the speaker in the minds of the listeners. An oration, in contrast to a speech, was the public display of a superior personality [. . .] The subject matter was sometimes even secondary to this display" (*Masters and Statesmen* 12). A rousing Fourth of July oration may not change our understanding of the United States, democracy, or the Declaration of Independence, but it may not be intended to do so. It may be intended to persuade us that the speaker is patriotic.

Among political theorists, some version of what is often called "deliberative democracy" seems to be the most popular; among historians of rhetoric (the academic discipline that traditionally taught the skills determined necessary for participation in public discourse), some version of classical (or, more accurately, neoclassical) rhetoric is favored. Neoclassical rhetoric, with its emphasis on debating both sides of a question on issues of civic concern, is liberalizing, not in the sense that it makes people vote for the "liberal" side on political issues, but in the sense that it challenges authoritarianism, questions tradition, and makes a merit of diversity (for more on this argument, see Sloane, especially 47). Advocates of agonistic rhetoric presume that deliberation among people with different perspectives enables both individuals and communities to understand a topic more thoroughly and to envision a wider variety of options. At least as far back as Aristotle, one of the arguments for rhetoric is that it enables a community or individual to come to better decisions.

Rhetoric is supposed to lead to better decisions in four ways. First, as a mental faculty, it (like studying dialectic) enables individuals to understand a situation better. Crassus, one of the ideal rhetors in Cicero's dialogue *De Oratore,* says that he argues both sides of a case before coming to a decision himself. Second, a public speaker who has considered the other side is better prepared to argue against the opposition, so there is a pragmatic benefit to a prospective rhetor. Third, even if people have no intention of becoming a public speaker, as citizens they will have to judge the rhetoric of others. If rhetoric teaches people to assess arguments critically, then the public is less likely to be persuaded by bad arguments. Finally, as Socrates argued in his defense speech, the unpopular opinions are often right; his voicing what no one wanted to hear was, he insisted, a service which should be rewarded by the state. This sense of public argument as agon—as a contest among points of view—presumes that difference of opinion is a fact to be celebrated, rather than bemoaned. Consequently, silencing points of view, even (perhaps especially) unpopular ones, hurts the community because it necessarily limits the deliberation.

According to scholars of pedagogy, neoclassical and agonistic rhetoric dominated antebellum pedagogy (Clark and Halloran, Johnson, Kitzhaber, T. Miller), especially in the slave states (Christophersen, Westbrook).[2] Newspapers were filled with long arguments that people read; congressional debates were lively and substantive; arguing politics was considered appropriate; student debating societies were popular; speeches were reprinted and discussed. Yet, when it came to debating slavery, there was a sense that the topic should be sacrosanct—the major thrust of proslavery rhetors was to get a strong (and, ironically enough, federal) support of slavery without a thorough discussion of its merits. As James Trecothick

Austin argues (in his 1835 attack on William Channing's *Slavery*): "The slave region has pronounced its decision. Within its borders Slavery shall not be discussed. The people do not mean by any affectation of liberality to endanger their social system. They believe it is right, but they mean to maintain it wrong or right. Upon this subject they ask no instruction and they permit none. They have taken their stand. They refute all argument by silencing it, and to all force they are prepared for resistance" (31). This passage is largely accurate, except for its equation of proslavery and "the slave region." Proslavery rhetors and the major slave-state politicians were agreed that slavery could not be criticized, and critics of slavery within the South faced boycott, shunning, and personal violence. The problem is that proslavery rhetors and politicians wanted federal policy changed (as in opening up new areas to slavery, censoring the mail, gagging abolitionists, strengthening the kidnapping of African Americans in free states), which necessitated congressional, and therefore public, policy making. They wanted to change public policy regarding slavery without public debate. They wanted decision making without deliberation.

And they did meet with considerable success, at least insofar as federal policy was predominantly proslavery, from the renegotiation of the Northwest Ordinance to the admission of California (see Richards, *Slave Power;* Ransom; Fehrenbacher). The dominance of proslavery policies was epitomized in the term "doughfaces" (for more on this term, and its meaning through the antebellum era, see Hans Sperber and James Tidwell). First coined in 1819 by John Randolph of Virginia, the term referred to northern politicians whose very face was as pliable as dough—they could be made to do whatever proslavery politicians desired.

Proslavery rhetors were less successful at silencing criticism of slavery outside of the slave South, but still troublingly effective. This success was generally achieved through calling for, threatening, enacting, or justifying individual and mob violence against any person accused of being an abolitionist, an insurrectionist, an amalgamationist, or disloyal. Like most inflammatory words ("communist," "terrorist," "liberal"), these terms were defined through negation (it means nothing more specific than "a position other than the rhetor's"), so that the charge could be disastrously and effectively applied with little actual argument. The most tragic of such smears was the accusation of insurrectionist, as it led to so many lynchings, but the equation of insurrectionist and abolitionist was nearly as tragic.

This reliance on violence is striking not merely in its oft-remarked hypocrisy—that people would behave in such an ungentlemanly manner to preserve their reputations as gentlemen—but in the antidemocratic nature of the major project of proslavery political action: that the interests of citizenry are best served by silence on what is universally acknowledged to be one of the most important issues. I do not mean the premise by which people like Daniel Webster operated (that preserving the Union necessitated keeping slavery off the table because the topic threatened party union and inevitably resulted in threats of secession), but slavery proponents' premise that it was not in their best interest to permit a thorough discussion of slavery.

To some extent, the reason for that political project appears obvious: the three-fifths compromise, made during the 1787 Constitutional Convention. That compromise granted that slaves, although they received no vote, would count toward population for purposes of determining federal taxation, congressional representation, and electoral college votes.[3] This compromise gave states with large slave populations a substantial political advantage; an immediate result was that a presidential aspirant depended upon slave-state electoral college votes. Mason Lowance says that, in 1856, a "free" state congressman represented 91,958 free white men and women, and a slave-state congressman represented 68,725 white men and women (xxxi).[4] Proslavery control of the presidency meant control of the Supreme Court, as well as the developing spoils system. Overrepresentation in Congress meant control of key congressional chairmanships, as well as the ability to prevent anyone hostile to slavery (such as John Quincy Adams) from attaining chairmanships that seniority and experience would suggest they merited.

While the unanimity of southerners on the issue of slavery is easily overstated, "aware that the slavery issue stirred up more excitement and enthusiasm than any other," southern politicians could and did rely on the bogeyman of abolitionism to rouse voters from the 1830s until and even through the war (W. Cooper, *The South and the Politics of Slavery* 68). Even many southerners who disliked slavery rallied behind the institution when it seemed attacked because "in its political form slavery became the cherished, visible symbol of independence, honor, and equality precisely because it embraced the most fundamental values of southern white society held in common by slaveowner and nonslaveowner alike" (W. Cooper, *The South and the Politics of Slavery* xiv). Jeffrey Young puts it even more vehemently: "Focusing political debate on sectional concerns about slavery, the planters transformed the threat against the institution of human bondage into an attack on the values of the entire South" (*Domesticating Slavery* 233). Southern culture was slave culture; southern society, as its rhetors reiterated, was slave society, and any attack on the latter was an attack on the former: "The identification of slavery as central to the preservation of Southern 'liberty' marked the intellectual as well as political hegemony of slave owners throughout the antebellum South" (Kolchin 182).

From the above argument, it may seem that the obvious explanation for rhetoric's failure is that it was up against an insuperable institutional advantage; the economic and political power of slave owners was simply overwhelming. But, that explanation just slightly evades the point. That the institution of slavery was powerful is not an explanation as to why its defenders would work as hard as they did to silence dissent. The underlying assumption is that slavers who worked to silence dissent simply pursued their own economic and political self-interest by preventing serious discussion of the demerits of slavery—that their self-interest was so completely on the side of maintaining slavery that rhetoric had no chance. The problem with this explanation is that it is not clear that proslavery politicians really were pursuing policies in the best interest of slave owners, let alone in the interests of the substantial number of nonslaveholding citizens in the slave states. This somewhat paradoxical point has to be explained in some detail.

If the pluralist vision of public discourse is correct, then the slavers striving for univocality was imprudent, not only for slaves, but for themselves. History suggests that slavers *were* imprudent, that a more thorough discussion of slavery that might have caused them to think about the long term would have been in their best interest for several reasons.

As is commonly observed by historians, proslavery rhetors' willingness to sacrifice basic rights (such as freedom of speech and the right to petition) in order to keep slavery secure from criticism alienated a significant number of citizens in non-slave states who had no interest in abolition. As Michael Schudson says about the gag rule, "The effort to deny [the right of petition] helped mobilize antislavery support; not a few people felt more strongly about preserving political liberties of citizens than about freeing slaves from bondage" (108, see also W. L. Miller 120–21; Ashworth 143; Russell 66; Parsons 248). Indeed, the gag rule so benefited abolitionists that Garrison's biographer maintains he worried about the "surge of new friends" it created (Mayer 217–18). Northern politicians' deference to slavers' policies, violence against their elected representatives, the gag rule, the congressional acceptance of the Lecompton constitution, the Fugitive Slave Act, the *Dred Scott* decision, and various other enactments of slavers' agenda created a large block of people who were convinced of a slave power conspiracy and committed to restricting it from new territories: "Nothing alarmed Northerners more than the aggressive demand of southern politicians that the western territories be opened to slavery; nothing lent more credence to the abolitionist charge that a Slave Power conspired to make slavery a national institution" (Stampp, *The Imperiled Union* 234). Abolitionists did not create this constituency; slavers did.

That is, Lincoln was not elected by abolitionists, but by people who firmly believed in the existence of a "Slave Power" determined to rob citizens of non-slave states of their rights. That this sort of person was opposed to the "slave power" does not mean they were pro-abolitionist (they sometimes accepted the notion that abolition within the slave states was unnecesary), and they were frequently openly racist. In fact, their opposition to slavery was typically grounded in a desire not to live with African Americans, whether slave or free. Members of this group believed, not without reason, that slave states were intent on spreading slavery to every state in the Union, and that the "slaveocracy" was willing to violate the rights of free whites—such as the right to petition—in order to preserve and promote slavery. While some scholars (e.g., David Davis, *Paranoid Style*) have minimized this perception, characterizing it as one example of the "paranoid style" (to be discussed later), the sense of a proslavery conspiracy was created by such proslavery federal policies as the gag rule, the Fugitive Slave Act, and, finally, the *Dred Scott* decision.

Further, the war cost far more than abolition would have. According to the economist Claudia Goldin, the most expensive form of emancipation considered at the time, one that included compensation for slave owners and "colonization" of the freed slaves, would have cost 3.634 billion dollars (in 1860 money, 85). Emancipation that involved neither colonization nor compensation to slave owners would have "cost" slave owners 2.5 billion dollars (not in the sense that they would have had to pay that amount, but that their ownership of slaves as capital and source of labor would have disappeared). According to Goldin and Frank Lewis, the total direct cost to the North of the Civil War was 3.4 billion dollars; the cost to the slave states was, at the very least, 2.89 billion dollars in direct costs ("direct" meaning not including the 2.5-billion-dollar "cost" of losing slave capital and labor).

The numbers may be even higher; Robert Fogel says that the war "devastated the southern economy, with per capita output in 1870 reduced to two-thirds of the 1860 level" (67). Such numbers point to the problem with the narrative that the Civil War was not about slavery, but economics. Had people been thinking in economic terms, they would have opted for abolition. On the contrary, they were making distinctly *un*economic decisions. It is interesting that some proslavery rhetors insisted that slavery was an uneconomic decision; this trend continued in the pro-South historiography. Coit, for instance, says, "All knew that the slave system, as such, gave 'the least possible return for the greatest possible expense'" (295). But, the commitment to slavery was neither rationally debated nor rationally examined; as Goldin and Lewis conclude, people at the time miscalculated the relative costs and benefits because they were not thinking very clearly or carefully about the various options. Public discourse, which should serve the role of opening up options, functioned to shut them down.

Fighting a war at that moment was neither politically astute nor necessary; slave states still had control of the federal government. The admission of California as a "free" state is sometimes described as having upset the "balance" in the Senate, but both Leonard Richards (*Slave Power* and *The California Gold Rush*) and Roger Ransom (*Conflict and Compromise*) point out the significant problems of reading Californian politicians this way (as they were notorious doughfaces).

It is common to assert that the election of Lincoln triggered secession, but that is far from accurate. Stripped of slavers' hyperbole about Lincoln's plans, Lincoln's election meant nothing for the institution of slavery or its expansion. He did not have control of Congress, and without that control, would have been able to do very little, especially considering the flimsiness of his electoral support and the weakness of the presidency. He clearly and repeatedly stated that he would not interfere with slavery in any existing slave state. His political mandate (which, as mentioned above, he would have had difficulty pursuing) was to limit the expansion of slavery. The slave states could easily have waited out Lincoln's term; all they had lost (for the first time since the election of John Quincy Adams) was control of the presidency. And they had almost certainly only lost it temporarily, due to their having split the Democratic vote. Ratner and Teeter explain the situation:

> The Democrats convened in Charleston, South Carolina, in late April. Stephen A. Douglas was the choice of northern Democrats, but the strong southern wing of the party rejected the Illinois senator who had opposed and ultimately defeated the Lecompton Constitution. The delegates endured fifty-seven ballots without determining a nominee. They reassembled in Baltimore some six weeks later. When many delegates from the Lower South walked out of that assembly, Douglas's supporters secured the nomination for him. Ten days later southern dissidents held their own convention in Baltimore and chose John C. Breckinridge of Kentucky as their candidate.
>
> Abraham Lincoln's opponents, by fighting among themselves

and by dividing, had assured his election in the fall. (*Fanatics and Fire Eaters* 86)

A politically savvy assessment of the situation would have suggested that proslavery politicians simply needed to wait out Lincoln's presidency, which, given the precarious nature of his electoral victory and his lack of control of Congress, would have been fairly easy. But, instead of looking carefully at what had been gained or lost (let alone why), proslavery rhetors exaggerated Lincoln's position regarding abolition, as well as the political and economic significance of his election. Thus, it was not his election that triggered secession, but their histrionic response.

Convinced by thirty years of alarmist rhetoric to the effect that the election of someone like Lincoln was unspeakably disastrous for slave states, several states appointed or elected secession commissioners immediately after Lincoln's election. Their charge was to go to other slave states attempting (in many cases, successfully) to persuade those states to call special secession conventions (the outcome of which was determined by the nature of the call). The secession commissioners' arguments, as Charles Dew's analysis shows, were extremely similar: "Over and over again they called up three stark images that, taken together, constituted the white South's worst nightmare" (C. Dew 77). The first was racial equality: "The commissioners insisted almost to a man that Republican ascendancy in Washington placed white supremacy in the South in mortal peril" (77). The second was race war (78), and "the third prospect in the commissioners' doomsday vision was, in many ways, the most dire: racial amalgamation" (79). Secession, they argued, was the only possible response.

Because these arguments were continually raised concerning abolition, they will be discussed in much greater length throughout this book. At this point, however, it is useful to note that they were obviously false. Slavery was abolished in the United States without the race war that slavers feared, without even undermining (in the long term) whites' political power or the oppression of African Americans. This is not just hindsight; that outcome could have been predicted at the time. Something continuously, probably deliberately, obfuscated throughout the slavery wrangle was that people knew what happened when slavery was abolished in a state because it had already been done several times. All the colonies had had slavery; slavery was abolished in New York and Pennsylvania without insurrection during the very era that bellicose proslavery rhetors were insisting that abolition necessarily meant race war. The British colonies, similarly, had abolished slavery successfully. The great hobgoblins of abolition—insurrection and amalgamation—were more common in slave states and rare in free states; an open debate that reminded the public of that fact would have been helpful.

There is an interesting irony in the race war topos: that it may have contributed to the defeat of the Confederate States of America (CSA). One of the puzzles of the Civil War is the collapse of morale in the CSA military. As long as the Confederate forces were doing well in the field, and as long as the hope for a short war could be maintained, Confederate soldiers had high morale. In 1864, when things began to go badly (but certainly not so badly that victory was impossible), desertions abounded. According to Richard Beringer and colleagues, "during the fall and early winter of 1864–65 desertion took away 40 percent of the Confederate armies east of the Mississippi" (197). By 1865, desertions in Lee's army in one month amounted to 8 percent (McPherson 820–21). One of the possible explanations for those desertions was that soldiers believed the race war rhetoric, and they believed that they were leaving their families in danger. Reid Mitchell points out that, as the war went on, the women and children left behind "faced the increasingly sure destruction of slavery; they lived among a people newly free. Southern institutions of racial oppression had been rationalized as a necessary means to control a savage people. Now the men who had been the force behind the laws of slave control were in the army, far from their homes" (Mitchell 128–29, see also Glatthaar 144–46). For thirty years, proslavery rhetors had been asserting that uncontrolled slaves would rape and murder; public policy had been grounded in that premise, and the war was supposed to be necessary because of it. It is reasonable to infer that soldiers fighting for the Confederacy believed that assertion.

Kenneth Stampp has suggested that morale may have collapsed because secession had been intended as a bargaining strategy, rather than an outcome sincerely desired (*Imperiled Union* 258–59). His argument is that proslavery politicians really wanted Republicans to agree to extend slavery into all territories below the parallel line of thirty-six degrees thirty minutes. When the Republicans refused (instead offering to support a constitutional amendment that the federal government would never abolish slavery in the current slave states), those who had made the threat had to make good on it. Some of the major figures at the time did say something along those lines, and one could argue that the degree of persuasion necessary to get the (sometimes more or less rigged) secession conventions to vote for secession suggests at least some ambivalence about secession. If many of those who favored secession did so as a bargaining chip, then, as Stampp says, "Those who had expected reunion through negotiation found themselves trapped in a war they had not anticipated, fighting for an independence they had never sought" (*Imperiled Union* 259). Stampp goes on to suggest that this ambivalence hindered their commitment to the war; "they may well have turned now unconsciously to reunion through defeat" (*Imperiled Union* 259). Stampp is clear that he is speculating, and it is highly speculative. For purposes of my argument, it does not matter whether Stampp is correct; what matters is that his argument is plausible, and, hence, represents a weakness in their position that proslavery politicians should have considered.

Similarly, it has been argued that the CSA lost the war due to the large, but politically silenced, antislavery contingent in the South. As Mitchell says, for the Confederate army, "far more so than in any other American war, the soldier in the field could not count on the unified support of the civilians back home" (125). According to Beringer and colleagues, "Guilt, from whatever sources, tormented enough consciences to influence collective behavior and provide a margin of shattered morale that led to Union victory" (163). It was not that such soldiers were so opposed to slavery that they refused to fight (although William Davis, in *Look Away,* argues that recruitment was a problem in the Confederacy from the beginning, see especially 226–40). But, it has been suggested that large numbers of southerners were ambivalent enough about the cause in the first place that they interpreted military setbacks as signs of God's displeasure (if that is correct, it means that they were not as persuaded by the scriptural argument as it might seem). Many southerners "came to believe that slavery should end and from that point they logically progressed to a sense of guilt over the war itself" (Beringer et al. 165).

One of many myths about the South that was created during the 1830s (and which continues) is that people in the slave states were unanimously proslavery—that "the South" and "proslavery" were synonymous. Granted, because proslavery rhetors were effective at creating a culture of legal and "extralegal" (i.e., mob violence) punishments for criticizing slavery, it is difficult to know how large that number was (for more on this see Degler, *The Other South,* and Ransom 143–44). Proslavery politicians did not succeed in exterminating southern antislavery sentiment, but they did succeed in making dangerous the voicing of such views (and, I will argue, the distinction between silencing and exterminating was lost on them, as it generally is in an authoritarian public sphere). Having more or less successfully muffled the antislavery contingent, slave-state politicians could not know how much support there really was for slavery. That is not a good situation in which to start a war.

The CSA's military success would have depended not only upon the sacrifices of nonslaveholding whites, but upon slaves themselves. Proslavery ideology could not permit open discussion of the loyalty or disloyalty of slaves (although both could be asserted, sometimes one after the other). Mitchell says "the ideological weakness and principal structural weakness was the fact that the Confederacy was created as a means to defend racial slavery," yet slaves' defense of the CSA was necessary for success (Boritt 124). Joseph Glatthaar points out that "Slaves who lacked opportunity to escape nonetheless found ways of contributing to Confederate defeat. At great peril to themselves, some slaves concealed, fed, and directed runaways or escaped Federal prisoners of war on the journey to freedom. Others sabotaged farm and labor equipment or assumed an uncooperative attitude with owners and overseers, to slow down work and promote widespread insecurity among whites at home" (145). If either of those explanations is even possible—if slaves and non-slaveholding whites were a sizable constituency who would not support the war—then southern politicians would have been wise to consider hostility to or ambivalence about secession. On purely pragmatic grounds, it would have been helpful to listen to dissenters enough to know how many there were, what their concerns were, and how they might react during a war.

It is easy for my point to be misunderstood. I am not arguing that secession was a bluff, the CSA was doomed to lose the war, or that it did so because of antislavery southerners. All that matters is that those outcomes and conditions were possible, because prudent policy makers should consider possible (not just wished-for) outcomes. But, those possibilities were not discussed, largely because the bellicose rhetoric and intimidating practices of proslavery rhetors successfully silenced the deliberation about slavery and abolition that slave states most needed. I am arguing that slavers' relentless efforts to suppress dissent may have caused them to overestimate their support in the South, exaggerate the negative consequences of abolition, overreact to Lincoln's election, and alienate huge numbers of northern voters who felt their own rights were threatened by slavers' political agenda. It is not that they silenced abolition, but that they did silence reasonable discussion of abolitionists' claims, the long-term prospects for the institution of slavery, and southern ambivalence about it, and silencing dissent hurt them.

From the 1787 Constitutional Convention up until the moment of secession, slavers had refused to deliberate about slavery, instead alternating between intimidating and bargaining. Secession had always been the trump card. Whatever their private conceptions—and whether proslavery rhetors sincerely believed that any concession regarding slavery was a step toward a race war—their short-term rhetorical success ensured that slavery could not be settled rhetorically. That is, the degree to which they succeeded in persuading people that the only two options were slave-state secession or federal deference to slavers' political hegemony was the degree to which they guaranteed the inevitability of war. If the 1860 secession threat was just another instance of that previously successful, and forty-year-old, bluff, then slavers were hoist by their own petard.

I am not suggesting that a more critical public sphere would have enabled slavers to see the injustice, hypocrisy, and irrationality of the slave economy, although that might have been nice. I am saying that it would have been in their best interest to engage in a *realpolitik* argument about the pragmatic long-term options available to the slave states. That was not what they did.

My suggestion of rational deliberation regarding slavery is hypothetical twice over. It is counterfactual to consider the outcome of a vigorous public discussion of slavery policy in antebellum America because it is counterfactual even to posit the possibility of the discussion itself—at least from the eighteen thirties onward. And so to return to the realm of the actual, the question is not whether slavers could have been persuaded to abandon slavery, but why nineteenth-century southern politicians were so determined to prevent the discussion at all costs. Why were they so hostile, not only to criticisms of slavery, but even to pragmatic discussions that might include acknowledging the sheer number of people who were critical of slavery?

One reason that proslavery rhetors gave for needing to silence critical discussion of slavery was that such discussion invariably provoked slave insurrection. For instance, *Negro Plot,* an "account" of the Vesey uprising published in 1822, asserts that the discussion of the "Missouri question" was "efficacious in producing both discontent and disillusion" (30). This line of argument does not hold proslavery rhetors responsible for the "Missouri question" (although it was only necessary because they wanted slavery allowed in Missouri); it blames the opponents for having resisted. There was not, and still is not, any reliable evidence that Nat Turner had read any abolitionist writings. It was simply conventional to blame insurrection (or insubordination) on abolitionists, so that the act of insurrection was, for many, all the evidence necessary of abolitionist infection. Many scholars accept the coerced confessions of participants in the Vesey rebellion who say Vesey had read the congressional debate over Missouri, but that, too, is deeply problematic.[5]

The "Report of the Joint Committee of Federal Relations" (*Communication from His Excellency, Governor McDuffie*) uses this consensus about the relation between abolition and insurrection to argue that free speech does not apply to abolitionists: "There is certainly some difference between the freedom of discussion, and the liberty to deluge a friendly and coterminus State with seditions and incendiary Tracts, Pamphlets, and Pictorial representations calculated to excite a portion of its population to revolt, rapine and bloodshed." The statement made by "Gentlemen of the South" at their July 20 meeting asserts that slaves read abolitionist pamphlets and therefore "concert schemes and conspiracies [. . .] which but for these publications they had never thought of" ("The Meeting Called by Gentlemen from the South" July 27 *U.S. Telegraph*). This is the argument explicitly made in an article in the *National Intelligencer* concerning a slave's attack on his mistress, entitled "The First Fruit":

> A circumstance of the most shocking character, and what was within a second of time of resulting in the perpetration of a most bloody tragedy, occurred in this city two nights ago, which viewing it as one of the effects of the fanatical spirits of the day, and one of the immediate fruits of the incendiary publications with which this city and the whole slave-holding portion of the country have been lately inundated, we have concluded it to be our duty to make public [. . . Mrs. Thornton was attacked] by a young negro man, her slave, which, from the expressions he used, was evidently induced by reading the inflammatory publications referred to above [. . .] During the whole time that he was endeavoring to force a second entrance into the house, he was venting the most ferocious threats, and uttering a tissue of jargon, much of which was a literal repetition of the language addressed to the negroes by the incendiary publications above referred to. (August 7, reprinted in the August 18, 1835, *Raleigh Register* and paraphrased in the August 8, 1835, *Niles' Register*).

According to the *Charleston Mercury*, among the resolutions of the citizens of Petersberg was "3. *Resolved.* That we shall repose no confidence in the good feelings of our fellow citizens of the North, however strongly and unequivocally expressed, if they confine their exertions in our behalf to mere declarations, as ineffic[i]ent as they are uncalled for; instead of arresting by prompt and vigorous acts the unhallowed proceedings of those unprincipled incendiaries, now engaged in organising amongst them, under the public eye, a system of insurrection, massacre and plunder, intended to be directed against the Southern States" (August 17, 1835). The August 23 *Raleigh Register* has a short article about a dentist who was circulating "seditious pamphlets." The article continues, "Another of these villains has been arrested in Caswell county, in this State. He was travelling on foot and stopped at the Blacksmith Shop of *Jas. Jeffreys,* Esq. He there exhibited one of his diabolical pamphlets, and after enlarging upon his plans and the extent of the combination of which he was a member, and the amount of means, physical and pecuniary at the command of his party, proposed to the colored blacksmiths to join in his project for the *immolation of the Whites*" (*Raleigh Register* August 23, 1835). The article mentions that he was later apprehended, and did not have any pamphlets on him; from this fact, rather than conclude that the story might have been false, the author infers that he had "gotten a hint from some quarter, which induced him to secrete or destroy the pamphlets, and a register of his recruits" (*Raleigh Register* August 23, 1835). When Harriet Martineau pointed out that it made no sense to blame Nat Turner on the abolitionist movement, as his rebellion predated abolition, William Gilmore Simms responded, it was not before the movement began, but "Before it was generally detected" (33).

The Petersberg Meeting of Citizens' second resolution refers to "the late attempts of the abolitionists inviting our slaves to insurrection and massacre" (*Charleston Mercury* August 17, 1835). Chapter 5 of Virgil Stewart's *The History of the Detection, Conviction, Life, and Designs of John A. Murel, the Great Western Land Pirate; Together with His System of Villany, and Plan of Exciting a Negro Rebellion* has John Murrell's (sometimes spelled Murel) explanation as to how he gets the slaves to murder their masters:

> We find the most vicious, and wicked disposed ones, on large farms, and poison their minds, by telling them how they are mistreated; and that they are entitled to their freedom, as much as their masters [. . .] and then refer them to their own degraded situation; and tell them that it is power and tyranny which rivets their chains of bondage; and not because they are an inferior race of people. We tell them that all Europe has abandoned slavery, and that the West Indies are all free; and that they got their freedom by rebelling a few times and slaughtering the whites, and convince them, that if they will follow the example of the West India negroes, that they will obtain their

> liberty, and become as much respected as if they were white; and that they can marry white women when they are all put on a level. (*Western Weekly Review* September 18, 1835)[6]

The speech which Stewart here gives to Murrell closely resembles the rhetoric conventionally attributed to Denmark Vesey. Paulding mentions this same argument: "Another of these pious incendiaries maintains the right and duty of the slave to cut the throats, or poison, or consume with fire, his master and all his family, if by so doing he can free himself from bondage" (Paulding 301). But, that is not what abolitionist literature actually said.

While the *Liberator*, the *Emancipator*, and literature of the American Anti-Slavery Society did often cite the examples of Europe and the West Indies, they were never directed at slaves and always explicitly rejected violence. Even Walker's *Appeal*, the least pacifist of abolitionist writing up to that point, did not make the argument Paulding paraphrases.[7] The basic (somewhat inconsistent) argument was that because such criticism provided "aid and comfort," so to speak, to people who plotted violence against the system, it was treasonous. This was the premise used for insisting that the rights to free speech and petition did not apply to critics of slavery. Most often the argument was made through repetition rather than ratiocination. As far as I know, only Richard Yeadon's *The Amenability of Northern Incendiaries, as Well to Southern as to Northern Laws, without Prejudice to the Right of Free Discussion; to Which Is Added an Inquiry into the Lawfulness of Slavery, under the Jewish and Christian Dispensations, Together with Other Views of the Same Subject, Being a Series of Essays, Originally Published in the Charleston Courier* actually argues that the definition of traitor applies, and it is a tortured argument. Yeadon argues that abolitionists are treasonous for two reasons. First, slavery is guaranteed by the Constitution (a complicated, but not entirely unreasonable argument). Because of this guarantee, anyone who condemns slavery is "betraying" the Constitution. Yeadon says, "It is a treason to the Union and to the Constitution, in any State, to permit any of her citizens, directly or indirectly, by word, writing, or printing, to disturb this sacred guarantee of Southern rights" (11). In other words, because the Constitution permits slavery, it is treasonous for anyone to criticize slavery, or to allow such criticism. Such an argument is logical only if the premise is true: that it is treasonous to criticize anything indirectly mentioned in the Constitution ("indirectly" because the words "slavery" and "slaves" were carefully and deliberately avoided in the Constitution).

Calling abolitionists traitorous may, to a modern reader, look patently insincere, if not actively silly. It was, after all, a smear made by nullifiers, who had not only advocated secession (a more obvious violation of the Constitution than criticizing slavery), but who criticized tariffs (something actually named in the Constitution, unlike slavery).[8] If abolitionists were treasonous for criticizing slavery, and if northern legislatures were traitors for allowing criticism of something mentioned in the Constitution, then nullifiers were treasonous for criticizing tariffs.

Indeed, the terms "treason" and "traitor" were used for nullifiers (several states passed resolutions characterizing South Carolina's stance as subversive of the Constitution; see Capers 156). Jackson, in his December 1832 "Proclamation Regarding Nullification" said that the nullifiers had brought their followers to "the brink of insurrection and treason" and not without reason (for more on Calhoun's awareness that his actions would be perceived as treason, see Niven 180, 189–90). During the nullification crisis, South Carolina had gone so far as to make military preparations for a war against the federal government. It may be, then, that the treason argument was an instance of cunning projection: nullifiers specifically and proslavery politicians generally took the strongest criticisms of them—that *they* were not particularly loyal to the Constitution—and projected the accusation onto their outgroup. A strange instance of this is the passage in Cooper's *Hints,* an argument for nullification, in which he argues that protectionism erects "in the midst of this republican country of equal rights, a favoured and privileged class, for whose sake the commerce of the nation is burthened and impeded" (7, repeated almost verbatim on 14), an apt description of what slavery did.

Some examples of projection involve what Gordon Allport called the "mote-beam" process—that the accusation was somewhat true of the object, but more true of the agent, such as in the "fanatic abolitionist" smear. As will be discussed, newspaper editors, in an era of relentlessly factionalized media, condemned other editors for factionalism. But, sometimes the accusation was simply not true of the object. For example, Duff Green, the pro-Calhoun editor of the *U.S. Telegraph,* who was clearly trying to use various issues (including anti-abolitionism) as devices to try to unify the slave states behind Calhoun, vilified Jacksonian Democrats for sectionalism. This is not the pot calling the kettle black: Green was engaged in sectionalism, on behalf of Calhoun, and Jackson papers were not. Calhoun biographers, even sympathetic ones like Margaret Coit, discuss Calhoun's attempts to rally the South behind him, and his failed use of slavery as the method (see especially 306). Niven says that "Calhoun's long-range political objectives were to consolidate his power in South Carolina and unify the slaveholding states behind his leadership" (Niven, *John C. Calhoun* 207; see also Capers 186, see especially his discussion of Calhoun's use of six resolutions in 1837 to encourage southern politicians to "follow the Carolinian's lead over to the Democrats and forced southern Whigs to take a stronger stand in support of his program in defense of slavery," 198). Jacksonians refrained from sectionalism not out of high-mindedness; it was not a viable option. Because of the disproportion created by the three-fifths compromise, a unified South could have dominance; a unified North could not, so neither Jackson nor Van Buren tried to use antislavery as a wedge issue.

Social psychologists use the term "defensive projection" for this kind of behavior, but I think "cunning projection" is more useful in this context. By using the term "cunning," I am not suggesting that proslavery rhetors were self-conscious that they were projecting. Social psychologists are perfectly persuasive that projection is generally an unconscious process, and that it gets much of its power from the way that it resolves unconscious, even suppressed, anxieties. Some research suggests that repression increases the attraction of projection; if that is the case, then one would see, as one does, the projection increase as the ability to voice guilt about slavery decreased. My educated guess is that there is an inverse correlation between the "necessary evil" topos and projection—the more that rhetors insisted that slavery was actively good, the more likely they were to scapegoat. I use the term "cunning projection," rather than "defensive projection," because I want to emphasize the rhetorical and political power that comes from this move: the most cunning politicians are not necessarily self-conscious about their strategies (and, in fact, one of the most cunning moves is to persuade one's self first), but seem capable of intuitive and unconscious cleverness. Whether Hitler *really* believed that invading Poland was a course of action forced on him by France and Britain is a question for psychoanalysts; but a rhetorician can say that it was a tremendously cunning way to frame the policy.

It is always tempting to pose the question of sincerity, and it is almost impossible not to speculate, but the process of self-persuasion (at the individual and cultural level) makes it very difficult to answer. For instance, what is particularly odd about the insistence that abolitionists cause insurrection is that proslavery rhetors intermittently indicated that they knew that insurrection predated abolition. The first major slave insurrection in what is now the United States was the 1739 Stono Rebellion in South Carolina; there were others in 1741 (New York), 1800 (Virginia), 1811 (New

Orleans), and 1822 (Charleston); it is conventional to date the beginning of strident abolitionism with Garrison's break with colonization in 1830, so all of these predate "abolitionism" in the sense historians use it now. There were also rebellions in other regions that terrified U.S. slave owners, such as the 1791 slave revolt in what is now Haiti, and the Demerara Rebellions of 1795 and 1823. This history was known; Holland, for example, has several pages narrating the history of insurrection in South Carolina, beginning with a 1711 one and remarking on three in 1739, the latter of which he blames on the Spaniards. The "Negro Act" of 1740 he attributes to these insurrections.

In addition, Holland says that, in the case of insurrection, "the *utter extermination* of the black race would be the inevitable consequence" (65). Yet, he is writing this pamphlet in response to an insurrection attempt, and narrating various other insurrections, most of which cannot be blamed on abolitionists, and none of which had the supposedly "inevitable" consequence of racial extermination. Yet he scapegoats abolitionists both for insurrection and for the "inevitable" consequence: genocide.

In listing Hitler's unification strategies, Kenneth Burke describes a "*Projection* device. The 'curative' process that comes with the ability to hand over one's ills to a scapegoat, thereby getting purification by dissociation. This was especially medicinal, since the sense of frustration leads to a self-questioning. Hence if one can hand over his infirmities to a vessel, or 'cause,' outside the self, one can battle an external enemy instead of battling an enemy within" (202–3). Scapegoating enables a community to promulgate a politically useful narrative of cause and effect. It is politically useful because it is much simpler—this bad situation has been caused entirely by bad people; killing them will solve it. Burke's analysis of scapegoating, much like the perspective of recent social and political psychologists, emphasizes the psychologically soothing properties of scapegoating—that an individual feels strangely cleansed by projecting one's shames onto something ritually killed (precisely the process that Orlando Patterson argues was, and is, behind lynching). And, certainly, it may well be that the rhetorical scapegoating of abolitionists (and occasional violence against suspected abolitionists) did serve to make slavers feel better about slavery. But it did something else as well. Projection is distracting in a politically useful way, in that it shifts the stasis. As will be discussed, Robert Montgomery Bird presents Indians as villainous for engaging in the same behavior as whites, with no acknowledgment of the potential contradiction.

Whether Duff Green made these accusations of Jacksonians and abolitionists to soothe his ethical discomfort seems to me impossible to know:

what matters is that this move works. Derek Rucker and Anthony Pratkanis have shown that people tend to believe that a person who makes an accusation is innocent of it. In their studies, they found that "Accusing others of a misdeed increased the blame placed on the target of the accusation and exonerated the accuser" (1505). In September 1835, various anti-Jacksonian southern newspapers called for a "Convention of Southern Merchants" which would boycott all northern products, engage in shipping direct to England, and use only southern factories—in short, what was conventionally called a "protective system." These resolutions and favorable editorials from various papers were reprinted in the *U.S. Telegraph* on September 26. In the next issue, Green accused the North, with the aid of abolitionists, of planning "the establishment of a protection system, necessarily consequent in their opinion, on the abolition of slavery." There is no evidence of such a plan on the part of northerners, but the evidence of such a plan on the part of southerners was present in the previous issue of the paper.

This cunning strategy of rhetorical projection rationalizes the bad behavior of the rhetor, in that it makes the aggressive behavior seem, at worst, defensive. Since the North is planning a protection system, it's acceptable for the South to do so; since the Indians slaughter women and children, it's acceptable for the whites to do so. This is moral relativism: the concept that certain actions are not bad because everyone is doing them assumes that the morality of an act is not determined in absolute terms, but is relative to who does it, and whether the opposition does: "The virtues of a freeman would be the vices of slaves" (Harper 111).

Proslavery ideology is inherently relativist (what is right for the owner is wrong for the slave), as is authoritarianism generally; yet, authoritarians often claim to be moral absolutists. Alexander Sims explains that the requirements of morality are "uniform": "What is right at one time or in one place, is right at all times and in all places. Also, of things in themselves wrong, neither time nor circumstance can change their moral complexion" (12). He later invokes a relativist argument to defend slave masters' failure to honor slave marriages. These marriages are "a *quasi*-religious obligation, assumed with a perfect knowledge of all the contingencies on which the connexion formed, must rest" (29)—not the same attitude one has about marriages among whites (see also his argument as to why the "degraded" state of the slave should be compared to the state of slaves in Africa, 30–31).[9] Authoritarianism is always morally relativist (regardless of the claims to be foundationalist) because the ethics of an act are not inherent to the act, but determined by whether the act strengthens or threatens the authoritarian's preferred hierarchy. Whether moral relativism is necessary for projection is an intriguing question; certainly, projection is extremely common among moral relativists who claim to be moral absolutists, like the proslavery rhetors.

The kind of projection common to proslavery rhetor has another odd quality. In the fall after the pamphlet mailing, apparently, the *Charleston Courier* had written disparagingly of the State Rights Party. A State Rights party member had objected, and the *Courier* printed an explanation. The *Charleston Mercury* (nullifier) letter writer, after saying that the explanation "is satisfactory" (meaning a duel is not necessary), goes on to say, "I regard the introduction of party politics as little less than absolute treason to the South" and that the original article had "the most unfounded and injurious imputations upon the character and principles of a party, of which I am proud to be a member, and which I know to be actuated by as much purity of purpose, and true love of country, as ever inspired the bosoms, or directed the movements, of any men on earth" (August 18, 1835). Of all the various puzzling aspects of proslavery rhetoric, this quality—which is difficult even to name usefully—has been the most muckling. The rhetor asserts something hyperbolic which is not literally true. Unlike mere hyperbole, however, the falsehood of the assertion is highlighted in the way the assertion is made. Clearly, the rhetor cannot actually know how his group compares to every other group of men on earth, as such a comparison is impossible to make. What we know, then, is that he is so passionately attached to his party that he will make absurd statements about it. The statement does not function as an assertion about reality, as much as a performance of his party loyalty. Had he said that he believed his party to be actuated by as much purity of purpose, and so on, as any other group of which he had been a member, or with which he was familiar, then the reader would have to be agnostic concerning his sincerity (perhaps he did think that proposition was an accurate representation of reality). Had he said that he considered party politics inappropriate or unethical, a reader could not know if the letter writer sincerely held that belief. To call party politics "little less than treason" is hyperbole—one would have the sense that a reader who responded, "Really, it's worse than murder?" had missed the point, yet a reader could not be certain that the author did not feel that strongly about party politics in principle—the proposition might be sincerely believed to reflect reality. But, as this hyperbolic condemnation of party politics is immediately followed by the rhetor's hyperbolic statement about his party—a statement that is propositionally meaningless, but performatively powerful—the reader *knows* he does not condemn party politics in principle: he has just demonstrated passionate attachment to party. My point here is not about the vehemence, nor about the hypocrisy, but about the way that the absurdity of the statement is self-referential.

In *1984,* the hero Winston Smith is given a book that explains the structure of Oceanic society, including the language rules. It explains the term *blackwhite:* "Like so many Newspeak words, this word has two mutually contradictory meanings. Applied to an opponent, it means the habit of impudently claiming that black is white, in contradiction of the plain facts. Applied to a Party member, it means a loyal willingness to say that black is white when Party discipline demands this" (175). One demonstrates one's loyalty to the party through one's use of language insofar as that language demonstrates one's willingness to believe, with perfect sincerity, both parts of what one knows to be a lie. Self-referential absurdity works in the same way (in fact, *blackwhite* is a better term for it): by making the statement in a manner that accentuates the logical absurdity of the statement, and with vehemence, a rhetor shows himself (or herself) to be more loyal to the group than to logic.

When South Carolina threatened secession over the tariffs, Jackson called the bluff, no other states joined the secession movement, the U.S. Senate voted almost unanimously to authorize Jackson to use force, and South Carolina was forced to submit in 1833 to "the highest tariffs ever to be charged in antebellum America" (Freehling, *Road to Disunion* 284); Capers points out that South Carolina had to wait "ten years for a reduction in the tariff equal to that which the Verplanck Bill at the outset [that nullifiers had rejected] had offered in two" (156). As Capers says, "The outcome was a definite defeat for Calhoun and his colleagues" (156); and "Calhoun and his colleagues were completely defeated" (164). This outcome is important to emphasize: South Carolina lost, yet pro-nullification journals typically asserted the opposite.

In the summer of 1835, the *Albany Evening Journal* had asked the question why the slave states threatened secession, when such an outcome would mean that slaves only needed to escape north (as the North would no longer have any motivation in enforcing fugitive slave laws). Duff Green's *U.S. Telegraph* quotes the passage from the *Albany Evening Journal,* "Why will the South be perpetually threatening a dissolution of the Union, when they must know that such a calamity would only hasten and increase the horrors which they all deplore?" and then replies:

> The South *know* the contrary. And they make no *threats* about the matter. They calmly tell the North what will be the result of a per-

> sistence in these measures, and this is distorted into *threats*. What will the Journal have the South do? Must we be silent, and kiss the rod that smites us? Is the Journal so ignorant of the character of the South, as to expect that because we have so patiently submitted to so much we will submit to every thing! The events of two years ago ought to have taught the Journal, and have taught the North, that there is a point beyond which the South will not be driven. We can tell the Journal that any hopes that may have been engendered in the North by the traitorous course of certain presses at the South, will be disappointed. (*U.S. Telegraph* Saturday evening, August 29, 1835)

Trying to describe this passage in traditional rhetorical terms of authorial intention and audience is surprisingly difficult. The "events of two years ago" refers to the Nullification Crisis, so the passage only makes sense had South Carolina successfully resisted high tariffs. Yet, surely, Green must have known that not everyone accepted that renarration. So, did Green "intend" that his audience would believe South Carolina had triumphed? The passage is strikingly close to the cliché "That's a promise, not a threat"—which is, of course, a threat that is made even more threatening by its denial of being a threat. In a similar way, the text denies itself: it claims that the South is calm, a claim belied by the histrionics of threatening secession over criticism of slavery. So, as with the reversal of the nullification narrative, should we believe that Green really intends to be understood as calm? Or that proslavery rhetors do not intend secession to be understood as a threat? Does he really believe that letting people dissent is a kind of humiliating homoerotic submission? How seriously can we take this? How seriously did they?

Janet Adelman, in her extraordinary discussion of Shakespearean hyperbole, says that, although a person engaging in hyperbole "does not believe himself and expects no one else to believe him, he means no less than what he says" (114). She goes on to say, "If we are to take it seriously, hyperbole must elicit some sort of belief or assent: that is to say that it demands of us the simultaneous perception of its literal falsehood and its imaginative relevance. It presents the spectacle of man making his own imaginative universe in despite of all reality, in despite of all human limitation" (114–15). I would go even further. It is not that we are certain that the speaker does not believe what he says—it is that the very question of the literal truth or falsehood is irrelevant—by using hyperbole, a speaker signals that he does not care whether it is true or not. The imaginative universe, *his* imaginative universe, is all that matters. In addition to thereby identifying himself as the sort of man described in the next chapter—a man willing to die for impractical ideals—hyperbole shifts the stasis away from the question of truth and falsehood to the question of *his* feelings. Hugh Blair's discussion of hyperbole emphasizes the feelings of the rhetor who uses it; hyperbolic expressions are, he says, "suggested by the warmth of passion" (153).[10] We are left unsure, and therefore left contemplating, just how strongly he really feels, and how far he will really go. Like the threats of secession, the rhetorical consequence of proslavery hyperbole is to make political issues ultimately about the feelings of the slavers, and specifically about their feelings for their group. Hyperbole functions in the same way that *blackwhite* does, as a demonstration of ingroup loyalty.

It is also intimidating, and intimidation is a very effective strategy in a politics of coercion or bargaining. By signaling that they are so passionately attached to the ingroup that they do not feel their language is restricted by the bounds of reason, such rhetors also signal that their actions are not restricted by reason. The 1828 South Carolina Special Committee report insisted that federal attempts to improve the situation of free or enslaved African Americans in South Carolina "is a subject in which there can be no reasoning between South Carolina and any other government. It is a question altogether of feeling" (29). The most controlling kind of violence is not controlled violence, but brutality that might have no causal or proportional relation to the catalyst. The more predictable and proportional the violence, the more it is subject to control by potential victims, thereby leaving them some autonomy. Random violence necessitates endless (or, in the words of Judge Thomas Ruffin's decision, discussed later, "perfect") submission; that relation of rationality and control creates the political power of irrationality. Lynchings (whether the antebellum lynchings of supposed insurrectionists or the postbellum lynchings of supposed insubordinates) were most controlling when the victims were innocent of the crime, when the reaction was completely irrational. In the 1830s, secession was an effective threat *because* it was irrational; if proslavery rhetors were crazy enough to secede, they were more than crazy enough to do the lesser acts that all politicians genuinely feared (such as creating their own political party). That the threat was simultaneously crazy and credible enhanced the ethos of the rhetors as people willing to do anything to get their way: a useful ethos in a bargaining situation.

The intimidation of this rhetoric is also present in the treason metaphor. A common smear to try to apply to one's opponents, it was consistently applied to abolitionists. This era seems to be the beginning of the accusation of "race traitor" (Philpot's 1839 piece calls them "wiggers"—a term still used by white supremacists). Dissenters were accused of "treason" and critics of the ingroup were regularly called "traitors." Dissent is resistance, and resistance is rebellion, so dissent is treason. Earlier, I briefly discussed the only text I've found that attempts to ratiocinate the connection (Yeadon); for the most part, it was simply a name abolitionists were called. It may initially have been the same kind of hyperbole as the state rights man calling party politics treason—a self-referentially absurd statement intended to draw attention to the rhetor's loyalty. But, after a time, and after the "abolitionists advocate insurrection" assertion came to be widely believed, this was hyperbole with potentially (and possibly intentionally) murderous consequences. The high degree of personal violence in the South was the background to every such accusation; the use of the term was a threat. If a dominant group can get a large number of people to accept that dissent is treason, then they implicitly justify violence against that group. To call dissenters traitors is to call for violence against them, while evading responsibility for the rhetoric.

The second line of argument was that criticism of slavery is treasonous because it is "the prosecution of an insidious but energetic war upon the slave-holding members of the Union" (Wm. Drayton 212). Criticism of slavery is war because it inspires insurrection. This argument is flawed in many ways, not least because it is insidiously circular. If the premise is that happy slaves could suddenly be transformed into nefarious plotters by reading abolitionist pamphlets (the assumption not only behind much of the anti-abolitionist political rhetoric, but an important point in the plot of Robert Montgomery Bird's *Sheppard Lee*), then repeating those arguments or describing insurrections would be equally dangerous. But, they *were* repeated; in newspaper articles, in celebratory speeches, in arguments for the gag rule or censorship of the mails, in defenses of slavery, proslavery rhetors discussed, sometimes in great detail, the prospects for slave insurrection. They also gave more publicity to abolitionist arguments than abolitionists could have, and through their exaggerated description of the power, wealth, and popularity of the abolitionists' supposed conspiracy to free slaves, publicized precisely the argument they said could not be made without inspiring insurrection.

So, it is not quite that abolitionist arguments could not be mentioned, but that any practical discussion of their merits, other than increasing control through heightened punishment and silencing dissent, was forbidden. This is what I mean when I say that the argument that proslavery rhetors silenced criticism of slavery because of fear that it might inspire insurrection is circular: proslavery rhetors were opposed to a practical discussion of slavery because they could only engage in fear-mongering, and not a practical discussion, regarding the possible consequences of abolition. We are still left with the question of why they were not opposed to a discussion, but to a rational one.

2
"With firm, undaunted resolution"
The Rhetoric of Doom

> So that instead of saying: What horrible things I did to people!, the murderers would be able to say, What horrible things I had to watch in the pursuance of my duties, how heavily the task weighed upon my shoulders!
>
> —Hannah Arendt

Scholars have often remarked on a striking quality of southern antebellum culture: its fatalism, sometimes called "the rhetoric of doom," "the myth of the lost cause," or the "rhetoric of defense." Although any and each of those terms is accurate, I will settle for the rhetoric of doom, an ideology (and practice) that precludes the consideration of particular historical context (and causality) by making all questions ones of eschatology, by valorizing impracticality, and by attributing victimhood to those who most benefit from (and promote) the system's injustice. The "rhetoric of doom" is Brian Dippie's phrase, who was writing about American attitudes toward Native Americans, but I will suggest it applies much more broadly. The "rhetoric of conservatism" and "fatalism" are both Dickson Bruce's terms for the quality he identified in defenses of slavery—the sense that proslavery forces were fighting for a dying world order and working against progress. The "myth of the lost cause" is the term historians use to describe the fantasy that the South engaged in a valiant, chivalrous battle against the forces of modernity, "that the war was a mawkish and essentially heroic and romantic melodrama, an honorable sectional duel, a time of martial glory on both sides, and triumphant nationalism" (Nolan and Gallagher 12). In its most familiar forms, ranging from *Gone with the Wind* to current debates over displaying the Confederate flag, that version of the Civil War downplays the role of slavery in the conflict, glamorizes plantation life (which is taken as synecdochic for southern culture), blames the extremism of the abolitionists for provoking the war, describes a southern aristocracy who gallantly took on a Civil War against all odds, romanticizes the war (thereby obscuring southern antislavery movements as well as the uglier sides of the war like Andersonville), and tries to shift the issue to one of states' rights, in which the southern states were trying to protect an older, nobler, and more chivalric political arrangement than the money-grubbing one toward which American political culture was inexorably slumping.

Alan Nolan and Gary Gallagher plausibly attribute this myth to the postwar need for pro-confederate politicians to regain credibility after having pushed the slave states into a devastating war: "The purpose of the legend was to hide the Southerners' tragic and self-destructive mistake" (Nolan and Gallagher 14, see also Gallagher). Proslavery politicians dragged the slave states into a ruinous war on the basis of certain arguments repeated nearly endlessly since the 1830s. When events proved these arguments to be false—one of those nasty things that history will do to rhetoric from time to time—the people who had made those arguments were left with a nontrivial amount of egg on their faces. Rather than admit that the arguments had been false, their former advocates simply claimed they had never made them, and concocted the myths of a southern culture separable from the slave economy, a war not fought for slavery, and the happy sharecropper instead of the happy slave.

Beringer and colleagues argue that losing the war created a kind of cognitive dissonance which the myth of the lost cause helped to relieve: "Confederates reduced the dissonance between the knowledge of defeat and the knowledge that their own doctrines had brought on an unsuccessful war" (184). Prior to the war, for instance, secessionists made no secret of the centrality of slavery to the secessionist cause; there was no debate as to what this war was about, and that they saw themselves fighting for slavery was clearly stated in the declarations of secession. As the *Declaration of the Immediate Causes Which Induce and Justify the Secession of South Carolina from the Federal Union* explains, secession is necessary because the recently elected Lincoln administration has announced "that a war must be waged against slavery until it shall cease throughout the United States" (something the administration, of course, had never announced). Georgia's declaration states, "For the last ten years we have had numerous and serious causes of complaint against our non-slave-holding confederate States with reference to the subject of African slavery." Mississippi's *A Declaration of the Immediate Causes which Induce and Justify the Secession of the State of Mississippi from the Federal Union* says, "Our position is thoroughly identified with the institution of slavery [. . .] There was no choice left us but submission to the mandates of abolition, or a dissolution of the Union, whose principles had been subverted to work out our ruin." The Texas declaration, after a long list of the wrongs of abolitionists, concludes, "And, finally, by the combined sectional vote of the seventeen non-slave-holding States, they have elected as president and vice-president of the whole confederacy two men whose chief claims to such high positions are their approval of these long continued wrongs, and their pledges to continue them to the final consummation of these schemes for the ruin of the slave-holding States." The Joint Resolutions of the General Assembly of Alabama begins,

> WHEREAS, anti-slavery agitation persistently continued in the non-slaveholding States of this Union, for more than a third of a century, marked at every stage of its progress by contempt for the obligations of law and the sanctity of compacts, evincing a deadly hostility to the rights and institutions of the Southern people, and a settled purpose to effect their overthrow even by subversion of the Constitution, and at the hazard of violence and bloodshed; and whereas, a sectional party calling itself Republican, committed alike by its own acts and antecedents, and the public avowals and secret machinations of its leaders to the execution of these atrocious designs, has acquired the ascendancy in nearly every Northern State, and hopes by success in the approaching Presidential election to seize the Government itself.

While I agree with Nolan and Gallagher's interpretation of the postwar political benefits of the myth of the lost cause, I will suggest that it predated the war (and may have even contributed to the war itself insofar as it discouraged practical discussion of the alternatives). In addition, while I do think this ideology is usefully characterized as proslavery, it was not peculiarly southern—I will rely on two rhetors whose "southern-ness" is problematic (at best).

It is common to look to antebellum literature for an explication of the politics of slavery; as long ago as 1950, Henry Nash Smith argued that 1830s southern literature was an attempt to justify slaveocracy through idealizing plantation life, by presenting a "picture of aristocratic masters, brilliant and charming heroines, and devoted slaves" (151). William Taylor replied that much southern literature was not about plantation life, and, further, that "Anyone expecting to find in these novels anything resembling a consistent celebration of the plantation economy, slavery or the Tidewater aristocrat is in for a surprise" (150). Taylor's argument is that southern literature does not idealize plantation life because it has a pervasive quality of tragedy. I will be taking Smith's side on this issue, but while granting that tragic quality, the point to be made here is how a tragic narrative apparently not about slavery could, in fact, serve as a defense and support of economic, political, and cultural commitment to slavery.

The Oxford Companion to American Literature summarizes the plot of Robert Montgomery Bird's *Nick of the Woods*:

> At the end of the Revolution Captain Roland Forrester travels through the Kentucky border wilderness with his beloved [sister] Edith, who is captured by Indians during one of their many raids and massacres. The only man who will not fight is the Quaker derisively called Bloody Nathan, an unctuous hypocrite who is really Nick of the Woods, the Jibbenainosay, or devil, feared by the Indians because he brutally kills them to avenge their murder of his family. When he finds Wenonga, a Shawnee chief, was the sole killer of his family, Nick, disguised as an Indian, slays him with a tomahawk, and disappears, to haunt the forests no more. George Rogers Clark saves Roland and Edith from the stake. (Hart 532)

As one can tell from the summary, the book is conventional in many ways, in both plot and characterization merging popular captivity narratives and the Walter Scott romances.

As with much antebellum literature (too much, according to Twain's famous comment), the prototype for Bird's hero, Roland Forrester, is the Walter Scott hero, a Romantic hero who is committed to a cause which, while in many ways the better cause, involves life-or-death conflict with a foe that is better armed, more cunning, better financed, and motivated by money. The main weapon on the side of the hero is the very virtue of the cause itself, in that the cause is more traditional, more picturesque, and nobler than the alternative. One is drawn to this cause through sentiment rather than practical concern (or, at least, the more genteel and sensible people are drawn to that cause; the cruder types lack the sensibility). If this myth is present in literature from the mid-1830s, then, long before the myth of the lost cause was a political narrative to justify the Civil War, it was an imaginative narrative that defined heroism: the noblest act of a hero is to enter a conflict even though he knows the forces of progress are against him.[1]

The political context in Scott's *Waverley* is clear—the expulsion of James and the resulting smoldering Jacobite cause—and would have been well known to Scott's readers. Even so, Scott emphasizes the ways that the political context has specific and identifiable consequences in the action of the novel. "I beg pardon, once and for all, of those readers who take up novels merely for amusement, for plaguing them so long with old-fashioned politics, and Whig and Tory, and Hanoverians and Jacobites. The truth is, I cannot promise them that this story shall be intelligible, not to say probable, without it. My plan requires that I should explain the motives on which its action proceeded; and these motives necessarily arose from the feelings, prejudices, and parties of the times" (63). In *Waverly,* the actions and motives are closely and explicitly tied to the particular historical and political context, but the closest that Bird gets to acknowledging a political context for the motives and actions of his characters is in an appositive phrase early in the novel: "The rich fields,—*the hunting-grounds of a dozen tribes of Indians,*—to be possessed, were first to be won, and won from an enemy at once brave and cruel, resolute and wily, who had shown no disposition to yield them except with life, and who had already stained them with the best blood of the settler" (Bird 2, emphasis added). The dates are vague, the precise nature of the specific conflicts with the Amerindians left unmentioned. Even in this passage—which is the most sympathetic to the Amerindians that one can find anywhere in the novel—one can see Bird's tendency to blame the Indians for their own destruction *and* for the deaths of any whites.[2] The Indians have stained the lands with the blood of the settler (but the settlers have not stained the land with the blood of Indians). The consequence, as Richard Slotkin has said, is that Indians are to blame for their own extermination, *and* they are to blame for fighting their extermination, *and* they are to blame for the moral and political consequences to the whites (514). This miasma of blame precludes a policy discussion of historical causation.

This shift to the mythic severely (perhaps deliberately) limits white responses; the absence of particular historical causation necessarily implies an absence of specific political solutions. Yet, the Indians do not have agency in this battle because they are tools in the hands of a white villain, Ralph Stackpole. Denying agency to the Indians preserves the honor of the combatants, in that, were the battle really between whites and Indians, Indians would, in a sense, be the equals of the whites. In addition, they would be capable of autonomy, a capacity that would invalidate the argument about their fundamental incapacity for political action. Making the Indians the tools of a white villain preserves the honor of the whites (in the same way that, I will argue, making slave insurrection the product of white abolitionists enables proslavery rhetors to deny African American agency and autonomy, while still scapegoating them for the conflict).

Scapegoating is often described as transforming "self-loathing into hostility toward others" (Glick 246). It is "denial through projection" (Landes 659); one can deny the trait in one's self *because* one condemns others for having it. It involves projecting an internal and shameful quality onto members of an "outgroup" who are then ritually (or literally) killed for possessing the quality. Social psychologists identify scapegoating as most likely to occur when a group of people is frustrated, and "aggression against the true source of frustration is inhibited" (Glick 247). Correctly directed aggression is inhibited because the true source is one's self (as in the case of homophobic self-defined heterosexuals with homoerotic impulses, see Adams, Wright, and Lohr), or the true source is a powerful group (as many have argued was the case with poor whites in postbellum South), or the true source is systemic and therefore extremely difficult to identify (as in the case of economic insecurity caused by a fluctuating cotton market).

The aggression and frustration are handled through projecting them onto a group that is unable to retaliate, so that projection is an early step in the narrative of scapegoating. Yet, there must be some sense that the group is powerful, either because some members of the group have enviable achievements or coveted possessions (Glick argues this was the case with Jews in prewar Germany), or because prominent members of the group can be associated with threatening movements (the presence of Jewish bankers and Jewish Marxists enabled Hitler to characterize Jews as doubly threatening). Yet, the group must also be weak enough that they cannot effectively resist or retaliate (physically, politically, or rhetorically) against the political and physical violence of scapegoating.

Multiple groups can be scapegoated at the same time; while abolitionists were scapegoated for slave insurrection, the English were scapegoated for slavery itself. Greenberg says: "The fears and panics that periodically swept the South during the years before 1860 seem an essential part of slave society, for they were firmly rooted in reality. Slaves did in fact resist, and masters were quite vulnerable to secret conspiracy—to a match tossed into a wooden town or to ground glass put in their oatmeal. In such an atmosphere, Anglophobia and later New Anglophobia served an essential function. The message of Anglophobia was that the real threat to masters came from outside the society rather than from within" (*Masters and Statesmen* 122; see also Dillon 168–70). Scapegoating is a narrative of contagion. It posits that there was a time when the community was pure, stable, peaceful, and secure. That community was infected by some external group, whose presence led to the current state of conflict, instability, and insecurity, as when the anonymous critic of Channing refers, falsely, to "the Garrisons, Thompsons and Follens (all alien born)" (23), or when southern proslavery rhetors insist that all abolitionists are northerners.

Describing the contagion as external enables a narrative of cleansing through expulsion and extermination. If, and only if, we expel or exterminate that alien group, and then close our borders to them and people infected by them, will we be safe. Interestingly enough, the scapegoating narrative is powerful only if it is practically impossible to cleanse the community of the infectious outgroup. Were the community genuinely able to exclude or isolate the infection, then the underlying premise—that the outgroup caused all the problems—could be proven wrong. The narrative is valuable *because* it cannot be tested.

Scapegoating is, social psychologists emphasize, powerful: "Scapegoat movements address frustrated needs for esteem, belonging, and transendence by reasserting the ingroup's superiority and offering membership in a wider social movement that promises symbolic immortality" (Glick 255). Hence, canny politicians often exaggerate the dangers posed by some group in order to present themselves as saviors of the ingroup: "A racist society may actually promote bigotry in order to unite ingroup members and distract them from real political and economic problems by sacrificing a historical scapegoat" (Tsesis 85). As early as the 1820s proslavery rhetors began falsely characterizing hostility to slavery as a "foreign or northern prejudice" (Kingsley 10), and to talk in terms of striving "to extinguish" it. John Niven has argued that "the perceived dangers of abolititionist literature unified Unionists and nullifiers in South Carolina" (*John C. Calhoun* 205). I am suggesting that was the intention behind alarmist rhetoric concerning abolitionists: to unify South Carolinians specifically and the slave states generally through scapegoating abolitionists.

In addition, scapegoating frees people from feeling responsible. Individuals (or communities) can deny responsibility for a situation by projecting that responsibility onto some outgroup (as when proslavery rhetors blame abolitionists for slave rebellions). This is an attractive way of seeing a situation both when the causes are complicated (and there is no clear villain), as well as when the community does not want to hold responsible the individual or group who caused the situation: "The scapegoat bears the blame, while the scapegoaters feel a sense of righteousness and increased unity. The social problem may be real or imaginary, the grievances legitimate or illegitimate, and members of the targeted group may be wholly innocent or partly culpable. What matters is that the scapegoats are wrongfully stereotyped as all sharing the same negative trait, or are singled out for blame while other major culprits are left off the hook" (Berlet and Lyons 8). To say that a rhetor scapegoats a group is not to claim complete innocence on the part of that group. Perhaps Denmark Vesey did read criticisms of slavery made during the Missouri Compromise, and perhaps he did read such speeches to co-conspirators (but, then again, perhaps such claims were coerced under torture). But, there is no reason to think he would not have rebelled had he never read those criticisms; as is clear from the history of slave rebellions, slaves did not need abolitionists to tell them that the system was unjust. The scapegoating of abolitionists for slave insurrection lets slavery (and slavers) off the hook for the consequences of slavery, just as scapegoating Native Americans for the conflict rationalizes the history of Indian wars, while letting white settlers and politicians who violated treaties off the hook.

This reframing of one's actions as justified because the opposition also engages in them means that the same behavior can be explained in opposite ways. With the exception of the appositive phrase quoted earlier, Bird attributes Indians' motivations not to a desire to hold onto land, nor to avenge the deaths of their families (the motivations of white killers); instead they desire to kill whites out of sheer blood lust. The Indians' motivations are uniform, simple, and animalistic, whereas the whites' motives are varied and complicated. This move is typical of racist rhetoric; Martin Reisigl and Ruth Wodak, in their book *Discourse and Discrimination,* note that racist discourse always presents the ingroup as complicated, with motives influenced by political, social, and personal context, but the outgroup is motivated by internal qualities: "The image of the [. . .] ingroup is more differentiated than the images of the others' groups, which, all in all, are much more characterized by 'internal attributions' than the ingroup. The outgroups' actions and behaviour are seldom explained by reference to external factors of communicative situation and historical, social, political and economic context, but primarily by pointing to alleged inherent and essential traits" (11). For instance, if people view one person hit another, they will describe the incident differently depending upon the group status of the attacker. If she is a member of the ingroup (or high-status group), the explanation will be in specific terms with external attribution of causality: she "hit the other person because she was provoked." This description makes the bad behavior of outgroup numbers atypical, and not an essential part of the ingroup member's identity. If the person is a member of the outgroup (or some low-status group), then the explanation will be in terms of the very identity, or internal attribution of causality: that person "is aggressive" (see especially Maas, Salvi, Arcuri, and

Semin). This description makes the bad behavior typical and essential. Michael Wilson describes the disparity in *Nick of the Woods:* "Indian men lack masculine self-control as a racial trait, displaying an ongoing slothful savagery and indolence, while white men lose their self-control only as a result of Indian violence, and do so only long enough to create a new white order out of the 'howling wilderness.'"

Similarly, success in the two groups is explained differently. Success (or virtuous behavior) on the part of an ingroup member is explained through internal attribution of causality ("she succeeded because she is a hard worker") whereas success on the part of an outgroup member is explained through external attribution of causality ("she was lucky") or nefarious motives ("she was greedy"). Thus, that the whites are willing to fight for land is a virtue, and it results from their concern for their families and their sense of honor; that the Indians fight for land is a vice, and it results from bloodlust.

There are important political consequences of this way of explaining behavior: one cannot reason or negotiate with people who are motivated by bloodlust so it is pointless to try. Were Americans to imagine that Native Americans were trying to hold onto land to which they had legitimate title, or had motives similar to and as complicated as white settlers, then the policy of genocide would have been clearly immoral.

This tendency to frame the conflict as Manchurian and eschatological rather than specific and political poisoned contemporary congressional debate about Amerindian policy. In May 1836, for instance, Congressman Samuel Vinton of Ohio objected to the ad hoc method of appropriating money to the secretary of war any time the secretary said, without any explanation, that there had been Indian depredations: "When the cry is sent up here that the people of the frontier are assailed by Indian hostility, we raise the means of making war upon them without a moment's delay; we crush them by our superior power. But we never inquire, while the war is going on, or after it is ended, into its causes; we make no investigation to learn who were the instigators of the war, or who was to blame" (Gales & Seaton, *Register of Debates* Pt. I, 3767). The first congressman to respond to him (Jesse Speight of North Carolina) began by saying, "This was not the first time the gentleman [Mr. Vinton] had stood up to advocate the cause of the Indians against the whites" (Pt. I, 3768). The next person to reply explicitly rejects the notion that one should think about historical causation: "I will not, and I hope the House will not, stop to inquire into the causes of this war. What, sir, shall we institute an inquiry into the causes of a war, and that an Indian war, when the war is already raging with all its horrors?" (*Register of Debates* Pt. I, 3772).

Vinton's move, to consider causes, is appropriate for effective deliberation. But, for some, all political and even cultural problems can and should be resolved through punitive measures, through violence or its threat. Because all problems are caused by willfulness, laziness, or just general wickedness, to look for causes of such behavior is pointless, as it would not lead one to a different policy. George Lakoff has described the "evil" frame in public discourse:

> To stand up to evil you have to be morally strong. If you're weak you let evil triumph, so that weakness in itself is a form of evil, as is promoting weakness. Evil is inherent, an essential trait, that determines how you will act in the world. Evil people do evil things. No further explanation is necessary. There can be no social causes of evil, no religious rationale for evil, no reasons or arguments for evil. The enemy of evil is good. If our enemy is evil, we are inherently good. Good is our essential nature, and what we do in the battle against evil is good. Good and evil are locked in a battle, which is conceptualized metaphorically as a physical fight in which the stronger wins. Only superior strength can defeat evil, and only a show of strength can keep evil at bay. Not to show evil overwhelming strength is immoral, since it will induce evildoers to perform more evil deeds, because they'll think they can get away with it. To oppose a show of superior strength is therefore immoral. (57)

Within such a frame, pausing to consider causes, or deliberate multiple policies, can only be motivated by an unmanly fear of punishment, or a desire to keep the wicked from getting the punishment they deserve. To ask why conflicts with Indians happen is to take their side.

Benjamin Hardin said that "the troubles with the Indians grew out of the opposition to the removal of the Indians" and that he "saw but one remedy, and that was to civilize them, and make them part of our own family, or else to exterminate them" (*Register of Debates* Pt. I, 3772). Hardin's slip of the tongue was significant—he says there is one remedy, but presents two. Since the first option was essentially unthinkable (as unthinkable as a large population of freed slaves), this was the rhetoric of doom (discussed below), that policy makers have no real choice in the matter, and are forced by circumstances into the (preferred) alternative.

Unlike Cooper's novels, which acknowledge political division among Indian tribes (which leads to a good Indian/bad Indian dichotomy), the Indians in *Nick* are universally brutal. In an oft-quoted passage in the preface to the 1853 edition, Bird explains his decision to demonize the Indians:

> We owe, perhaps, some apology for the hues we have thrown around the Indian portraits in our picture—hues darker than are usually employed by the painters of such figures. But we confess, the North American savage has never appeared to us the gallant and heroic personage he seems to others. The single fact that he wages war—systematic war—upon beings incapable of resistance or defence—upon women and children, whom all other races in the world, no matter how barbarous, consent to spare, has hitherto been, and we suppose to the end of our days will remain, a stumbling-block to our imagination; we look into the woods for the mighty warrior, the 'feather-cintured chief,' rushing to meet his foe, and behold him retiring laden with the scalps of miserable squaws and their babes. Heroical? *Hoc verbum quid valeat, non vident.* (v)

Probably because Bird described himself as the alternative to Cooper, much critical discourse has assumed the same dilemma—that Cooper's view of Indians is compassionate and kind. Yet, as Dippie has argued, Cooper's good Indian/bad Indian dichotomy could hardly help Americans come to a reasonable policy regarding Native American nations. Cooper's "good" Indians are the ones who see the deaths of their peoples as inevitable, and "bad" Indians try to fight for their lands and peoples (just as good slaves submit and bad slaves resist).

Dippie has called the former attitude the "rhetoric of doom," the notion prevalent as early as the first part of the nineteenth century that the Native Americans were doomed to die, and all one could do was to pity the "good" ones who submitted tragically. Instead of acting on their behalf, one should *feel.* To restrict views of the Amerindian to the range between Cooper and Bird is to efface exactly the pragmatic political solutions the United States did not consider, such as honoring treaties or deferring to the U.S. Supreme Court.

Bird's use of the rhetoric of doom is slightly more complicated in that Dippie's rhetoric of doom concerns the future of the Indians, but in Bird, the doom hovers over the whites as well. The hero Roland and his sister Edith, symbols of the Virginia aristocracy, must learn to accept their own incompetence at frontier life. Roland, who had been a Revolutionary War hero, cannot even save himself, but must be rescued by the frontiersmen with their brutal tactics. When the book is over, he and Edith return to Virginia, leaving settlement to the hardier and cruder types. Their presence has not raised the manners or education of the frontier settlers—they do not stay to marry, or serve as leaders of the new communities, or even teach; they go home. Their life is, quite literally, barren—they cannot marry each other, and they do not marry anyone else. Roland and Edith are all fine and good, and Roland may have been a hero in Virginia, but Virginia standards do not apply in the wilderness.

They do not apply because, as we are told and shown ad nauseum, the Indians are a different kind of foe from the kind faced in the Revolution. Fighting Indians requires methods that are more brutal, and it requires that the whites adopt precisely the tactics for which the Indians are condemned. The whites scalp, massacre, sneak up on unsuspecting Indians, and, in the final battle, murder women and children—exactly the crimes for which Bird says in his preface he cannot admire the Indian. The contradiction goes unremarked, as Bird repeatedly tells us that scalping is justified and necessitated by the brutality of Indians (see Winston on this point, 87). As Michael Wilson says, "scenes of white Americans either performing or allowing violence that would seemingly illustrate a lack of proper masculine self-control are either carefully obscured or rationalized away." It is the Indians who entrap the Virginia aristocrats, and it is only the crude, uneducated, and uncouth frontiersmen—men willing to engage in savage brutality—who can save them. This is partially the ingroup/outgroup thinking previously described: Indians and frontiersmen engage in exactly the same behavior, and that behavior is a sign of inherent evil in the outgroup, but a sign of goodness in the ingroup. Indians are condemned for doing what the frontiersmen also do because it is not a question of policies—what one does—but who one is.

At first glance, this binary of good (but impotent) and ruthless (but effective) is not the rhetoric of doom. In the first place, while fictional, it is not entirely a myth. The American political scene generally and the South specifically were, at the time of Bird's book, undergoing a reconsideration of the Revolutionary ethos, typified in Virginia aristocrats like Jefferson, Madison, and Washington. In the early part of the nineteenth century, as several historians have said, the Revolution versus frontier ethos was a vivid dilemma, as the kind of political and even military figure of the Revolutionary era was increasingly displaced by a newer, cruder kind of figure, personified by Andrew Jackson. William Taylor summarizes much of the

1830s southern literature on this point: "If these writers have anything to say about the place of the Cavalier gentleman in the nineteenth-century South, it is to call his usefulness into question. His characteristic improvidence, his lack of enterprise and his failure to move with the times—in sum, his inflexibility and inadaptability—spell his doom" (154, see also Cmiel, Kimmel, and Freehling). James Cobb says, "The perception of the planter-Cavalier as not quite up to the demands of a rapidly changing contemporary world suggested someone who, however noble, was also flawed, someone whose admirable intentions were often neutralized by ineffectual behavior" (25).

Jackson was not a Cavalier like Washington, Jefferson, or the Revolutionary heroes; he was notoriously badly educated, his manners were rough, his financial past was problematic, and his marital status even more so. He did not share the Revolutionary heroes' ambivalence about violence or slavery, nor did he emulate their mistrust of faction (his willingness to use all the powers of government to further his own party was renowned). Jackson lacked the education and gentility of the earlier presidents, and the cruelty of his military practices offended even many of his contemporaries. Washington had been famous in his era for his refusal to violate contemporary notions of the rules of war, such as respecting the lives and property of noncombatants, and restricting, as much as possible, the violence to the military. A recent military historian says, "Washington eschewed the way of the guerrilla, and where he was in personal command the revolutionaries never resorted in any significant measure to blurring the rules of war, particularly the distinction between combatants and noncombatants" (Weigley 410). Jackson, on the contrary, was equally famous for his refusal to follow such rules. In 1812, he went to war against the Creek Indians, and "in the subsequent peace treaty, the harshest ever made with the Indians, he not only stripped the Creeks of half their lands, but wrenched great tracts away from tribes who had actually fought on his side" (Brogan 227). Particularly in regard to his brutality, he typified the new kind of southerner: "The Southern frontiersman had a reputation for barbarism exceeding that of anyone else, and it grew out of some very real and very brutal practices in his community" (Bruce 5).

David Grimsted has shown that although the North and South were more or less matched in terms of numbers of riots and mob actions, southern mobs were much more violent, more likely to be directed at persons than property, and much more tolerated, or, as he says, "Being a Southern rioter meant seldom having to say you were sorry" (15). Faust attributes southern students' tendency to riot to the honor culture: "Any dissatisfaction with college life or supposed mistreatment by the faculty provided an occasion for student uprising, for notions of honor seemed to these young Southern gentlemen adequate justification for any act of violence" (*Sacred* 9). William Freehling remarks on the importance of physical violence in southern culture, and its connection to seeing discourse as violent: "Terroristic violence was also the natural extreme of a system which often used verbal intimidation to inhibit dissenters" (*Road to Disunion* 98). Eugene Genovese and Elizabeth Fox-Genovese argue that this violence was not in contrast to the ideally genteel paternalism of slave culture, but that both were entangled in the southern construction of chivalry: "As a standard of properly Christian and chivalric conduct, paternalism bade masters accept duties, responsibilities, and a code that made the ultimate test of the gentleman the humane treatment of his slaves. Yet all knew that slaveholding paternalism, when faithfully observed, also followed the chivalric mode: It included violence. Historically, chivalry—medieval, southern, or other—has rested on violence or, what comes to the same thing, the threat of violence" (*Mind of the Master Class* 337). Taylor notes the sense of having moved from the Revolutionary era, saying, by the 1830s, "Southerners had become obsessed by feelings of social decline, by a conviction that the civic values and ideals of the Revolutionary generation had been eroded away by a half century of democratic change and territorial expansion" (146). Whereas Taylor explains the fatalism as a consequence of historical forces, Faust attributes the fatalism and pessimism to external conditions (soil depletion and consequent westward migration).[3] Both such explanations might be seen as another instance of the very quality they are trying to explain: the rhetoric of doom.

This rhetoric depends upon seeing people's options as severely limited, if not entirely controlled, by imperious external circumstances. The people who have made certain political, economic, or personal choices are thereby exempt from responsibility for those choices; they are even exempt from responsibility for having themselves created the imperious circumstances. James Henry Hammond overworked his slaves so much that "they experienced an appalling mortality rate" (Rubin xi), yet he blamed their deaths on God: "If God would only allow my negroes to live and thrive and give me reasonable health" (Bleser 107). God is the agent and he is the object of his slaves' health. "If my negroes increased as they ought," he writes later in the same diary entry, as though dying of overwork were willful behavior on the slaves' part. When he reflected on his first ten years as a planter, he excused himself from responsibility for the high death rate, emphasizing that the fault is nature's: "My negroes have *decreased* in the *course of nature* and in spite of every exertion a man could make" (80).[4] His passion for profit, carefully noted in his diary, is not greed, but something forced upon him by his desire for his family, and the questionable practices in which he engaged, such as "wearing out my negroes on poor land where they do not increase" (41), were forced upon him by the need for money. He was forced into cruelty by circumstance, the settlers were forced into violence by the Indians, the southern intellectuals were forced into pessimism by the exhausted soil.

This bifurcation of roles—the kind but ineffectual Roland Forrester and crude but ruthless George Clark—was present in the rhetoric of slave mastering as well. There was a patina of aristocracy, a claim to gentility, and possibly even a sincere desire to replicate the always fictional image of the British landed aristocracy, but slavery was systematically dependent on brutality. I don't mean the individual acts of brutality directed against individual slaves, on which the scholarly debate has focused, although that was important, but the role of systemic and yet random terror (a point to be pursued later). As Sally Hadden has shown, this brutality, in the form of slave patrols, involved the whole community, not just slavers, thereby giving non-slave owners a stake in the racial and power hierarchy created by the institution of slavery. As much as slave owners might announce their hopes to control slaves through love, they bemoaned their dependence on violence and terror. The slave South was long noted for its strange intermixture and interdependence of violence and claims to gentility. Its high tolerance of personal violence was so extreme that, when South Carolina congressman Preston Brooks beat Senator Charles Sumner into unconsciousness on the very floor of the Senate, he was lionized. For many critics of slavery, the claims to gentility and obsession with honor on the part of southerners were absurd, hypocritical, and dishonest because they were belied by the personal, communal, and institutional brutality of slave culture. But it is not clear to me that proslavery rhetors saw one as belying the other; as in Bird, gentility's dependence on brutality is not presented by slavery apologists as hypocrisy or dishonesty, but as further evidence of the chivalry of slavers—because they felt bad about, and victimized by, their own brutality.

My argument is that *Nick of the Woods* perfectly displays a way of thinking about history, politics, and deliberation that was foundational for slavery. That the policies have never been deliberated is recast as manly decisiveness, that they are based on inaccurate premises is transformed into nobility, that they are brutal becomes a reason to pity the one engaged in (and who profits from) the brutality. And all of this is attached to a view of history that, in various ways, conceals the practical and particular historical causes of and long-term solutions to political problems by framing them as issues of group loyalty. This frame severely limits the role that rhetoric—that is, public argument—can play in identifying the range and relative merits of various options open to a polis. That the ethical system is morally relativist means, further, that any kind of rhetoric that appeals to principles of reciprocity, egalitarianism, or human rights is excluded *a priori*.

If *Nick of the Woods* is the sort of Sir Walter Scott–inspired historical romance common to nineteenth-century literature, Theophilus Fisk's speech "On the Bulwark of Freedom" is the sort of historical romance common to epideictic occasions, and I want to use it in order to lay out the characteristics that typify epideictic rhetoric. It was a speech in honor of the sixtieth anniversary of the May 1779 Revolutionary War naval battle in which Sir Henry Clinton attempted to land in Charleston, hoping to inspire the Loyalists to retake the city. Robert Leckie attributes the South Carolinians' success to several factors: careful planning by Colonel William Moultrie (who, among other preparations, built a redoubt of palmetto logs and mud, with walls sixteen feet thick), the large number of troops on the American side, Moultrie's remaining unperturbed by General Charles Lee's disruption of his plans, and Clinton's error in thinking that troops could wade across "the Breach" (a decision which might, Leckie speculates, have been the result of deliberate patriot misinformation concerning the depth of the water). As Leckie says, "In all, there were about six thousand men in Charleston holding what was nothing less than a fine and bristling series of fortifications" (229). That is not the way that Fisk tells the story, however.

In Fisk's version, the redoubt was inadequate: "So slight were the works that General Lee called the fort a slaughter pen" (4). Supplies were minimal: "lead was so scarce that the windows of the dwelling houses were deprived of their weights to supply the soldiers with bullets" (7). Moultrie had too few troops: "with only three hundred and forty four regular troops and a few volunteers" (7), "a few American troops had effectually resisted a British army" (9). The victory was Providential: "Here again Divine Providence which so often has interposed in our behalf, was again manifested in a most remarkable manner" (6). The success, so much against all odds, was the result, not of careful handling of logistical problems, but of "unshaken faith and gallant deeds" (11): "With firm, undaunted resolution, they determined to meet their ruthless invaders at the waters' edge. With hearts as true to the cause as their own rifles were to the aim, they determined on victory or martyrdom—to preserve their city, or to find a grave beneath its crumbling ruins" (8). In Fisk's version, it is not the careful and pragmatic planning of Moultrie that won the battle, but the romanticism of the soldiers; Moultrie's impressive command of logistics is shrouded by the romance that Fisk wants to tell. The battle becomes something out of Walter Scott, but with the romantic hero(es) victorious (although the audience knows it was a temporary victory, as the British would later succeed in taking the city).

In addition to having to hide Moultrie's impressive and important grasp of tactics, this version necessitates an odd interpretation of the British motives and actions. According to Leckie, the British plan to attack Charleston "was based upon [George Germain's] conviction that the South was full of Tories who would flock to the king's service once the Union Jack were unfurled" (Leckie 226). Germain believed that revolution had been forced upon the people of Charleston, so that they could take the city with little fighting. Fisk, however, asserts that British intentions were to devastate Charleston, to "lay waste your borders with fire and sword" (4) so that Charlestonians had to fight to defend "their hearth-stones from pollution" (4). The inaccuracy of Fisk's characterization of British plans should have been obvious to South Carolinians, since Charleston did, in fact, capitulate to the British on May 12, 1780, and it was under British control for the rest of the war. The British did not lay waste the city (see J. F. C. Fuller 312). In fact, Clinton rejected the military and Loyalist arguments for vengeance, "adopting instead a conciliatory policy of granting pardons and paroles. His clemency was so successful that no fewer than two thousand Patriots volunteered to fight for King George if they could oppose French or Spanish soldiers, rather than their own countrymen" (Leckie 518). Leckie says that Charleston did become "a cockpit of murder, arson, rape and robbery" (519), as a consequence of rebel and loyalist colonists fighting one another, not British vindictiveness, and it continued long after the war (see Phillips, *The Cousins' War* 320–22). This was even acknowledged at the time of Fisk's speech; according to Genovese and Fox-Genovese, "Simms, in his *Life of Marion* and *History of South Carolina,* recorded atrocities committed by both sides" (*Mind of the Masters* 33). So, Fisk scapegoats the British for what the South Carolinians colonists, rebel and loyal, did.

One would hardly expect to find tremendously correct retellings of battles in celebratory speeches, so my point is not that Fisk's version is historically inaccurate. The interesting point is the *way* it is inaccurate—Fisk makes the battle a narrative of gallant, if impractical, men who improbably win against a much stronger and more brutal foe because their hearts are in the right place and their cause is just. All practical considerations—military as well as political—are obscured in the light of this grander narrative.

In certain important points, this narrative is the same as that of *Nick of the Woods:* just as the settlers are forced by the Indians to engage in violence (as opposed to acknowledging that the settlers have chosen to violate treaties), so the South Carolinians are forced by the British to fight (as opposed to acknowledging that Patriots chose rebellion). The practical, political causes of the fight are obscured, as is the very range of pragmatic responses available to the combatants. There are differences, as well. Fisk's narrative does not have the tragic overtones of Bird's, so there is not the sense that even the heroes are degraded—at least, not the heroes of the Revolutionary naval battle. But, there is still a tragic and victimized Romantic hero: the slave owners.

Having finished his narrative of the battle, and his encomium of Moultrie, Fisk brings the speech to the present day, and he then introduces the subject of abolitionists. The abolitionists, like the British, intend to "scatter wrath and desolation—mildew and blight—havoc and death, in the Eden bowers of the sunny South" (13). Like the Revolutionary-era South Carolinians, current southerners are threatened with complete destruction: were abolition to happen, "Your lands would be covered with ruin, and your altar-stones with blood and desolation" (15). And, like the Patriots of the Revolution, southerners have formidable opponents; they are besieged: "And shall our proud barque founder upon the breakers which threaten her from every point, and the black billow of fate roll over the shipwrecked crew—shall some future historian ever record the decline and downfall of this our land, the wonder and admiration of the world?" (18). This battle against the abolitionists, like the Patriots' battle against the British and the settlers' battle against the savage Indians, is a battle of good against evil. Abolition is "the frozen viper" (16), an "insidious vine" (16), the result of "stagnant pools of priestcraft" (16), a "black wave" (17), "the serpent in the Eden of the South" (17), and "the misty veil of a gloomy superstition" (17).[5] Like Bird's Indians, abolitionists' motives are purely evil: "The hawk when he pounces upon the trembling dove, has as much real genuine philanthropy at his heart, as a modern abolitionist [. . .] There is not an abolitionist in America but would hold slaves tomorrow, if he could buy them with wooden nutmegs" (15).

When Fisk considers the argument that slavery is evil, he counters, "But if it is an evil—an evil to whom? an evil to the Master if any body.

It may be an evil for him to toil hour after hour, from the morning light to evening shade, at his counting room, to earn the wherewithal to enable his negroes to live like Nabobs in comparative indolence [. . .] It may be an evil to the country, and to the owner—but it is a blessing to the slave; if it is an evil, it is one of God's own appointing, and we should submit to it without murmur" (15). While Fisk's narrative is not as tragic as Bird's—there is no equivalent of the white settlers slaughtering children and taking scalps—Fisk's argument, like Bird's, turns whites into the victims of the very system they perpetrate.

As bizarre as this may seem to us, it was a common argument. Freehling, Young, and others have discussed at length the ways that southern slave owners justified the brutality of slavery through invoking familial metaphors. Slave owners identified themselves as loving fathers, and insisted that they would rather have foregone violence altogether, but were forced to discipline slaves. In that rhetoric, slave owners engaged in torture, murder, and rape only because they were forced into it by the laziness, dishonesty, and rebelliousness of slaves. Slave owners were victimized by slaves, in that they were forced to engage in the behavior about which they were ashamed; they scapegoated slaves for the cruelty inherent to slavery.

Because abolitionists are evil, and motivated simply by a desire to do evil, there is no need to consider their criticisms; there is no reason to think carefully and critically about slavery. Because it is an issue of good versus evil, this is not a topic that should be treated in policy debates. And even when Fisk reaches the exhortation, when the genre would suggest that he should say what policy his hearers should follow, he keeps the discourse in the realm of the eschatological: "Let us see in every heart a shield, and in every hand a sword to guard the ark of our privileges from profanation" (18). As in Bird, there is no specific history, there are no political causes, and, therefore, there are no political solutions; the language of eschatology occludes the political, and the language of religion prescribes submission to a system from which they happen to benefit.

This is epideictic rhetoric, and, for the reasons listed above, a poor foundation for public debate of important issues. That a piece of literature, and an epideictic speech, should be epideictic is not surprising, nor even troubling, but I will argue that proslavery public discourse was dominated by this mode, and that *is* troubling. Slavery was a political institution and an entire set of policies, from the personal to the national. At the personal level, every moment that a slave owner continued to own slaves was a policy decision. At the national level, policies like the three-fifths clause, the Northwest Ordinance of 1787, Indian removal, the Missouri Compromise, the annexation of Texas, acceptance of the Lecompton constitution, and so on, all served to protect and promote slavery. The consensus among historians is that the majority of people in the non-slave states acquiesced, with some undetermined amount of grumbling, as long as it was restricted to existing slave states; abolitionism was not a popular movement. William Miller summarizes the situation in 1836: "The support for abolition was miniscule; the abolitionist orators were being stoned and mobbed even in the North [. . .] They didn't have any support" (120). A large number of citizens who had been anti-abolitionist became antislavery because they were alienated by the aggressive tactics of proslavery rhetors and politicians. Whereas abolition had no support, "Civil liberty, on the other hand, free debate and free press and the sacred right of petition, taken in the abstract at least, had wide and strong support [. . .] To take action that seemed to contravene these fundamental American liberties was not very prudent" (W. L. Miller 121). The problem, then, was not abolitionists' aggression, but proslavery, and it was imprudent.

My argument is that prudence is exactly the virtue obscured in the heroes of people like Bird and Fisk. One might argue that it is unreasonable to look to literature and epideictic rhetoric for thorough discussions of policy options, but that is not quite my point. It is not unreasonable to look to historical romance for a sense of historical causation—in Scott's *Waverley*, characters end up in the situations they do because of specific decisions that are made, not because they are locked in a battle between good and evil. It is precisely that sense of personal responsibility and historical contingency that is absent from Bird and Fisk. Fisk's recasting of Moultrie's actions supports the argument that the southern conception of honor saw something mildly dishonorable in being prudent.

Southern culture's bifurcation of honor and practicality is very complicated, so that this point about the prudent can easily be overstated. As critics of Genovese's argument in *The Political Economy of Slavery* have shown, slave owners were very practical when it came to pricing slaves, allocating tasks, breaking up families, and turning a profit (see especially Fogel and Engerman; for a general review of the issue, see Smith, *Debating Slavery*). But, this ability to be prudent in regard to their self-interest does not disprove that they *claimed* not to be concerned with profit—one of the supposed distinctions between slavers and slave owners was that the former was only out for profit, while the latter put his paternal responsibility for the slave first. That this was a distinction without a difference does not mean it was not a consequential ideological distinction. Slavers claimed that their practices, unlike sharp and shrewd Yankee treatment of factory workers, were unprofitable. They claimed not to break up slave families, but empirical research shows that they did when profits were sufficiently attractive (see Tadman); they claimed to control through love and affection, but empirical research shows they (or their overseers) relied heavily on physical punishment and its threat (see Seabrook, *Essay* 10–11); they claimed to think of slaves as family, but made a tidy profit from them.[6] In rhetorical terms, they privileged an *ethos* of the impractical gentleman who thinks about honor rather than profit, so that prudence was excluded from the realm of public discourse as a goal of public policy, but not behavior.

The consequence was (and is) that the possible prudence or imprudence of policies and practices was not pursued in public discourse, and that to consider such questions was potentially shameful and unmanly. Michael Kimmel, following William Taylor, has argued that American antebellum culture had three possible models of manhood. The "Self-Made Man" was the man who supported his family through careful attention to economic triumph, but this was a deeply problematic model due to its emphasis on money. The "Heroic Artisan" was the ideal, but increasingly less plausible as industrialization increased (and I would suggest impossible in a slave culture, as the association of skilled artisanship and African Americans had the notorious effect of deskilling artisanship). The "Genteel Patriarch" was, in many contemporary plays and novels, presented as an effete, effeminate, and artificial man, the English (or Anglophilic) whose day was over. Southern culture was the last stand of "the Genteel Patriarch" (whom Taylor calls "the Cavalier"): "To the Genteel Patriarch, manhood meant property ownership and a benevolent patriarchal authority at home, including the moral instruction of his sons. A Christian gentleman, the Genteel Patriarch embodied love, kindness, duty, and compassion, exhibited through philanthropic work, church activities, and deep involvement with his family" (Kimmel 16). But, as Kimmel argues, this was a model of inherently impaired manhood, as contemporary literature made the Genteel Patriarch an object of disdain, at worst, and criticism, at best, as in the case of Forrester.[7] It could not be redeemed through economic success, as that was precisely what it was defined in opposition to. As Genovese and Fox-Genovese say, "Southerners themselves harped on the contrast between their chivalric values and the typically bourgeois values of Northerners" (*Mind of the Master* 97). Thus, manhood had to be demonstrated in (apparent) lack of concern for profit and self-preservation; that is, risk.

This disdain for profit has been explained in various ways, but I think it is worth considering as yet another example of projection. Despite the paternal ethos, slavers did think about slaves as economic properties, and this way of thinking was intermittently admitted. Whitemarsh Seabrook, in his *Essay on the Management of Slaves,* says: "To their owners, our slaves yield two distinct interests: the one annual, or that which arises from their labour; the other, a contingent or prospective interest, the issue of the females" (5). Calhoun argues that, if a master treats his slaves well, "the Planter will have reason to be satisfied; he will always obtain seven or eight per cent upon the value of his slave" (qtd. in Coit 286). If slavers were open about the institution of slavery, they would have had to admit that their sense of manhood and achievement depended upon the enslavement of other humans, something that violated the *ethos* of paternalism, so they condemned northerners for what they were actually doing: being more concerned with profit than persons.

It is not so much that one cannot be prudent (one should, after all, turn a profit with one's plantation), but that one could not seem to be motivated by prudence. Bruce and Greenberg have each argued that this need to show that one was not prudent had disastrous consequences: "Nineteenth-century men of honor felt compelled to risk everything in many different fields [. . .] When Confederate strategists repeatedly preferred to attack rather than to assume a more prudent defensive posture, they were only giving expression to another form of their powerful cultural impulse toward risk. It was a losing strategy—but it was a strategy few Southern gentlemen could resist. The Confederacy may well have lost the Civil War as a result of lessons learned at Southern card tables and racetracks" (Greenberg 138, see also Freehling, *Prelude* 34–35). To say that this version of proslavery ideology idealizes idealism is not to say that it denigrated practicality. It is to say that there was a dichotomy between impractical (Roland Forrester) and practical (George Clark and the other frontiersmen). The former is idealistic and unrealistic, and the latter are brutally realistic. And there is nothing in between the two.

This, too, maps onto the complicated roles of slavery: the ideal of a loving father and the reality of an overseer. As Norrece Jones says in regard to slave-mastering practice in South Carolina, "because of the feared sickly season and 'country fever' between May and November, most ruling-class planters from the eastern and middle portions of the state departed for healthier climates" thereby leaving their slaves to the care of overseers alone for more than half the year (28). The ideology of slavery characterized the slave owner as a patriarch who loved his slaves as family members. According to Kingsley, slavers should "consider the slave as a member of his family, whose happiness and protection is identified with that of his own family" (Kinglsey 16; see also Young, especially 181–83). In reality, slavers had to rely heavily on overseers, who had no clear role in the patriarchal melodrama. Greenberg says, "Those who could afford it placed the burden of punishment on the shoulders of overseers—and then hated them for their brutality" (*Masters* 22, see Scarborough 161–63 for instances of conflict over outrageously brutal treatment by overseers). Overseers "undercut domesticity" because "they made paternalism dependent on the very sort of wage slave that domestic patriarchy had allegedly obliterated" (Freehling, *Road to Disunion* 68; see also Young, especially 180–82; Wiethoff, *Crafting the Overseer*).

A particularly disturbing quote in James Breedon's collection of slave-mastering advice is from a planter who recommends maintaining the ethos of loving father by having the driver do all the punishment: "I rarely punish myself but make my driver virtually an executive officer to inflict punishments that I may remove from the mind of the servant who commits a fault the unfavourable impression, too apt to be indulged in, that it is for the pleasure of punishing rather than for the purpose of enforcing obedience and establishing good order that punishments are inflicted" (79–80).[8] Perhaps there was reason for the impression; another entry in Breedon's book says, "More punishment is inflicted on every plantation by the men in power from private pique than from a neglect of duty" (78). Seabrook advises planters that "the object of punishment is the reformation of the criminal and the preventing of others from committing the like offense. It is manifest then, that such punishments and such a mode of inflicting them ought to be resorted to, as make the strongest and most lasting impression on the mind" (9). This reliance on the performance on punishment generally, and especially on overseers to enact it, made southern slavery much closer to northern factories than proslavery ideologues liked to admit, so the role of overseers is erased from proslavery rhetoric. Defenses of slavery emphasize how much owners love their slaves and the proslavery visual rhetoric shows owners tending them, but fail to mention overseers.[9] So slavery as an institution is kind because slave owners of large plantations do not often punish slaves. While not an outright lie (like the myth that the swamps were healthful for slaves), this was certainly rhetorical mis-direction.

Norrece Jones's interpretation of relations between owners and overseers suggests an even grimmer reading of the function of this idealism/brutality split. He argues that "overseers were expected to do the impossible: planters demanded slave compliance without slave injuries, bountiful crops with limited resort to lashings, and faithful service despite poor pay" (33). By setting out impossible goals, *while* refusing to think clearly about just how they were to be attained, owners could congratulate themselves on their high ideals, and take the profits from the low practices. Setting out goals which can only be attained through unethical practice, without actually calling for that practice, enables an owner (or manager, or legislator) to escape responsibility for the very actions she or he is actually requiring. Wiethoff has argued that there almost certainly were abusive scoundrels among the overseers, but he has also pointed out that a common way of paying overseers (giving them a cut of the crops) was continued although it was known to increase abusive practices. Widely condemned for encouraging overseers to overwork slaves, it was still widely used because it was profitable (*Crafting the Overseer's Image* 3–4). So, again, slavers engaged in a practice they knew encouraged abuse because they put profit first, but they did so in a way that enabled them to imagine someone else was responsible.

Slavers' rhetoric of victimhood kept the policy discourse off slavery, in that it shifted the political definition of "the problem" from slavery to antislavery. The more that political discourse made slavery the issue, or talked about the true condition of slaves, the more likely public policy would do something about slavery; slavers' rhetoric of victimhood helped keep the discourse focused, not on slavery, but on its critics. If slavery is the problem, the solution involves policies about the institution of slavery; if abolitionists are the problem, then the solution involves policies about them.

Until the 1830s, the most common southern defense of slavery was that it was an evil, but something impossible to resist, "an incongruous though necessary evil" (Tise 286), or, in Kingsley's words, an "iniquity [that] has its origin in a great, inherent, universal and immutable law of nature" (14). "No one will deny," says Alexander Sims in 1833, "that Slavery is a moral evil" ("Preface"). This view was not restricted to southerners. James Trecothick Austin, the Massachusetts attorney general, after arguing that slavery cannot be abolished, says, "I utter the declaration with grief; but the pain of the writer does not diminish the truth of the fact" (25). The necessary evil is a self-serving fatalism about slavery—while pronouncing it evil (and thereby showing that one has the right feelings), this position excludes any action to end slavery: "Public sentiment in the slave-holding States cannot be altered" (Austin 24).

One would expect that the "evil" inherent to slavery would be the condition of Africans and African Americans. Instead, southern defenses of slavery attribute the victimization to the slave owners. Made most famously by Thomas Jefferson, this argument asserts that slave owners are corrupted by slavery, have been forced into it by someone else, and are its true victims. Holland, in 1822, after narrating Britain's long history of involvement in the slave trade, said, "If then, we are unhappily afflicted with an evil, the curse of which is felt and acknowledged by every enlightened man in the Slave-holding States, it should be a matter of sympathy, rather than of rebuke particularly when it is recollected that it was not of our own creation. It must be conceded by every fair and candid reasoner, who is at all acquainted with the history of our country, that the introduction of this mischievous and unhappy institution is not imputable to the present generation, nor are we answerable either to heaven, or to earth, for its existence" (22). In the 1830s and later, rhetors began to assert that slavery was an economic burden, that it was more expensive than free labor, and that the institution frustrated manufacturing and industrialization, thereby harming the South's overall economic development (an issue still debated by economic historians). In areas with high slave population, defenders of slavery described themselves as endangered by the presence of slaves and ex-slaves, a threat that victimized them. And, like Bird's white settlers who were forced into brutality by the Indians, slavers described themselves as further victimized by slaves because slaves' lazy and duplicitous nature forced owners into savage punishment.[10]

Earlier, I mentioned William Taylor's argument that southern literature was not a defense of slavery; I am saying, however, that the tragic narrative of novels like *Nick of the Woods* does serve as a defense of slavery and slaveocracy, while barely mentioning the institution, through reinforcing the imaginative foundation for that system. This view served to rationalize a system that had a dreamy, noble, and tragic ethos that was actually protected and supported by a brutal practicality; left out is something in the middle, the practical but principled argument about long-term politics and policies. In other words, left out is open deliberation.

The notion that slavery was imposed upon the South was a cliché in the political discourse on slavery. By turning themselves into helpless victims of the very institution they were, on the contrary, deliberately trying to expand, slavers could absolve themselves of responsibility for the course of action they were aggressively pursuing. Like Bird's settlers, forced into cruelty by the Indians, so slave owners were forced into owning slaves by the English, and are forced into cruelty by slaves. But, there was a rhetorical danger to that line of argument—if slavery was so harmful, why not abandon it? (In fact, much of the abolitionist Theodore Weld's *American Slavery as It Is,* published in 1836, argues that slavery should be abandoned because it is harmful to slave owners and the South as well as to slaves.) And it is in that light that the extraordinary rhetorical and political importance of the rhetoric of doom becomes clear: the very attachment to falsehood becomes idealism, impracticality is transmogrified into romanticism, ethical principles are abandoned in favor of moral relativism, personal responsibility for choices is evaded, and deliberation is displaced by epideictic.

3 "A deep conviction, settled on every bosom"

Alarmism, Conspiracy, and Unification

> And often we must think of rhetoric not in terms of some one particular address, but as a general *body of identifications* that owe their convincingness much more to trivial repetition and dull daily reënforcement than to exceptional rhetorical skill.
>
> —Kenneth Burke

One reason scholars tend to accept the narrative of calm waters broken by the pamphlet mailings is that there was an impressive amount of anti-abolitionist agitation in the summer and fall of 1835. There were meetings of concerned citizens who passed belligerent resolutions, condemning abolitionists as "mischievous" ("The Union Must Be Preserved," *Western Christian Advocate,* September 11, 1835); there were politicians who berated the abolitionists for their "mischievous purposes" and "fanatical schemes" ("Speech of Governor Tyler," *African Repository and Colonial Journal* October 1835); there were alarmist editorials and articles that called for "a spirit of concert and of action among the Slave-holding States" and "a firm determination to resist, at the threshold, every invasion of our domestic tranquility" ("Extract from Governor Wilson's Message," *Charleston Mercury,* August 7, 1835). The "Report of the Joint Committee of Federal Relations" (*Communication from His Excellency, Governor McDuffie*) says that "the present condition of the slave question in the States of this confederacy, presents one of the most extraordinary spectacles which, your committee will venture to assert, has ever challenged the notice of the entire civilized world." The *Charleston Courier* said of the public meeting called in response to the pamphlets, "one of the most imposing assemblage of citizens in respect of numbers, intelligence and respectability, that had ever been witnessed" (qtd. in *Niles' Weekly Register* August 22, 1835). However, if these reactions should be seen as evidence of something catalyzed by abolitionists, then the alarmism, hyperbole, and agitation should have been specific to the pamphlet controversies, or to the post-July 1835 slavery debate. And, I will argue, looking carefully at southern rhetoric shows that anti-abolitionism was on the rise before the AAS mailing, and that hyperbole was the norm for southern public discourse.

There was a long series of events before 1835 to which proslavery rhetors and politicians, especially in South Carolina, responded with predictions of race war, fearmongering about the terrible crisis, bellicose demands for extreme measures, and combative threats of secession.[1] As early as Holland's 1822 *A Refutation,* proslavery rhetors began threatening secession over slavery, while, interestingly enough, blaming the North for that outcome (see especially Holland 9–11).[2] In the spring before the pamphlet controversy, it was such a common threat that northern newspapers remarked on it (discussed in an earlier chapter). As in the sixth and seventh resolutions of the Committee of Twenty-one, secession was threatened if critics of slavery were not silenced: "6) Resolved. That in the event of no effectual measures being adopted either by the general or state governments, or by the people of the non-slaveholding states, for the suppression of the great and growing evil of which we complain, it will become the solemn duty of all these states having a common interest with us on this subject to adopt the most decisive and efficacious measures TO PROTECT THEMSELVES" (qtd. in *Niles' Weekly Register,* August 22, 1835). It is important to point out that proslavery rhetors did not threaten secession only if abolition were enacted, but if criticism of slavery continued.

Matthew Mason points out that "the conventional view" that slavery burst upon the political scene during the Missouri Compromise "as if out of nowhere" (3) is false, and that "there was never a time between the Revolution and Civil War in which slavery went unchallenged" (5). Merton Dillon says, "At no time could the American slaveholding society be called secure" (6). Even during the Missouri Compromise, when there was a massive fire in Savannah, the issue of to whom aid went led to outrage on the part of northerners and southerners alike. Some northerners required that their aid be extended to African Americans, and some southerners rejected the money; Savannah's mayor said that requirement was "throwing among us the fire-brand of discord" (qtd. in Mason 2).

In 1822, after the failed Vesey rebellion, Thomas Pinckney refers to the citizens of the "Northern states, who directly or indirectly instigate our Black population to such scenes as they lately mediated" (7). Pinckney insists that they must "stop all incendiary publications" that come from the free states (8) and cease "the most dangerous of these indulgences, [slaves] being taught to read and write" (7–8). Seabrook's 1825 *A Concise View of the Critical Situation, and Future Prospects of the Slave-holding States, in Relation to Their Coloured Population* begins by saying that "a momentous crisis in the history of our country, is rapidly approaching" (3). This crisis is created by "the poisonous shaft [. . .] still grasped by the fanatic" (3). Slave ownership, Seabrook says, "is daily becoming less secure, and more the subject of acrimonious animadversion" (3). Seabrook blames this crisis on, among others, fanatics, the Hartford Convention, England, colonizationists, and Rufus King.

In 1827, it was proposed that the federal government use some of the money generated by the sale of public lands to pay for colonization of free African Americans. Although scholars now generally accept Garrison's characterization of colonization as effectively proslavery (as I do), that is not how it was always seen at the time. In 1827, Charles Hayne, of Georgia, condemned colonization with the kind of superlatives common in the summer and fall of 1835: "of all the extravagant schemes that have yet been devised in this country, I know of none more wild, impracticable, or mischievous" (*Register of Debates,* 19th Congress, 2nd session, 290). He argued that the Senate should not receive the petition (precisely the proposal that would lead to the "gag rule" controversy in December 1835), and it was withdrawn (295, 296), but not before Smith, of South Carolina, had described it as "an entering wedge, which they should oppose" (296; see Freehling, *Prelude* 124 for the South Carolina legislature's panicked response to the American Colonization Society). In 1828, the *General Assembly Senate Report of a Special Committee of the Senate of South Carolina* was created to report on the tariff issue but also to determine "whether Congress can extend its legislation to the means of meliorating the condition of the free colored or slave population of the United States" (29).[3] The committee reports: "Should Congress claim a power to discuss and to take any vote upon any question connected with the domestic slavery of the Southern States, (excepting it be to devise the means of prohibiting the slave trade, the only power which it has by the terms of the Constitution,) it is not for your Committee to prescribe what course ought to be adopted to counteract the evil and the dangerous tendency of public discussions of this nature" (29). The Nullification Crisis (which proslavery politicians tended to refer to as "the Force Bill" controversy, thereby shifting the stasis to Jackson's actions rather than their own) was notorious for its aggressive rhetoric and threats of secession. The threats began with uproar over the tariffs of 1828, and came to a head with South Carolina's November 24, 1832, "Ordinance of Nullification" that threatened secession from the Union should the federal government attempt to enforce the tariffs. The penultimate paragraph of the ordinance stated that any military response would be held "as inconsistent with the longer continuance of

South Carolina in the Union; and that the people of this State will henceforth hold themselves absolved from all further obligation to maintain or preserve their political connection with the people of the other States; and will forthwith proceed to organize a separate government, and do all other acts and things which sovereign and independent States may of right do." The ordinance also

> ordained, that all persons now holding any office of honor, profit, or trust, civil or military, under this State (members of the legislature excepted), shall, within such time, and in such manner as the legislature shall prescribe, take an oath well and truly to obey, execute, and enforce this ordinance, and such act or acts of the legislature as may be passed in pursuance thereof, according to the true intent and meaning of the same, and on the neglect or omission of any such person or persons so to do, his or their office or offices shall be forthwith vacated, and shall be filled up as if such person or persons were dead or had resigned; and no person hereafter elected to any office of honor, profit, or trust, civil or military (members of the legislature excepted), shall, until the legislature shall otherwise provide and direct, enter on the execution of his office, or be he any respect competent to discharge the duties thereof until he shall, in like manner, have taken a similar oath; and no juror shall be impaneled in any of the courts of this State, in any cause in which shall be in question this ordinance, or any act of the legislature passed in pursuance thereof, unless he shall first, in addition to the usual oath, have taken an oath that he will well and truly obey, execute, and enforce this ordinance, and such act or acts of the legislature as may be passed to carry the same into operation and effect, according to the true intent and meaning thereof.

Just as with the slavery controversy, those with the greater political power tried to use that power to extinguish the other side completely.

This is the kind of behavior that makes me skeptical of Greenberg's argument that southerners hated faction (*Masters and Statesmen*). Greenberg is right that southern rhetors constantly condemned faction, but I'm not sure those condemnations should be taken at face value, as it looks very much like cunning projection. For instance, Henry Laurens Pinckney, the editor of the factional *Charleston Mercury,* in his 1833 Fourth of July speech, moves from bemoaning the entrance of faction into the Fourth of July celebrations to arguing that Whigs should become State Rights Party members: "But why is it that this day, so peculiarly dedicated to our ancestors, and endeared by the remembrance of their toils and triumphs, should have been made an occasion, in this community, of political contention and party strife? Why is it that on this political Sabbath, the people of this city, descended, as they are, from the same illustrious source, and enjoying, as they do, the same glorious inheritance, no longer unite as brothers around the tombs of their fathers, nor offer fraternal and harmonious oblations upon the common altar of their common country?"

The pronouns shift at this point; whereas "our" had meant "the people of Charleston" of both factions, "our" has come to mean his party: "Did we denounce our brethren as unworthy of political communion with us?" For the rhetorical question to make sense in the context, the answer should be "no." But, in fact, it was the nullifiers who instituted the test oath, which prohibited political office to people who would not swear loyalty to nullifier principles, so, in fact, they had denounced their brethren as unworthy of political communion with them. He continues: "Or is it, as they kindly intimated by their conduct, that the purity of their patriotism would be sullied by continued confraternity with anarchists and rebels? What say you, Whigs?" (*An Oration* 4). This leads to a paean to "a State Rights man" and what makes them more patriotic, more loyal, and less submissive than the opposition (and why all Whigs should be nullifiers). He condemns the opposition for doing something it has not done, but which he is doing in the same speech in which he condemns the behavior.

Regardless of whether members of the pro-nullification faction saw themselves as engaged in faction, their behavior in this instance is puzzling insofar as it was unnecessarily—even self-destructively—combative, and grounded in unrealistic assessments of the situation (Capers frequently uses the term "self-delusion" in reference to Calhoun and his supporters). Yet it exemplifies much of how proslavery rhetors would respond in the antebellum era. Freehling explains this overreaction as anxiety about protecting slavery (*Prelude* 309–13), and it may have been. It may also have been simply that they were obsessed with controlling the discourse. Having lost the political battle, they were determined to win the local discursive battle, thereby changing the way that people were allowed to talk, as though that would change reality. As I will discuss in the conclusion, authoritarians love loyalty oaths, even (especially?) when they have little impact other than outing people who put truth above party loyalty.

After losing the tariff battle with Jackson, pro-nullification forces still tried to enforce the oath part of the ordinance, and they often asserted that they had triumphed against Jackson, as when Henry Laurens Pinckney told his Charleston audience in 1833, "Liberty has emerged from the ordeal, not only uninjured, but strengthened and refined [. . .] we meet in peace and in victory" (*An Oration* 4). The first move was a failure: "All in all, the nullifiers' attempt to enforce state unity by enacting test oaths formed the most unsuccessful part of the postnullification reaction" (*Prelude* 321). The second may have been partially successful; I earlier quoted the Duff Green article that narrates nullifiers as victorious (yet Calhoun biographers generally insist that he learned from the disaster, suggesting he knew it had failed).

Both moves were consistent with dueling behavior. Greenberg points out that the dance of a duel enabled both sides to claim that they had "triumphed" (*Masters and Statesmen* 142). For the potential duellist to admit that he made concessions in order to avoid a fight "would have been an acknowledgement of a willingness to abandon principles" and "have even acknowledged inferiority" (142). The nullifiers had been forced to make concessions, and their secession threat had been shown to be empty posturing, so they redeemed their honor through claiming they had triumphed and demanding submission from the closest thing they could get to Jackson—Unionists (those who had opposed secession). They lost, they insisted they hadn't, and they prohibited anyone else saying anything different.

Alarmism was often the result of slave insurrections, real or imagined. The Denmark Vesey conspiracy almost immediately followed the Missouri Compromise, and, as Freehling has said, "The tragic slave conspiracy which Vesey inspired, although completely crushed in 1822, remained in 1832 and long thereafter a searing reminder that all was not well with slavery in South Carolina" (Freehling, *Prelude* 53). Indeed, various sources—including the city of Charleston's report on the Vesey uprising, *Negro Plot: An Account of the Late Intended Insurrection among a Portion of the Blacks of the City of Charleston, South Carolina*—all concluded that the insurrection plot was the logical outcome of criticisms of slavery made during the Missouri Compromise debate, specifically speeches by Rufus King (see 27, 31, 46; Holland blames black missionaries, see especially 11). The significance of this argument in regard to the congressional debate over the Missouri Compromise cannot be emphasized strongly enough. Pinckney and others who make the argument are not calling for the silencing of marginalized and radical *abolitionists*, but the silencing of criticism of slavery everywhere, including in congressional debates over whether it should be allowed to expand. The logical conclusion is that proslavery rhetors believed that free discussion of slavery in any public place was incompatible with slavery in slave states.

In the confessions extorted through torture, one of the accused conspirators implicated free African American sailors, so South Carolina passed a law requiring that free black sailors be jailed while their ships were in port. The issue was "a major obsession of the South Carolina Association, a self-created, extralegal organization founded by the wealthiest and most influential members of the planter gentry" (Greenberg, *Masters and Statesmen* 112–13). This obsession was probably unnecessary, but the alarmism over sailors of African descent continued, with nontrivial political consequences. Because the ships were often foreign, these laws caused conflict with the federal government and other nations, a controversy that, according to Greenberg, flared up from time to time.

This anxiety about sailors was part of the fantasy that insurrection was always and only the consequence of external contagion. Like the equation of "northern" and "abolitionist" this fantasy obscured southern sources of antislavery and resistance. Internal dissent and resistance—regardless of the race or gender of the dissenter—demonstrated that the repressive policies had not ended the ability of people to resist slavery. So, rather than acknowledge the limits of oppression, people could look for narratives that rationalized it, and they could demand policies that presumed it. The Negro Seaman laws are an example of such a policy.

The Nat Turner rebellion of 1831 had tremendous impact on southern debates about, and perceptions of, slavery. The subsequent debate in Virginia over abolition contributed to panic, not only about abolition, but about the cracking of a solid slave-owning South. Those who advocated emancipation (mostly from the western section) argued that Turner's rebellion showed that slavery endangered everyone; they assumed that rebellion and slavery were necessarily entwined. Responses to that argument, therefore, had to disentangle rebellion and slavery, and look for other sources of resistance. Some, like Thomas Dew (discussed later), argued that Turner was insane, and so had no rational motive. More commonly, it was asserted that Turner had been motivated by reading Garrison's *Liberator,* something never proven.

Fears about slaves were manifest in the rumors and accounts of slave conspiracies to rebel, set fires, or poison whites that were, as Herbert Aptheker has shown, recurrent in southern newspapers, diaries, and reports through the 1830s. These "insurrections" have the same pattern: someone claims to have overheard slaves or free people of color "plotting," there is a panic which may or may not be reported in the papers as an actual insurrection, the militia is called out, various slaves or freedmen are scapegoated and murdered, and the papers praise the authorities for restoring order. Jones describes this pattern: "No matter how unfounded the claim or how spurious the source, the threat of an insurrection could trigger interstate hysteria that rarely was quelled until some black body had been sacrificed. And so that cycle went: deadly fear, black deaths, and appeals for more funds toward slave control" (25). Even in regard to actual insurrections, the aftermaths saw more African Americans murdered than there had been whites killed in the initial insurrection: "Indiscriminate murder and torture characterized efforts to suppress revolts and uncover conspiracy" (Dillon 157). Whites did not admit that they might have behaved precipitously, that they panicked, or that the murders might have been unnecessary.

Slavers' fear of slaves was sometimes admitted, but more often denied, even in the midst of arguments for public policy based on fear. So, there was, simultaneously, a fear-based public policy and a rhetoric of fearlessness. In the midst of his discussion of insurrections, Holland says, "With regard to any very serious or permanent effects resulting from the insurrectionary movements of our negroes, we must confess that we feel little or no apprehension" (65). If that is the case, if they really feel little or no fear, then why worry about criticism of slavery? Appomattox insists that the people of Southampton did not panic during the Turner rebellion (6) although he grants that "under the excitement produced by the sight of murdered neighbors and relatives [. . .] some few slaves were slain" who were innocent (5).

After the Nat Turner rebellion, there was a spate of insurrection panics, which then receded. Rather than admit that these panics were the consequence of white fear (rather than black action), Simms explains, "The moment that the south grew angry at the abolitionists and drove their laborers away, and burned the pamphlets and papers, the insurrections, which had 'broke out as often as once a month before,' entirely ceased" (33). One such panic was in Wilmington. The *Niles' Weekly Register* reports:

> A letter dated Raleigh, Sept. 13, was received by Mr. Barnum, of the City Hotel, Baltimore, by yesterday's southern mail, saying that expresses had arrived announcing that *Wilmington was in the hands of the blacks and burnt!*—that it was reported they *were advancing on Raleigh*—that the citizens had been all night under arms—and the women, almost distracted, were flying all directions. All business was stopped, except in preparation for events. At the instant of writing an express arrived from *Johnson county*, (adjoining that in which *Raleigh* stands), demanding arms and ammunition! Wilmington *was,*

> (must we say?) a large town, and had a great commerce. ("Awful" September 17, 1831)

There was no insurrection; nor was there either a correction or a retraction on the part of the *Niles' Register.* Instead, the newspaper (like others) reported it as an insurrection plot that was only barely foiled.

There was, however, a panic, during which wild rumors circulated, and newspapers reported the rumors as fact. Even when events proved the rumors false, neither whites in the area nor newspapers were willing to admit that their judgment or perception might have been (or would ever be) fallible. When evidence demonstrated the panic was unfounded, as Grimsted eloquently puts it, "then followed a determination, equally blinding to the truth, to present the action as heroic, not hysterical" (142). Moreover, the article in the *Wilmington Recorder* demonstrates that the faith in whites' judgment remained unshaken by facts; they could still be certain:

> Summary justice was executed yesterday morning by the PEOPLE, on four of the *ringleaders,* engaged in the Conspiracy, the frightful disclosures respecting which, now agitate the public mind. The guilt of these monsters in human shape is established beyond a doubt. A deep conviction settled on every bosom—that the measure was indispensable to the safety of the community—called for their execution. If ever stern necessity required a prompt and vigorous course in making public examples, this necessity exists in our country. Two ringleaders were executed at Kenansville, Duplin Co. about a week ago. ("The North Carolina Plot," reprinted in the *Workingman's Advocate* October 1, 1831)[4]

In addition to exemplifying the unshakeable faith in the accuracy of white perception, this passage exemplifies the political practice of privileging the feelings of the powerful, and the real political power of hyperbole. The slaves had to be executed because of the "conviction settled on *every* bosom" (emphasis added), but, surely, not everyone was convinced. This mythical universality of sentiment is not an intellectual one—it is not "the conviction of every mind" let alone "the conviction of everyone who saw the evidence." These people were killed because of how some people *felt.*

The feelings of slavers and proslavery rhetors were always of central concern in proslavery rhetoric.[5] *Communication from the Governor, Transmitting a Preamble and Resolutions Adopted by the Legislature of Mississippi, Relative to the Persons Denominated Abolitionists* begins, "Whereas, the citizens of the state of Mississippi, have witnessed with apprehension of the deepest solicitude" (3). Although the 1835 Georgia Report and Resolution begins by saying that the committee has brought to the subject "that dispassionate deliberation its importance demands," the first paragraph concerns the "community of sympathy and good feeling" that currently exists between the North and the South and which the abolitionists "will inevitably" convert into "deadly hostility." The rest of the document is about feelings: the "spontaneous expression of feeling which has burst forth" in response to the pamphlets is "a matter of heart-felt congratulation"; that they "hail the sentiments expressed by the resolutions of some of the recent meetings of the North"; and so on. *The Communication from His Excellency, Governor McDuffie,* a "Report of the Joint Committee of Federal Relations," says that the committee has "given to this subject the deep and anxious consideration" which the topic and situation "so obviously demands." Seabrook's 1825 *A Concise View* says that anything that rouses strong feelings threatens the Union: "Whatever individual, or legislative acts, have a tendency to create or eternize the implacable feelings, usually incident to geographical distinctions, should be viewed, as positive attempts, *de facto,* to sap the foundation of our confederacy" (4). He also condemns the African Colonization Society, and various pro-colonization resolutions and proposals, because of how they make slavers feel: these actions "generate a state of feeling, hostile to our tranquility and interests" (13). Furman's 1823 *Exposition* makes the fear slavers' feel about criticism of slavery as important as insurrection; he says that the convention attendees, the sentiments of whom he is explaining, "are particularly unhappy" that the Bible has been used to argue for emancipation, "both on account of its direct influence on those, who admit it; and the fear it excites in others" (16). The *Joint Preamble and Resolutions of the General Assembly of the State of Alabama, in Favor of the Annexation of Texas to the United States of America* begins, "The General Assembly of the State of Alabama, have witnessed with feelings of deep mortification." Slavers' feelings exempt them from political (and historical) responsibility; Frederick Dalcho says about slavery: "We are ready to confess that, the present state of things, is not in accordance with our feelings. We deprecate the evil which attends it. It has descended to us; we have not produced it. We would most willingly apply the remedy, if we knew what it was" (6). The mistake continually made throughout proslavery rhetoric is to present evidence of strong feelings about a proposition as though it were evidence that the proposition were true; it is only evidence that powerful people feel strongly about it.[6]

Scholars like Young and Freehling point out that one consequence of slave insurrections was that they demonstrated that whites did not really see into the hearts of their slaves; slaves were not actually transparent, and whites did not really *know* what was going on. So, it's interesting that the major consequence of these panics was a reassertion of the supremacy of whites' knowledge—they could engage in what many called a "reign of terror" (then and now) by insisting on the power of their feelings. Their feelings constituted knowledge, and their knowledge constituted reality. This reality, regardless of its accuracy (that is, whether it referred to an external world rather than the internal one of slavers' feelings), becomes the basis of political action.

In the context of antebellum rhetoric generally, even the rhetoric of that spring specifically, alarmist rhetoric was the norm. In his inaugural address delivered in December 1834 (seven months before the mailing), South Carolina governor McDuffie called for the death penalty for abolitionists (qtd. in Julius, 134). In response, the South Carolina legislature immediately passed a resolution calling on northern states to suppress abolitionist activity in their borders (Julius 135). During that same session (again, months before the mailing), the legislature passed an antiliteracy law. Henry Laurens explained, in an open letter to Whitemarsh Seabrook, that this law was necessary because "there is hardly a publication which reaches us from other lands, or even from our sister States, which does not contain, in a great or less degree, inflammatory matter" (8).

Southern newspapers from 1835 have alarmist accounts of George Thompson's 1835 speaking tour of the United States, the British seizure of the slave ship *Enterprize,* and conspiracies by gamblers, Catholics, lawyers, and slaves. Alarmism was not restricted to the south. In January, an out-of-work (and almost certainly disturbed) Richard Lawrence attempted to assassinate Jackson. For reasons that are too complicated to narrate in the space limited here, the Mississippi senator George Poindexter was implicated in the assassination attempt. There were accusations and counter-accusations of plots and fabrications serious enough that the Senate appointed a committee to investigate (see February 21, 1835, *Congressional Globe* for the Senate, 582; for a detailed discussion of the incident, see Miles). George Bourne's anti-Catholic newspaper, *The Protestant,* had been agitating against Catholics since 1830 (which almost certainly contributed to the 1834 riot at the Ursiline convent in New York); Samuel Morse's anti-Catholic *Foreign Conspiracy against the Liberties of the United States* was published in 1835 (and was serialized in many papers), as was Rebecca Reed's *Six Months in a Convent* (Maria Monk's more explicitly pornographic *Awful Disclosures of Maria Monk* was published in 1836). In addition to those articles, with details of oaths, elaborate networks of spies, lists of conspirators, and detailed codes of behavior, the *Western Weekly Review* published an article entitled "Secret Club of Lawyers," which described a secret conspiracy of thirty-three lawyers, whose leader, "called the Tetrarch, is invested with the most absolute and irresponsible power" (May 8, 1835). Although the article begins by claiming that this is a society "differing in design and organization from any one we ever heard of," it is, in fact, exactly like all the others. It has complicated rituals, oaths "of unconditional submission in all mat[te]rs relating to his duties in the society," a multistate organization, detailed codes of behavior, and so on.

In March 1835, several newspapers announced that war with France was imminent (see especially the *U.S. Telegraph* and the *Western Weekly Register*), while others predicted war between Ohio and Michigan (see the *Charleston Mercury*). The 1830s began with near panic about a solar eclipse, and the summer of 1835 saw many northern newspapers consumed with the "moon hoax."

It may be that a pervasive air of crisis meant that any local grievance could explode into violence. The 109 riots that Grimsted says occurred between July and October of 1835 were antibank, anti-Jacksonian, antiabolitionist, antigambling, antislave, antiblack, anti-Catholic, and sometimes simply unfathomable, such as the riot of Pennsylvania College medical students who, the newspaper report speculated, rioted because their teacher's lectures were outdated (*Raleigh Register* June 2, 1835).

A good example of the culture of conspiracy and alarmism is the series of articles in newspapers during the spring and summer of 1835 concerning the supposed slave insurrection plot of John Murrell. Virgil Stewart (whether a charlatan or lunatic remains an interesting question) claimed that Murrell had confided in him an incredible plot, the details of which Stewart revealed in a series of articles for a tidy sum. These articles generally began in late July or early August, and ran through October (see, for instance, the *Western Weekly Review,* August 14 through October 9). The first few articles narrate a fairly plausible account of a petty criminal who specialized in stealing horses and slaves (sometimes, according to Stewart, with the complicity of the slaves). In a late installment, Stewart claimed that Murrell confessed to being head of a vast conspiracy comprised of abolitionists, slaves, and a criminal organization, intended to start a slave insurrection that would murder all whites from Maryland to Louisiana.

The plot is implausible in the extreme—as David Grimsted aptly says, it "needs only to be read to be disbelieved" (149)—but it was taken as "unquestioned fact" (150). Grimsted, quite persuasively, connects this series of articles to a major insurrection scare in Mississippi in July, saying that the article primed the pump for the subsequent lynchings. A widely reprinted article in the *Clinton Gazette* (called "Horrible Conspiracy") about that latter scare begins:

> A few days anterior to the 4th of July, various circumstances excited some suspicion in the minds of a few respectable citizens of Madison county, in the neighborhood of Beattie's Bluff, of an insurrection among the slaves of that settlement being about to occur. Several slaves were at different times overheard, whilst engaged in secret conversation relative to the proposed plot. A scrutiny, such as the crisis seemed to demand, was forthwith instituted, which led to the development of facts of a most startling and extraordinary character. It was very soon ascertained in the progress of the examination which ensued, that two individuals by name Cotton and Saunders, both of them steam doctors by profession, were prominently concerned in this nefarious scheme. Both these individuals were immediately apprehended. A large meeting of the citizens of Madison county was held, to deliberate upon the momentous crisis which had arisen, at which it was unanimously resolved that a committee of investigation should be immediately organized in the name, and upon the responsibility of the whole body of the citizens, to use all necessary means for ferreting out this nefarious plot, and bringing the offenders to a speedy justice. This committee thus organized, composed of 13 of the most respectable citizens of the county, men of elevated standing in the community, for moral worth, integrity and discretion, proceeded as soon as possible, to the task assigned them; and discovering that the evidences of a conspiracy having been formed, were perfectly conclusive, and that the guilt of Cotton and Saunders was placed beyond doubt, with but little delay, ordered them to a public execution, by hanging, which took place in the town of Livingston, on Saturday, the 4th day of July. (*Niles' Weekly Register,* August 8, 1835)

This is the *most* melancholy duty, the facts were the *most* startling, the meeting was *unanimous,* they used *all* means, the men were the *most* respectable, they went *immediately,* the evidence was *perfectly* conclusive and beyond doubt—the reliance on superlatives is striking. It is also striking that the author claims they *deliberated:* it was a lynch mob, and there was very little likelihood that the meeting would have decided the steam doctors were innocent, or that the meeting would have had a vocal minority arguing for the rule of law (for more on the role that gamblers played in southern culture, see Fabian). There is a tendency to attribute the Murrell panic to the mailings, as when Ann Fabian reverses the chronology in a footnote: "Early in the summer of 1835 northern abolitionists had also stepped up their propaganda campaigns in the South. With abolitionist attacks ringing in their ears, with rumors and hangings fresh in their minds, 'prominent' citizens (read slaveholders) of Vicksburg set about to celebrate Independence Day" (207n33). On the contrary, they could not have had anything ringing in their ears about the pamphlets, as the hangings took place weeks before the pamphlets were mailed. In most southern papers that I read from the summer and fall of 1835, the Murrell/Stewart "conspiracy" generated much more coverage than the abolitionist pamphlets, which were not even mentioned in some papers.

The *National Intelligencer* has two contradictory versions of the events. The first, published July 25, and reprinted from the *True American,* described the incident as a "mobocracy" lynching gamblers who had misbehaved at a Fourth of July celebration. On July 27, the *Intelligencer* reprinted an article with the slave insurrection version. This version was printed with a preface, but not one that acknowledged the discrepancy between it and the earlier article. Instead, it says, "THE FRUITS OF FANATICISM.—Behold, ye 'Liberators,' 'Emancipators,' 'Abolitionists,' the fruits of your extravagance and folly, your recklessness, and your criminal plots against the lives of your fellow-men!" The article itself does not claim that the plotters were inspired by abolitionist writing, and there was never any evidence to this effect. As Grimsted says, almost immediately, "Southerners began to revise this story to blame abolitionists for the trouble, or, more commonly, to insist that abolitionism and the criminal clan were a unified conspiracy" (147).[7]

I don't want to be understood as arguing that there was no panic over abolitionists in 1835; I am saying that we may have pushed back onto the era our own, very specific, meaning of the term "abolitionist," and so we misidentify the nature and catalyst of that panic. Current historians use "abolition" to identify the policy advocated by immediate abolitionists like Garrison, Tappan, and Weld—immediate, uncompensated emancipation of slaves, with full citizenship rights. That policy is distinguished from "emancipation," which is used to cover various plans of gradual emancipation, some involving compensation, and some not, and most not specifying citizenship rights to ex-slaves. Given that usage, if we look to the summer of 1835 for the activities of abolitionists, we look to the things we believe they really did, and plotting a multistate slave insurrection is not one of them (whereas the pamphlet mailing is). But, usage in the 1830s was not so careful. "Abolitionist" was a devil term, and the notion that abolitionists explicitly advocated insurrection so pervasive that abolitionists' interference could be, and was, read in to any rebellion or resistance, real or imagined. As absurd as this connection is, it was so widely accepted that I think we need to understand that when proslavery rhetors refer to abolitionists' activities in the summer of 1835, they probably mean Murrell's fantastical plot.

Further, I will suggest that panic over abolitionists was politically useful, and consciously fomented throughout the spring of 1835. In 1835, Jackson's party was immensely powerful. According to the *Congressional Biographical Dictionary,* the 1833–34 Congress (23rd) had 242 congressional representatives, of whom 143 were Jacksonians; the others are variously identified as members of the Whig, Anti-Mason, Know-Nothing (Native or American Party), Republican, Democrat, Anti-Jacksonian, or Nullifier parties. Of the forty-eight Senate seats, twenty were held by Jacksonians, and the others by a mixture comparable to Congress. The Twenty-fourth Congress had a similar makeup—approximately 120 Jacksonians. Could the various non-Jacksonian parties unify (as many of them eventually did), they had a shot at dominance, but, divided, they were nearly powerless; they needed a unification device. Michael Holt has pointed out the dilemma faced by the Whigs: the very condition that enabled the unification of disparate groups (hostility to Jackson) was not an effective rallying point for voters (*Rise and Fall* 33–37). The problem is that their major motive for working together was animosity to Jackson himself, which, while motivating for them, was not an issue on which they could build a unifying coalition of voters. Anti-Jacksonian papers (like the *Telegraph*) tried to rouse readers with alarmist articles about Jackson's usurpation of political power, buying off of the press, and factionalizing of government, but (perhaps because their own behavior on those points would not withstand much scrutiny), those issues were not effective unifying devices. The Whigs had to find something other than Jackson-hating to unify voters, or what William Cooper calls "a galvanizing issue," and they found it, he says, in anti-abolitionism: "The rise of an organized abolition movement in the North matched the growth of anti-Jackson sentiment in the South. The southern anti-Jackson men, the Whigs, went after the abolition issue with unabashed vigor and glee" (*The South and the Politics of Slavery* 58).

In 1835, Jackson was at the end of his second term. At the time, the nomination and election systems were fragmented, party control was far from absolute, and the process extended over most of the spring. Early in 1835, Jackson indicated his preference that his vice president, the New Yorker Martin Van Buren, succeed him. Anti-Jackson papers, who already openly accused Jackson of being a tyrant, presented this move on Jackson's part as an attempt to perfect the Jacksonian takeover of American government. Duff Green, the pro-Calhoun editor of the *U.S. Telegraph,* appears to have held out hope that it might be possible to prevent the planned Democratic Convention in Baltimore from happening, or to prevent it from selecting Van Buren. I will suggest that close analysis of Duff Green's anti-Jacksonian *U.S. Telegraph* over the spring of 1835 shows that Cooper was correct—anti-abolitionism was an attempt to unify the various anti-Jacksonians through the wedge issue of abolition. As the spring went on, and as the Van Buren nomination went ahead, the *Telegraph* published more, longer, and increasingly alarmist articles about abolitionists, sometimes explicitly accusing Van Buren of being abolitionist, and sometimes implicitly doing so, such as through emphasizing that the abolitionists were from New York.

The first article about slavery was January 26, called, significantly, "The Next Presidency—The Anti-Slavery Question," which accused New York politicians of trying to "connect" the presidential election to slavery, a striking instance of cunning projection. As discussed in an earlier chapter, Green here accuses the Jacksonians of doing something that they are not doing, but he is. The same tactic is central to the January 27 article called "Emancipators." The article, with extracts from a speech a Mr. Stone had made at a colonization meeting, tells its readers that these extracts "show the spirit with which the religious Fanatics are carrying on their incendiary movement." The extracts were prefaced with this marginally coherent comment: "Let them be joined by those whom the Van Buren organ at Boston is endeavoring to enlist under the cry of 'Free labor and Slave labor,' and by those whom it hopes to gain by representing the contest for the next Presidency as one to be decided upon the principle of interference or non interference with the slaves of the south, and it will be found that the country will have still stronger reasons to curse the influence which the New York Politicians have over the administration and the Government." The article shows no connection between Stone and Van Buren, nor does it quote the "Van Buren organ" (presumably the *Statesman* or the *Post*) advocating abolition of slavery in the slave states.[8]

That same day, there was an article attacking the *Liberator* reprinted from the *Boston Courier,* a Whig paper (Mott 187), which organ was praised because it was "conceived in the right spirit" and it expressed "fears [. . .] founded in true wisdom" ("The Liberator and the American Union" January 27). On January 31, the *U.S. Telegraph* reprinted a three-paragraph article from the *Petersburg Intelligencer* attacking a January 16 Anti-Slavery Convention held in Boston. The main point of the article was that "the people of the South owe it to themselves to watch the course of these fanatics with a jealous eye, and be prepared to counteract or to resist their efforts whenever a more perfect organization shall enable them to throw off the mask with which they now endeavor to conceal their true objects" ("From the Petersburg Intelligencer"). Although rarely mentioned, there was a brief skirmish over antislavery petitions in the House in mid-February of 1835. On February 18, the *U.S. Telegraph* published a two-paragraph letter from "the Washington correspondent of the Journal of Commerce" on the abolitionist petitions ("The Slavery Question"). On February 20 and 21, there were somewhat longer articles sniping at Virginian congressman Henry Wise (at this point still Jacksonian) for the inconsistency of his giving a long speech condemning others for paying attention to the petitions, an inconsistency in which the *Telegraph* regularly engaged.

In March, the Virginia elections began, about which the *Telegraph* had announced that "Our opinion is that the next Presidency depends upon the elections about to be held in Virginia" ("The Presidency" March 14). Because of the complicated system of elections in that era generally and Virginia specifically, the elections were not completed until May, and the *Telegraph's* continual tallying of votes suggested Green did not give up hope until the very end. Two days after announcing how important the election was, the *Telegraph* had the first of many articles tarring Van Buren with the brush of abolitionist. This article, "Virginia," had a somewhat tortured argument that Van Buren must be abolitionist because he had written a pamphlet supporting Rufus King, and King had been an opponent of violating the Northwest Ordinance to admit Missouri as a slave state. Proslavery rhetors successfully managed the rhetorical equation of anti-expansionist (sometimes called "restrictionist") and abolitionist, a cunning misnomer of considerable political benefit.

Something deliberately elided during the antebellum era, but which has remained obscured in current discourse about the slavery debate, is that the major policy conflicts (such as the admissions of Missouri, Texas, and Kansas; the Fugitive Slave Act; the gag rule; and the *Dred Scott* decision) were created by proslavery politicians agitating for additional privileges for slavery, either through expanding slavery to areas from which it was prohibited by previous agreements, or by trying to put an end to the "balance" of slave and free states, or by undermining the very distinction between slave and free states. But, to emphasize that the conflicts arose not from slavery, but from the expansion of slavery, would make it clear that proslavery rhetors were the instigators of the conflict, and that wasn't the narrative that they wanted to tell. The story they wanted to tell was not of the most powerful force in America demanding more power, but of David resisting Goliath. To name the people who were resisting them—people opposed to expansion—accurately, would mean to call them anti-expansionist, a name that would draw attention to the proslavery political agenda of expansion. Hence, they needed a different name: instead of calling them anti-expansionist, proslavery rhetors called them abolitionist.

This smear of Van Buren as abolitionist for having been opposed to the expansion of slavery is doubly flawed: in addition to relying on the misnomer "abolitionist" for "anti-expansionist," Green had no evidence as to what Van Buren's stance had been regarding Missouri. To explain this point requires a digression about Van Buren's tendency to try to stand on both sides of fences. Van Buren had never publicly opposed (or supported) the admission of Missouri as a slave state. While he was a member, the New York state legislature had passed a resolution opposing the admission, but it remains unclear whether he was present when the vote was taken. He had recommended a resolution on the issue, but was too busy to sign it when the time came. Ted Widmer, in his biography of Van Buren, describes Van Buren as having "had a remarkable ability to absent himself from a contentious slavery vote just before it was called" (111). For instance, in regard to another topic of which Green would make much, Van Buren fought the explicit disenfranchisement of African American men in New York, but supported the requirement that they have at least $250, "which removed many of them from the rolls" (Widmer 50). So, he did, and did not, support the disenfranchisement of African Americans.[9] Niven, in his sympathetic biography of Van Buren, says he was opposed to the expansion of slavery to Missouri, although it's striking that Widmer gives no evidence of Van Buren having said so in public (*Martin Van Buren,* 385). But Green didn't wait for evidence: later articles refer Van Buren's opposition to the expansion of slavery as though it had been proven. As Kenneth Burke says, "often we must think of rhetoric not in terms of some one particular address, but as a general body of identifications that owe their convincingness much more to trivial repetition and dull daily reënforcement than to exceptional rhetorical skill" (*Rhetoric of Motives,* 26).

Van Buren's pamphlet did not, the author grants, mention King's stance in regard to Missouri, but the author asserts that Van Buren's silence on that topic was simply part of a strategy "to accomplish by indirect means what he could not do by direct means." Obviously, according to the author, the pamphlet "was written for the purpose of inducing the democratic party to unite on the support of Mr. King, as a first step towards that consolidation which actually took place on the slave question." This "real object," "carefully [kept] out of view," was to unite the North "as a political interest" on antislavery; that object can be inferred because the only other interpretation of Van Buren's silence on the subject of King's attitude toward Missouri would be that he did not know it. The author thereby set up a false expeditio—because Van Buren must have known of King's stance, he must have suppressed it in order to further his sectionalist scheme—that does not exhaust the possibilities. Van Buren may have neglected to mention King's stance because he was embarrassed by it, because he disagreed with it, because he thought it was a political liability for his party, because he didn't know it. But, the accusation of a despicable plot removes the claim from the realm of argument; any counter-evidence can be dismissed as more evidence of just how subtle Van Buren is.

This same attempt to smear Van Buren as abolitionist because of his support of King appears in the March 18 article, "Martin Van Buren and His Claims on Virginia." It quotes heavily from the New York Legislature's resolution, promising to provide evidence later that Van Buren supported it: "It is asserted in the Charlottesvi[l]le Advocate, and we have no doubt it is so, although the proof is not at this moment before us, that Mr. Van Buren voted for them." This "proof" was never produced (nor did Green ever acknowledge the long articles in the Jacksonian *Enquirer* that refuted these claims). Van Buren's stance on the admission of Missouri was raised again on March 26 ("Signs"), April 6 ("Mr. Van Buren and the Virginia Elections"), and April 7 ("The Columbia [S.C.] Telescope").

The March 18 edition of the *Telegraph* had a long and very alarmist article about the seizure of an American slave ship by the British. The April 8 *U.S. Telegraph* had a long article on a report concerning "the colored population of Ohio," which noted the committee's perception that putting "colored and mulatto" citizens on an equal footing with whites would encourage slaves to escape and thereby lead to "a disruption of that fraternity of feeling that now exists" between Ohio and the two bordering slave states. Thus, Ohio should not treat its free African American citizens in a way that would anger slave owners in other states. Or, to put it another way, the state of Ohio should consider the feelings of citizens of other—

slave—states when making laws. Yet, slave states need not consider the feelings of non-slave states. There is a language of fairness, but it is only invoked to enforce hierarchy.

A March 27 article, "Black Spirits and White," was part of a vicious exchange with the *Winchester Virginian* over whether Van Buren had wanted the suffrage extended to African Americans, the *Telegraph* asserting he had supported that proposal when he was in the New York state legislature, and the *Virginian* insisting he had not. The April 15 article, "Van Buren's Vote for Negro Suffrages," presents no evidence that he actually supported the proposal, but says that their point is that "The whole current of Mr. Van Buren's public conduct and sentiment previous to his lifting his aspirations to the Presidency, was steadily against the opinions and feelings of the South, on the subject of Slavery." This same article referred to Van Buren as "an abolitionist in disguise," and "an approver of the Missouri Restrictions."

The use of passive voice in the April 6 article is especially interesting: "Mr. Van Buren is admitted to have been a restrictionist in 1820. He does not pretend that his opinions have undergone any change." *He* didn't admit to having been a restrictionist, nor did his supporters, but the unstated agency in the first sentence, coupled with his agency in the second, and his name in the subject position in the first sentence, could make it seem on a quick reading that he had made the admission and still did not regret the decision.

In a good example of the "friend of my enemy is my enemy" thinking that is so loved in binary ethical systems, the article quotes a passage from the *Wheeling Gazette* (a West Virginia paper that had advocated the abolition of slavery in Virginia) that argued that the first step in attaining abolition is getting a northerner elected president (mentioning Van Buren or Webster as examples). This same strategy—condemning Van Buren by pointing out that critics of slavery liked him—was repeated in the April 18 "Mr. Van Buren and Mr. Webster," in which the same passage from the *Courier* is repeated twice, once in a mixture of caps and italics, and once in all caps: "*Van Buren is a* NORTHERN Man; *he is* NOT A SLAVEHOLDER." Green liked this passage, as he quoted it (in full caps) once again May 5 in "The Succession."[10] This passage was also used in a different article that same day, in which readers were reminded of Van Buren's having supported African American suffrage (which, as has been pointed out, he did not) in "Mr. Van Buren's Negro Voters," a title that implies African Americans voted for Van Buren.[11]

On April 21, the *U.S. Telegraph*'s "Northern Fanaticism—Duties to a

Civil Government" reprinted and excoriated a letter from the *New York Emancipator* that argued "that a just man will never believe himself bound to obey (what he considers) an unjust law," a position quite close to that promulgated by the *Telegraph* and other nullifiers in regard to duties. In apparently unrecognized irony, Green not only condemns the sentiment, but advocates responding to such people by breaking the law: "The fittest answer to this will be a halter to the first man who attempts to propagate these principles in the slave-holding states."

On April 23, the *Telegraph* reprinted an April 17 letter to the *Charleston Mercury* that said, "He stands committed, as a *Tariffite* and an ABOLITIONIST" and asked "is it not the duty of every Southern patriot to interpose to save the destinies of the South from this man, and the Northern Tariff and Abolition party that support him?" ("From the *Charleston Mercury*," *Charleston Mercury* April 17, see also April 20). The term "committed" is significant, in that it evokes the authority of a trial, when evidence of Van Buren's supposed abolitionist sentiments (even granting the tenuous definition of "abolitionist" as anti-expansionist) never was produced. But he was committed, in the sense that a conclusion had been reached; once again, repetition served the function of proof.

On April 28, the issue of abolitionists rejecting human government was again raised, in a two-paragraph untitled article that expressed wonder that abolitionists have "arrived at the conclusion, that if the 'government is destroyed' in the attempt of the Abolitionists to free the slaves, it will be the fault of the people of the South."[12] The *Telegraph* rehashes Van Buren's supposed opposition to slavery in "A Word to the Friends of States Rights—Mr. Van Buren on Internal Improvements" (April 30). After saying that the South is united in regard to three issues—improvements, the tariff, and slavery—the article asserts that Van Buren had been "the steady foe" on these issues "in every vote and act of his public life." It's worth emphasizing that this claim was false in every way; "the South" was not united on those issues, and Van Buren's stance in regard to them had not been steady, let alone steadily in opposition to "the South."

The May 2 edition has two fairly short articles about abolitionists: "Anti-Slavery Movements," about a meeting in New York, and "The Object Openly Avowed!" The latter article begins with a paragraph from an antislavery paper calling the abolition of slavery in the District of Columbia the "first step" toward universal emancipation. The editor responds, saying that "the moment Congress passes any act of emancipation for the District of Columbia, they will shake off the Union, and all connection with the abolitionists, as the worst of curses." He goes on to a series of rhetorical questions about the apathy and indifference of southerners to their danger, ending with, "Will they never awake from their infatuated apathy, but to perish as they first open their eyes [?]"

The May 6 article, "From Jamaica," reports that "accounts from this island continue to be anything but favorable as to the effects of the gradual abolition system recently adopted," noting, paradoxically, that the major trouble is from the poor white laborers brought in to replace slaves. Like the May 14 article "West India Abolition," which insisted that the successful abolition of slaves in West India was not a relevant example for the possible consequences of abolition in the South, these two articles are intended to dismiss the clear examples of successful emancipation.

A May 8 attack on a then-recent biography of Van Buren has a long paragraph asserting his (still unproven) opposition to admitting Missouri as a slave state ("The Presidency"); and in a May 9 article reiterates his "opposition" to "the peculiar interests of the slaveholding States" ("A Watch Case"). The May 10 article, "Mr. Van Buren," reprinted from the *Lehigh Union,* begins: "Do our readers know that little Van voted in the New York Convention for conferring the right of suffrage upon free negroes?—the most degraded species of our population—literally the filth and offscoring of all things—men without either moral or political principles, or patriotic feelings, and almost as ignorant as the brutes that perish [. . .] A free negro put on an equality with an American freeman!"[13] By May, Van Buren's support of African American suffrage and his opposition to the expansion of slavery had become stock issues in the anti-Van Buren rhetoric. These charges were included in resolutions passed by anti-Van Buren and pro-White (Green's preferred candidate) meetings and self-appointed vigilance committees. The full resolutions of such committees were published in a very long (four-column) article called "Public Meeting" May 12, as well as in a one-column article June 4 ("Public Meeting").

On May 14, there was a longer, untitled, article concerning the threat some northerners made not to enforce the fugitive slave laws. This threat "was considered as a rod which had only to be shaken over the South, and they would at once be quiet and submissive." The problem is not the use of threats in political discourse—I've mentioned the number of times the *Telegraph* threatens secession—nor the desire to make the other side submit (after all, the northerners' objection to the Fugitive Slave Act was that they were forced to submit to citizens being kidnapped); but, this transforming of a political question (does the Fugitive Slave Act violate the concept of a "free" state?) into a question of domination and submission is useful for shaming rhetoric.

There was a short (three-paragraph) May 19 untitled article on an antislavery meeting, reprinted from the *New York Commercial.* The May 18 article, "Anti-Slavery Movements in New York," was much longer—one and a half columns—and asserts that New York "is the great central point from which all the Anti-slavery movements diverge and receive their impetus." This fantasy of New York as the single source of contagion is politically useful in two ways. In addition to amplifying the sense of a single source (which could, therefore, be exterminated), this narrative implies that a successful New York politician must, of necessity, be infected.

Much of the article was reprinted from an antislavery speech that argued that the South would be harmed by secession, since the North would no longer have to enforce fugitive slave laws. The editor of the *Telegraph* glosses this argument to mean "that the South is in such a position, that it cannot do otherwise than yield and submit to any measures which the Free States choose to dictate to them upon the subject!", again framing a political question as one of manly domination or shameful submission.

May 20 had two long articles, amounting to one and a half columns, almost entirely reprinted from the antislavery paper the *Emancipator.* The point of printing this material is, the introductory paragraph from the editor says, to "show the feelings and the objects of the two hundred Anti-Slavery Societies now formed" ("Anti-Slavery Movements"). It should be remembered that Green had condemned Henry Wise (the congressman) and the *Enquirer* for publicizing antislavery arguments.

A May 21 article, "A Remark on Irony," part of an exchange with the Jacksonian *Globe,* ends with a four-paragraph accusation of collusion between abolitionists and Jacksonians—referred to as the "*gallantry* between the Abolitionists and the Van Burenites." In the nineteenth century, the term "gallantry" often implied an adulterous sexual liaison, so this article should be seen as another instance of the long, and unfortunate, tradition in American public discourse of associating one's opposition with shameful sexual practices. In contrast to one's own policies, which are manly, upright, rigid, straight (and so on, I could continue with the metaphors evoking tumescence), one's opposition is deviant (as I would suggest we should understand the accusations of submissiveness and submission), flaccid (as in accusations of weakness, vacillation, and indecisiveness), or, as in the case of accusations of gallantry between abolitionists and Van Buren, illicit. One of the odder instances of this tradition is the amalgamation smear, used throughout the spring by Green, but also crucial in the extended defenses of slavery (discussed in a later chapter).

May 25 had a moderately long article, with two paragraphs reprinted from the *Emancipator* and another from the *Western Herald,* which is, the editor explains, "a thorough going Webster paper" ("Anti-Slavery"). "Anti-Slavery Movements," published May 30, begins, "The Emancipator, the principal organ of the Anti-Slavery interest of New York, is openly out for amalgamation" and goes on to emphasize the work of abolitionists in New York, quoting heavily from them (which is important, as Green condemned other newspapers for reprinting abolitionist writings).

There were odd side issues as well. In Pennsylvania, a new newspaper was founded supporting "agrarian" principles, which the *Telegraph* announced amounted to anarchy because it advocated granting full rights to paupers. Even that gets dragged back to slavery: paraphrasing an argument important in Dew's 1832 defense of slavery (to be discussed later), Green explains that pauperism is not an issue in the slave states because slavery "necessarily excludes pauperism": "In the South the distinction between master and servant is color. The serviles as a mass are excluded from the polls. Color constitutes a *caste,* and the *white* man is free. The white man is the master. He is the property holder, and as such is interested in the preservation of property" (June 5, "Mr. Van Buren and the Northern Confederacy"). How any of this argument about *herrenvolk* democracy relates to Van Buren remains unclear to me, but the article begins with a passage reprinted from the *New York Evening Post* ("credited to the Hampshire Republicans") in which the author argues for supporting Van Buren because "For the support of SLAVERY at the South, we are called upon to vote for Mr. White" (June 6). This is all very confusing (as many of these articles are), but, what it seems to mean is that the un-named author of the quoted passage claims that a major argument for White is that he supports slavery—a fair and accurate description of the arguments made by papers like the *Telegraph.* So, this author is saying, an opponent of slavery should not vote for him. The *Telegraph* glosses this kind of argument (precisely the same kind that Green had been making about Van Buren): "Here we are told that 'no *Northern* man can hesitate to prefer Mr. Van Buren;' that before the writer would vote for Judge White, he would 'cut off his right hand'—because to vote for him would be to countenance SLAVERY [. . .] This is the not the idle ranting of a religious zealot—of a fanatic. It is carried into the columns of the Evening Post; a paper endorsed by the Globe, and one of the orthodox expounders of the new political faith." The rather tenuous line of reasoning is that this author is anti-white; he is also opposed to slavery. This writer has been published in the *Evening Post,* and the *Post* is endorsed by the *Globe*, and the *Globe* is a Van Buren paper. The inference I think the reader is to draw is that to vote for Van Buren is to vote against slavery.

This article goes on to condemn the Van Burenites for appealing to sectional prejudices (i.e., antislavery) in service of a unified region. As mentioned earlier, this accusation is not only incoherent—antislavery was such a marginal position in 1835 that unification on such a basis would have been impossible—it is also untrue; Van Buren was careful to espouse anti-antislavery, if not actively proslavery, sentiments. However, the accusation was a good description of precisely what Green was trying to do in these various articles: inflaming sectional prejudices for purposes of his faction.[14]

Johnson was a controversial choice for vice president because of his openly treating his African American mistress (or possibly wife) Julia Chinn and their children as his family. On June 9, Green engaged in the kind of amalgamationist-baiting that would later typify pro-segregation rhetoric. The title of the article, "The Amalgamating Republican in Baltimore," refers, not to Johnson, but to a newspaper editor who had argued that Johnson's family affairs were irrelevant. This piece of billingsgate is repeated June 27, when the editor suggests that the editor of the *Georgetown Sentinel* must be one of Johnson's "mulatto sons," and again in the June 30 "The Georgetown Sentinel—Col. R. M. Johnson." The basis of Green's objection to Johnson's behavior is made clear in "A Sketch of the New Candidate for the Vice Presidency," which begins:

> Richard M. Johnson is offered to the Northern Fanatics as a man after their own heart. Are they *abolitionists?* Are they AMALGAMATIONISTS? What more would they have than a man whose life illustrates, whose practice carries out the maxims of their school? A man who has never had any wife but a negress? Who has reared up a family of mulatto children under his roof? Who has recognized their mother as the mistress of his household? Who has endeavored to force them into the highest circles of fashionable society?—Who has done, and is daily laboring to do, more than any other man, to realise the dangers which afford his Northern allies a pretext for meddling with our affairs?

Johnson's crime is not having sexual relations with an African American woman, nor with fathering "mulatto" children, but with his open acknowledgment of them, and his insistence on their being treated with respect. Even more explicit is "The Georgetown Sentinel—Col. R. M. Johnson" (June 30), when the editor says, "If Col. Johnson had the decency and the decorum to seek to hide his ignominy from the world, we should disdain to lift the curtain; but he seeks nothing of the kind. His chief sin against society was in the publicity and barefacedness of his conduct. He scorns all secrecy, all concealment, all disguise. He affects no squeamishness, no sensibility to public opinion." The latter article also accuses the *Georgetown Sentinel* editor of wanting "a wife, who, like the offence of the King, in Hamlet, 'is rank and smells to heaven.'"[15] Just as Nazis accused all their critics of being Jews, and right-wing authoritarians accuse all their critics of being communist, so Green tries to smear his opponents with the amalgamationist term. What makes his use even stranger is that it would be a smear at all: there is something about a proslavery rhetor feigning outrage at race-mixing that must give a reader pause. Yet, that was what Green did.

The majority of a column-long June 9 article on abolitionists is a reprint from a Baltimore paper. This excerpt is prefaced by two paragraphs, ending with the statement that the article "will no doubt be hailed at the North by the *fanatics,* as evidence of the rapid extension of liberal feelings at the South." Another instance of the polarizing move, whether abolitionists would actually hail the original article is irrelevant; it, and its author, have now been placed on the side of abolitionists. Green found this a useful article; he reprinted portions of it the next day in "Questions. Moral, Physical, and Physiological."

The June 10 edition also has a fairly long article reprinted from the *New York Courier and Enquirer,* arguing that a recent antislavery article in the *Edinburgh Review* was part of an English anti-American campaign begun after the war of 1812, originating in "a common fear of the influence of the principles of our government, and the contagion of our example." English antislavery "is the way they make war against us," a theme that Greenberg emphasizes in *Masters and Statesmen* (see especially chapter 6). The argument is that England, being afraid of the spread of democratic principles, agitates on the antislavery question in order to destabilize the United States.

The June 11 edition has two articles devoted to attacking abolitionists and warning "Southerners" of their danger. One, reprinted from the *Boston Gazette,* called "The Union of the States," concludes, "We do not feel inclined to brood over melancholy anticipations, or to 'borrow trouble and evil before it approacheth the threshold;' but when we behold a fanatical party rapidly increasing among us, whose motto and watchword are destruction and violence, and when we see men of character and standing—men who ought to understand our social relations, casting their wealth and influence into the treasury of fanaticism, to enable it to sap the foundations of the republic, we confess that we are not slow to believe, that the day which shall produce the disruption of these United States, is not remote." The *Telegraph's* preface to this article takes it to task for being too sanguine that "Southerners" are roused to the danger. In other words, this article is not alarmist enough for Green.

The second June 11 article, "Anti-Slavery Movements in the Church," is a long report of antislavery "petitions and overtures" presented at the general Assembly of the Presbyterian Church at Pittsburgh. The article's point was that "Great exertions are now making [*sic*] to connect the Anti-Slavery movements with the Church." June 19 has a column-and-a-half article defending slavery, attacking abolitionists, and emphasizing how happy slaves are ("Slavery: The Condition of the Slaves at the South Not Understood, and Misrepresented at the North"). And an untitled June 25 article describes "a riot of the blacks to prevent the recovery of a slave" and says the riot was "one of their [the abolitionists'] movements. They wish to get up a spirit at the North so as to prevent the restoration of any person fleeing from labor in the Slave States." This may be referring, not to the race riot of June (when whites attacked the black community) but to the earlier incident when "a mob of blacks and whites attacked some people trying to remand a woman falsely alleged to be a runaway" (Grimsted 30). A proslavery rhetor like Green would never admit that the fugitive slave laws enabled (and may have been intended to enable) the enslavement of free African Americans. His attributing the incident to the abolitionists, without any evidence, rather than to a community outraged at the kidnap of a free person, keeps agency to a small group of whites who use African Americans (the same way that *Nick of the Woods* keeps agency to whites). This move both reflects and reinforces proslavery rhetors' ability to blame abolitionists for any unrest without providing any evidence.

The June 27 attack on Van Buren ("The Presidency") says, "The man is blind to the signs of the times as daily exhibiting themselves who does not know that there is in the State of New York a powerful band of fanatical enthusiasts bent upon the entire extirpation of slavery from this land [. . .] Mr. Van Buren is particularly acceptable to those meddlers, because of his active exertions in striving to impose upon Missouri an unconstitutional restriction in relation to slavery. *He is their candidate.*" Van Buren's passive endorsement of King's stance on Missouri (because he did not condemn King) has now been transmogrified into active exertions.

The July 3 edition has an article attacking abolitionists ("Anti-Slavery Movements" reprinted from the *Boston Courier*), another defending slavery as scripturally sanctioned (reprinted from the *Southern Christian Herald*), and an untitled article again raising the issue of Johnson's relationship to Chinn. "The Anti-Slavery Movements" refers to "the Apostate at Richmond" (the newspaper's term for Thomas Ritchie, the pro-Jackson editor of the *Richmond Enquirer*) "and other like traitors" who claim that the abolitionists are small and marginal (July 3).

July 8 has a long article reprinted from the *New York Commercial* reporting on the meeting of the British Anti-Slavery Society. The editor, before describing and quoting from the various speeches, says Thompson (a British abolitionist speaker then on tour in New England) should be sent to the West Indies, "instead of prowling about New England, for the purpose of inflaming the passions of the people, where a slave has not been seen these twenty years, against their brethren of [t]he South." July 9 has an anti-abolitionist article, "The Anti-Slavery Question" (mostly reprinted from the *Democratic Herald*); an article called "Negro Law in Philadelphia," that reports two crimes committed by African Americans; and a short paragraph concerning an African American performer that enabled the editor to take a swipe at "Northern Amalgamationists."

July 14 has two long articles (one untitled, one called "Anti-Slavery Movements—A New Proposition"), the first of which was almost entirely material reprinted from the *Emancipator,* and the second of which begins, "The people of the South have no idea how very much the minds of their brethren at the North are engaged in inventing projects by which they may be released from the *burthen* of having slaves."

"The *True,* and *Only* Issue," published July 18, reports the proceedings of an antislavery meeting at great length and in great detail. After giving the detailed report, the editor apostrophizes:

> We have been told that there was no danger. Mr. Ritchie, an avowed abolitionist himself, has told us that there is no danger; that when there is danger he will sound the alarm, and that before he will permit an interference he would secede!! Thus making secession our only remedy against plunder.
>
> Is there no danger now? We put the question directly to the Editor of the Enquirer. Do you not know that the abolitionists have already become a most formidable political party? and are you not

> acting with that party? Is not your candidate for the Presidency their candidate? and will not his election consolidate their power and influence?

This long article (over two columns) ends: "To the South we say awake, awake for the enemy is upon you." This same day has a long (full-column) article called "The Late Riots in Philadelphia," which claims that "The consequence of immediate emancipation would be to drive the white man from the South. It would become a black colony." This consequence would, the author insists, harm the white laborer of the North, who would have no market for their products. The result will be a race war, in which "The laboring *whites* will combine, and MURDER the laboring *blacks*."

July 21 has another article defending slavery ("Boston Gazette—Anti-Slavery"), and July 22 had a long article largely consisting of quotes and resolutions from speakers at a Boston antislavery meeting ("Abolition Movements"). July 23 there was an article consisting of two letters previously published in the *Richmond Whig* attacking abolitionists and calling for meetings of young men "in every county, city, town, corporation and borough" ("Virginia and Abolition"). On July 25, the *Telegraph* published an entire pamphlet consisting of a kind of abolitionist catechism, forwarded to the paper by the person to whom it had been mailed. The recipient said he hoped the pamphlet would receive wide publicity "that the planters of the middle and Southern States may know what to expect from a portion of their Northern brethren" ("To the Editor of the Telegraph"). July 27 the *Telegraph* published an attack on the "Southern meeting at New York"—a meeting the paper had previously supported—because the meeting concluded there was no real danger from abolitionists; there was another article the same day, "The Meeting Called by Gentlemen from the South," quoting the preamble and resolutions initially proposed by a committee, and which calls for an anti-abolitionist convention.[16]

July 28 has two articles about abolition ("The Abolitionists" and "From the Richmond Whig"), the first of which argues that the pro-Van Buren press has decided not to "warn the people of the dangers ahead" in regard to abolition because it might hurt his election. July 30 has three articles on abolition ("Anti-Slavery Publications," "Progress of Anti-Slavery," and "The Fanatics and the Van Buren Press"). The last article again accuses "the Van Buren Press" of intentionally playing down the dangers of abolition out of party interest. July 29, the day the pamphlets were received (and, hence, *before* the *Telegraph* knew of them), the *Telegraph* has a long article from the *Richmond Whig* claiming that "Step by step the misguided and miserable Fanatics of the North, are approaching our institutions" ("The Northern Fanatics"), a shorter article praising the *Telegraph* for its attempt to warn southerners about abolitionists ("Southern Meeting in the City of New York" originally published by the *Journal of Commerce*), and a long "dialogue" between two voters about their horror at Johnson's openly acknowledging his relationship with an African American woman.

There was another way in which slavery was mentioned during those months: as a shameful situation into which the country was slipping. In highly alarmist passages of mixed metaphors, these articles (written by the editor of the *U.S. Telegraph* or reprinted from elsewhere) sometimes simply called for supporting White against Van Buren, and sometimes called for committees of vigilance or clubs: "clubs or associations, combining as many young men as possible, meeting as frequently as convenience will permit, kindling the flame of patriotism in every breast by collusion, examining in their meetings the measures of Government, communicating with each other throughout the State, and inspiring all with the resolution to conquer at the polls, and arrest at all hazards the rapid tendency towards consolidation and slavery" (May 15, "Appeal to the Young Men of Virginia, Friends of States Rights," reprinted from the *Richmond Whig*). The irony of slavers denouncing slavery was often noted (especially during the Revolution). It is often explained, not as a condemnation of slavery, but as a condemnation of *their* being enslaved. While other scholars have come to different conclusions, this explanation seems to me the most sensible. As will be argued later, proslavery ideology depended heavily on arguments about hierarchy, and liberty (which was always conceived of as freedom *from* control) was imagined as limited to people highest on the hierarchy.[17]

As in many other cases (such as the gag rule debate), this alarmist and exaggerated rhetoric is coupled with the assertion that the rhetoric is not exaggerated and the speaker is not alarmed: "We exaggerate nothing. We set down nought in malice. We wish not to communicate a panic to others, feeling no apprehension ourselves." Two sentences later, the author writes, "The cause for alarm would be greatly reduced." When I characterize proslavery rhetoric as irrational, it's because of those sorts of internal contradictions. They *are* exaggerating, and they *are* writing in malice, and they *are* trying to create a panic, and they *are* alarmed (as indicated in granting two sentences later that there is a cause for alarm), so what they say contradicts what they say.

This is a kind of rhetorical having your cake and eating it too, of making certain arguments while denying the logical implications and rhetorical consequences. In *The Human Condition,* Arendt argues for the importance of responsibility in public argument, of risk taking. Making public arguments necessitates existential risk because taking a stand means that one might be wrong. But, what rhetors like the authors of this "Appeal" want is to take a stance in such a way that they cannot be wrong. Condemning others for alarmism, they can engage in alarmism while denying they are. This kind of discourse makes critical argumentation impossible, as argumentation necessitates that people acknowledge the underlying premises of one's arguments. If rhetors refuse to do so, then any possibility of the discourse moving people in new directions is gone; deliberation is not possible, and all that is left is some form of coercion.

The extent to which such meetings were used (if not motivated) by political parties is indicated in the *U.S. Telegraph's* coverage of the July 20 meeting. Initially hailed by the paper as necessary, and intended to call for anti-abolition meetings all over the South, it was condemned afterwards as an "abortion" (July 27), presumably because the meeting did not endorse that call. Ritchie, pro–Van Buren editor of the *Richmond Whig,* said that the meeting had been planned as part of a Nullifier strategy: "a new panic was to be played off upon the South, like the Bank Panic" (qtd. in "Abolition Movements" August 5, 1835, *U.S. Telegraph*). Green was furious, according to Ritchie, because the meeting backfired and did not play itself into the hands of nullifiers. He had made the accusation at least once before that spring: "The *Evil Genius* of the South, ever since his hopes of the Presidency were blasted, has been continually plotting some mischief against our happy Union. His Nullification Convention being balked in its progress towards revolution, by the sternness of Gen. Jackson, supported by the virtue and patriotism of the surrounding Southern States, the Disorganizer immediately set to work, through his engines, to get up suspicion and hostile feeling between the North and South on the slave question" (May 26, 1835).[18] I think Ritchie was right. Throughout the spring of 1835, Green used abolitionism as a scare tactic in a failed attempt to prevent the Van Buren nomination. When the summer of 1835 arrived, Green was openly looking for an issue that would alarm the South. I am saying such editors found two: the pamphlet mailing and the Murrell conspiracy.

4
“For the sake of your wives, children and their posterity”
Manly Politics

> History *is* a conspiracy, set in motion by demonic forces of almost transcendent power, and what is felt to be needed to defeat it is not the usual methods of political give-and-take, but an all-out crusade.
>
> —Richard Hofstadter

Many of the rhetorical qualities of the newspaper articles discussed in the previous chapter are ones that Richard Hofstadter has identified as elements of the “paranoid style,” which was tremendously popular in the 1820s and 1830s. He says that writers of that era “illustrate the central preconception of the paranoid style—the existence of a vast, insidious, preternaturally effective international conspiratorial network designed to perpetrate acts of the most fiendish character” (Hofstadter, “Paranoid Style” 14). As Hofstadter and David Brion Davis have said, one of the functions of the paranoid style was to unify a diverse group: “The paranoid style would thus appear to be a psychological device for projecting various symbols of evil on an opponent and for building emotional unity through a common sense of alarm and peril” (*The Slave Power Conspiracy* 4).[1]

Anti-abolition was, in Burke’s terms, a perfect “unification” device. Abolitionists were not very well known, at least not directly—they were “known” in a corrupted form that attributed to them slyness, religious fanaticism, sexual deviance, and the plotting of mass murder. This “knowledge” was false, but the fear was based in real events. Nat Turner’s rebellion killed over fifty whites, which was the largest massacre of white civilians on American soil in living memory (granted, the retribution for his rebellion killed more, but that would not have been on the minds of the general public). Defending abolitionists was therefore political suicide in most parts of the country, as one could easily be characterized as sympathetic to terrorists like Turner. Resisting the policies, such as the abrogations of constitutional rights, that anti-abolitionists insisted were necessary for the security of people in slave states necessitated arguing from constitutional principles. When people are afraid, and when politicians find it useful to foment that fear, trying to get the public to think in terms of constitutional principles is rhetorically difficult. And it was not in the short-term best interest of either the Jacksonians or the anti-Jacksonians to have a thorough discussion of constitutional principles, the role of slavery in American policy, or the three-fifths compromise. It was easier for both sides to appeal to anti-abolitionism.

Anti-abolitionism was a topic that lent itself to demanding increasingly strident demonstrations of loyalty to slavery forces. And that is what proslavery newspapers, or newspapers with editors who seemed to think they could benefit from rousing proslavery forces, did. They did not simply criticize abolitionists, nor even just demonize them, but they used them in the service of rousing party unity through the equating of particular policies (or political parties) and demonstrations of loyalty to the institution of slavery. Thus, it was not the abolitionists who disturbed the calm waters in 1835, but they were useful tools in the hands of politicians intent on doing so.

The contradictions, irresponsibility, and hyperbole of the articles discussed in the previous chapter are, unhappily, the same qualities that one sees in newspaper coverage of the AAS pamphlet mailing. The first mention of those pamphlets in newspapers outside of South Carolina tended to be August 8 through 11, and they were generally quite brief. This is not to say that there was no uproar over the pamphlets, but that it took over a week to develop, was strongest in South Carolina, and was not even mentioned in many southern newspapers. The *Charleston Mercury,* in typically hyperbolic fashion, identified the pamphlet controversy as "one of the most important questions that could possibly arise in the progress of human affairs" (August 10, 1835). Such superlatives were common; the Charleston "meeting of storekeepers" unanimously adopted a statement that the abolitionists had "the vilest purposes that have ever animated the hearts of men" (*Charleston Mercury* August 4, 1835).

At the same time that the *U.S. Telegraph* printed and reprinted such flowery attacks on Jackson, Van Buren, and Colonel Johnson, it also had alarmist articles about the tragic consequences of faction: "The bitterness, the virulence, the vulgarity, and perfidy of factious warfare pervade every corner of our country;—the sanctity of the domestic hearth is still invaded;—the modesty of womanhood is still assailed" ("Party" *U.S. Telegraph,* June 24, reprinted from the *Sunday Morning News*). In "Politics and the English Language," Orwell complains about a certain kind of political writing in which "words and meaning have almost parted company. People who write in this manner usually have a general emotional meaning—they dislike one thing and want to express solidarity with another—but they are not interested in the details of what they are saying" (165). This is just such a passage: condemning faction by saying that it invades the sanctity of the domestic hearth and assails the sanctity of woman is incoherent (at best); his meaning, in that sense, is completely unclear. But it is clear that the author wants to be seen as vehemently condemning faction. Similarly, the *Charleston Mercury* April 13 article asserts that "The Constitution is literally at its last gasp," the same confounding metaphor used in an anti-Van Buren letter published January 6 in the same paper.

Orwell argues that mixed metaphors result from "dying metaphors" (so that the author wasn't thinking about "last gasp" as a metaphor at all, and therefore could claim that the Constitution was "literally" doing it). He describes the use of dying metaphors as a sign of lack of thought, giving examples like "ride roughshod over, stand shoulder to shoulder, play into the hands of" (159), and one could make a similar list of dying metaphors for 1830s political rhetoric. For instance, the cliché of "entering wedge" (a constant in anti-abolitionism) could be used by both sides in exactly the same debate. The *Gospel Messenger and Southern Episcopal Register* published a letter calling the practice of Sunday mail an "entering wedge" for establishing atheism (January 1932); a letter in the *Gospel Messenger and Southern Episcopal Register* called it the "entering wedge" for an attack on Sabbath-keeping (January 1830); the Kentucky *Reformer* published a letter calling the ending of the Sunday mail the "entering wedge" for establishing a national religion (March 1830).

Even past the syntactic absurdities, there are logical, if not ethical, problems with these relentlessly factionalized papers condemning faction, and yet they continually did so. The anti-Jackson *Raleigh Register,* which had the motto "Ours are the plans of fair delightful peace, *unwarp'd by party rage,* to live like brothers" (emphasis added), spent the spring and early summer of 1835 in vitriolic exchanges with the Jacksonian *Standard.* One letter in the exchange, for instance, begins, "The writhing, twisting and screwing—the protestation, subterfuge and unfairness and the lamentation, complaint and outcry displayed in this famous production" (*Raleigh Register* February 10, 1835).

The day *prior* to the discovery of abolitionist pamphlets in the mail, the *Charleston Mercury* bemoaned that, concerning the danger of abolitionists, "the people of the South are sunk in such apathy" and "the people at the South are deceived." This apathy has been generated intentionally by Jacksonians: "The syren song that all is safe, is sung in their ears by the Abolitionist of the *Richmond Enquirer,* and some of his treacherous coadjutors; and they think that there is no danger, until the avalanche falls on their heads" (*Charleston Mercury* July 28, 1835).[2] The argument that abolitionists are a fringe group, and not a genuine threat, is also part of the plot: "The syren song of the Enquirer, that they are in a minority at the North, should not deceive the South. A minority can stir up sedition as well as a majority" (reprinted from the *Whig,* August 5, 1835). An article in the highly partisan *Charleston Mercury* says, "In the South, the excitement is universal, embracing all states, and embracing all parties, with a few worthless exceptions of party hacks, who look upon every movement with a view to party consequences, instead of the public good" (August 5, 1835). In other words, failure to respond with horror and terror to the pamphlets is a sign that one is a party hack.

Greenberg has argued that the antifaction rhetoric was sincere, and came from a sense that "to become a devoted member of a party was severely to reduce one's autonomy, to submit to an external authority, to be 'at the will' of other people (*Masters and Statesmen* 51). Parties were especially bad, but factions were little better.[3] Southern statesmen liked to see themselves as the true Republicans who thought independently about issue, but, in fact, southerners demonstrated a "remarkable loyalty" (Greenberg 46). Faust quotes Hammond and others claiming that they abhorred faction, and, like Greenberg, takes those disclaimers at face value. If so, then they may be examples of defensive projection. It may be that the disparity between their ideals and their behavior created an ethical dissonance that scapegoating the "other" party resolved. If so, then this projection had the added bonus of shifting the stasis—nullifiers' behavior is no longer the issue.

I am much more skeptical: to me, these claims look like cunning projection. Cunning projection functions in multiple ways at the same time. Because of ingroup/outgroup thinking, the same behavior is a virtue in the ingroup and a vice in the outgroup: loyalty is shameless factionalism; coalition-building is pandering to extremism; passion is fanaticism. Some number of the intended audience will not notice the moral relativism (because the relative viciousness and virtue of the outgroup and ingroup seem to them absolute). If the audience does notice the contradiction, then it becomes *blackwhite:* it is open, ranting, and ruthless partisanship. The more glaring the contradictions in one's party's rhetoric, the more blazing one's own loyalty. That one will carry water for people whom one knows to be unworthy is the sign of true loyalty.

After the nomination of Van Buren, a committee of citizens assembled in Rowan County, North Carolina, and, saying it was their "duty" to "give the alarm" to their fellow citizens, passed various resolutions regarding the dangers of Jacksonians. They resolved that "the rapid *progress* which the Federal Government, within a few years past has made, and is still making in the usurpation of power not granted by the Constitution—in the abuse of powers that are granted—in the extravagance of public expenditures, and in the corruption of Republican principles—is such as ought greatly to alarm all patriotic and thinking men, not only for the safety of our Republican Institutions, but even for Liberty itself" (*Raleigh Register,* June 2, 1835). That liberty itself was in danger was repeated throughout the various resolutions: citizens must "save our institutions from the fate that now threatens them"; they must form vigilance committees which would, among other things, set forth, "in plain and earnest language, the dangers that now hang over the country, and particularly over the Southern States"; and that the "late attempt of the President of the United States, to DICTATE to the People who shall be their next President, in our opinion is an open assault on the freedom of elections, and daring outrage on the constitutional rights of the people—and as such, ought to arouse the patriotic indignation of every citizen who is worthy of the name of FREE MAN" (*Raleigh Register* June 2, 1835, emphasis in original). A person who is not worthy of the name "FREE MAN" is either a woman or a slave.

That the Constitution itself was in peril was a common theme, and, as in the previous quote, often connected to attacks on manhood; this metaphor is significant, especially in regard to its association with hermeneutics. A marginally coherent article in the *Richmond Whig,* reprinted in the anti-Jacksonian *U.S. Telegraph,* lists the offenses committed by the Jackson administration. The list (too long to finish here) begins:

> To emasculate, and reduce to a mere dead letter, our sacred Constitution, by latitudinarian constructions—to desecrate it by the open violation of its most vital provisions—to merge the rights of the States in the assumptions of the General Government—to gather into the hands of the Federal Executive, the powers and responsibilities originally distributed among many—to claim the custody of the national purse not only, but actually to grasp and keep it, by what is tantamount to violence; to wage war with, and contemplate the destruction of, a co-ordinate branch of the Federal Government—to use the immense patronage of the Executive office, for cementing and perpetuating the ascendancy of the faction which brought him into power—to demoralize the nation by transforming the ancient spirit of personal equality and independence into abject ser-

> vility and man-worship, and by relying upon self-interest instead of principle as the motive for political preference and action—to relieve the people from all share in the burden of public affairs—to substitute the will of the Executive for law—to constitute the President a King in all but the name—and finally to introduce the usage of designating his successor. ("The Van Buren Letter" June 16; reprinted from the *Richmond Whig*)

The metaphors of violence (grasping the national purse by what is tantamount to violence, waging war), domination/submission (abject servility, man-worship), and masculinity (that the Constitution is emasculated) are associated with latitudinarianism (that is, broad-mindedness in regard to textual interpretation). So, in some obscure fashion, latitudinarianism is unmanly; for a manly hermeneutics insists that texts have one and only one meaning.

Any issue might be described as life and death, with the lives of women and children at stake. The *U.S. Telegraph* reprints a speech from the *Richmond Whig*, in which the speaker raised the alarm regarding the potential tyranny of New York, and the editor apostrophizes: "Read this picture of the overpowering strength of New York—of the spirit which governs those who rule her destinies—of the designs deep laid, pursued with indefatigable toil, refined art, and unscrupulous means, for her political aggrandizement, and for your political degradation! Read it we say, and tremble, if not for your independence, for that of your children and successors" ("The 'Empire State'—The Whale and the Little Fishes" February 17, 1835). An article in *Southern Agriculturist* has a passage: "Depend upon it, not only your prosperity; but your independence, nay, probably, your very existence rest on the exertions now recommended. We shall not say, Gentlemen, for your own sake, but for the sake of your wives, children and their posterity, and for you[r] own posthumous fame" (Volume 9, January 1836, 10). The article concerns the need to manure one's fields.

During the summer of 1835, the *Charleston Mercury* has articles and letters on the decision of the trustees of the South Carolina College not to hire a Dr. M'Auley, an ordained minister, to teach literature. The person whom they did hire was not a minister. One letter on this issue predicts dire consequences of such an act, including the spread of atheism, more ruinous than war, pestilence, and famine:

> The facts of the past history and influence of that Institution (the College) are too flagrant to be denied, and too alarming to be con-

> cealed. On whom rests the inexpiable guilt of sustaining such a School of vice and impiety, for so many years to spread pollution and atheism throughout the State?
>
> The reply must be, that the dreadful responsibility belongs originally to those Trustees who rejected Dr. M'Auley, and deliberately established an influence hostile to the most sacred principles, and destructive to the most precious interests of a Christian People. By this decision, the classic grounds of Literature were given up to the unhallowed use, marshalling the forces, and preparing the weapons to assail the Gospel of Christ. Not for the wealth of worlds would I bear the responsibility of one of these men, who had the power to prevent this terrible calamity, but did not. By that single act those Trustees entailed upon this State the deadliest curse to which a community can be subjected.
>
> Had they caused war, pestilence, and famine, to spread their united ravages through the land for seven years, the consequences would not have been so hopelessly ruinous, so irretrievably destructive, as those produced by converting the College into a fortress of irreligion, and training up hundreds of our most prominent men in a hot bed of infidelity.
>
> Other public calamites are temporary and remediable in their influence—but the horrid murderous effects of such a system of education are remediless as the second death—illimitable as eternity. (qtd. in *Charleston Mercury* August 31, 1835)[4]

Comparing this passage to the previously quoted attack on Jackson ("The Van Buren Letter") is instructive. In addition to the concern with blame, and the connected accusation of a deliberate plot against the morals of the country, both assume the entanglement of sacred and secular, and a polarized world of good and evil people (and the evil people know that they are doing evil). The attack on the Trustees assumes, but never argues, that having a non-minister teach literature is the same as deliberately promoting atheism; the attack on Jacksonians not only refers to the Constitution as "sacred" and to violating it as to "desecrate" it, but also calls the opposing interpretation of the Constitution "latitudinarian." Using that term as abuse is significant, as it generally means having a pluralist scriptural interpretation (a point to be pursued later). In addition, both assert the undeniability of their interpretation (the "open violation" of the Jacksonians, and the previous actions of the college being "too flagrant to be denied"), rely heavily on metaphors of war ("to wage war with," "marshalling the forces," "a fortress of irreligion"), and use superlatives ("most vital," "relieve from the people all share," "most sacred," "most precious interests," "deadliest curse").

The *Raleigh Register* begins an article on public lands with this statement: "There is no subject now agitated in this country, of more deep and enduring interest to the people, than that of the Public Lands" (April 7). The Yorkville, South Carolina, *Patriot* says that the test oath bill "strikes a death blow at our liberties" (reprinted in the *Western Weekly Review* January 2, 1835). The *Raleigh Register* predicts that a particular bill (intended to allow Catholics to serve in public office) will necessarily lead to an established (presumably Catholic) church (July 21, 1835). The *Charleston Mercury* condemns the North Carolina Legislature and called for all individuals "to endeavor, if possible, to roll back a tide, which threatens, in its mad career to destroy all that is valuable and beautiful in the institutions of our country" (January 1, 1835).[5] The Pleasant Hill Temperance Society resolves that the liquor traffic "is productive, not only of immorality, but frequently, of the most diabolical offences of which the criminal law of the land has cognizance" (*Raleigh Register* August 23, 1835). Numerous fires are the most devastating, several murders the most horrific, various crimes the most diabolical. The April 24 *Charleston Mercury* has one article that begins "It has seldom fallen to our lot to record a more affecting incident than the one we are about to detail" a few columns over from another article that begins "Never have we been called upon to record so shocking an event as that which occurred last week." In other words, a hyperbolic and bifurcated rhetoric of good (ingroup) or evil (outgroup), submission or domination, broadmindedness or masculinity, loyal or traitorous, was conventional in such papers, regardless of topic—the anti-abolitionist rhetoric has to be seen in that context.

This is not to say, however, that the anti-abolitionist frenzy was "mere" rhetoric, simply a handy stick with which to beat Jacksonians. It has become conventional to break antebellum historians into the two camps of "irrepressible conflict" (those who argue that a war over slavery was inevitable) and "the bungling generation" (those who think the war was created by a series of bad choices on the part of a generation of politicians).[6] Freehling characterizes the latter as: "Revisionist historians who have long thought that 'irresponsible agitators' used 'mere demagoguery' to cause a 'needless' Civil War" (*Road to Disunion* 301). This explanation, Freehling says, "contains vital truth. Ambitious political candidates especially exploited fears about disloyalty, for exciting the multitude was the path toward electoral victory. Sometimes no rhetoric worked so well as indicting one's opponent as soft on slaves" (*Road to Disunion* 301). The problem with this line of argument, Freehling argues, is that labeling proslavery southern discourse as demagogic does not explain why it worked. Freehling says that McCarthy's anticommunist fearmongering (and his appeal to loyalty) eventually produced a backlash, but the southern "charges of treachery rang on and on," from the beginning of what he calls aptly "loyalty politics" in 1835 (301). But, McCarthy was not the beginning or end of anticommunist demagoguery. Red scares were especially effective in the South, frequently getting entangled with civil rights for African Americans; each of the various civil rights movements was rebutted with accusations of communist agitation (still a central tenet of racist attacks on Martin Luther King Jr.). The examples in *Twentieth-Century American Demagogues* are almost entirely southern politicians, and there is a sense that demagoguery has long had more power in ex-slave states. Honor-motivated violence remains twice as high in ex-slave states (Nisbett and Cohen), and lynching remained an effective method of social control. These factors suggest that there was something cultural about slavery, an ideology (meaning both a belief system and political practice) that was very deep, very powerful, and very attractive, and long entangled with demagoguery.

An individual demagogue rarely creates the unification device, but relies on a preexisting and culturally powerful set of in- and out-groups. So anti-Jacksonian papers did not invent anti-abolitionism any more than Hitler invented anti-Semitism or McCarthy invented anticommunism. And, while McCarthy's anticommunism did flare up and burn out in a relatively short period of time, it remains powerful in some regions (including my current state), and among some groups (as indicated in right-wing authoritarian demagogues referring to CNN as "the Communist News Network"). The anti-Semitism on which the Nazis drew was hundreds of years old, albeit potently infected by the racial "science" of the late nineteenth century (and, like anticommunism, anti-Semitism is alive and well).

Any of these unification devices works by defining a shared identity as against an outgroup identity. As in the case of proslavery demagoguery, there may seem to be more than two groups: slavers, docile slaves, abolitionists, insubordinate slaves, Jacksonians, nullifiers, Whigs. But, fundamentally, the narrative is of two groups (ingroup and outgroup) and their respective minions. The demagogue tries to get his group (and, usually, himself) identified as the true representative of the ingroup; this is generally done through persuading the public (through repetition) that his specific faction most perfectly represents the ingroup—any competitor for that representation is actually part of the outgroup.

Ingroup and outgroup identities are ideologically defined, presenting readers with a stark choice between discrete and opposed (often almost mirror-image) worlds. What world did anti-abolitionist demagoguery present? A rigid, stable, hierarchical world in which the rhetor's group was entitled to dominate, a bifurcated (but very clear) world of evil or good, submission or domination, broadmindedness or manliness, nuanced intellect or decisive action, chaos and certainty, villains or heroes, terror or security. Thus, the anti-abolitionism of the 1830s was part of the construction of a group identity; my goal in this chapter is to lay out some of the tenets of that identity.

Crucial to proslavery ideology was the contrast of shameful submission and manly domination. To permit abolitionists to criticize slavery was, in some obscure way, to submit; the *Charleston Mercury* reprinted a letter originally in the *Boston Atlas:* "We Virginians are greatly excited at the progress of your Northern abolitionists. You will hear before long of such a storm in the South produced by these fanatical fools in the Northern States, as will jeopardize if not dissolve this Union. There is scarcely a man among us that would hesitate a moment between a dissolution of the Union and a submission to the slightest interference with our slave population on the part of the citizens of another State" (August 17, 1835). After the Baltimore Convention, at which Van Buren's nomination became official, the citizens of Mecklenberg County, North Carolina, met to protest what the politicians at the convention had done: "To acquiesce in their nomination and sanction their proceedings would be a tame surrender to the control of factious and designing men, interested in perpetuating public abuses" (*Raleigh Register* June 16, 1835). The *U.S. Telegraph,* on the same topic, writes, "We prefer an honorable defeat to a base abandonment of the great cause in which we have so long fought" (*U.S. Telegraph* June 21). The *Niles' Weekly Register* says, "The colonists of Texas are not disposed to submit quietly to the military despotism of Santa Anna, but are arming themselves for resistance" ("Texas" August 1, 1835).

The tendency to see the only available political roles as dominant or submissive means that one cannot use political discourse to come to entirely new policies or ideas—one enters the political arena to force the others to submit to one's precommitments. Coming to new commitments implies that one has, in some sense, submitted to the other side. Edward

Ayers summarizes this view: "To be undecided and open to persuasion was to be less than a man" (137).

Unfortunately, that was a common way for proslavery forces to frame discourse about slavery—that to permit criticism of it was to "submit." Earlier, I quoted Duff Green comparing allowing abolitionist criticism to kissing the rod that smites one, and his equating threats not to enforce the Fugitive Slave Act with shaking a rod over the South. A *Charleston Mercury* article on the North Carolina Legislature's instructing a senator how to vote says that the U.S. Senate alone has not submitted to Jackson: "That body, and that alone, would neither bend the knee, nor kiss the rod" (January 14, 1835). John Forsyth, a Jacksonian senator from Georgia, characterized the Senate's hostility to Jackson in the same way: "Are we to use the rod without mercy, and treat the executive as a whipped school-boy; charge him with audacity if he does not kiss the rod which has been mercilessly applied to his shoulders for his own good?" (May 6, 1834, reprinted *Niles' Weekly Register* June 7, 1834). This is not a criticism of anyone kissing the rod: like slavers' use of the "they are making slaves of us" rhetoric, it is not disapproval of domination and submission, nor a complaint about hierarchy in the abstract; it is a complaint that the appropriate hierarchy of domination and submission is being inverted.

Christopher Olsen has described the "fatal" consequences of southern tendencies to frame political issues in terms of submission and domination. Olsen has described the ways that secessionists successfully labeled the opposition as "submissionists" and various other terms that suggested anyone who disagreed "groveled in the lowest, most unmanly fashion and was willing to submit to humiliation and disgrace. Unfailingly, State-Rights men used the code words—*humiliating, degrading, insulting*" (*Political Culture* 49). The consequence was to make secession the only honorable policy: "Once the voters defined Republicanism as an insult to individual and community honor, they had to seek satisfaction" (169; for the role of the "submission" metaphor in South Carolina politics, see especially Ford 338, 360–73).[7] During (and after) the Nullification Crisis, both sides characterized the other as submissive: H. L. Pinckney characterizes the tariffs as "domestic subjugation" and Richard Yeadon said nullifiers "submit" to their party (qtd. in Sinha). To the degree that rhetors succeeded in equating deliberation with submission, they succeeded in precluding a political solution to slavery, because they effectively framed the conflict as a duel.

In the 1830s, proslavery rhetors paired permitting abolitionist criticism with submission, and demanding satisfaction from northern states with manliness: "We are justified in repeating, again and again, that a failure on the part of the Northern States, to legislate against the Agitators and disturbers of our peace, will be considered as an acquiescence in their designs and movements—and will compel us to hold them as enemies, against whom we must arm for resistance and defence. And we say again, and time will prove that we are right, that 'we can recognize no fellowship, either political or social, with communities which send forth amongst us cut-throats and incendiaries" (*Charleston Mercury* August 26, 1835). This language frames the conflict as a duel. In an honor culture, the distinction between calling someone a liar and disagreeing with him is almost impossible to maintain. Slavers wanted to define themselves and their relation to their slaves a specific way; abolitionists said that definition was not true, thereby (implicitly) calling proslavery rhetors specifically and slavers generally liars. I think it is this sense of having been contradicted that explains proslavery rhetors' emphasis on their hurt feelings. The article "Incendiary Tracts" ends with the following: "It requires no prophet to foretell what is to be the consequence of this feeling engendered in the minds of the people of the North. There will result on their part a total disregard of the feelings and wishes of the South in all its political relations, and strife will beget [s]trife until the Union be dissolved" (*Charleston Mercury,* reprinted from the *U.S. Intelligencer* August 26, 1835). Just as an individual accused of lying must redeem his honor through a duel, so a group accused of misrepresenting themselves (that is, lying about who they are) must redeem their honor through a fight.

Yet, if they do secede, they will not be responsible for secession (a person who provokes the duel is responsible for the duel, not the person who makes the challenge). Immediately after threatening secession, another writer asks, "And who will be to blame for this result? Not the South, certainly" (*Charleston Mercury* August 26, 1835). Another *Mercury* correspondent says, "It is but too evident, that the day is fast approaching, when the Southern people will be obliged to stand to their arms in defence of their property; that day, it is true, will burst asunder this United Republic—but the fault will not be *ours*" (August 1, 1835). The South was threatening secession *and* blaming the North for that possible outcome. They were not claiming that the North would declare secession, but that the North would not have acted in such a way as to prevent the slave states' secession. In other words, the North is responsible for managing the feelings of the South. In contemporary literature, it was a convention that a good wife with a hot-tempered husband was responsible for managing his feelings; if he lost his temper, it was her responsibility for having done something to provoke him. Similarly, slaves provoked punishment, and abolitionists provoked slave owners. A letter to the *Boston Commercial Gazette* reprinted in the *Charleston Mercury* says that "if the mad career of the hot headed abolitionists should lead to acts of violence on the part of those whom they so vindictively assail, who shall be accountable for their acts?" (signed by "a Southerner" August 5, 1835). The 1828 *General Assembly Senate Report of a Special Committee of the Senate of South Carolina* says that the persistence of Congress in certain claims "must inevitably cut us off, limb by limb, from the great body politic" but, if it so alienates the "feelings" of South Carolina, "South Carolina, in such an event, will have at least the consolation to know that the fault will not be hers" (29). The slaver was in control of the situation because he was only barely in control of himself; he was certainly not responsible for his actions.

It seems to me that several scholars, such as Faust, have misunderstood the resulting emphasis in southerners' diaries and letters on self-mastery—they wrote a considerable amount about how they could barely control themselves. Rather than a statement of desire for self-control, these kinds of statements should, I argue, be seen as taking pride in being someone whose feelings are so strong he can barely control them. The *Charleston Mercury* reprints an article from the *Aiken Telegraph* which ends:

> The disease has been permitted to run till the tokens of DISSOLUTION are clearly seen in prospect—dissolution, not of Slavery, but of the UNION. *And when that is done, we shall have lost the hold which we now have upon the South by political ties and social influence, and the prospects of the slave will be rendered more hopeless than ever.* How much would the condition and prospects of the slaves in the West Indies have been improved by a *dissolution of the Union* between these Colonies and the mother country? We will not insult the understandings of our readers by a reply. (*Charleston Mercury* August 7, 1835).

This point, repeated elsewhere, that having slave-holding states in the Union gives northern states some kind of control over them is a somewhat confusing argument. It is never specified just what kind of control it gives northern states, and it is even fairly hard to guess just what the nature of that control would be, although it does bring to mind contemporary stories written for women (e.g., Lydia Sigourney's "The Drunkard") in which women reform men extremely indirectly, without overtly criticizing, but perhaps by shedding a tear at the right moment, or giving a mournful look, or by crying when a child dies.

In an honor culture, one is dishonored, not by one's actions, but by people speaking of those actions, or by one's own public acknowledgment of the behavior, as exemplified in Green's outrage at Johnson being open about his relationship with Chinn. Dueling is an appropriate way to settle the resulting controversy, because one can silence the person; while, as Franklin famously said, violence does nothing to settle the question of accuracy, it does serve to shut up the accuser and end his ability to speak the accusation. For Franklin, this was a condemnation of the practice of dueling. Silencing the accuser, for him, left open the question of its veracity. For advocates of violent responses to criticism—of which dueling advocates are just one type—removing the accusation from the realm of discourse enables people not to think about it. That which is not spoken ceases to exist.

Such a view of the relation of rhetoric and reality necessarily connects violence and public discourse. If something does not exist unless and until it is mentioned in public discourse, one need not control one's own behavior, as much as control others' talk about that behavior. To the degree that one confuses discourse and another world to which discourse refers, one can believe that controlling discourse controls the world: that one could make slaves' unhappiness disappear by not letting it be mentioned; that slaves are happy until someone tells them they are unhappy; that the flaws of slavery would disappear if we could make the criticisms of it disappear. By this logic, one can declare the pamphlets false, not by refuting their specific accusations, but by showing that they dishonor the privileged group, and contradict what good people say. This method of argumentation is authoritarian thrice over. Authorities determine the "meaning" of texts. They do so on the basis of the consequences the interpretation will have for maintaining the current social order (that is, their authority). The authority of the authorities is then used to coerce submission to this authoritatively derived "meaning."

The manly position is to refuse to argue. The 1835 Georgia Resolutions of the General Assembly say that they "declare their unalterable determination" to prevent interference with slavery: "Upon this point there can be no discussion—no compromise—no doubt." The Committee of Twenty-one (the Charleston committee formed after the pamphlets were received) said they "abstained from any labored argument on the subject of slavery, not from any inability to sustain, on moral and scriptural grounds, its existence and toleration as now established in S. Carolina, but from a deep conviction of the fixed resolution of the people of this state, to permit no discussion within her limit of RIGHTS, which she deems inherent and inseparable from the very existence of the state" (qtd. in *Niles' Weekly Register* August 22, 1835). The committee that authored the March 21, 1836, Kentucky resolutions also refuse to present "a formal vindication of the justice and propriety of the institution of slavery. To do so, would involve a recognition of the right of those northern abolitionists to question it." The Petersberg meeting of citizens resolved "That we not only disdain discussion on this subject, but claiming to be, to all intents and purposes, the exclusive judges of our own concerns, we scorn to make terms with our enemies, and declare our purpose to retain our property just as long as we please, without pledging ourselves to any form or measure of concession or melioration, or bringing our free action and violation under any constraint whatsoever" (reprinted in *Charleston Mercury* August 17, 1835). A public statement composed at a public meeting claiming that the people present "disdain discussion" is initially puzzling, but the paradoxical goal (public discourse without discussion) was commonly held by proslavery rhetors. A letter (signed "A South Carolinian") to the *Charleston Mercury* begins, "It is surely a subject of just gratulation that the people of the South are at length thoroughly aroused to a sense of their danger and a firm vindication of their rights. From every quarter of the South we hear of popular meetings, all holding the same language, and all animated by the same spirit." In the next paragraph, the author goes on to say, "And first, *of our Right to our slaves.* Upon this point, we should say distinctly to our Northern brethren, we allow no argument whatever. It is not a subject for discussion. Whether slavery is an evil or not, is for ourselves, and not for others, to determine" (August 19, 1835). These two arguments may seem contradictory—the writer is happy that the issue is being discussed in numerous meetings *and* says it is not a subject for discussion, but this pairing demonstrates an authoritarian view of public discourse: appropriate public discourse is not disagreement, or argument, but expression of the correct view.

Explaining that last point is complicated, as many people today share the same sense about the limitations of discourse. I am saying that many of the participants in 1835 public discourse saw three possible roles in the public sphere: epideictic, threats, bargaining.[8] For authoritarians, the preferred mode of public discourse is epideictic, discourse that reinforces "the" cultural values. Because a community in perfect agreement is, for authoritarians, the ideal, a rhetor, regardless of whether what he or she is saying is controversial, *claims* to be stating undisputed (and undisputable) universal truth.

But, there are circumstances in which the disagreement is so present that one cannot plausibly claim to be speaking what "everyone" knows. In that case, one asserts (or implies) that it is not *real* disagreement; the apparently disagreeing interlocutors secretly agree, but pretend not to out of nefarious motives. This move is typified in Fisk's comment that all abolitionists would own slaves if they could (but they are simply too poor—a problematic assertion given the common characteristic of them as dangerous because they are so wealthy). Or, as will be discussed later, they are of a category that somehow does not count—"everyone" agrees because those who disagree have removed themselves from community membership by disagreeing. The strategy of denying that people disagree while in the midst of a disagreement is surprisingly effective, as in the case of silencing southern abolition. One consequence of the proslavery rhetoric regarding the pamphlet controversy, for instance, is that proslavery rhetors effectively presented the pamphlets as imposed upon unwilling southerners by northern abolitionists (a representation apparently accepted by many scholars). The pamphlets mailed to the Charleston post office were, apparently, unsolicited. By making them epitomize all abolitionist pamphlets, one can obscure that some number of antislavery pamphlets were distributed to and by southerners who wanted them and agreed with their sentiments.

If possible, those who disagree are silenced; one uses whatever power one has (institutional, cultural, or even physical) in order to enforce the unanimity. One politically useful consequence of the pamphlet controversy was that southern postmasters received permission from the U.S. postmaster to seize antislavery material, and to take names of anyone who might have requested such material. They were able to increase their surveillance of internal dissenters. While the public *discourse* described a flood of unwanted material, the public *policy* involved all people, including that unknown number who wanted abolitionist pamphlets. The rhetoric of security enabled the suppression of dissenters' rights.

Proslavery rhetors threatened abolitionists with violence and northerners with secession. They also relied on loyalty oaths, anti-sedition laws, gag rules, financial support for party organs, the factionalizing of government itself (using government appointments and contracts to reward party loyalty). More subtle methods included explicit or implicit calls for violence against dissenters, the use of enemy or criminal metaphors for the outgroup (such as calling them traitors) so that violence against them can be rationalized as self-defense, and threats of violence against anyone who dissented. The goal of this form of discourse is to gain the submission of the other parties—whether they really agree, or simply acquiesce, is irrelevant; getting one's way is all that matters.

Another approach is to bargain. While this was not very obvious in the newspaper rhetoric of 1835, one can see it in the gag rule controversy, discussed later. As with epideictic and intimidation, participants do not use discourse to investigate or explore decisions; they enter the realm of discourse with ideological and policy precommitments. The goal is to coerce others to submit to one's policy preferences as much as possible; to the extent that discourse changes the minds of participants it is in terms of their perception of how likely they are to succeed, and how much they might have to compromise. Since the nature of a compromise is determined by the severity and credibility of the threats one brings to the table, there is never a point when one tries to reason with one's opposition (although one will almost certainly claim to be reasonable).

For the most part, southern anti-abolitionist rhetors alternated between confirming and intimidating, with particular emphasis on the former. Rhetors continually insisted that "the South" must and did speak with "one voice" on the issue (whatever the issue happened to be). The *Charleston Mercury* reprints a piece from the *Whig,* which asserts that "the South can do much by union, concert and firmness, in putting down the Abolitionists and their bloody designs. It needs but that the South should speak in *one voice,* for that voice to be heard and obeyed" (August 5, 1835). Sometimes it is asserted that the unanimity already exists; the Petersberg Committee of Citizens reports, "The abstract question of Slavery is one on which no candid difference of opinion can exist among an enlightened and Christian people" (*Charleston Mercury* August 17, 1835). Yet, it goes on to make the "necessary evil" argument, and to insist that the southerners are already taking care of the problem, both of which are controversial assertions. That is, it goes on to assert as universally held an opinion about which there is actually considerable disagreement.

The denial of disagreement is necessarily connected to the authoritarian view of textual meaning. Authoritarianism premises and promises stability and certainty, whereas pluralism implies multiple sites of authority, often envisioned as a continuum ranging from nearly certain to completely uncertain. Not only does the continuum model presume multiple sites of authority, it also implies that, at many places on the continuum, one could be mistaken. Auhoritarianism posits, instead of a continuum, a binary opposition between certainty and uncertainty, so that denying complete certainty means embracing a paralyzing uncertainty. This is the reason that "latitudinarianism" is a devil term. Latitudinarianism promotes a broad, inclusive, and tolerant approach to the problem of meaning in scripture—it presents certainty and uncertainty as ranges on a continuum—which allows for multiple authorities in perpetual and productive conflict.

In struggling to come to terms with proslavery ideology, I have found this authoritarian epistemology/hermeneutics particularly difficult. It is conventional to describe authoritarians as naïve realists (that is, to reject the role that interpretation plays in understanding, and to believe that knowledge comes directly and easily from direct perception). There is no difference between hermeneutics and epistemology: it is no harder to interpret a text than it is to perceive a sensory phenomenon. Certainly, that is the epistemology explicitly advocated by authoritarians, who have a strong tendency to reject arguments for complexity or nuance as obfuscation. For instance, the March 21, 1836, Kentucky Legislature's "Resolutions Respecting Abolition Societies" (*Communication From the Governor, transmitting resolutions from the Legislature of Kentucky on the subject of abolition societies*) abuses abolitionists because they "imagine themselves the special executors of the divine will" (4). This is not a condemnation of that stance; the third paragraph of the communication asserts that it is through God that "dominion has been given to the white man over the black" (3). Slavers are executors of God's will; abolitionists are not. Authoritarians generally say that reality (including any text) has one specific meaning; this one interpretation is accurately perceived by some people and not others; there is no process of interpretation or possibility of their making a mistake.[9]

Yet, oddly enough, at other moments, proslavery rhetors seem to endorse the principle that reality can be constructed through using coercion to create consensus. For instance, if one considers the problem of whether proslavery rhetors *really* believed that criticizing slavery was a violation of the Constitution (or the Constitution prohibited the abolition of slavery in the District of Columbia, and so on), then the possibility arises that what they really believed was that, given sufficient credible threats about secession or sectionalized politics, they could manufacture agreement on those points. Whether that was an accurate reading of the framers of the Constitution would be displaced by whether that reading was acceptable to the people threatening violence.

Naïve realism and epistemological authoritarianism appear to be opposite, but both share a conflation of perception, truth, belief, and ingroup consensus. Naïve realism presumes that, because truth is easy to perceive by good people, and ingroup members are good people, then ingroup consensus is true. With authoritarian social construction, the causality is slightly different: it presumes that ingroup consensus is truth, and that changing a community's belief will change their perception. With either epistemology, one answers the question of "How do you know this is true?" with evidence of ingroup members' strong feelings of conviction.

The possibility of manufacturing consensus through repetition and intimidation is demonstrated in the spread of the belief that abolitionists advocated and incited slave insurrection. When it was pointed out that the pamphlets did not call on slaves to engage in violence, one proslavery editor responded in a telling way: "The Abolitionists have published a card denying that their papers and pamphlets are insurrectionary in their tendency. Fortunately the pamphlets and papers speak for themselves *to all who can read them,* so that none can mistake their infamous character" (*Charleston Mercury* August 21, 1835, emphasis added). But, who could read them? The whole point of the, apparently successful, seizure and burning of the pamphlets at the Charleston post office was to keep anyone from receiving them. Rather like people today who argue for banning books they brag never having read, this editor appears not to be troubled by the logical tangle.

The various laws that banned abolitionist pamphlets did so on the grounds that they would lead to murder and rebellion. North Carolina's 1830 antiliteracy law begins, "Whereas the teaching of slaves to read and write, has a tendency to excite dissatisfaction in their minds, and to produce insurrection and rebellion." The Missouri law (signed February 1, 1837) titled, "An Act to prohibit the publication, circulation, or promulgation of the abolition doctrines," begins: "If any person shall publish, circulate, or utter by writing, speaking, or printing *any facts, arguments, reasoning,* or opinions, tending directly to excite any slave or slaves, or other persons of color, in this State, to rebellion, sedition, mutiny, insurrection, or murder, with intent to excite such slave or slaves, or other persons of color, to rebellion, sedition, mutiny, insurrection or murder" (emphasis added, see also the Virginia law called "An Act to suppress the circulation of incendiary publications and for other purposes" passed March 23, 2836; and "An Act to prevent the publication or circulation in this State of seditious, pamphlets and papers" passed in Tennessee, February 15, 1836). It is striking that the law indicates the possibility that such rhetoric might have facts, arguments, and reasoning: it does not matter whether abolitionist rhetoric is true. As Arendt says, "Contemporary history is full of instances in which tellers of factual truth were felt to be more dangerous, and even more hostile, than the real opponents" ("Truth and Politics" 255).

Anti-abolitionists could know that abolitionist rhetoric called for violence because, in the paranoid style, all opponents are engaged in a fiendish plot. As Hofstadter says,

> The distinguishing thing about the paranoid style is not that its exponents see conspiracies or plots here and there in history, but that they regard a 'vast' or 'gigantic' conspiracy as *the motive force* in historical events. History *is* a conspiracy, set in motion by demonic forces of almost transcendent power, and what is felt to be needed to defeat it is not the usual methods of political give-and-take, but an all-out crusade. The paranoid spokesman sees the fate of this conspiracy in apocalyptic terms—he traffics in the birth and death of whole worlds, whole political orders, whole systems of human values. He is always manning the barricades of civilization. He constantly lives at a turning point: it is now or never in organizing resistance to conspiracy. Time is forever just running out. (30)

Thus, like the writer bemoaning the deliberate plot to loose atheism upon the land through hiring a non-minister to teach literature, so the contemporary readers know the final, and evil, goals of the abolitionists without having to read them.

Slavers were never responsible: "We of the South regret the necessity that compels us to keep a portion of the human family in bondage; but the evil is not of our seeking—it was entailed upon us—it is deep rooted in our system" (*U.S. Telegraph* July 29, reprinted from the *Richmond Whig*). The Petersberg resolutions say that "we are nowise answerable" for slavery (*Charleston Mercury* August 17, 1835). That same document begins by "appealing to the history of our country for our acquittal from its stain" (*Charleston Mercury* August 17, 1835). George Freeman, in his sermon on slavery, begins by saying that slavery "may be regarded as one of the penal consequences of sin—an effect of that doom pronounced upon the human race in consequence of the disobedience of our first parents, whereby perpetual labor was entailed upon man as the only means of sustaining life" (5). That southerners continue slavery is irrelevant; what matters is that they did not start it.

Similarly, slavers are not responsible either for their feelings or their reactions, no matter what those reactions are, including genocide. According to one article, "a sudden emancipation, either by *force* or through *principle,* would be a calamity that *must* desolate the south, *and cause a terrific destruction of both masters and slaves!*" ("The South," *Niles' Register* September 24, 1831). The Charleston Committee Of Twenty-one said that emancipation would "produce the utter destruction of that class of persons, for whose welfare [abolitionists] pretend to be so solicitous" (*Niles' Weekly Register* August 22, 1835). The July 29, 1835, *U.S. Telegraph* threatens that the "*whole race will be put to the sword*" (italics in original). A September 1835 article in the *Baltimore Literary and Religious Magazine* holds abolitionists responsible not only for the various anti-abolitionist meetings but also "Have they observed the state of matters at New Orleans? Have they noticed the horrid events, deemed indispensable to suppress a servile war, in Mississippi? Have they examined the detail of Murrel's plan for the universal butchery and plunder of the twelve slave-holding states? Do they know that a large meeting in the city of New York, has recommended a movement of the entire south, against them and their principles,—and against the north, if it will not suppress them? Are they then *now* satisfied, that they are doing, and have done infinite harm?" (283–84). The "servile war, in Mississippi" is, it should be emphasized, a reference to the Murrell conspiracy fantasy, showing that Grimsted is correct in arguing that the incident was read as an abolitionist plot. Abolitionists will harm African Americans because they will do something that will cause slavers to massacre blacks. Proslavery rhetors were threatening race war, *and* condemning abolitionists for such a threat, *and* blaming abolitionists for proslavery reactions.

This insistence on the irresponsibility of proslavery rhetors is deceptively powerful. The extent to which proslavery rhetors could persuade the public that they were not responsible for any of the ills of slavery was the extent to which the causal narratives in proslavery ideology, and the consequent political agenda, could be protected from disproof. No matter what the outcome, slavers were not responsible, so there could never be evidence that they had done the wrong thing. Even when free-state politicians deferred to proslavery fearmongering and agreed to violations of free speech, the right to petition, and states' rights, proslavery rhetors came to the conclusion that it was not enough (rather than the more accurate conclusion that it had been too much). The great tragedy of an ingroup making history a matter of honor is that, because one is forbidden from narrating history in a way that dishonors the ingroup (the fact that it dishonors the ingroup is taken as proof that it is untrue) the group silences the very information that might help them make better decisions in the future. Coupled with the obsession with feelings (the sense that one can triumph through firmer faith), this denial of self-criticism means that the solution to every problem is to continue to do what one has been doing, but with stronger conviction. To continue to make a mistake is more manly and a greater display of loyalty than to rectify errors and set a new course.

The view that the north had to placate the south was a premise of proslavery rhetor's insistence that northern states take action against abolitionists. In the course of making such demands, proslavery rhetors cheerfully ignored any principle of states' rights. William Wiecek summarizes this position: "The northern states would have to amend their constitutions to comply with slave-state concepts of civil liberties" (180). Vindex begins his text by articulating a general principle of state sovereignty, but throughout argues that northern states are obligated to punish their citizens for violating slave states' laws. A letter to the *Charleston Mercury* says: "We have a right at least to demand, and to expect, such legislative action as will ensure our quiet for the future. Let us then call upon them for it. I have no doubt of our success" (*Charleston Mercury* August 24, 1835). The "Report of the Joint Committee of Federal Relations" (*Communication from His Excellency, Governor McDuffie*) recommended that the South Carolina legislature "make an explicit demand on the non-slaveholding States, for the passage of penal laws by their Legislatures, providing for the punishment of the incendiaries within their limits" (see the third and fifth resolutions for this demand). In February 1836, the state of Virginia passed "Resolutions relative to the interference of certain associations in the northern states with domestic slavery in the south." The second says "that the state of Virginia has a right to claim prompt and efficient legislation by her co-states to restrain as far as may be, and to punish those of their citizens, who, in defiance of the obligations of social duty and those of the constitution, assail her safety and tranquility, by forming associations for the abolition of slavery, or printing, publishing, or circulating through the mail or otherwise, seditious and incendiary publications, designed, calculated or having a tendency to operate on her population" (*Communication from the Governor, transmitting a copy of certain resolutions of the General Assembly of the State of Virginia,* see also the second paragraph of *Communication From the Governor, transmitting a preamble and resolutions adopted by the Legislature of Mississippi, relative to the persons denominated abolitionists*). If a citizen from a northern state criticizes the legislation of a southern state (i.e., slavery), it is a violation of states' rights. But, a southern legislature can criticize the legislation of a northern state. The notion that the proslavery politicians were concerned with states' rights was one of the most successful cunning misnomers of proslavery rhetoric. By insisting that *they* were committed to protecting the rights of states, proslavery rhetors could misdirect the public from their political commitment to violating the sovereignty of free states.

Such violation was done, interestingly enough, with a rhetoric of loyalty. Yeadon, as quoted earlier, insisted that it was treasonous to allow criticism of slavery; defending the right of someone to make a certain argument is the same as making that argument: "The dominant party in each Northern State has now to *act* upon the matter, and prove whether or not they are allies of the Abolitionists" (*Charleston Mercury* August 20, 1835). Those who are not with them are against them, so that those who support the Constitution are transmogrified into traitors, and those who wish to violate it are not. A *Mercury* correspondent says, it is clear that "it is the duty of the Northern States to interfere, and that, if they do not, they virtually justify the fanatics, and assume the responsibility of encouraging their villainy" (August 24, 1835). A long quote from the *Charleston Mercury* displays this "us against them" logic:

> We have viewed the first movements of the Northern Abolitionists with no other than feelings of scorn and derision. We felt that a crusade commenced against the South by such heroes would be as contemptible as its motives were ostentatious and its spirit hypocritical. We quietly looked forward to see this unprincipled design smothered by patriotic and humane spirit in the people among whom it displayed itself. But when these misguided wretches are allowed by public opinion and the municipal authorities of some of our sister States in the North to organize their fiendish band with the avowed object of invading rights guaranteed to our Citizens by the Constitution, and by stirring up revolt among the Slaves of the South, to levy a servile war upon a large portion of these United States; and when, moreover, one of the Departments of Federal Government, instituted as the national channel of friendly and commercial correspondence between the citizens of this union, is employed as a known agent of these hostile plots, it threatens to become a question of no distant consideration in the South in what relation we will stand towards our present fellow citizens of the North, and whether we may regard the Union as the means of our protection or of our destruction. (*Charleston Mercury,* reprinted from the *Petersberg* [Va.] *Intelligencer,* August 10, 1835, regarding a public meeting—this was the statement of that meeting, in the *Charleston Mercury* August 17, 1835).

The "South" must doubt their relation to the North because the North has not responded as histrionically as these rhetors.

In addition, proslavery rhetors could slip a specific political philosophy into the discourse. Burke remarks on this strategy in *Rhetoric of Motives:* by associating a commonly shared stance (abolitionists are evil) with a specific political agenda (nullification), a rhetor can make it seem as though the two (the stance and the agenda) are identical. The audience first participates "in the form, as a 'universal' locus of appeal, and next by trying to include a partisan statement within this same pale of assent" (59). In many of the anti-abolitionist arguments (and some of the resolutions), especially ones published or authored by South Carolinians, the nullifiers' theory of the Constitution was asserted. Hence, someone either had to reject the argument (and thereby sound like a defender of abolitionists) or grant the nullifiers' constitutional interpretation. When this kind of strategy works, and it often does, one can get people to believe that, for example, instead of the situation being pro- or anti-slavery, it is nullifier or abolitionist (or, later, secessionist or abolitionist).

Much of what is obviously illogical in proslavery arguments fits with the logic of the rhetoric of doom. The slaves play the part played by the Indians in *Nick of the Woods*—tools who can be used by the diabolical abolitionists. Just as the Indians have no legitimate grievances against the whites, and, hence, their violence must be explained by a combination of their essential bad natures and a manipulating villain, so slave insurrections are not the result of particular circumstances of American slavery or any actual injustices, but must be explained by the essential bad natures of slaves (Murrell, it should be remembered, is supposed to have selected the "most vicious" and "wicked" slaves to work on) and the nefarious plots of abolitionists. Were it not for abolitionists, so this story goes, slaves would be perfectly happy.[10] If this is the case, then the impracticality of their policies would not have given proslavery rhetors pause. What would matter is not whether or not they could succeed, but how manly they could look in the course of trying.

The anti-abolitionist rhetoric discussed in this and the previous chapter did not genuinely respond to abolitionist arguments; it is very possible that none of the rhetors (other than Drayton) ever saw, let alone read, any of the pamphlets which they were condemning. But, the stasis was not really about abolitionists' arguments. It was about which political party could respond in the most manly way to the "threat" supposedly presented by their criticisms of slavery. Freehling has said about this era that "the real issue [. . .] was not so much whether slavery should be abolished but rather whether slavery could be discussed" (*Prelude* 52). And the answer was no.

5
"Careless of the Consequences"
Extended Defenses of Slavery

> Societies minimize group conflict by creating consensus on ideologies that promote the superiority of one group over others.
>
> —Felicia Pratto

Traditionally, rhetoricians describe a triangle of author (intention), text (strategies), and audience, set against a background of context; rhetorical analysis means to explain a text in regard to each of those relations, how the author has shaped a text in order to have a particular intended impact on a certain kind of reader within generic and historical contexts. To categorize the kinds of intentions an author might have, rhetoricians often use an essentially Aristotelian taxonomy (epideictic, deliberative, forensic) or a more Ciceronian one (informative, persuasive, convincing). Briefly, deliberative is rhetoric for the decision-making assembly, what we would call "political" discourse; forensic is judicial; epideictic is praise or blame speeches (such as funeral orations). The Ciceronian taxonomy is more audience-oriented: we inform people who are ignorant on the topic, persuade people whose position on an issue we wish to change; and convince people who more or less already believe what we want them to believe, but whose actions we seek to change. In each category, what's important is what we *change* in the audience, so rhetoric is about change.

The historical question—what caused proslavery agitation to increase—can usefully be pursued through rhetorical analysis. Initially, my thought was to infer proslavery rhetors' intentions (in calling for more extreme anti-abolitionist policies, in publishing attacks on abolitionists, or in publishing defenses of slavery) through rhetorical analysis: Who was the intended audience? What was the context for this rhetoric? But, it quickly became clear that these questions can be answered in ways that are unintentionally circular—if one describes the summer pamphlet mailings as the context, then, at least implicitly, the authors must have been intending to respond to those pamphlets. To put this rhetoric in the context of anti-Jacksonian political dilemmas is, at least implicitly, to suggest that the rhetors intended to resolve their political problems through defenses of slavery and attacks on abolitionists. In addition to this potential circularity (one gets to the interpretation one wants by shifting the context), as critics of traditional rhetorical analysis have argued, such analyses seem to posit an autonomous, even atomistic, author who is in perfect control of a text, a fully conscious agent who surveys the field and deliberately arranges a text like the ideal general arranges troops. This fantasy of a deliberate rhetor, like the fantasy of an excellent general who takes in everything with a single glance (discussed briefly in chapter 7), is, as any writer knows, obviously counterfactual.

There is a kind of ambiguity in the very question of whether or not a rhetor *really* believes the assertions of a text, an ambiguity at the center of factionalized public discourse. That question can mean: does the rhetor believe that this assertion accurately reflects reality; or, does the rhetor believe that this assertion accurately reflects his/her conviction? For people who privilege ingroup loyalty over all other virtues, only the second question matters—the first is irrelevant. For people who care about the first question, a whole series of other questions immediately follows: about perception, interpretation, cognition, and language. All of those questions arise from the perception of at least the possibility of a disjunction between what is and what one believes—whether one answers with a mild or radical form of skepticism is not here the point; the point is that not everyone sees the need to pose the questions in the first place, because they acknowledge no disjunction. For naïve realists (perception is always accurate), or epistemological authoritarians (reality is made by the powerful), the personal convictions of the ingroup *are* reality; they don't reflect it; they don't represent it; they *are* it. For either of those approaches to discourse, what matters about a text is not what it says about any kind of external reality, but what it says about the rhetor's loyalty to the ingroup. Hence, to engage in anything other than wishful thinking about the ingroup and its policies is disloyal.

To talk about authorial intention seems to necessitate remaining in a realm of deliberate strategies and conscious decisions, and that entangles us in questions of sincerity: either the rhetor makes a deliberate decision to express sincere sentiments *or* deliberately decides to make an insincere appeal to prejudices of the audience. We associate cunning rhetorical decisions with insincerity, so, to say that a rhetor cunningly appeals to a certain sentiment seems to imply that he or she did not share that sentiment. From my argument up to this point (that proslavery rhetors used anti-abolitionism as a wedge and unification device), readers may infer that I imagine proslavery rhetors deliberately, and insincerely, deciding to foment a fear they did not feel. And that is not my argument, nor am I arguing that the various intentions ascribed to these texts are mutually exclusive. The very nature of textual analysis means that, since we can talk about one text at a time, we tend to describe a situation in which a single text has a certain kind of impact on an audience, but, in political discourse, a single text does very little. The paradox for which I want to argue in this chapter is that the extended arguments for slavery, as a whole, had a profound impact on political discourse precisely because no single one did.

As Greenberg says (previously quoted), an important function of oratory is to draw attention to the speaker. By confirming dominant values (the traditional description of the effect of epideictic), the speaker shows he shares those values—he is a member of the ingroup. This is not a trivial act; Faust argues that several authors of proslavery texts craved public recognition, and that "Hammond, Simms, Tuckers, Holmes, and Ruffin soon discovered that their essays won recognition other intellectual endeavors failed to secure" (*Sacred Circle* 116). Tise says that "a relatively large number of southern intellectuals did indeed use proslavery as a means of drawing attention to their abilities and work" (125). If so, it's interesting that these essays were praised and recognized, as they are fairly poorly argued. It does not take close analysis to conclude that the texts are internally contradictory, sometimes in obvious ways and sometimes more subtly, even within a few pages. William Drayton, for example, begins a chapter on abolitionists by saying, "The abolitionists never deign to weigh the consequences of their actions" (201). The chapter goes on to discuss slave insurrection, alternately accusing abolitionists of intentionally choosing such a consequence—abolitionists have "deep and dangerous designs upon the slaves" (202)—and reasserting their ignorance (and lack of concern for) that outcome ("careless of the consequences, [abolitionists] go on)" (206). Drayton characterizes abolitionists as calculating *and* uncalculating. Paulding reprints a letter from a judge who, in describing local practices regarding punishing slaves, says, "Our laws are mild, and make little discrimination between slaves and free whites, except in a few political offences" (215), fourteen pages after that same correspondent had described at length the laws peculiar to slaves (202–3), and fifty pages after Paulding's twenty-page discussion of the slave code (140–60). In this same discussion, the anonymous judge mentions that no slave owner has been prosecuted for mistreating his slaves, an admission that does not stop Paulding from claiming that slaves are protected from cruelty by various laws (165, see also 171).

Having argued that freed blacks would never work (228), Drayton then argues that they would work at such low wages as to lead to massive unemployment among poor whites (237–38). He goes back to asserting that they would not work, and describes the devastating economic effects (240–43; Harper's argument that free labor is unprofitable *and* cheaper is similarly problematic).

Defenses of slavery often rely on privileging the hypothetical over the actual. Having argued the disastrous consequences of freed slaves remaining in the South (most of chapter 19), he then asserts that they would all move north (chapter 20).[1] That freed slaves *would* rape "the daughter or the wife" is adequate reason to reject emancipation; that whites *do* rape the daughters and wives of slaves is not adequate reason, however, to reject slavery. Harper first argues that slave owners would not beat their slaves because that would not be in their economic best interest (98), then he argues that they love their slaves too much (99), then he says "It is true that the Slave is driven to labor by stripes" (100). So, slave owners *would* not beat their slaves, despite the fact that they *do*.

Early in his chapter on "Laws for the Government of Slaves," Paulding discusses a case in which a master was convicted of "immoderate, cruel, and excessive beating of his own slave" (144) and which was dismissed, not because the court ruled the accusation false, but because "this court has little hesitation in saying that the power of correction does not belong to *it*" (144–45). Twenty pages later, after arguing that the only punishment that works with slaves is whipping (162–64), Paulding then asserts that owners love their slaves too much to abuse them (165–66), then grants that such abuse exists in isolated instances (167, see also 169), and then says "we never saw or heard of any such instances of cruelty" (168). The reader has just heard of such a case, twenty pages earlier, and from Paulding himself. He goes on to quote from an owner who describes his system of punishment: "Vicious and idle servants are punished with stripes, moderately inflicted; to which, in the case of theft, is added privation of meat" (197). A reader may quite likely conclude he has just heard of a second such incident, again from Paulding himself.

Harper also argues, like Simms, that slaves don't like to read; Harper says, "Of the many Slaves whom I have known capable of reading, I have never known one to read any thing but the Bible" (101). Were that the case, then there would be no reason to be concerned about abolitionist pamphlets, but, when it comes to that topic, then suddenly Simms and Harper are tremendously concerned about the number of slaves who would willingly read something.

Harper's argument on the raping of slave women is an especially interesting instance of kettle logic. He begins by stating the abolitionist proposition he intends to prove wrong: "that marriage does not exist among slaves." He grants that "the chastity of [slave] wives is not protected by law from the outrages of violence. I answer, as with respect to their lives, that they are protected by manners, and their position. Who ever heard of such outrages being offered? At least as seldom, I will venture to say, as in other communities of different forms of polity. One reason doubtless may be, that often there is no disposition to resist. Another reason may be, that there is little temptation to such violence, as there is so large a proportion of this class of females who set little value on chastity, and afford easy gratifications to the hot passions of men" (104). Slave women are not raped; they aren't killed if they resist; no one has heard of their being killed for resisting; well, maybe they are sometimes killed for resisting, but no more often than anywhere else; they don't resist; they have little sense of chastity, so men don't need to rape anyone. This argument is, apparently, intended to refute the abolitionist argument that "marriage does not exist among slaves" (104). Yet, it confirms that very argument, in that he makes it clear that white men like him see slave (and "coloured") women as appropriate victims for sexual exploitation.

It was common for proslavery rhetoric to go through three moves in regard to a criticism made by abolitionists: first, deny that the problem exists; second, say the problem is just as bad somewhere else (usually the North); third, say it's better in the South. The consequence is that the internally contradictory rebuttal inadvertently grants the argument it is supposed to be refuting. The conclusion one must draw from Paulding, despite his assertions, is that slaves are not actually protected from violence; the conclusion one must draw from Harper is that white men do not respect the marriages of African American women.

Another example of arguing from known counterfactuals is the amalgamation threat. Some defenses of slavery acknowledged interracial sex. Harper grants that "the passions of men of the superior caste, tempt and find gratification in the easy chastity of his females" (105, see 104, previously discussed). Like other proslavery rhetors, he argues that white men's easy access to slaves protects the chastity of white women: "Can it be doubted that this purity is caused by, and is a compensation for the evils resulting from the existence of an enslaved class of more relaxed morals?"

(107). Simms lists as one of the benefits of slavery that "the negro and the colored woman in the south, supply the place, which at the north is usually filled with factory and serving girls" (Simms 40). Simms goes on to praise the consequences of this amalgamation:

> The result of illicit intercourse between the differing races, is the production of a fine specimen of physical manhood, and of a better mental organization, in the mulatto; and, in the progress of a few generations, that, which might otherwise forever prove a separating wall between the white and the black,—the color of the latter,—will be effectually removed. When the eye ceases to be offended, the mind of the white will no longer be jealous, and that of the colored person will gradually approximate to the general capacity, the inflexible courage, and directness of purpose, which, at present constitute the moral difference between the two people. (40)[2]

Kingsley, in his *pro*slavery text, advocates amalgamation, and Simms admits that mulattoes "have been made free in consequence of their relationship to their owners" (51).

Yet, as in the newspaper articles, proslavery rhetors relied heavily on amalgamation as a smear and scare tactic. Paulding begins his fourth chapter saying, "The advocates of immediate emancipation, aware of the consequences sketched in the preceding chapter, have sought to obviate them by recommending amalgamation; that is, indiscriminate marriages, between whites and blacks, accompanied of course by a communion of social and civil rights" (61). If amalgamation happened, Paulding goes on to argue, "such a mixture would at once destroy the homogeneous character of the people of the United States, on which is founded our union, and from which results nearly all those ties which constitute the cement of social life" (64). He may have gotten that argument from de Saussure's 1822 *A Series of Numbers,* which says that blacks would try "to create a new race, in violation of nature" and that this "would tarnish the national reputation, as well as colour, and humble it in the dust" (16). Austin, after arguing that emancipation would necessarily result in race war, says, "Is it supposed they could amalgamate? God forbid!" (45). Proslavery rhetors regularly evinced horror and nausea (W. Drayton 235) at the notion of amalgamation, and accused abolitionists of lacking the "natural feelings, to endure a prospect at which ordinary human nature sickens" (235). The logic of these rhetors' arguments all presume that amalgamation was not already happening, something which was false, and which they must have known was false. The antislavery societies did not advocate amalgamation, but slavers did practice it, and had for some time, and the United States had not been destroyed by it. Whether abolitionists were nauseated at the notion of amalgamation is a red herring; many slave owners, quite obviously, were not.

Harriet Martineau remarked on the hypocrisy of the amalgamation smear in a long passage in her 1837 book:

> A gentleman of the highest character, a southern, planter, observed, in conversation with a friend, that little was known, out of bounds, of the reasons of the new laws by which emancipation was made so difficult as it is. He said that the very general connexion of white gentlemen with their female slaves introduced a mulatto race whose numbers would become dangerous if the affections of their white parents were permitted to render them free. The liberty of emancipating them was therefore abolished, while that of selling them remained. There are persons who weakly trust to the force of the parental affection for putting an end to slavery, when the amalgamation of the races shall have gone so far as to involve a sufficient number! I actually heard this from the lips of a clergyman in the South. Yet these planters, who sell their own offspring to fill their purses, who have such offspring for the sake of filling their purses, dare to raise the cry of amalgamation against the abolitionists of the North, not one of whom has, as far as evidence can show, conceived the idea of a mixture of the races. It is from the South, where this mixture is hourly encouraged, that the canting and groundless reproach has come. I met with no candid southerner who was not full of shame at the monstrous hypocrisy. (10)

If Martineau is right, then not only did southerners engage in hypocrisy in making the accusation, but they knew they did so. What should one make of this deliberate repetition of an assertion which the rhetors knew to be false? One response is that ideology is characterized by its falsification of reality. Hannah Arendt, for instance, says of masses: "They do not believe in anything visible, in the reality of their own experience; they do not trust their eyes and ears but only their imaginations, which may be caught by anything that is at once universal and consistent in itself. What convinces masses are not facts, and not even invented facts, but only the consistency of the system of which they are presumably part" (*Origins* 351).[3] But, Arendt describes the attraction of the system that is, although false, internally consistent, and I am emphasizing its *in*consistency. Others (most famously, Marxist theorists like Althusser) have said that ideologies are marked by internal contradiction, something which would seem to contradict Arendt. I will suggest that these extended defenses of slavery were, and were not, consistent, and they were, and were not, effective.

In most ways, the proslavery ideology of the extended defenses is the same as that manifest in the newspaper rhetoric. The situation was a crisis caused by abolitionists (two mentioned the pamphlets that abolitionists had sent across the South like a disease, although there is reason to doubt that they meant those sent by the AAS). These rhetors assumed or posited a polarized worldview—those who are not with us are against us. Sometimes this was presented as a racial issue; Drayton, for instance, implied and asserted that the interests of blacks and whites are necessarily at odds, so that any assistance to (or empathy for) African Americans (slaves or not) is hostility to whites; and criticism of whites is necessarily some kind of taking sides with African Americans. Drayton and Harper both slipped the nullification theory of the Constitution into the argument, so that one was either on the side of abolitionists or a nullifier.[4] Whether the nullifier position was adopted or not, slavery was asserted as an inviolable right, sometimes unspecified, and sometimes as the right to property, and southerners were presented as the promoters of an absolutist theory of property rights.

Abolitionist criticism was a violation of slavers' "rights," but it was never made clear just what "right" was violated. It appears to have been some kind of right not to have their feelings hurt. Drayton says, after discussing abolitionist criticism, "The very act of interference itself is a violation of [slavers'] rights, and an outrage on their feelings" (201). Paulding, in his list of the terrible consequences of abolitionists' actions, begins with southerners' feelings: "The feelings and good name of millions of our fellow-citizens have been grossly assailed, their rights invaded, their firesides and social institutions disturbed, and their lives endangered" (6). Later, the feelings of slavers is the first item in a list of what is at stake in the issue of abolition: "It is a question involving their feelings and their reputation; their domestic quiet; the peace of their household; their property; their safety, and that of their wives and children" (53). As in the newspapers, rhetors also assumed a binary opposition of submission and domination, with the sense that to permit criticism is to submit; as Drayton says, "The people that submit to such wrong will submit to any thing" (xvi).

The manliness of the proslavery rhetor, as well as of the southern position, was contrasted to the effeminacy of the abolitionists: "The notorious Thompson [. . .] is known to be a missionary from a society of venerable spinsters" (Paulding 135). Drayton refers to the "frothy effusions" of the abolitionists (xviii), and explains Tappan's success among abolitionists by saying "Weak men are generally vain" (163). He says that abolition "has ministered so successfully to the little vanity of a feeble and contracted mind" (163), and that Tappan (and Garrison) "caressed and honoured" the British abolitionist Thompson (166).

One part of the slavers' manly ethos was that he was calm and in control (yet in grave danger of losing his temper and control), while the outgroup was out of control, irrational, and emotional (yet coolly plotting murder and insurrection). Thus, for instance, it was conventional to describe the abolitionists as Paulding does: "foaming at the mouth with a ferocious abhorrence of the civil institutions of a free people, or writhing with envy at their own innate insignificance, and sighing for notoriety" (303, see also 108). He says that abolitionism is as "deaf to argument as it is blind to the dictates of common sense" (307). Proslavery, on the contrary, is addressed "to the rational, reflecting citizens of the United States" (Paulding 307). He summarizes the two sides: "The institution has been assailed on one hand with violence and obloquy; on the other defended with invincible determination" (5). Drayton says, "the incendiaries appeal only to the passions" (xvii), but also says that this "crisis is one which calls for the aroused and excited energies of the nation" (xvi). So, the excitement on the part of abolitionists is inappropriate, but on the part of anti-abolitionists is necessary. And, of course, a rhetor who threatens slavery, genocide, or the lynching of abolitionists does not seem especially calm.

In general, abolitionists were held responsible for slave insurrection, but also for any other ills of slavery (which the same rhetors denied to exist at all *and* blamed on abolitionists). Secession was constantly threatened, at the same time that it was asserted that abolitionists (and those who would not take a sufficiently strong stance against them) would be responsible for such an outcome. So, once again, others were made responsible for catering to the feelings of slave owners. As with the newspaper rhetoric, the issue of responsibility for slavery was tremendously important, and always solved historically—current owners of slaves are not responsible for slavery because slavery was imposed on the United States (Drayton spends all of chapters 5 and 6 arguing that England was responsible for slavery; see Simms 19–20). Paulding says that abolitionists throw "unmerited obloquy on millions of innocent people. We say innocent people, because slavery in the United States, whatever may be its influence on the happiness of mankind, is not the product of this soil of liberty. It is not our work. It is not the offspring of our independence. It is the bantling laid at our doors by its mother, England" (125, see 126–28; if it was so good, it is not clear why rhetors were so anxious to lay the responsibility elsewhere).

That England forced slavery on the colonies was part of a narrative that Jefferson tried to include in the Declaration of Independence—a narrative that characterized colonists as hostile to slavery and the slave trade. But, in this narrative, colonist (and U.S.) agency slips in and out. Henry de Saussure and Robert Walsh, who both use this narrative to excuse the southern states from responsibility for slavery, also praise the United States for ending participation in the international slave trade. England had imposed both on the colonies, yet the United States had exerted agency to end one of them. The slave states could end slavery—several did—so history demonstrated agency in regard to the institution of slavery. This flickering sense of agency means that agency is denied in situations in which rhetors want the credit for desiring the action but not the consequences of the action.

The proslavery stance (and, generally, whatever the rhetor was arguing) was asserted as undeniable, and obvious to all, as was the univocality of the South: Drayton says, "The views of the South on this subject are distinctly understood. The people of the slaveholding States [. . .] are prepared to act, as one man" (Drayton 223), and Paulding refers to "the universal feeling of the South" (53, see also 54). The authority of the proslavery stance comes from this unanimity. Yet, in regard to colonization, the annexation of Texas, amalgamation, and other issues, these authors took different positions. That a single text could both endorse and reject the perpetuity of slavery means that even individual rhetors were not univocal. So the assertion of universal agreement on the proposition was, like the assertion of calmness, or disdain for faction, belied by the very texts asserting it.

Drayton, Freeman, and Harper all begin with a history of slavery, asserting its beginning in prehistoric times, and its basis "in the nature of man" (Harper 80). Dew discusses the history of slavery immediately after the introduction, and ends with historical examples regarding the prosperity of slave civilizations (771–76). Simms does not have an extended discussion of the beginnings of slavery, but, toward the end, a paragraph begins, "Every primitive nation, of which we have any knowledge, in the whole world's history, has been subjected to long periods of bondage" (71). That paragraph goes on to assert, at a high level of abstraction, that periods of bondage improve a people (just as the previous section argued, at an equally high level of abstraction, that civilizations necessarily enslave less civilized tribes). This argument, openly taken from Thomas Dew (whom Harper, Simms, and Drayton cite), asserts that "the institution of Slavery is a principal cause of civilization" (Harper 81). Harper says that "nothing can be more evident than that it is the sole cause" (81). There is no real evidence for this assertion (so a reader can likely think of many things that are more evident), and, of course, providing evidence for an assertion about something being a *sole* cause is notoriously difficult.

But, the authority of this assertion comes not from its relation to evidence; instead, it derives from the authoritativeness of the assertion itself. In this view, a statement is true because it *cannot* be disputed (as opposed to the notion that a statement is true only to the extent that it can be tested). The authority of the statement comes from its (albeit unsupported and unsupportable) claim to be a universally valid statement that thereby enhances the authority of a preexisting consensus. That is, this kind of authority is circular.

Rhetoricians have long struggled with how to describe argument from authority, a line of argument that logicians reject as inevitably fallacious. In rhetoric, the validity of an argument from authority is assessed by the credentials of the authority being cited, the relevance of his or her expertise for the topic, and the accuracy of the view attributed to them: whether he or she is an expert in a relevant field and has actually said what is being quoted. At the same time that theorists in rhetoric describe how appeals to authority should work, there is acknowledgment that this ideal is far from the practice. What typically happens is, as Elliot Aronson and Anthony Pratkanis say, along the lines of a celebrity endorsement: "By shaving with the right razor or eating the right cereal, we are saying, 'I am just like that ballplayer; I am part of the attractive in-group.' By purchasing the 'right stuff,' we enhance our own egos and rationalize our inadequacies as we 'become' just like our favorite celebrity" (131). The rhetorical force of the appeal comes from the attractiveness of the authority being invoked, so that we buy the product as a consequence of being attracted to the person. But, as one can see from the proslavery rhetors' use of authority, that is not actually how this appeal works in authoritarian discourse: causality is reversed, so that authority is the consequence (not cause) of our desire for the policy.

Robert Walsh, for instance, whom I mentioned in the introduction, wrote two major texts on slavery. One, a response to criticism of the United States' pretensions to republicanism when it protected slavery, was cited by proslavery rhetors as an authority; the other, an argument that the Northwest Ordinance should not be abrogated to enable Missouri to be a slave state, was not. Walsh was an authority (and praised as such) when his arguments could be used by proslavery rhetors and was not an authority when they could not. The anonymous hostile response to Channing's *Slavery* is, the author says, intended to show that "Channing's theories are wrong in relation to the established and unchanging order to human society:—wrong as to slave owners:—wrong as to slaves:—wrong as to the whole of the American people:—and therefore, morally and religiously wrong" (33). But, Channing's chapter condemning abolitionists "is decidedly the truest and most practical of all his opinions" (22). Channing is entirely wrong, except when he agrees with the author.

Agreeing with some things that an author says, and disagreeing with others, is not necessarily a contradiction, if there are other ways that one is supporting an argument. But, it is a problem if one is engaged in argument from authority. As mentioned earlier, an argument is an assertion with support. If the support for one's assertion is that an authority has endorsed it, then attacking that authority undermines one's own argument. The "endorsement" is no longer a *reason* to support the proposition.

This problem of erratically endorsing and rejecting the same authority is particularly vivid in regard to arguments from scripture. When scripture can be used to endorse their arguments, proslavery rhetors insist on complete deference to it; when it contradicts the argument they want to make, they reject the authority of scripture. So, like Walsh, scripture is an authority when (and only when) it confirms their precommitments.

Dew and Drayton argue for their version of history by taking bits from scripture, secular histories, and even Voltaire. Drayton concludes: "From the facts, stated in this and the preceding chapter, it will be seen that slavery has always prevailed; and is so intertwined with the necessities of life, that while man exists, slavery will probably exist also" (30).[5] Certainly, every incident that Drayton used (from those various sources) exemplifies slavery, but, were he to accept scriptural history as authoritative, he could not have concluded that slavery has always prevailed: Adam and Eve did not have slaves. As I will argue later, proslavery rhetors had to work very hard to achieve the reading of Genesis 9 that they wanted; it was a far-from-"literal" reading.

Scholars have debated the relation of scripture and slavery, with some recent major scholars taking the position that proslavery ministers made "a solid scriptural case for slavery" while "the antislavery spokesman failed to demonstrate that the Bible repudiated slavery" (Genovese and Fox-Genovese 490).[6] On the contrary, the proslavery case for scriptural authority was incoherent and inconsistent, invoking and rejecting literal readings (even sometimes insisting that the dominant Christian version of scripture is unreliable), alternating between biblical and secular histories, appealing to mutually exclusive authorities. The problem is in the term "demonstrate," a verb which, logically, requires an indirect object. To thousands of people, abolitionists did demonstrate that the Bible repudiated slavery; as even Genovese and Fox-Genovese say, some proslavery ministers "set out to refute the abolitionist argument only to end up accepting it" (490).

The argument that slavery supports scripture relies on accepting a skilled stasis shift that proslavery rhetors introduced into the debate: moving the discussion away from specific practices of slavery to slavery in the abstract. Southern U.S. slavery was called "the peculiar institution" (a proslavery term, it should be emphasized) because it was known to be unique in world history. As Peter Kolchin says, "'The 'slave South' stood increasingly alone, joined in the Western Hemisphere only by Brazil and the Spanish islands of Cuba and Puerto Rico. Slavery had become the South's 'peculiar institution'" (93, see also Davis, *Slavery and Human Progress* 109).

There were three levels at which slavery was attacked by abolitionists. First, at the most abstract, abolitionists disputed the ability of one human to own another.[7] This was a problematic argument in that scripture does have examples of that practice. Second, at the still fairly abstract level, they argued that scripture neither exemplifies nor endorses race-based and perpetual slavery, the condition that made nineteenth-century southern U.S. slavery increasingly "peculiar." Third, and this was where abolitionists had the strongest case, they argued that the specific practices common to southern U.S. slavery violated scripture: failing to recognize slave marriages, breaking up of slave families, sexual exploitation of slaves, violence against and mutilation of slaves, kidnapping of free African Americans, denying direct access to scripture. Abolitionists particularly emphasized the sexual exploitation and mutilation because the sections to which proslavery rhetors appealed (that is, the laws regarding slavery) forbid those practices, in some cases requiring that slaves who were treated in those ways must be freed.

My point (and the point of much abolitionist discourse) was that Old Testament slavery, while exemplifying slavery, did not exemplify the practices of southern U.S. slavery; in fact, scripture prohibits them. And many of the most egregious violations were incorporated into state laws (such as selling free African Americans into slavery, prohibiting emancipation, forbidding literacy). How to define and defend the actual condition of slaves in ways that accounted for the state laws was always a problem for proslavery rhetors. They might deny the existence of cruelty, they might insist upon the ideal version of slavery, they might reject slave narratives as fictions and instances of abuse as trivial exceptions, but the state laws were there for anyone to read. And they were not the laws of Moses, which was the point that abolitionists kept making.

For instance, the twenty-first chapter of Exodus describes how to treat one's servants. Among those laws are that:

26. And if a man smite the eye of his servant, or the eye of his maid, that it perish; he shall let him go free for his eye's sake.
27. And he smite out his manservant's tooth, or his maidservant's tooth; he shall let him go free for his tooth's sake.

Drayton refers to these laws, but only as evidence that slavery is permitted, not to claim that southern states follow the laws that sanction slavery (see especially chapter 9); similarly, Paulding refers to the rules to show that the Israelites had slavery (19). Freeman mentions the law that one should free one's servants (Jubilee), but rejects its application on the grounds that it only applied to slaves who were themselves Hebrew (the same argument that Drayton makes about another passage).

What proslavery rhetors could do was to argue that scripture did not condemn slavery in the most abstract form (one human owning another). They did try to defend it at the second level—race based and perpetual—but here the argument became vexed. Scripture specifies that the slaves are such due to debt or war (not race), and it dictates the periodic freeing of slaves (through erasing their debt). Proslavery rhetors argued that the various rules dictating freeing slaves applied only to fellow Hebrews.

Even if one grants that distinction, it does not actually solve the rhetors' hermeneutic problem: Christian exegesis, grounded in Paul's arguments concerning circumcision, emphasized that membership in the Chosen People was not ethnic, but spiritual. So, passages regarding promises to Hebrews were understood to apply to Christians. If proslavery rhetors used that hermeneutic, then the rules regarding Hebrew slaves applied to any converted Christian slaves. Hence, what proslavery rhetors had to do was reintroduce race to scripture. Their entire argument about scripture relied on the race argument, and the race argument relied on Genesis 9.

This passage (Genesis 9, in which Noah says that Canaan shall be a servant because of something that Ham did), as Stephen Haynes has explained, was crucial for justifying the racial basis of American slavery, but it is also very confusing in several ways. First, it is unclear exactly what

Ham did that would merit such punishment; second, it is unclear why Canaan would be punished for something Ham did; third, it is not clear that the punishment should be perpetual, and apply to Canaan's children as a marked race. So, proslavery rhetors who worked with this passage all used the same argument, and it is actually somewhat remarkable for people who claimed to read scripture literally; they rejected Christian versions of scripture in favor of Muslim ones.

They asserted that "the *Arabic version* contains the *true* reading" (Freeman 14; see Dalcho 9, who attributes the argument to Bishop Newton 16). Dalcho paraphrases Bishop Thomas Newton's argument on this point: "We have explained the prophecy according to the present copies of our Bible: but if we were to correct the text, as we should any classic author in a like case, the whole might be made easier and plainer" (16). Genovese and Fox-Genovese grant that proslavery ministers' reliance on Noah's curse was "their scripturally weakest suit" (523). But, without that card, they lost the argument for the racial basis of U.S. slavery being justified by scripture. And, if they lost the race card, they also lost the argument about Jubilee, as they lost the argument for rules regarding the freeing of slaves applying to other races.[8] It seems likely that many readers of scripture did not realize that this application of "Noah's curse" to Africans was a tenuous interpretation; Drayton simply refers to it.[9]

Freeman, Dalcho, and Newton (from whom Freeman and Dalcho have taken the argument) are explicit that they are rejecting the Christian tradition in favor of the Muslim; others made the same move without the admission. Alexander Sims, for instance, claims, "When the Word of God plainly declares his will (which is his Law), there is no need to consult the more dubious exposition of his works [. . .] This Word is plain in its declarations, and clear in its inferences on the subject now under consideration" (12). On the next page, he refers to a secondary source (Milman's *History of the Jews*) to support his reading of the laws in question, as he does throughout his discussion of scripture. Claiming to get a reading in scripture, he has drawn it from expositions other than scripture. To refute the abolitionists' use of the "Do unto others" principle, Sims says, "No interpretation of the Bible can be correct which makes that sacred volume contradict itself. It reveals to the world, the will of God respecting his creatures in a harmonious manner. Where, therefore, two interpretations may be made, one consistent and harmonious, the other contradictory, the former must prevail" (17). Scripture is harmonious; portions which seem not to be harmonious must be interpreted in such a way as to make them harmonious—up to this point, Sims and the abolitionist exegetes are in agreement. The disagreement is that they interpret the rules regarding slavery in light of that principle, and Sims (and most proslavery exegetes) do the reverse. Slavery is the principle, so that the authority of a particular interpretation of scripture comes, not from its method, but from the extent to which it confirms the consensus.

This is a confusing point for many people, as it typifies how scripture is used in political debates now, particularly by people who claim to be engaged in a literal reading. Religious rhetors demand submission to an interpretation that is asserted to be *in* the text (even when it relies on interpolation) while ignoring other, less amenable, passages. People who do not follow Mosaic laws in regard to polygamy, farming restrictions, or clothing, suddenly invoke literal and decontextualized readings to condemn their pet vice or to defend their sacred cow—but that is precisely my point. This is a method of *using* scripture to defend precommitments. These rhetors are not unique in that use, but are good examples of it.[10] And that method of using scripture involves first privileging what authorities already say is true (and what, not coincidentally, happens to be in their economic and political best interest), and then looking to scripture to support it. One reading of scripture is posited as the authoritative one, and it supports an authoritarian view of government.

The myth of asymmetric insight fuels this sense of authorities being able to construct reality. Asymmetric insight is the assumption that the more privileged can see into the minds of the less privileged; in proslavery rhetoric, it is the myth of slave transparency. Paulding reprints a long letter which describes slaves' internal states: "The slaves generally look upon their masters and mistresses as their protectors and friends. They seldom, I am persuaded, think of the injustice or cruelty of being held in bondage, unless they have tasted of the tree of knowledge to which they are invited by some Satanic abolitionist" (205, see also 200).[11] Drayton assumes, first, that all slaves feel the same, and, second, that he (and other whites) know what those feelings are. W. J. Cash famously noted the political power of this myth. Cash "knew that any master class's confident knowledge of what its underclass wants is a subtle and hence powerful way of exercising social and personal control" (Clayton 21; Cash 326).

Asymmetric insight justifies giving (and refusing to take) advice and criticism from others "without adequate attention to *their* thoughts, feelings, interpretations, and motives" (Pronin et al. 639).[12] It is only to the degree that the powerful know the subordinates that they can legitimately claim to represent them. The justification of a representational democracy in which one kind of person (white male property owner) represents all kinds (women, nonwhite, and so on) is that that sort of person, because of asymmetric insight, knows what is best for everyone. The fantasy is that men can rule women (or whites can rule minorities, or the rich can rule the poor) because they know what they think *and* what women think (whereas marginalized groups do not even really know what they think). To say that person does not really know all the others is to say he is not fit to rule.[13]

Not only does one know the world better, but one's knowledge creates the world. To be powerful means the ability to create the identity of groups. Stereotype formation "is a joint endeavour through which groups develop shared explanations of the world that allow them to represent social relations veridically and manage them appropriately, partly by orienting group members to ideologically-relevant goals" (Haslam, Turner et al. 184). That a consensus was achieved on the stereotype of abolitionists (as inciting insurrection) had real political consequences. Proslavery rhetors who defined "the" slave as incapable of economic autonomy could make that group identity true insofar as they could legally prohibit economic autonomy.

Hence, abolitionists' dissenting from proslavery rhetors' representation of "the" slave was not just a point of disagreement about slaves. It dishonored powerful proslavery rhetors because it disputed the basis of their political power—it suggested that they did not have asymmetric insight. If they did not *know* their slaves, they had no right to rule them, and that is precisely what abolitionists argued.

To attack the practices of southern slavery (which are presumed to be the same in all slave states), then, is to attack the economic *and* political hierarchy of the South, and that is to attack hierarchy itself. The first part is accurate—abolitionists did intend to attack the political, economic, and racial hierarchy of the slave states—but it's interesting that this was taken to mean that they would institute chaos. Kingsley says, "Slavery is a necessary state of control from which no condition of society can be perfectly free" (11); so a society without slavery has no hierarchy and, therefore, no order. The *Niles' Weekly Register*, in an article called "Detestable Villainy," accuses abolitionists not only of exciting sedition, but of trying to "overturn the existing social and political relations of the country" (August 8, 1835).

A particularly strong abolitionist critique of slavery practices in the American South was that they violated the Christian precept of "do unto others as you would have them do unto you." Abolitionists argued that whites would not want their children sold into slavery, and would not want to be illiterate, and so on. Proslavery rhetors responded to this call for empathic perspective-shifting by saying it violated the very notion of social order. Freeman says that "do unto others" cannot be taken literally, but must be understood to mean that one should behave in a way appropriate to one's place in hierarchy (see also Furman 9–10). Harper explicates that same passage, "We just suppose, that the Creator will require of man, the performance of the duties of the station in which his Providence has placed him, and the cultivation of virtues which are adapted to their performance" (102–3). Drayton says that the abolitionists' interpretation of the golden rule "strips it of its golden attributes, and makes it sanction all it was intended to condemn" (98) because it requires "that the authority of the father over his child, of the master over the apprentice, of the tutor over his pupil, should [. . .] be given up" (98, for ministers' endorsing of this interpretation of hierarchy, see Snay 69–72). It would, Drayton says, "abrogate all law, would place the innocent at the mercy of the guilty, involve right and wrong in indistinguishable confusion, and render society a chaotic and jarring mass of wretchedness and crime" (98).

At first I thought that this insistence on the chaos necessarily consequent on emancipation was another instance of self-referential absurdity (after all, Pennsylvania and New York were not in chaos), but I have come to think it is more complicated than that. Were there not slavery, there could not be slavers, and owning slaves was white manhood. So, without slavery, white manhood would be impossible—it would be chaos for these writers' sense of identity. The term that the civil rights historian Jason Sokol repeatedly uses for whites' reaction to demands like enfranchisement is "unthinkable"—too many whites could not imagine changing the racial hierarchy of the South, and so fought it. Proslavery ideology, similarly, was both an excess and deficit of imagination. Public policy was too affected by the imaginative realm of the loving slave owner, the happy slave, the cunning abolitionist, but was tragically constricted by a cultural inability to imagine a different model of manhood—one not racially inflected and not created by domination.

The consequence of abolition, the proslavery rhetors insisted, would be political and social equality between "coloured" and whites. An article in the *Baltimore Literary and Religious Magazine* called "Abolitionism" lists as the third, and final, tenet of abolitionism: "That the distinctions of colour, *odour,* &c. between the white and black races, are to be disregarded entirely; and that all the coloured people with the least possible delay, are to be placed on the same footing in all respects, personal, social, and civil, as if they were white" (285). Proslavery rhetors reminded their readers that abolitionists socialized with African Americans, and several rhetors invoked the image of a black congressman (quoted previously).[14] Harper says, "It is the order of nature and of God, that the being of superior faculties and knowledge, and therefore of superior power, should control and dispose of those who are inferior" (89).

So, alternately, abolitionists are condemned for wanting to get rid of all order (and have perfect equality) and for wanting the wrong hierarchy (in which African Americans might be able to demand deference). The first resolution quoted by Cooper (*Hints*) says, "All power exercised by one man or set of men over others, is of necessity either delegated and entrusted, or usurped" (3). Africans were not enslaved by delegation and trust; it was usurped. Although Cooper condemns attempts to usurp power from people like him, he does not condemn it in regard to slaves. This political theory is, and is not, an appeal to power politics; it is, simultaneously, justification by an appeal to amoral power politics *and* justification by claiming moral superiority. That Africans have become enslaved through violence is a sign that they deserved it; were whites to become enslaved through violence, however, it would not have the same signification.

It is easy enough to say that such a view is hypocritical, or that it involves a double standard, but that criticism is lost on people with this sense of ethics. For them, ethical behavior is not universally applied. Principles of good conduct depend upon where one is in the hierarchy. The same act is bad if done to a freeman, but not if done to a slave (e.g., Harper on whipping, 111); it is bad to enslave whites (the rhetoric of enslavement on which Roediger remarks) but not blacks. Even right and wrong are relative to who one is: Harper says, in response to the abolitionist argument that slavery necessitates degraded morals on the parts of slaves, "If we estimate their morals according to that which should be the standard of a free man's morality, then I grant that they are degraded in morals" (102). Paulding says, as to why jail is not an effective deterrent for slaves, "disgrace is no punishment to those who have lost the sense of shame [. . .] Hence a resort is had to corporal punishment, the only effectual mode of reaching the feelings of a race whose situation naturally places them out of the reach of those restraints and inflictions, which operate most effectually on those who have preserved the sense of honour and the safeguard of shame" (163–64). It is not clear to me whether this is why such documents simultaneously assert that slavery is not violent toward slaves and rationalize that violence (because slaves have neither shame nor honor, violence against them does not count as violence), or if this is simply another instance of *blackwhite*.

In general, proslavery rhetors' sense of history is puzzling. There is a tendency to try to narrate a perfectly static history, as though things (at least in the slave South) are as they have always been. Yet, such rhetors also sometimes praise progress and insist that things are different (and better) than they were. Harper, for instance, at one point insists that "mutation and progress is the condition of human affairs. Though retarded for a time by extraneous or accidental circumstances, the wheel must roll on" (93). The rhetoric of doom, and discourse of imperious circumstances, implies a world with very little human agency. The only good act is to resist change (hence the identification as "conservative"). Genovese and Fox-Genovese describe this: "Following the logic of cyclic interpretation, Southerners accepted in theory the inevitability of their own empire, even as they strove to extend its life as far as possible in practice" (154). Calhoun, in a letter to the *U.S. Telegraph,* explains what is required of his political followers: "The task that remains for us to perform, is a difficult one. It involves the exercise of the passive, much more than the active virtues—to stand prepared to maintain what has been acquired, rather than to make new acquisitions—to preserve our principles and doctrines in full vigor and purity, ready to be called into action when the emergency may raise, without having them actively and continually exercised" (*U.S. Telegraph,* "Mr. Calhoun" April 3, 1835. A letter from Calhoun). *This* social arrangement is intended by God; any change to it is a rejection of God's will.[15] Yet, the political agenda that comes from this resistance to progress is not conservative, as it almost always involves new ways of doing things.[16]

The kind of slavery practiced in the U.S. slave states was a very new kind of slavery, for instance, and proslavery rhetors increasingly began advocating new policies (such as rejecting the ability of a "free" state to forbid slavery within its borders). Granted, they often denied that this was new behavior and did (and do) often create fictionalized histories to legitimate the practice, but those are reasons to insist that "conservative" is a misnomer. The accurate term is "authoritarian," and an even more accurate term is that such people are high in "social dominance orientation."

Definitions of authoritarianism usually rely on Adorno and others, who argued that certain characteristics tend to correlate. Hostile toward minority groups (essentially, any group other than themselves), drawn to defensive projection of what they consider "deviant" emotions, reliant on rigid all-or-nothing mental categories, authoritarians are submissive to others in authority and demand submission of others to them. Social psychologists have found this model difficult to test empirically, however, and generally rely on a modified version, such as Bob Altemeyer's *Right Wing Authoritarianism.* Felicia Pratto and colleagues' concept of social dominance orientation "postulates that societies minimize group conflict by creating consensus on ideologies that promote the superiority of one group over others" (Pratto et al. 259). People with this orientation "favor social practices that maintain or exacerbate inequality among groups and [. . .] oppose social practices that reduce group inequality" (Pratto et al. 262). People high in social dominance orientation tend to be ethnocentric, racist, nationalist, intolerant of diversity (of various kinds), supportive of punitive social policies, and not very empathic (Pratto et al.; for a summary of the research on social dominance orientation, see Nelson 103–9). For such people, rigid hierarchies *are* social order.

Because the hierarchies are rigid, they are fragile: this house of cards must be strengthened and defended, but cannot be rebuilt. The world is as it is, and significant change is unthinkable—not in the sense that people do not contemplate it, but in the sense that one should not permit them to do so. Thomas Dew concludes his discussion of the riot in Saint Domingue: "The great sin of that revolution rests on the National Assembly, and should be an awful warning to every legislature to beware of too much tampering with so delicate and difficult a subject, as an alteration of the fundamental relations of society" (824). For reactionaries, thinking of alternatives is dangerous, simply because it implies criticism of the current hierarchy. Education should be oriented toward teaching respect for, and deference to, the current arrangement; policies should be oriented toward protecting and defending it; and public discourse should be oriented toward confirming peoples' good feelings about it.

In an era of religious sentimentalism, when religious faith is explicitly not subject to rational proof, empirical evidence, or any kind of reason, authoritarianism makes it a religious duty to accept political beliefs without question. The sacred and secular are combined not simply in what Young calls "the marriage between Protestant and sectional doctrine" (219) (that is, the assertion that supporting nullification is a religious duty, or any other conflation of God and a particular political party), but also in the sense that one has a religious duty to hold political beliefs without asking for rational proof, empirical evidence, or any kind of reason other than revelation from authority (and something is an authority if it confirms the current hierarchy). This is not, it should be emphasized, the way that all religious people hold religious beliefs, but a way that correlates strongly to authoritarian thinking and stereotyping (so that those with a "quest" orientation toward religion, for instance, tend not to be as prejudiced and authoritarian; for a summary of this research, see Nelson 94–99).

The abolitionists, especially the AAS, argued about specifics—specific practices, specific people to whom these things had happened, specific laws, specific experiences. They had already begun publishing what would be the cornerstone of their rhetoric—detailed personal narratives of slaves, slavers, and visitors to the south. Like proslavery rhetors, they were striving to make a point about the inherent qualities of the institution of slavery, but the relation of specific and general was different for the two groups. The distinction that used to be made in rhetoric (until it turned into a fairly trivial way to identify sentence order in paragraphs) was between inductive and deductive reasoning. In inductive reasoning, one uses data to infer a principle; in deductive, one uses the principle to infer the specifics. Few rhetors use one or the other exclusively (abolitionists reasoned deductively from principles concerning universal rights, the inner light, and so on), but, for the most part, abolitionists relied on inductive reasoning and proslavery rhetors on deductive. Thus, those specific episodes, so important to abolitionists, were simply dismissed by proslavery rhetors; they sometimes mentioned a few of the kinds of incidents to which abolitionists referred (e.g., the breaking up of slave families) but presented them as incidental, as signs that individual slavers should behave better, and not as signifying anything about slavery itself.

Simms, for example, grants that Martineau makes several good criticisms in her chapter "Morals of Slavery": "It is painful, because it is full of truth. It is devoted to the abuses among slaveholders of the institution of slavery; and it gives a collection of statements, which, I fear, are in too many cases founded upon fact, of the illicit and foul conduct of many among us, who make their slaves the victims and the instruments alike of the most licentious passions" (38). Martineau's calling attention to these abuses will, he trusts, "have that beneficial effect upon the relations of master and slave which the truth is at all times most likely to have every where" (39). That these abuses occur is not, for Simms, an indictment of slavery; for him, those incidents should be understood in the light of the already established definition of slavery; the reality of day-to-day experience is superseded by the socially constructed reality of proslavery ideology. As Jeffrey Young has so eloquently put it: "Had the slaveowners focused on the brutal reality of plantation slavery with any measure of objectivity or detachment, they would have recoiled in shame. Instead, they gazed at the master-slave relationship through a prism of romantic, often fictive ideas articulated in novels, travels accounts, histories, and religious tracts" (133). Just as the specifics of slavery are subsumed to the idea of slavery itself, so the particulars of abolitionists—their methods, arguments, even identities—are subsumed to some abstract construct of abolitionism. In other words, in Arendt's terms, the reality of experience does not matter, but the constructed and imagined story does. This is the same phenomenon described in an earlier chapter—one demonstrates one's nobility by one's commitment to that imagined story, by one's ability to ignore reality.

For instance, the AAS maintained that they had only mailed pamphlets to South Carolina, so that this image of a southland "flooded" with pamphlets directed at slaves was false. Martineau mentions this charge, saying

> I was told so universally in the south and west that the abolitionists of Boston and New York were in the habit of sending incendiary tracts among the slaves, that it never occurred to me to doubt the fact; though *I was struck with surprise at never being able to find any one who had see any one who had actually seen one of these tracts* . . . Mr. Madison made the charge, so did Mr. Clay, so did Mr. Calhoun, so did every slave-holder and merchant with whom I conversed. I chose afterwards to hear the other side of the whole question; and I found, to my amazement, that this charge was wholly groundless. No Abolition Society of New York or Massachusetts has ever sent any anti-slavery paper south of Washington, except the circulars, addressed to public officers in the States, which were burnt in Charleston. (I: 124, emphasis added)

Simms quoted this entire passage in his review, and pointed out that she believed abolitionists "at the expense of the first names in our country" (19). For Simms, the argument from authority is more important than the specifics—the word of Clay should matter more than the fact that no one has seen the pamphlets.

He does not actually answer her accusation; she asked for an example of someone who had seen them, and he does not claim to have seen the pamphlets, nor to know anyone who did. Instead, he says that he does know someone who saw some other abolitionist writings (but he didn't see those either), thereby unintentionally confirming her argument.

His description of the pamphlets is significant. Simms says that drawings "are sometimes put upon manufactured cottons, such as are employed entirely for negroes, and insinuated here and there, at decent intervals, among the bales intended for the southern market. Such bales were discovered in a merchant's collection in Charleston, to the knowledge of the writer, but a few years ago" (19). Since the AAS was only recently formed, and since they were condemned for *mailing* pamphlets, these were not their pamphlets. This strategy of putting pamphlets into bales of old clothes was, according to Peter Hinks, an important means of distributing David Walker's *Appeal to the Colored People of the World* (145). So, Simms responds to Martineau's insistence on personal observation about the AAS pamphlets by referring to general knowledge that someone else has sent something else at a different time and via a different route.

In an authoritarian culture, to question the assertions of authorities is to question their goodness. So, the truth of their assertions can be supported through reasserting their goodness as men. Drayton favorably quotes a long passage (from another text) that argues that the framers of the Constitution were "conversant with the rights of men," "they had as much philanthropy," and "as much Christianity," yet they did not abolish slavery. "Shall it be said that such men put a blot and stain upon our country?" (84). The author uses this argument to reject the text of the Declaration ("all men are created equal"). In other words, the author rejects one text (written by someone who did bemoan slavery) on the grounds that good men implicitly endorse slavery. Various foundational texts are thereby merged into the opinions of different people whose actions must be followed because they were good men.

Harper, similarly, dismisses criticisms of slavery by moving to an abstract argument about evil itself: "The condition of our whole existence is but to struggle with evils—to compare them—to choose between them, and so far as we can, to mitigate them. To say that there is evil in any institution, is only to say that it is human" (Harper 85, see also 96). Ericson has called this kind of argument deontological, and that is not an inappropriate term. But, he pairs it with abolitionists' abstract arguments, and the two are very different. The abolitionists' abstract arguments involved what might be considered a deontological view of rights—that rights are not grounded in socially constructed law, and may not be represented in the actual behavior of real nations, but transcend such constructions.[17] Proslavery abstract arguments, however, are along the lines of Harper's comments about evil, or their tendency to refer to "the man" and "the woman" and "the slave." It is as though there is a realm of Platonic forms which are the appropriate subject for argument—that those ideals have little or no basis in the day-to-day lives of actual men, women, and slaves is irrelevant. In fact, assertions about actual events can be dismissed on the grounds that they contradict the hypothetical or abstract. Slave owners do not hurt their slaves, Simms says, because they would not hurt them.

As discussed earlier, proslavery rhetors often argued in the hypothetical, about what people *would* have thought or *would* have done. This line of argument came up particularly in regard to two issues about which hypothesizing was not even necessary: how emancipation could be brought about; what southern politicians would or would not have done in regard to joining the Union. Dew, Paulding, and Drayton do engage in detailed argument showing that emancipation is "impracticable," speculating on various ways that emancipation *could* happen. What both ignore in their discussions is that emancipation *did* happen in all the other states. Their assertions about how emancipation *would* have to happen are contradicted by what *did* happen in those states; the possible precedent is dismissed in an aside by both Dew and Drayton. All Dew says about the example of the other states is: "It is enough to say that paucity of numbers, uncongenial climate, and the state of agriculture to the north, together with the great demand of slaves to the south, alone accomplished the business" (818). This assertion is true of some, but not all, of the northern states; more important, it ignores that some "slave" states had very few slaves, as few as some of the northern states did at the time they began emancipation. Thus, the actual, and very practical, historical precedent is dismissed in favor of hypothetical abstraction.

This rejection of the actual in favor of the hypothetical is an important part of the "race war" argument. Slavery had been abolished in various states, and several of them had substantial free African American populations, and they did not have the same rate of slave insurrection as slave states. Were one to compare the number of insurrections (real and imagined) in slave versus free states, one would have to conclude that insurrection is a danger in slave states and not in free. Yet, the opposite was continually claimed: that race war was the necessary consequence of emancipation without colonization (see Drayton, chapter 19; Harper 87). Both Drayton and Dew argue that freed blacks, inherently too lazy to work, "would *wrench* the means of existence from the white man, and in case of resistance, resort to the torch and the knife" (Drayton 228).

Drayton acknowledges that the North has not yet had a slave insurrection, but tries to turn various incidents into signs that race war is still inevitable. He insists that the tendency that freed blacks have not to help officers of the law take a fugitive slave proves that "they are still insolent and arrogant to a degree which renders them dangerous to the community" (229), so African Americans are to blame for being victims. The recent race riots (in which whites attacked African Americans), he says, were caused by the "presumption of the blacks" (231). The riots would have resulted in a race war if African Americans had been more numerous. That race war is "inevitable, cannot, we think, be doubted" (244). It must result from the very nature of African Americans: "The gratification of their ungoverned passions, their lust, their love of blood, and their hatred of the whites, would combine with the desire to secure the wealth of the citizens, possess their cities, seize their plantations, and prosecute those pursuits which, in the hands of the whites, have been attended with such great success and profit" (244). This is, it should be remembered, the same group previously characterized by Drayton as childlike, affectionate, innocent, unambitious, and devoted to whites. Thus, although there had never been an insurrection in a free state with a large free African American population, and although African Americans are devoted to whites, it cannot be doubted that race war is "inevitable."[18]

This is not to say that abolitionists never made abstract arguments (assertions about the universality of human rights were crucial to their rhetoric) nor is it that proslavery rhetors never talked in specifics (Drayton and Dew are very specific when it comes to the cost of colonization, the number of slaves in the United States, and other, generally economic, issues; Drayton goes into great detail about the rebellion in Saint Domingue; Freeman is very specific in discussing the prophecy of Noah). It is a question of rhetorical tendency—proslavery rhetors tend to use the abstract to explain or understand the specific, and antislavery rhetors tend to use the specific to explain or understand the abstract. In other words, Martineau demonstrates her abolitionist tendency, not by being offended by slavery, but by trying to find someone who had seen the pamphlets, by insisting on a particular, real, example.

Slavery, Dew and Drayton say, aids and heightens civilization because it "impel[s] the master onward in the career of civilization" (Drayton 101) by giving him comfort, leisure, and luxuries. As it did so, "man became a refined and intellectual being" (Drayton 101). The word "man" in the last quote does not refer to all men, because he is not claiming that slavery refined or intellectualized slaves. Manhood is denied men of African descent. And womanhood is denied the women. Drayton, in an argument lifted from Dew (784–85), says "One of the most pleasing incidents of slavery is its amelioration of the condition of the female sex. Among all savage people women are degraded into slaves, the abject drudges of their brutal lords [. . .] One of the first fruits of slavery is the rescue of the gentle victims from their undeserved and wretched fate. The slave relieves the woman" (104). Of course, slavery does not relieve the slave woman, but, just as African American men don't count toward what constitutes the experience of "men," so one can make generalizations about "women" that exclude the experience of free or enslaved African American women. It is significant that both "man" and "woman" are in the singular (just as proslavery rhetors talk about "the slave," "the slaveowner" and capitalize Slavery). Drayton is not talking about real men and real women, but an abstract conception of man and woman-ness, one prohibited to African Americans.[19]

Social psychologists have discussed the epistemological significance of this tendency to argue in the abstract in regard to ingroup and outgroup identity construction. People "encode and communicate desirable in-group and undesirable out-group behaviors more abstractly than undesirable in-group and desirable out-group behaviors" (Maas et al. 981). Hence, the Slaveowner and the Abolitionist that Simms and other proslavery rhetors discuss are inherently good (for the first) and evil (for the second). Slavers who behave badly are individuated, as are slaves who learn to read, or rebel, or engage in any other kind of disruptive behavior. This language use "renders disconfirmation of preexisting ideas about in-group and out-group difficult" (981). Or, as Van Eemeren and Grootendorst argue, because the assertions are so abstract, they are hermetic; an infinite number of counterexamples does not disprove the abstraction because each one is dismissed as particular.

In one regard, though, this argument about what slavery does to (slave-owning white) man and (slave-owning white) woman was rhetorically problematic. As was discussed in an earlier chapter, since Jefferson, it had been a convention to bemoan the effect of slavery on slavers. Jefferson had argued that it made slave owners tyrannical, haughty, and prone to violence. These rhetors do and don't reiterate Jefferson's argument. While they reject the implication that slave owning damages slave owners, they, possibly unintentionally, grant, and even demonstrate, that he was right.

Drayton, for instance, condemns "the north" for claiming moral superiority: "Has the north a right to decide that she is superior to her sister south, in political virtue; to say *stand aside, for I am holier than thou?* Is this modest assumption of superior virtue creditable to her?" (107). "The north," of course, has made no such claim, and even Jefferson's argument, reiterated in the criticisms of abolitionists, was not a comparative claim—neither Jefferson nor the abolitionists presented the issue as a moral competition between regions. But, in much proslavery rhetoric, criticism of an aspect of southern life by a nonsoutherner is taken as "the north" claiming to be better than "the south"—criticism is an act of moral domination. Appomattox, apparently from western Virginia, after granting that the New England states do have better educational systems, transforms that fairly specific criticism of the slave economy into a general attack on the relative merits of regions; his region "may challenge a comparison, for purity of manners and morals, for kindness, generosity and honesty, with any people under the sun" (23). He goes on to dismiss Jefferson's famous characterization of the pernicious consequences of slavery on the grounds that Jefferson was from *"eastern"* Virginia (24), so Appomattox does not object to sectionalism on principle. Similarly, the beginning of the Drayton passage might make one think that Drayton objected to anyone claiming moral superiority; that is not his point—he goes on to claim moral superiority for the south: "To him who contemplates the 'high and haughty' virtues of the south, and then recurs to the treachery and tergiversation, the degrading appeals to popular errors, the corrupt arts of electioneering, the servility and indifference to principle, and the universal and ravenous appetite for office, exhibited in the politics of the north" (108). Drayton does not dispute that southerners are more prone to violence or more haughty; it is just that he will not accept those characteristics as vices to be bemoaned.

Southerners' attempts to prove that the south is better than the North ran them into some troubles. One of the cliché criticisms of the northerners was their obsession with profit. Dew characterizes northerners as having "that cold, contracted, calculating *selfishness,* which withers and repels everything around it, and lessens or destroys all the multiplied enjoyments of social intercourse" (Thomas Dew 821). A major argument against emancipation was that it would be too expensive (an argument made as early as by Walsh, in 1819). A conventional argument as to why slave owners cannot be cruel to their slaves is that it is not in their economic interest: "If he inflicts on him such punishment as will permanently impair his strength, he inflicts a loss on himself, and so if he requires of him excessive labor" (Harper 98).

Slavery, as mentioned above, is presented as the only possible social arrangement because it is a necessary extension of hierarchy, which constitutes social order (Harper 82–83; Freeman; Simms 61–66). Simms says that "the definition of true liberty, is the undisturbed possession of that place in society to which our moral and intellectual merits entitle us. *He is a freeman, whatever his condition, who fills his proper place*" (65). The anonymous critic of Channing concludes his text: "Society is man's necessary condition. Its members *must* be governed. Governing may be the exercise of power by a few, that all may have and enjoy the benefits of existence. It may be, the exercise of power by a few, to control and oppress the many, so that these few may wanton in luxury, and delight in their supremacy. This latter has been the common lot, in most nations, and in all ages" (60). J. H. Guenebalt, in his "Dedication" section of his collection of extracts from European racialist scientists, says, "Let the distinctions of rank be destroyed, and society can exist no longer—chaos begins, and all is confused" (vi). Farley says: "One man is born to labor, working with his own hands from morning till night for a scanty support—while another is born to ease and affluence; he may lay if he please on a bed of roses. There is no help for it. God has ordered it so" (14). John Drayton's discussion of slavery ends with an argument that "Nature, governed by unerring laws, which commanded the oak to be stronger than the willow, and cypress to be taller than the shrub; has at the same time imposed on mankind certain restrictions, which can never be overcome" (148). This view of society—hierarchical, stable, authoritarian—is consistently invoked in proslavery ideology.

Yet, one of the things which, according to Drayton, makes the North inferior to the South is that the North is a hierarchy, whereas slavery has created a perfect equality among whites, an argument he notes he has taken from Thomas Dew (823). Many of the most prominent proslavery rhetors (such as Hammond) were *arrivistes,* and Ingraham's discussion of slavery emphasizes the social mobility it enables (discussed later). This may appear to be a contradiction, and it may indeed be one, but it is one that W. J. Cash described in his analysis of southern culture, remarking that poor whites, often related to the planter aristocracy, could, if handled correctly by members of that class, glow "with the sense of participation in the common brotherhood of white men" (41).[20] The South, if one believes Dew, Drayton, or Cash, had perfect equality among whites *because* there was a racial caste system—no matter how low on the economic hierarchy, a white, any white, could consider him- or herself in the same racial category as the highest. In Burke's terms, the unification of the whites was dependent on and reinforced the division between whites and African Americans. So, somehow, the ideal society has social mobility *and* a rigid social hierarchy.

Of more importance than the logical inconsistencies in this competition with the North for the moral high ground is the move itself—a discussion of slavery is turned into an issue of regional rivalry. And, as in *Nick of the Woods,* issues of causality become issues of blame. Dew, for example, concludes a long discussion blaming other countries for imposing slavery on the United States: "If ever a nation stood justified before heaven, in regard to an evil, which had become interwoven with her social system, is not that country ours? Are not our hands unpolluted with the original sin, and did we not wish them clean of the contagion the moment our independent existence was established? Where is the stain that rests upon our escutcheon? There is none!" (789)[21] The perception of discourse as trying to establish a hierarchy of goodness means that criticism is an attempt to dominate someone. Therefore, criticisms of southern slavery can be answered by pointing out that the North does not have the moral high ground, as though that were the issue in the first place. I don't think that this is a cunning attempt to shift the stasis (although the move, which logicians call *tu quoque,* is a fallacy and does have that consequence), as much as it is a sign of how discourse works in what I am calling authoritarian approaches to discourse. As much as abolitionists tried to distinguish criticisms of slavery from criticisms of slave owners, as much as they had prologues and prolepses saying that they were not attacking slave owners, they were always heard as doing so, because they were criticizing the beliefs of such people. If abolitionists were right, slavers were not who they claimed to be.

I have emphasized the inconsistencies within the same authors—that one proslavery rhetor would disagree with another is only an indictment of *the* proslavery ideology if one assumes that there was only one, and that is not my assumption. It was, however, the assertion of the proslavery rhetors, so the diversity of views among them is a problem for their argument. Simms says that his book "contains principles which no sophistry can subvert, and no misapplied ingenuity, whether of cunning or of self-blinding philanthropy, could keep from the ultimate reception of mankind" (3); it is taken from "the inevitable sense of mankind upon the subject of which it treats" (4).

Simms also says that he, like thousands of other southerners, is not in favor of annexing Texas, and that he disagrees with the recent decision to forbid Carolinians to free their slaves. Both of these positions are controversial; so, despite his initial promise to his readers, he has not kept to an "inevitable sense of mankind." Again, that proslavery rhetors disagree is a problem, not because I think they should agree, but because they assert that there is no disagreement on these issues.

It is tempting to assume that this internally contradictory logic comes from the defensive position. Being "on the defensive," as Mason says, "rendered their attempts to defend slavery hesitant and confused" (7). Rhetors defending a popular ideology are not subject to the same scrutiny as those attacking it, but that situation only explains why they would not perceive the logical problems in their arguments; it doesn't answer the question of whether they sincerely believed every part of their logically contradictory arguments. For instance, what should we make of Paulding's argument that abolitionists want to "overturn the social relations of nations, and establish a universal brotherhood" (306)? I think it quite possible that they were sincere in their equation of that political and economic hegemony with social order, that they really believed that it was a question of doing exactly what they were doing or total chaos. *That* is what has to be explained.

And it is partially explained through reconsidering the question of effectiveness. These texts were ineffective at constructing a logically sound (i.e., internally consistent) explanation of southern U.S. slavery in light of the Bible, the laws, and the practices, and they were (therefore) almost certainly ineffective at persuading an informed, intelligent, opposition audience. But, there is no reason to think that the rhetors were striving for either of those goals. These texts were, probably, effective at what scholars of communication call immunizing. By presenting a weak version of opposition arguments to precommitted readers, an immunizing text ensures that the readers will resist the stronger version should they ever be exposed to it. These texts were probably very effective at persuading already proslavery readers that abolitionist arguments were both worthless and dangerous, and deserved to be silenced with violence. And they were almost certainly effective at reinforcing an authoritarian view of politics and discourse.

Authoritarianism assumes that slavery is necessary for social order, especially in that it preserves hierarchy, so that an attack on slavery is an attack on social order; that order itself is fragile, in constant (and imminent) danger of collapsing into anarchy; because anarchy is always simply one false move away, we are always in a crisis that requires extreme measures; among the extreme measures required by the fragility of social order is complete agreement (dissent is treason, in other words); social order is preserved only if people are completely controlled; people are controlled through enforcing deference to established authorities, and, when that is insufficient, through punishment or its threat; authorities dictate correct doctrine (which is absolutely clear) in texts, whose meaning is unambiguous; because the truth is obvious, disagreement is only explained through willful obtuseness on the part of dissenters, or through their conscious participation in an evil conspiracy; at the same time, because order and control are so important, the actual truth of the situation is always less important than the extent to which a particular belief or policy enforces/

enables the authorities' control or threatens it. What fosters loyalty is true, whether or not it is accurate. Proslavery rhetors consistently supported authoritarianism; that they did so with inconsistent and contradictory arguments is, by their ideology, irrelevant.

6
"Our laws to regulate slaves are entirely founded on terror"
The Political Theory of Slave Codes

> Indeed, these laws show that almost nothing could be created in the antebellum South without taking slavery into consideration.
>
> —Paul Finkelman

In the previous chapters, I have emphasized how public discourse both appeals to and creates consensus about group identity, with sometimes tragic consequences. Thus far, I have relied on the fairly conventional understanding of public discourse as discourse about policy; in this chapter I want to consider policy itself as a form of public discourse. Specifically, I want to look at laws related to slavery in various states in two, closely related, ways: the issue of causality (why they were passed when they were); and, the theory of causality implied by the laws themselves (their implicit political theory). According to Paul Finkelman, "Legislators probably passed more acts on slavery than on any other subject." The prevalence of the topic of slavery in statutes shows that slavery "affected virtually everything legislators did [. . .] Indeed, these laws show that almost nothing could be created in the antebellum South without taking slavery into consideration" (x). Laws concerning hunting raised questions about slaves' access to weapons; regulations over boating touched on anxieties about free African American sailors; laws about liquor evoked concerns about poor whites and blacks consorting together.[1]

The sheer number of the laws suggests the considerable anxiety that people felt about slaves, free African Americans, and even slavery itself. Literate slaves meant, not just slaves who could read abolitionist literature (the typical justification for antiliteracy laws), but slaves who could forge passes; it also meant slaves who could do something that many poor whites could not (therefore threatening white supremacy). But, antiliteracy laws belied central tenets in the case for slavery: that it was good for slaves, that slaves were not incapable of autonomy, that they loved being slaves. Such laws also presented a rhetorical problem: how do people who want to see themselves as loving, and loved, patriarchs presiding benevolently over affectionate slaves rationalize (in both senses of the word) oppressive slave codes?

The checkered history of antiliteracy laws—that they were passed (often in the wake of an insurrection scare, and in the midst of controversy), then repealed, then reinstituted, then modified to give exceptions, then intensified, and often imperfectly enforced—demonstrates that citizens in slave states were anxious about literate slaves *and* anxious about oppressive slave codes.[2]

Scapegoating the abolitionists was rhetorically helpful for trying to allay one part of that anxiety; claiming that the rigid laws were necessitated by abolitionism could enable proslavery rhetors to evade responsibility for the logical consequences of slavery. The *Report and Resolutions of Georgia General Assembly* says that "if a rigor heretofore unknown to our domestic legislation be found in the features of the bill they have introduced, it has been forced upon them, by the movements of men, who, assuming to be the friends, are indeed the most cruel enemies of those whom they have taken under their especial care." Paulding says,

> Influenced by a just apprehension of the consequences of the rash and intemperate interference of the abolitionists, and their perservering attempts to instigate the slaves to violence and insurrection, it thus appears that the people of the South are compelled, in self-defence, to close up to them every avenue of religious knowledge, and to adopt all the rigorous measures of a jealous policy. They will no longer wear their chains so lightly as scarce to feel them; they will no longer be permitted the indulgences which ever result from a generous confidence that they will not be abused to bad purposes, nor allowed the freedom of action which was gradually becoming more extensive. The free blacks are still greater sufferers by the efforts of their over zealous friends, for it is proposed to repeal almost all the laws conferring on them any of the privileges of freemen. They have become objects of the most rigid and severe scrutiny; and there can be no doubt that the slightest suspicion will draw down on their head additional penalties. The master cannot trust his slave—the slave hates his master; on the one hand is seen a watchful jealousy, ever the precursor of severity to the dependant; on the other, a spirit of stubborn refractory pride, mingled with one of a still more dangerous and malignant nature. Thus, on the one side confidence, on the other, gratitude and affection, are irretrievably lost. All that contributed to render the relations of master and slave a reciprocity of

> mutual benefits, and gave the institution of slavery in the South the leading features of the patriarchal state, in which, as the head of the tribe possessed all the property, so he was under the solemn obligation of maintaining and protecting all his dependants; all these will give place to a contest of jealous apprehension and secret revenge. That master will be obliged to act the tyrant in his own defence, and the slave will resort to the only weapons of weakness; deception, fraud, conspiracy, and over acts of vengeance. (294–95; see also Ingraham 293)

Paulding's defense relies on casting the slavers as victims of abolitionists, as forced into an antagonistic relationship with their slaves by abolitionists. This strategy attempts to reverse the cause and effect (so that, rather than abolitionism being a consequence of the oppressions of slavery, the oppressions of slavery are the consequence of abolitionism). Yet, he has unintentionally granted the abolitionist argument: if, as he says, abolitionists have so changed the conditions that compassionate slavery is impossible, then compassionate slavery is impossible, and slavery cannot be defended on the grounds that it is compassionate. But, this sort of criticism of Paulding's argument would have seemed irrelevant (or worse) at the time, as it presumes that deliberation is the goal of public argumentation, and that such deliberation is aided by a pragmatic analysis of the situation. On the contrary, such pragmatic analysis—which depends upon airing criticism—would have seemed to proslavery rhetors to be indecorous, as it dishonored privileged people, and disloyal, as it would involve negative comments about an existing institution.

Obviously, such a sense about the limitations of public discourse limit the possibilities of deliberation. Deliberation is further limited by the ways that proslavery rhetors used the topos of blame. Aristotle famously insisted that "no one deliberates about things that cannot vary, nor about things not within his power to do" (*Nicomachean Ethics* 337); he is not claiming that people never discuss such things, but that such discussion cannot be *deliberation* because the discourse could not result in any change, and deliberation is not just about judgment, but about action (see *Nicomachean Ethics* 339). To the extent that abolitionists discussed blame (which might more appropriately be called responsibility) it was to hold slavers responsible for owning slaves, breaking up slave families, refusing to teach them to read, exploiting them sexually, and so on—actions which could be different, and in which slavers themselves were engaged, thereby meeting both of Artistotle's criteria. Proslavery rhetors, however, wanted to place the blame on people who were dead, whose actions could not be changed, thereby making slavery beyond deliberation.

It forecloses any real policy discussion insofar as it lays out, instead of a practical discussion of actual options, an impossible goal. By positing a time when things were better, when slave codes were not oppressive, this narrative suggests that our goal should be to return to that time (this is the sense in which it was a reactionary, not conservative, narrative). Before looking closely at that nostalgia, it should be noted that this strategy is rhetorically and politically powerful: set up impossible goals that simultaneously rationalize current conditions of oppression *and* relieve those enforcing the conditions from responsibility.[3] Were the goals achievable (that is, could slave states have completely eradicated the abolitionist movement), it would have become clear that repressive slave codes had nothing to do with abolitionists like Garrison and Tappan, so slavers needed abolitionists. In fact, they needed a different kind of abolitionist from the ones that were actually active: they didn't need Quakers who advocated emancipation through moral suasion; they needed violent insurrectionists who practiced amalgamation and advocated uncompensated emancipation forced on slave states by the federal government.[4] That is the "abolitionist" that proslavery rhetoric discursively created.

Determining what caused state legislatures to pass repressive laws is very complicated. While, on the whole, the history of laws concerning slaves is one of increasing state control and restricted personal freedom (especially, but not exclusively, for the African Americans—slave laws also restricted slavers' behavior), it is not a straight trajectory at every point along the way. In 1804, Virginia passed "An Act further declaring what shall be deemed unlawful meetings of slaves," which said "that all meetings or assemblages of slaves, at any meeting house or houses, or any other place or places, in the night, under whatsoever pretext, shall be deemed and considered an unlawful assembly." This law was revised in 1805 to exempt meetings for religious worship (if led by a "licensed, white minister"; "An Act to Amend and Explain an Act further declaring what shall be deemed Unlawful Meetings of Slaves"). This pattern represents the dilemma that legislatures had—a fear of African American churches, but a desire to permit religious worship.

Delaware's 1827 laws prohibited attendance at "riot, rout, or unlawful assembly" (see section 8, chapter 1). Mississippi's 1799 slave code said, to "prevent the inconveniencies arising by the meetings of slaves" owners and overseers were not allowed "to permit or suffer any slave not belonging to him or her, to be and remain upon his or her plantation above two hours at one time, without leave of the owner or overseer of such slave." In 1805, "An Act respecting slaves" extended the time to four hours and clarified that this act did not restrict slaves' "going to church, and attending divine service, on the Lord's day, and between sun-rising and sun-setting." Mississippi's June 1822 "An act to reduce into one the several acts concerning slaves" allowed masters to send their slaves "any place or places whatever, for the purpose of religious worship" as long as the worship was conducted by a white minister (a similar law was passed in 1804). In December 1822, however, that section of the law was repealed. The 1805 law prohibited attendance at an unlawful assembly, a term clarified in the December 1822 law which said, "All meetings or assemblies of slaves, or free negroes, or mulattoes, mixing and associating with such slaves, above the number of five, at any place of public resort, or at any meeting-house or houses, in the night, or at any school or schools, for teaching them reading or writing, either in the day or night, under whatsoever pretext, shall be deemed and considered as an unlawful assembly" ("An act to alter and amend an act to reduce into one the several acts concerning slaves").

In 1800, South Carolina defined "an unlawful meeting" as "all assemblies and congregations of slaves, free negroes, mulattoes, and mestizoes, whether composed of all, or any of the above description of persons, or of all or any of the above described persons, and of a proportion of white persons, assembled or met together for the purpose of mental instruction, in a confined or secret place of meeting, or with the gates or doors of such place of meeting barred, bolted, or locked, so as to prevent the free ingress and egress to and from the same." This same law outlawed any meeting of African Americans, "even in company with white persons" to meet together for any purpose before sunrise or after dark. Tennessee's law forbidding slaves from assembling without written permission was passed in 1803. All of these laws were passed before there was any significant abolitionist movement, let alone a "strident" one.

According to Thomas Morris, both Virginia and North Carolina forbade manumission by last will in the 1700s, and both states later relented; Virginia permitted such manumission in 1782. But, both states then later passed more restrictive laws. My research suggests an even more complicated history. In 1801, North Carolina passed a law requiring that people who freed slaves post a bond for their good behavior ("An Act to amend, strengthen, and confirm the several Acts of Assembly"), and vested "exclusive power of emancipation" in the state superior court in 1818 ("An Act to invest in the Supreme Court of this state exclusive power of emancipation"). Alabama, which appears to have required legislative action for emancipation until 1833, then passed a law authorizing judges of the county court to emancipate slaves ("An Act to authorize the Judges of the County Courts to emancipate slaves"). Tennessee, likewise, empowered county courts to emancipate slaves in 1801. South Carolina forbade all manumission except by deed in 1800, and passed another antimanumission law in 1820 (that law, it should be noted, also prohibited bringing into the state "any written paper, with intent to disturb the peace or security of the same, in relation to the slaves of the people of this State," meaning anything that criticized slavery; qtd. in M. Johnson, 969). Florida greatly restricted the ability of an owner to free slaves in 1829. Kentucky restricted the ability of an owner to emancipate slaves in 1794 ("An Act concerning the Importation and Emancipation of Slaves"), and further restricted them in 1823 ("An Act to amend the law respecting the emancipation of slaves"). Mississippi passed "an act to prevent the liberation of slaves" in 1805 which was partially repealed in 1805 and amended in 1815.

The amendments were not consistently more restrictive, as in Virginia and North Carolina; they seemed to operate in a pattern of restriction, partial reconsideration, restriction, partial reconsideration. Because the reconsideration was rarely a complete rescinding, the end result was that the slave owner's ability to free his or her own slaves was increasingly limited by states' laws—in some slave states prohibited and in others severely restricted—*before* Garrison broke with colonization or started the *Liberator.* Not only does this complicate the narrative that abolitionists caused a backlash, but it is fairly ironic given that the slave South claimed to be the place where property rights were sacrosanct. If they had been sacrosanct, and had slaves really been seen as subject to property right principles, state legislators would not have passed so many laws controlling what slavers did with their slaves (for more on this contradiction, see Morris 378–80).[5]

Slave-state legislators made no pretense of respecting the property rights of free African Americans. Many cities and states forbade them from certain kinds of jobs (e.g., the Georgia law mentioned below that prohibited them from working in printing establishments, or the many laws, such as Alabama's 1822 law, that prohibited them from running stores or selling liquor). States struggled with prohibiting gun ownership among free African Americans and slaves, often passing such laws generally after an insurrection scare, but then having to reconsider them when owners wanted slaves to hunt, or in light of efforts to have wolves killed (see, for example, the difference between Mississippi's 1799 "A law for the regulating of slaves" and 1804 "An Act respecting slaves"). A law passed by Kentucky in 1808 is especially interesting in regard to states' and individuals' rights. Some African Americans in Kentucky, who, it appears, had been brought from Virginia and Pennsylvania against the laws there, were suing for their freedom. "An Act limiting actions in certain acts" simply prohibited them from being able to make such suits. Had the Kentucky Legislature respected either the property rights of the African Americans or the states' rights of Virginia and Pennsylvania, they would not have passed such a law. The institution of slavery was sacrosanct, and the rights of anyone (including whites) were infringed or eradicated if they conflicted with the security of slavery.

This is not simply ugly hypocrisy or greed, although it was both, but a theory of rights. Rather than seeing rights as natural, transcendent, and universal, southern legislators acted as though rights were derived from one's place in the hierarchy, and granted by the state. As Faust says, southern intellectuals believed that "men did not possess natural rights [. . .] Freedom was not a right but a privilege" (84). This perception is related to the notion of positive law—that rights are posited by the construction of a constitution and body of laws; they are socially constructed (although proslavery rhetors did not consistently appeal to positive law—they did sometimes assert innate rights for themselves).

If things like free speech are socially constructed privileges to which people are entitled to varying degrees, then the higher on the hierarchy, the more free speech one has. One's ability to practice that privilege is severely restricted to things that do not disrupt the system. During the gag rule controversy, Owens explained that the right of petition "was not an abstract position and unqualified term; that in the exercising of every right there were corresponding duties" (38). Kentucky's "Resolutions Respecting Abolition Societies" uses "right" and "privilege" as though they were synonymous: "When the constitution of the country guarantees to every citizen the right to publish and speak his opinions upon all subjects, it wisely fixed the limitation that he shall be responsible for the abuse of that privilege" (4). As several people said during the gag rule controversy, if someone misuses a right (such as through petitioning to have slavery abolished), they forfeit it. When proslavery rhetors complain that the federal government is "trampling on our rights," the emphasis should be on "our" rather than "rights."[6]

For instance, Mississippi's 1822 "An Act to reduce into one the several acts concerning slaves, free negroes and mulattoes" permitted up to thirty-nine lashes "if any negro or mulatto, bond or free, shall, at any time use abusive and provoking language to, or lift his or her hand in opposition to any person, not being a negro or mulatto." This is, obviously, not operating on the principle of equality before the law, but of *in*equality before the law; a "negro" or "mulattoe" is even forbidden self-defense. The purpose of these laws was to preserve the existing hierarchy, which was seen as identical to order, so that insubordination and insurrection are more or less the same thing.

A major focus of anxiety concerned the free African American population. Alabama's 1833 law, which permitted emancipation if approved by a county court judge, required that emancipation take place after the slave had left the state and required that he or she never return. But, slave states passed laws trying to rid themselves of freed slaves long before Garrison began agitating. In 1806, Virginia passed a law requiring that emancipated slaves leave the state within twelve months, or risk being sold back into slavery ("An Act to amend the several laws concerning slaves," January 1806). North Carolina prohibited "free persons of colour" from emigrating in 1826, as did Florida. South Carolina passed a death penalty for free African Americans who migrated to the state in 1820. This same law, "An Act to restrain the emancipation of Slaves, and to prevent free persons of colour from entering into this State, and for other purposes," required that free African Americans in the state pay fifty dollars a year to remain—or be subject to the death penalty.

Some state slave statutes do demonstrate fear of abolitionists, but, again, the dates do not support a simple causality claim that the supposed shift in abolitionist rhetoric led to them. Alabama, Tennessee, Virginia, and Missouri all passed resolutions or memorials condemning abolitionists in 1835, 1836 (Virginia), or 1837 (Missouri). Tennessee passed "an act to prevent the publication or circulation in this State of seditious pamphlets" in 1835, which may have been as a result of the pamphlet controversy. But Tennessee had already passed a law "to prohibit any person from using words in the hearing of any slave or person of colour, either publicly or privately, that may have a tendency to inflame their minds, or induce them to insurrection" in 1803 ("An Act to prohibit any person from using words in the hearing"), and another law forbidding seditious speeches by slaves in 1806 ("An Act to amend the law in force and use concerning free negroes, mulattoes and slaves"). South Carolina's "An Act to restrain the emancipation of Slaves, and to prevent free persons of color from entering into this state, and for other purposes" made it a high misdemeanor "if any white person shall be duly convicted of having directly or indirectly circulated or brought within this state, any written or printed paper, with intent to disturb the peace or security of the same in relation to the slaves of the people of this state." This law was passed in 1820. Georgia passed a law which was intended "to prevent the circulation of written or printed papers within this State calculated to excite disaffection among the coloured people of this State, and to prevent said people from being taught to read or write" in 1829 ("An Act to be entitled an act, to amend the several laws"). That same year Georgia prohibited slaves or free "negroes or mulattoes" from working in printing offices ("An Act to prohibit the employment of slaves"). Mississippi and North Carolina both passed laws regarding "seditious" pamphlets in 1830 (MS: "An Act to prevent the circulation of seditious pamphlets"; NC: "An Act to prevent the circulation of seditious pamphlets"). So terror of abolitionists precedes the advent of radical abolitionism.

Laws prohibiting the teaching of reading and/or writing to slaves were especially controversial, and there is no clear pattern to their passage (for more on this issue, see Cornelius). In 1830, North Carolina outlawed teaching "slaves to read or write, the use of figures excepted." Georgia prohibited the teaching of reading or writing to any "slave, negro or free person of colour" by a white person, slave, negro, or free person of colour December 22, 1829 (Section 11 of "An Act to be entitled an act, to amend the several laws now in force in this State, regulating Quarantine"). South Carolina's law forbidding the teaching of reading and writing to slaves was passed in January 1835, so one might claim it was caused by the increase in abolition activity, but it was passed six months prior to the pamphlet controversy. South Carolina had already passed such a law in 1740 and another in 1834, and Georgia had one as part of its 1755 slave code.

There is not a strict linear progression to these repressive laws year by year or state by state. The condition of slaves, in regard to the likelihood of manumission, ability to earn their own freedom, access to skills like reading and writing, capacity to marry or testify, and the ability of free African Americans to vote, travel, remain safe from kidnapping, and own property all declined substantially between 1790 and 1859, but not in a straightforward pattern across slave states. Whatever slave-state legislatures were reacting to was local, rather than regional, let alone national. So, one has to wonder: what were they reacting to?

Missouri's 1837 law has been explicitly attributed to the pamphlet mailings (Savage 313). The law was proposed in November 1836 and, apparently, went through its required three readings with minimal debate. There was no reporting of it in Missouri newspapers at the time, the Governor's fall 1836 Message says nothing about a need for anti-abolitionist laws, and the Missouri *Argus*'s early 1837 summary of that session's legislative actions does not even mention the act. It was not, apparently, a noteworthy event. But, neither had the pamphlets been noteworthy in Missouri: I can find no mention of the AAS pamphlet mailings in the summer or fall of 1835 in Missouri newspapers. There was, however, agitation about the Murrell conspiracy, which was, it should be remembered, perceived as an abolitionist plot. There was agitation about abolitionists and abolitionism unrelated to the pamphlets, such as the spring 1836 agitation over the perception of Marion College as a source of antislavery sentiment.[7] Elijah Lovejoy's activities in St. Louis had already been blamed for the lynching of an African American steamboat worker; anti-Mormonism was tied up with Mormon's opposition to slavery (the June 30, 1836 *Far West* reports an anti-Mormon meeting that condemned them specifically on those grounds); a summer 1836 camp meeting in Palmyra became violent when a proslavery audience member stabbed an antislavery speaker; and that same year two colonizationists were threatened with lynching if they didn't leave the state. Since there is no evidence of Missouri uproar over the pamphlets, it's more reasonable to infer that any one of these events—or all of them together—inspired the anti-abolitionist law.

Even when the causality seems clearly implied by the order of events, it may not be so simple. After the Vesey rebellion, South Carolina passed various laws (such as the Negro Seaman laws, previously discussed), so it's reasonable to infer that the first led to the second. That explanation, however, ignores that there was significant anxiety about a slave uprising in 1818, and in 1820 "up and down the southern coast" (Dillon 130–31). While any individual uprising (or rumor of one) has significant impact, it *creates* neither the desire for repressive laws, nor the fear of uprising. South Carolina had passed a law forbidding private emancipation in 1820, two years before the Vesey rebellion. Maryland's anti-insurrection law was passed in 1778, Kentucky's in 1811. The Stono Rebellion of 1739 almost certainly led to the 1740 "Negro Act." But, because South Carolina had passed the restrictive "Security Act" before the Stono Rebellion, some have argued that the act caused the rebellion. So, it may be that rather than repression being the consequence of rebellion, it is both the consequence and the cause.

In addition, it is difficult to distinguish between an actual insurrection and a panic. Political action is always in response to *perceived* political problems, which may or may not have anything to do with actual events. North Carolina passed a law regarding insurrection in 1795, which was amended in 1798, and passed additional laws in 1802. The 1795 law may have been passed as a consequence of anxiety arising from the 1791 revolt in Haiti, or the Maroon Wars. The Demerara Rebellion of 1795 may have contributed to the 1798 law. The 1802 laws were as a consequence of a nonexistent rebellion; an insurrection panic stormed through the eastern part of the state beginning in May. Guion Griffis Johnson's *Ante-bellum North Carolina* says: "During the heat of the excitement, a report circulated in Winton that the town of Windsor had been burned by the Negroes. The town council sent a messenger by fast horse to determine the truth of the report. On his way he met a messenger coming from Windsor, and on questioning him found that he had been sent to Winton for the same reason" (G. G. Johnson 510). The scare had essentially the same pattern as other insurrection panics, or that the Salem witch trials had had: a panic, coerced confessions which were then used to extort other confessions, which were then used to rationalize executions. Herbert Aptheker's research on newspapers, letters, diaries, and government documents turned up reports of plots, if not incidents, of insurrections, arsons, and poisonings in virtually every year from 1800 to 1840. Johnson, in addition to the 1802 panic (which she refers to as the "so-called insurrection of 1802" [510]), discusses other major insurrection scares in 1805, 1811, 1818, 1821, 1825, 1830, and 1831 in North Carolina alone (see her chapter "Slave Conspiracies"). My point here is rather complicated: because legislation would be in reaction to the perceived threat of insurrection, rather than the actual event, and because the threat was nearly constant, it is difficult to know whether any specific set of laws stemmed from fear of insurrection.

It is easy to focus on the dramatic, and fairly appalling, laws passed regarding the teaching of reading and writing, restricting emancipation, enabling the kidnapping of free African Americans and so on, but it does not seem to me that those represent the bulk of slave laws. Reading the laws, one comes to see the major concerns expressed in attempts to control some of the more mundane behavior, such as restricting trading. Arkansas' 1825 law is typical; it says, "That no slave shall be suffered to buy or sell any article of property whatever, unless such slave shall have, in writing, particularly specifying in his or her pass, such article or articles; and any slave found in possession of any article of property, without such writing as aforesaid, shall be subject to suffer any number of lashes, at the discretion of the captain of the patrol, not exceeding ten." One might be tempted to conclude that such laws were intended to restrict or prevent "stealing."[8] But, I would suggest that these laws are related in intention to those various laws that specifically prohibited paying slaves for their labor, or owners permitting them to hire themselves out. The 1829 Georgia law, "An Act to regulate slaves and free persons of colour in the towns of Clinton and Macon," typifies this latter kind of law. The second section of the law says, "That no slave shall be allowed to hire his or her time from his or her owner or manager, nor shall any slave be allowed to work or carry on any traffic upon his or her own account, or for the purpose of procuring a livelihood, or raising money to pay his or her hire wages."[9] In the early days of American slavery, such hiring out enabled slaves to earn enough money to buy their freedom. Hence, reducing their opportunity to get access to money reduced their chances of being able to buy their freedom (or pay someone to help them run away). That these laws were passed more frequently than anti-insurrection (or anti-abolitionist) laws may suggest that African American economic autonomy was even more terrifying than insurrection.

These laws restricting what slaves and free African Americans could own and what businesses they might pursue probably had another function as well—protecting the racial hierarchy. A recurrent argument for slavery was that African Americans could not handle freedom. Prosperous African Americans threatened that argument; the solution was to make reality fit the rhetoric by closing off any avenues to prosperity. The "natural" hierarchy of races could thereby be maintained. Like the Mississippi laws that prohibited insubordination, laws that restricted freed African Americans to certain kinds of employment preserved the economic hierarchy (or tried to). So, ideology created the need for a particular law in order to create the reality the ideology claimed was "natural."

Tennessee's 1806 "An Act to amend the law in force and use concerning free negroes, mulattoes and slaves" prohibits "riots, routs, unlawful assemblies, trespasses, and seditious speeches by a slave or slaves, or any insulting or provoking language used by such slave or slaves to any white person." Insulting language is just as forbidden as riots, and, in some obscure way, in a similar category. According to Wiethoff, Virginia passed a statute forbidding African Americans (free or not) from raising their hands against a white or "abusive and provoking language" (qtd. in *Insolent Slave* 32); Mississippi passed a law against insolence in 1822, and Louisiana had a similar law by 1816 (*Insolent Slave* 33, 34).

The cluster of laws passed in 1829 and 1830 is especially interesting for considering cause and effect. In those two years (before the Nat Turner rebellion, Garrison's publication of the *Liberator,* or the pamphlet mailings) Maryland, Georgia, Mississippi, and North Carolina all passed an unusual number of laws, or an unusual kind of law, especially in areas reached by David Walker's *Appeal to the Coloured People of the World.* Mississippi's November 1830 law, "An Act, to prevent the circulation of seditious pamphlets, papers and magazines in this state, and for other purposes," threatened with a fine of between one and one thousand dollars, and a jail term of three to twelve months, any white person who "shall print, write, circulate or put forth, or cause to be printed, written, circulated or put forth any book, paper, magazine, pamphlet, handbill or circular in this state, containing any sentiment, doctrine, advice or in[n]uendoes calculated to produce a disorderly, dangerous or rebellious disaffection among the coloured population of this state, or in anywise to endanger the peace of society, by exciting riots and rebellion among said population." A "slave, negro, mustizo, or free person of colour" who circulated such material would be punished with death. In December 1830, the North Carolina General Assembly passed a series of laws forbidding African Americans from gambling, attending muster or election days, or being taught reading or writing, and it required that plantation owners have a white overseer (the last was part of a law passed in South Carolina in 1800). I want to look carefully at the North Carolina laws, in order to argue that repressive laws signify an authoritarian political theory, not white abolitionist activity. To the extent that they were a reaction to abolitionist activity at all, it was not to people like Garrison, but to Walker.

The laws were proposed December 1, 1830, by William Meares, on behalf of the "joint select committee on that part of the Governor's Message which relates to Slaves, &c." in secret session (*Raleigh Register* December 9, 1830; *Niles' Weekly Register* February 5, 1831).[10] That joint committee was formed, apparently, on a motion of Stedman on November 19, who requested that the committee "enquire into the expediency of preventing the education of slaves and the dissemination of incendiary writings among them" (*Raleigh Register* November 25, 1830). This action was almost certainly a response to the Governor's Message, which had the following section concerning an "incendiary" publication:

> I transmit to the Legislature, a copy of an incendiary publication which has been circulated very extensively in the Southern country, the design and mischievous tendency of which, cannot be mistaken.
>
> The discovery of this inflammatory production in Virginia, South-Carolina, Georgia and Louisiana, and more recently in our own State, can leave no doubt upon any rational mind, that a systematic attempt is making by some reckless persons, some too, who under the cover of pious exertion to enlighten the ignorant, and lead them from sensualizing darkness, are willing to sow sedition among our slaves, and this book, artfully distorting, the peaceful doctrines of the Bible, is intended, and well calculated to prepare the minds of that portion of our population, for any measure, however desperate.
>
> It is fruitless to complain of the relation between master and ser-

> vant, and it would be criminal in the Legislature to attempt to avoid any responsibility growing out of this relation (inherent in the political condition of the Southern country, by which either the security of property, or its value, may be effected—for in the same proportion as these are secured, will the general protection and comfort of the slave be regarded.
>
> As it has been satisfactorily ascertained, that some of the free persons of colour in the State, have permitted themselves to be used as agents for the distribution of seditious publications, it is respectfully recommended that all this class of persons residing within the State, be required to give security for the faithful discharge of those duties which they owe, in return for the protection they receive, from the laws of the State. This regulation cannot prove onerous to those who have sustained a good character, for the ease with which they will be enabled to give the security required, will serve as an exemption to them from any unpleasant operations of the law. (*Raleigh Register* November 18, 1830, and *North Carolina Star* November 18, 1830).[11]

The Governor's Message makes the same arguments previously discussed—the assertion of obvious meaning to a text, the positing of a calculated conspiracy to rouse slaves to insurrection. The comment about the general protection of the slave seems to me an implicit threat of violence, if not race war. The governor's comment that "it is fruitless to complain," like Judge Ruffin's comment in *State v. Mann* that "It is useless, however, to complain of things inherent in our political state," typifies how the rhetoric of doom was applied to the institution of slavery. The last paragraph quoted is, I would infer, calling for the kind of law passed in many other slave states that required that free African Americans post a prohibitive bond to remain free; if actually enforced, such laws would make it too expensive for most (perhaps all) free African Americans to remain within the state. They were not consistently enforced, but the possibility that they might be was a useful form of social control.

The Governor's Message would seem to suggest that the causality is quite clear: these restrictive laws were the reaction to the increased agitation of the abolitionists. Samuel Ashe's *History of North Carolina* explains them and the Governor's Message in exactly that way:[12] "At this period a great campaign was conducted in England for the emancipation of slaves in the British West Indies, which was successful in 1830, and then some English orators made addresses in Northern States. And coincident with their coming the basis of Northern opposition to slavery seemed to change. Formerly it had been political; now the moral question became more prominent. Conscience was awakened; and fanaticism knew no bounds" (II:341). This history is, however, wrong. Britain abolished slavery in 1833, "some English orators" presumably refers to Thompson, who visited in 1835, and the change in American abolition is usually attributed to the *Liberator,* which began publication in 1831. These incidents cannot have been the catalyst of the laws.

The most obvious place for an explanation of the need for the laws is the Joint Select Committee's "Report Relative to the Government of Slaves and Free Persons of Color." This report was presented December 1, accompanied by the following bills:

A bill to prevent the gaming of slaves, and to prevent free persons from gaming with slaves, or suffering them to game in their houses.
A bill to prevent the circulation of seditious publications and for other purposes.
A bill to prevent slaves from attending muster or election grounds.
A bill to prevent all persons from teaching slaves to read or write.
A bill to re enact a part of the first section of an act passed in 1787, for hiring out persons on indictment or presentment, not being able or willing to pay the fees of office and jailer's fees.
A bill to amend the several laws in this state concerning slaves and free negroes.
And a bill to regulate the emancipation of slaves. ("Senate," *Greensborough Patriot* December 4, 1830)

A legislative report is a classic (if not classical) example of the affirmative case in debate, in which southerners were supposedly well trained. It should describe a problem and propose a solution that purports to solve that problem. So, what was the "problem" that these laws were intended to solve?

The *Report* begins with the statement that the members of the committee "have examined with attention the subject committed to their consideration, and are fully impressed with the belief that a period has arrived which imperiously requires of the Legislature the adoption of some more rigid system of government for the conduct of slaves and free persons of color" (*Report* 2). The use of the word "imperiously" is interesting, as it was used in that era and in that kind of situation to suggest that the circumstances themselves absolutely demand something, as though these politicians have no choice but to do what they are doing.

Also familiar is the use of the word "rigid," invoking the hope that the problem is looseness and flacidity, that a more manly and controlling response is required. The *Report* goes on to describe exactly what it is that the committee members have seen that demonstrates this need for more rigid government: "Upon examination, it appears evident to the committee that the conduct and behaviour of this description of our population, generally speaking, for several preceding years, has been from better to worse" (*Report* 2). While this document has the language of studied consideration, it must represent sheer reaction, a reassertion of precommitments. The committee had twelve days between when they were charged with making the report and when they presented it, so their "examination" was not, obviously, tremendously rigorous or thorough. They examined, at best, their own preconceptions, which imagined a decline from a more golden era. This is a part of conservative rhetoric, almost by definition, and it is so much a part of that rhetoric that it is accepted without question—there is more crime than there used to be, people are less moral than they used to be, the center does not hold.

They describe just what that "worse" behavior is: "a spirit of uneasiness and insubordination among the slaves has been increasing; whilst the free persons of color appear to have relaxed from labor and industrious pursuits, and subsist, in most instances, by corrupting the slaves to steal from their owners" (*Report* 2). The primary problem is not how slaves behave (it is not that they act with insubordination), but how they *feel* (something transparent to slavers).

As noted earlier in the chapter, in regard to laws that forbid insolence as well as insurrection, there was a clear connection between the two in proslavery ideology. Presumably, the more that slaves feel uneasy and insubordinate, the more likely they are to engage in insubordination: "In the minds of many articulate Southrons, they were one step closer to revolution each time a slave was insolent" (Wiethoff, *Insolent Slave* 20). Holland's 1822 explanation of the Vesey uprising says, "A general spirit of insubordination among our slaves and free negroes—springing from the relaxation of discipline on the part of the whites—had been long discernable" (83). The 1836 Kentucky "Resolutions Respecting Abolition Societies" uses a gradatio: the pamphlets tend to "produce a spirit of discontent, insubordination, and perhaps, insurrection" (3). Defining the problem of insurrection in terms of slaves' feelings means that legislators have to find a way to change how the slaves feel, so that they will return to a state of ease and subordination—whether legislators sincerely believed such a prelapsarian state could again be achieved is impossible to tell (and, given the rhetoric of doom, may be irrelevant).

If the slaves were feeling less easy and subordinate is impossible for us to know, just as it is not known to us if the free persons of color were less industrious than they had been. Nonetheless, it is not impossible that that *was* the case. Aptheker, for the most part, accepts that perceptions of resistance and insubordination were indicative of slave behavior, attributing changes to mechanisms of control. That the prospect for manumission was fading may have led slaves to see less benefit in subordinate behavior, and the increasing economic restrictions on free persons of color may have caused them to turn to an underground economy. It is quite possible that the situation was such that those were sensible decisions.[13]

It is equally likely that there was no change in spirit or behavior and that the committee members were summoning the political cliché of a decadent spirit abroad in the land. They also appeal to a false universalism. The *Report* concludes a paragraph insisting that the slave laws have been mild, saying, "But the committee believe they will be sustained by the observation of every person, that in proportion as [slaves'] treatment has been mild and humane, their conduct has been turbulent and disorderly" (*Report* 2). This was not the observation of every person; North Carolina had a sizable population of Friends (Quakers) who were deeply ambivalent about slavery at best, and many of whom were profoundly opposed to it. The Quakers had objected strongly to various laws passed regarding slaves and free persons of color, and the *Greensborough Patriot* continually printed editorials and articles in favor of manumission. The dissenting view of Quakers was so well known that it was proposed that they should not be allowed to own slaves.[14] And a representative from a predominantly Quaker region dissented during the (secret) legislative debate and "moved to strike out that clause of the bill which prohibits slaves from being taught to read. Many of his constituents considered it to be their duty to teach their Servants how to read, that they might obtain a knowledge of the Scriptures, and he thought if Slaves were not taught to write, so that they could hold no correspondence with each other, the purpose of the friends of the bill would be answered" (*North Carolina Journal* December 15, 1830). My point is simply that the committee report was not appealing to universally held beliefs, and that fact was evident to the very people making the report. Like assertions of dissent being treason, the rhetor's horror of faction, or Africans' resistance to swamp diseases, this assertion of universality was not *just* untrue, but *obviously* untrue.

False assertions of universally held beliefs irrationalize dissent. Paulding asserts that "all rational reflecting men believe" emancipation is bad for slave and master (10). Thus, those who believe differently are, by definition, irrational. Their argument can then be dismissed on the grounds of its being rational, without having to be answered. In addition, the rhetor asserts (without having to show) the rationality of his audience; it's a kind of pandering. As Aristotle says, "To declare a thing to be universally true when it is not is most appropriate when working up feelings of horror or indignation in our hearers [. . .] people love to hear stated in general terms what they already believe in some particular connexion" (*Rhetoric* 1395). When successful, this move makes the values of a single group "the" community (if not human) values.

Universalizing is, in ways not always seen, dehumanizing. If every "person" is in agreement, then those not in agreement must not be "persons." This is an extremely important point, and too often unnoticed because the move to assert one set of views as universal premises is so common. It is not simply a fallacy, although it is that, but a move in community definition, and, if successful (as it too often is), enables a consensus position to become unanswerable without high cost to the dissenter. If "we" all agree on something, then to disagree is to identify oneself as "them." Simply disagreeing requires abandoning one's membership in the ingroup and taking on membership in the outgroup.

In speech act terms, an assertion has a word-to-world fit, meaning that an assertion is judged as true by whether the words fit the world. In a performative (sometimes called command), the discourse has a world-to-word fit, meaning that, if the act is correctly performed, the world will be made to fit the word: a chair adjourns a meeting by saying it is adjourned. But, a person who pulls a loaded gun and announces that the meeting is adjourned has engaged in a strikingly similar performative act; the meeting is almost certainly just as adjourned that way as the other. In both cases, the assertion enacts the reality it describes; in the latter case, it does so by simultaneously threatening to insist on the assertion. I am suggesting that these kinds of speech acts are performative in two mutually reinforcing ways. An openly irrational rhetor who vehemently asserts something obviously false performs the identity of a loyal ingroup member; if the assertion is the consensus of a violent and irrational group, the very vehemence (and irrationality) of the performance implicitly threatens any potential dissenters.

My argument that newspaper rhetoric, as well as the extended defenses, relied most heavily on the epideictic and intimidating is not intended to imply that there is an absolute distinction between the two. Epideictic is always at least somewhat intimidating because it functions to define ingroup identity. The more that the ingroup values loyalty over truth, the more that the power of the ingroup is inherently coercive. If outgroup membership is in any way associated with active persecution—formal or informal boycotting; personal violence; economic, political, or social ostracism; civil or criminal prosecution—then epideictic is an extraordinarily important form of social control. It tells people what they are allowed to say.

Epideictic also tells people whom to hate. It is often said that epideictic "confirms" cultural values, but what that description misses is that this confirmation is not happening to an autonomous mobile in space. People have these values, and people are the objects of these values. Proslavery epideictic rhetoric confirmed the "value" that criticism of slavery necessarily leads to violence against whites; such a confirmation had tragic policy consequences. It also, as I suggested in the first chapter, had real consequences for supporters of slavery. It limited their ability to think carefully about the actual costs of slavery, and it led them down the road to an unnecessary and devastating war. Whether slavers managed to construct slaves' knowledge in the way they desired is doubtful at best; it appears that they did, however, manage to construct their own. They constructed a world in which they could not imagine alternatives to authoritarian approaches to government, discourse, and education. They could not, because they would not let themselves, imagine a world with a large population of freed slaves.

But, to return to the *Report,* the major thrust of it is that "spirit of insubordination" must be curtailed. This spirit has four causes: "First, by the circulation of pamphlets; secondly, by the black preachers; thirdly, by slaves exercising the privileges of freemen; and fourthly, by the free persons of color" (*Report* 2). Of those causes, the third merited special mention—half of a paragraph is spent on the presumptive behavior of some slaves because "to this state of things is to be attributed, in a great degree, that daring spirit of insubordination so obviously increasing amongst this description of people" (*Report* 2). On the next page, when the *Report* goes into more detail concerning each of that class of dangerous person, the longest paragraph begins:

> As to the slaves who exercise the privileges of freemen—these privileges excite dissatisfaction in the minds of those to whom they are not extended. They receive and entertain other slaves in their houses, and seduce them every way from their duty; they tempt others to steal, and receive the property; they instill into other slaves the injustice and rigour exercised by the master; and by their exemption from all control in the application of their time, they possess the best op-

> portunities of communicating with other slaves, and arranging every preparation necessary for a common design. To those who own horses, as the fact is in some instances, there is afforded additional means. This description of slaves generally make a pretence of raising a crop. This renders their detection more difficult; and though it may be easy to establish that they sell and consume more than they grow; yet the impracticability of showing, by legal evidence, how or in what way they have violated any existing law, has hitherto left them in the full and open enjoyment of this injurious traffic, and which cannot, as the committee believe, be effectually prevented but by the enactment of additional laws. (*Report* 3)

The *Report* goes on to say that much the same is true of "free persons of color," an assertion that leads one to wonder why the *Report* separates the two kinds of people, and spends more time on the not-free slaves.

It is possible that this was a pet peeve of one of the committee members, perhaps because he suspected a nearby free-acting slave of aiding his slaves in stealing crops. It is also possible, though, that this type of person bothered the committee in the way that Mary Douglas describes fears regarding people who violate boundaries. Douglas argues that beings who violate rigid "natural" boundaries are imagined to pollute a community: "Pollution is a type of danger which is not likely to occur except where the lines of structure, cosmic or social, are clearly defined. A polluting person is always in the wrong. He has developed some wrong condition or simply crossed some line which should not have been crossed and this displacement unleashes danger for someone" (113). Slaves who act free (but are not) transgress a boundary imagined to be natural (between slave and free). They are, for that reason alone, almost magically able to be sources of infection in the community; by being transgressors, they are inherently dangerous. Part of their danger comes from the fact that they can transgress—people who break rules of behavior that are imagined as "natural" thereby show that the rules are not natural, but social constructs. The greatest danger, then, presented by slaves who act like free men is that they demonstrate the distinction between slave and free is a legal construct, and not an ontological division.

Wiethoff discusses this issue in regard to rhetorically skilled slaves: "Having denied the possibility of an artful insolence among slaves, the gentry faced a problem when slaves demonstrated rhetorical sophistication. In effect, the gentry was challenged to preserve a traditionally bright line between rhetoric and reality, style and substance. If the institution of slavery was as credible as they insisted, then slave insolence should not be as credible a threat as trespass or assault" (*Insolent Slave* 168). If the line really could not be crossed, there would be no need to pass laws forbidding the crossing of the line. Slaves who behave in ways that violate boundaries don't just threaten the boundaries; they threaten to expose the ontological status of the taxonomy.

Although we might condemn the laws that the committee recommended, and as much as we might like to see the logic of the committee as tortured and unjust, it actually serves as the logic underlying much current policy (especially educational and welfare "reform"). The *Report* defines the problem as the insubordinate attitude of some people; that problem has been exacerbated by a recent practice of mild and humane laws. Once the situation has been defined that way, the solution is relatively obvious: replace the mild and flaccid (and implicitly, if not feminine, then at least impotent) laws with inhumane and rigid (thereby implicitly manly) laws that will keep people in a submissive and obedient attitude. Restrict their exposure to people who might have or encourage any other attitude, thereby "producing that certain obedience which is the object of all laws" (*Report* 4). That last comment, to which I will return, is significant—this is not just about slaves, nor just about pamphlets, but indicative of a way of thinking of the function of law. In this view, an authoritarian view of government, the object of all laws is not to protect people from one another (the classically liberal position), nor to enable people to prosper (what Isaiah Berlin famously called "freedom to"), but to produce obedience.

The session was secret, so reporting of the debate is impossible to find, and newspaper coverage is consequently sparse. The *Greensborough Patriot* has a highly critical article concerning the various laws, saying that the intention of prohibiting slaves from attendance at muster or election day was to keep slaves from observing the military training, which, the article says, "we deem to be entirely unnecessary, as our militia trainings are so miserably conducted, that slaves, even if they had the capacity, would not be able to gain any *insight!*" (December 15, 1830).

Neither the North Carolina *Star* nor *Raleigh Register* names the pamphlet which the Governor included with his message, but the North Carolina *Journal* and *Niles' Weekly Register* both say that it was David Walker's *Appeal.* Guion Griffis Johnson's *Ante-bellum North Carolina, A Social History* also says it was Walker's *Appeal.* This is quite likely the case, since copies of the *Appeal* had been distributed in North Carolina the previous spring. According to Hinks, Walker, who had come from Wilmington,

North Carolina, had sent copies to Jacob Cowan, who used a network of escaped slaves to distribute the pamphlet throughout eastern North Carolina. Johnson's version of what happened upon authorities' discovery of the pamphlets is:

> When news of Walker's *Appeal* reached Washington, the town commissioners promptly doubled the night watch; forbade meetings of Negroes except during the day to hear white preachers; disarmed all free Negroes in the town; sent "an address to a select few in every Captain's Company" of the county militia; ordered immediate musters for a strict examination of the arms required to be held by state law; called out the Washington Guards who "made such a display of strength & discipline as must put a damper on the hopes of all seditious persons present"; ordered the Guards to stay under arms, equipped with twenty rounds of cartridges, and to come fully armed in case of an alarm of fire; and dispatched a wagon to Raleigh for an additional supply of public arms. (516)

To put it another way, they panicked.

To conclude that this panic led to the reactionary laws is quite reasonable, so one explanation of the 1830 North Carolina laws is that whites were terrified by David Walker's pamphlet, and its successful distribution. At the same time, though, Johnson mentions a significant fact about the set of laws passed in December 1830 and the additional restrictive measures passed in 1831 in the wake of the Nat Turner rebellion:

> Most of the restrictive measures passed with regard to the slave in 1830 and 1831, because of the missionary efforts of abolitionists within the State, were proposed as early as 1800 in a bill "for the better regulation of slaves" which originated in the Senate. This bill would have prevented a Negro from keeping or carrying any kind of weapon; from engaging in "riots, unlawful assemblies, trespasses, and seditious speeches"; from engaging in meetings for religious worship unless conducted by a white preacher "of good morals"; and from buying or selling any goods. The bill would also have forbidden an owner to permit slaves of others to come upon his plantation; to teach or cause to teach his slaves to read or write; or to permit a slave to hire his time unless a license be obtained from the county court. The Senate rejected the bill on its first reading. (499–500)

In other words, even before the insurrection panic of 1802, there was a significant group that wanted these sorts of laws. Walker's *Appeal* did not create that desire, but it did serve as the occasion (in rhetorical terms) the "reactionary group" (Johnson's term) could use to get passed laws they had long wanted.

My argument is that there were really two "causes" for the laws. They were a response to fear engendered by David Walker, whose role in this is often obscured by more abstract talk about "abolitionists." In an earlier chapter, I suggested that Simms refuted Martineau's assertion about the American Anti-Slavery Society's mailing of pamphlets by pointing to Walker's *Appeal,* thereby demonstrating his tendency to conflate all abolitionists. Here, I would like to elaborate on that suggestion, by describing it not as a conflation, but as a substitution, with emphasis on its rhetorical power. Almost certainly, the *Niles' Weekly Register* is correct. Walker's pamphlet had been distributed in North Carolina in 1830, and had caused considerable panic (see Hinks 137–45). But, for the governor to name the pamphlet, or for the legislators to debate the issue openly (that is, not in secret session), would mean that they would have had to admit in public that they were terrified of a black man.

Such an admission would have been, at best, dishonorable. Displacing Walker with "abolitionists" as historians do, or refusing to name Walker, as did contemporary coverage, protects the honor of slavers by obscuring the scrambling panic inspired in them by an articulate black man. Dillon maintains that slaves took pleasure in the terror that whites demonstrated after insurrection scares; whites certainly thought slaves laughed up their sleeves at the panics (which may have been part of the motivation for the vindictive quasi-judicial lynchings). Slavery worked by inspiring either fear or awe (or both); paternalistic slavers liked to think it was awe, but theorists like Ruffin (discussed below) said it was fear. Either way, white fear of black men reversed the power, and therefore could not be admitted.

Autonomy (called insubordination in slaves) was always associated with insurrection (for more on this point, see Wiethoff *The Insolent Slave).* An editorial in the *Southern Agriculturist* demonstrates the intimate connection between African American autonomy and insurrection, and the extent to which the need for terror and control precludes appeals to self-interest. It says: "a slave in a state of insubordination is an enemy; [. . .] in a state of perfect subjection, he is a kind, willing, good-humored, and useful friend" ("Our Slaves," December 2, 1829). Breedon's collection of slave advice has masters commenting on the need for complete submission: "It greatly impairs the happiness of a negro to be allowed to cultivate an insubordinate temper. Unconditional submission is the only footing upon which slavery should be placed" (35). Johnson paraphrases the view held by those people who wanted a rigid slave code: "the slave must be kept down 'if the whites expect to live, much less rule'" (499). This is exactly the argument made by Judge Ruffin in his 1830 decision on *State v. Mann,* in which he ruled that an owner could not be prosecuted for assaulting a slave. Slavery, Ruffin said, requires the complete subjection of the slave. Unlike the relation of teacher to student, parent to child, or master to apprentice, in which the end (or goal) of the institution is partially to the benefit of the student, child, or apprentice,

> The end [of slavery] is the profit of the master, his security, and the public safety; the subject, one doomed in his own person, and his posterity, to live without knowledge, and without the capacity to make anything his own, and to toil that another may reap the fruits. What moral considerations shall be addressed to such a being, to convince him what, it is impossible but that the most stupid must feel and know can never be true—that he is thus to labour upon a principle of natural duty, or for the sake of his own personal happiness, such services can only be expected from one who has no will of his own; who surrenders his will in implicit obedience to that of another. *Such obedience is the consequence only of uncontrolled authority over the body.* There is nothing else which can operate to produce the effect. The power of the master must be absolute, to render the submission of the slave perfect [. . .] The slave, to remain a slave, must be made sensible, that there is no appeal from his master; that his power is in no instance, usurped; but is conferred by the laws of man at least, if not by the law of God. (emphasis added)

Ruffin is here discussing the issue which recent political theorists often describe as the problem of governmental legitimacy.

Political theorists often identify three (interwoven) sources of governmental power: coercion, blind faith, and legitimacy. A government can use violence and its threat to *coerce* people to obey its dictates. As Lakoff characterizes this sense of politics, it is a familial metaphor, in which "what is required of the child is obedience, because the strict father is a moral authority who knows right from wrong. It is further assumed that the only way to teach kids obedience—that is, right from wrong—is through punishment, painful punishment, when they do wrong" (7). This is a tremendously expensive strategy if the government tries to do it through a clear statement of laws, with appropriate punishment for each violation. Even if the government pays the costs necessary for complete surveillance and perfect punishment, this strategy leaves the citizens considerable agency, as they can take calculated risks regarding compliance. A less expensive, and more effective, means of coercion is to have extreme punishments, unwritten or ambiguous laws, and random enforcement. If there is little correlation between behavior and punishment (such as if citizens are sometimes extremely punished for minor infractions, or if the innocent are just as likely to be punished as the guilty), citizens will internalize the coercive power of the government, constraining themselves more than the government could. If the penalties are disproportionately directed at outgroup members (as a result of being accused of being a member of a demonized outgroup), then the ingroup/outgroup basis of the economic, cultural, and political hierarchy is rationalized through essentially criminalizing the outgroup. So, for instance, the random lynching of free African Americans (as part of fantastical insurrection plots) was a far more effective means of coercive social control than only punishing those who rebelled. If the people chosen as victims were actually chosen for having hierarchically threatening qualities, such as being autonomous, economically successful, or educated (that is, they inspired *ressentiment*), the lynchings served as warnings to the African American communities generally.[15]

People who have *blind faith* that the government's policies are correct have never questioned the basis of the laws, but not because they feel endangered by doing so. They simply haven't bothered, out of apathy, deference to tradition, or "although we do not like a situation (it is not satisfactory and far from ideal), we cannot imagine things being really different and so we accept what seems like fate" (Held 195). It is, in a sense, a failure of imagination.

In conditions of governmental *legitimacy,* citizens accept the policies either because they have been thoroughly considered and genuinely seem to be the best, or because, although we do not like the outcome, we believe that the method by which they were reached was legitimate. Jurgen Habermas's more recent work defines rationality in exactly that way: a statement is rational if it was debated openly.

> Thus the rational acceptability of a statement ultimately rests on reasons in conjunction with specific features of the process of argu-

> mentation itself. The four most important features are: (i) that nobody who could make a relevant contribution may be excluded; (ii) that all participants are granted an equal opportunity to make contributions; (iii) that the participants must mean what they say; and (iv) that communication must be freed from external and internal coercion so that the "yes" or "no" stances that participants adopt on criticizable validity claims are motivated solely by the rational force of the better reasons. ("Genealogical" 44, see also the "pragma-dialectical" theorists like Van Eemeren and Grootendorst)

The important point is that dissent and debate enhance *legitimacy* but weaken *blind faith* and *coercion.*[16] Because, as Ruffin says, legitimacy is not possible for slavery (since no reasonable slave would grant that it was a good system), it must be grounded in blind faith or coercion. In an authoritarian (i.e., coercive) system, the law controls through threat, so lessening the threat lessens control.

It should not be a shock to anyone—that slavery is a coercive system—but it did (and does) make some people uncomfortable, so that this was intermittently admitted. Obviously, the hope was that the system could be maintained through blind faith, but that was problematic. Thomas Clay insisted that religious instruction could serve to make slaves submissive, a plan that Seabrook rejected as "Utopian" and a "wild and fantastic project" because it proposed that slavers "rule our slaves by perpetual prayer and exhortation, instead of the practical exercise of the master's authority" (24). Or, as Kingsley puts it, "Our laws to regulate slaves are entirely founded on terror" (12).

While several proslavery rhetors condemned Ruffin's decision, especially when antislavery rhetors took to quoting from it (for more on the reaction to the decision, including abolitionists' use of it, see Tushnet; for more on Ruffin's [unnecessary] use of the rhetoric of imperious circumstances, see Greene), the sentiment was commonly expressed (see especially Wiethoff's discussion of this issue in regard to legal cases regarding overseers and excessive punishment; see also Dillon 88). The whole reason that "insolence" was so threatening, and so consistently interpreted as a precursor to insurrection, was that it signaled intellectual independence, it proved the "family" metaphor was sheer fantasy, and it showed slaves did not have blind faith in the system (see especially Wiethoff, *Insolent Slave* 162). Dillon says, "Few owners could fail to know that their labor system rested ultimately on force—the threat of reprisal—and the willingness of slaves, however extorted, to remain in bondage" (2).

Proslavery rhetors sometimes tried to articulate other ways of gaining authority for slavery. Michel Foucault (and Habermas, in substantially different terms) argues that systems gain cooperation by getting people to internalize the means of coercion and control, either through moral systems that tell people what is right and wrong, or through threats of future punishment. Essentially, coercion can be used to create a system of blind faith, at which point the coercion is no longer necessary. Clearly, some proslavery ideologues thought they could achieve something like this: to make criticism of slavery unthinkable by making it unspeakable.

It was sometimes asserted that slavers were successful in creating this perfect consensus. The February 1836 *Southern Agriculturist* reprinted a passage from Joseph Holt Ingraham's *The South-West* in which two slaves brag about their market value. Ingraham moralizes on this exchange:

> Yet thus do negroes view slavery. Thus do they converse upon; and are as tenacious of the limited privileges, (yet to them unlimited, because they know, and can therefore aspire to no other) which, like flowers, are entwined among the links of their moral bondage. [. . .] Do such men "pine in bondage" and "sigh for freedom?" Freedom of which they know nothing, and cannot, therefore, feel the deprivation; a freedom of which they have heard only, as the orientals of their feebled genii, but to which generally they no more think of aspiring than the subjects of the caliph to the immortality and winged freedom of these imaginary beings. (79–80)

The editor of the *Southern Agriculturist* concurs: "Such indeed is the condition of the slave. He views his slavery as a thing born with him and to die with him. He has never known of any other condition for himself or his ancestors, and if left to himself would live contented and wish for no other" (80).

Paulding quotes from a letter in which a correspondent asserts that "Born slaves, and familiarized with their condition, they have no wish to change it when left to themselves [. . .] They take pride in their master's prosperity; identify his interests with his own; frequently assume his name, and even his title, and speak of his farm, his crops, and his possessions, as their own" (205). Paulding himself argues that "the slave neither knows nor has ever known any other state of life, and to him custom has become a second nature. His mind revolves calmly, and, if you please, sluggishly, within the unvarying circle of his wishes, hopes, and fears" (182–83, see also 179). This was precisely the hope that was put to the lie by insubordinate behavior, especially calculated and rational behavior like the successful distribution of Walker's *Appeal*.

This is why it was so crucial to claim that abolitionists cause insurrection—the implication is that the structure of slavery works because slaves do not realize they have any choice in the matter; as long as there is complete unanimity that slavery is good, and slaves must be slaves, they will never hear otherwise. General Flourney explained: "The interpositions of [abolitionists'] causes [*sic*] t[h]e slave to be disobedient, and his master is obliged to chastise him; and thus the slave and his owner are mutually injured [. . .] Let the man alone, and he knows not that he is a slave" (*U.S. Telegraph,* July 27, 1835, "The Meeting Called By Gentlemen From the South"). Because abolitionist writings crack the consensus, they weaken the compliance of slaves to the system: "It is easy to persuade the ignorant that they ought to be miserable; and it is not more difficult to render them so, by making them discontented with their situation" (Paulding 183).

As, in a sense, it was. It is probably true that slaves can only assent to slavery by believing they have no choice in the matter. Kevin Bales discusses this issue in regard to modern slavery, pointing out that slavery depends upon coercion. It is unreasonable to expect that slaves would feel apathetic about slavery (however much proslavery rhetors then and now may try to persuade themselves of slaves' laziness and lack of interest); the attempts to narrate slavery into the beginnings of history were efforts to make it a tradition but were belied by slaves' own oral traditions (as well as by the first chapters of Genesis); and Ruffin points out that it was hopeless to try to pretend that slavery is to the long-run advantage of slaves. Slavery was a stable institution only as long as slavers could maintain perfect physical and ideological control. Like Norrece Jones, I am saying that the purpose of the restrictive laws was to try to control African Americans, that preventing African American autonomy was an end in and of itself. What, then, caused the repressive laws? Slavery. As is demonstrated by their presence long before any abolitionist movement, they are inherent to the system of slavery. Any sign of autonomy on the part of African Americans—slave or free—signaled the fragility of slavers' control, and, hence, was met with increased attempts to make criticism unthinkable and autonomy impossible. Because the basic premise was false—that slaves could not and did not imagine freedom and autonomy without "outside influence"—it was certain to fail. But slavers tried.

7
"The Sweet Waters of Concord and Union"

Proslavery Rhetoric in a Deliberative Setting

> Wherefore the speaker should endeavor to guess how his hearers formed their preconceived opinions and what they are, and then express themselves in general terms in regard to them.
>
> —Aristotle

In the 1830s, abolitionism was a good example of what Nancy Fraser has famously called a "subaltern counterpublic." Politically marginalized (every single speaker in the gag rule controversy distanced himself from abolitionists, even the one who spoke in favor of the petition), made up of the legally marginalized (such as women and free African Americans), abolitionism was further hampered by the dominant constitutional theory.[1] It was generally accepted that the federal government had no right to pass any laws concerning slavery within a state; only a state legislature could abolish slavery. The major strategy of abolitionists was what Garrison termed "moral suasion"—they would appeal to the consciences of slave owners, trying to persuade them to free their own slaves voluntarily. Another strategy was to abolish slavery in the District of Columbia, since, because it was not a state, it could be directly controlled by Congress. Because it was not a state, it had no "state" right to slavery.[2]

The conventional practice was that the first few days of each session, after various preliminary pieces of business, were given to the presenting of petitions. Sometimes speakers read them, and sometimes they summarized them. Petitions, except for ones praying for abolition in the District, were read or summarized, and then referred to the appropriate committee. Antislavery petitions were read and tabled. The Twenty-fourth congressional session began on December 14. On December 16, the first petitions were read. Among the first was an antislavery petition concerning slavery in the District of Columbia. It was not referred to a committee, but, after a brief argument, laid on the table, the conventional practice at that time for antislavery petitions (they were read and immediately tabled). On Friday, December 18, congressional representative Jackson, of Massachusetts, "presented the petition of sundry citizens of Massachusetts, praying the Congress to provide for the immediate abolition of slavery within the District of Columbia; which he moved be referred to a select committee" (27). Hammond "moved that the petition be not received" (27), a motion that set off a procedural and political uproar, taking up the rest of that day, the next six weeks, and, in a sense, much of the next eight years.

According to Habermas, political deliberation involves three aspects of practical reason; it is "'pragmatic' to the extent it deals with achieving practical ends, 'moral' insofar as it is concerned with achieving the fair resolution of interpersonal conflicts, and 'ethical' when it is concerned with the interpretation of cultural values and conflicts" (Bohman 175). The gag rule controversy ranged over these three areas. There was, first, the very practical question of whether the argument itself was a violation of House Rule #45—that petitions could not be discussed on the day petitions were presented. There was also the practical question of the best way to silence abolitionists, in the words of more than one speaker, to "meet the question in some form which could by no possibility be considered either equivocal or evasive" (Franklin Pierce, December 18, middle column, page 33). This was not raised as a moral or ethical question (whether they should be silenced, whether an "equivocal" response did any harm), but the best means for achieving that apparently agreed-upon end. There was also the question, both pragmatic and ethical, of whether the House could refuse a petition. After Hammond made his motion, "The Speaker said he was not aware that such a motion had ever been sustained by the former practice of the House" (27). This "pragmatic" question was difficult to resolve; the debate continued to get hung up on procedural questions, as to which motion had precedence, and what it meant, in practical terms, to vote a particular way. At various points, someone would have to explain what was going on, as when Aaron Vanderpoel said, "What was the question before the House? It was upon the motion of the honorable gentleman from Maryland [Mr. Thomas] to reconsider the vote taken this morning, to the end that that honorable gentleman might move (as he had promised to do) the question, whether the House *would consider* the petition" (32). This was also an ethical question, whether rejecting the petition was a violation of the constitutionally protected right to petition. There was the moral question as to how the right to petition could be balanced with some often unspecified "right" of slavers (when it was specified, it was sometimes the right to own slaves in slave states—an issue not actually raised by the petitions—and sometimes a vague right not to have to hear criticism).

The question actually posed by the petition was whether Congress had the will to abolish slavery in the District of Columbia. One might say that that question involved a prior one of whether Congress had the legal or constitutional right to do so. And, in fact, that was sometimes how speakers responded to the question—Congress had no right, various speakers said, to "interfere" with slavery in the District. This was untrue, as well as beside the point. Whether Congress had the right to interfere made no difference if they did not have the will, and they did not. For reasons explained by Leonard Richards, having to do with the disproportionate power given to proslavery politicians by the electoral college imbalance, there was no danger of Congress voting to abolish slavery in the District. Thus, had the issue been phrased in practical terms—will these petitions endanger slavers' ability to practice slavery in the District of Columbia—it would have been answered in the negative, and the argument would have been settled without any need for showdowns, meeting the question, or the high drama (which is probably why many rhetors did not want it framed that way).

Instead, to the extent that anyone stuck to the specific plea of the petitions (with the exception of William Slade, who argued for their merits), rhetors framed it as a question of ability, as when Balie Peyton says that the problem with the petition is that "it asked Congress to do what every man in the country knew it had no power to do" (28). Obviously, the signers of the petitions did not know that Congress had no such power, nor did the lower House of the New York State Legislature, which had passed a resolution stating that Congress did have such a power. But, "every *man*" knows Congress cannot do that, so those who disagree are not really men. This framing of the issue as a question of manliness and ability rather than pragmatics enabled proslavery rhetors to demand demonstrations of submission to proslavery ideology—something a pragmatic discussion would have evaded.

Henry Wise, when making the same demand for a show of loyalty, says what "the South" will do if the North does not submit: "He hoped gentlemen who professed to be friendly to the South would come out and show their principles and their opinions. If the House desired to evade the question, let the South know it. If it was the opinion that Congress had the right to interfere in this question, let the South know it at once, and it would know what to do. Their predecessors had told them what to do. They had no longer any business there. Their business was at home to report to their people. He would go home, never to return there again, if that House were to say, directly or indirectly, that Congress had that power" (Wise 31). "The question" which might be evaded is whether Congress has the right to make laws concerning slavery in the District of Columbia. Wise engages in classical bargaining behavior—he threatens to leave. That is a strategy available only to parties whose presence is necessary, which is usually the more powerful, so it is a show of force. And it's interesting that he makes it in order to force a particular constitutional interpretation on the House. The combination of such arguments and behavior suggests, as argued previously, that proslavery rhetors assume that the meaning of texts is simultaneously stable *and* determined by coercive power.

Like Hammond, Wise responds to disagreement with coercion. Both Hammond and Wise were trying to get his policies through without visible evidence of disagreement: "Mr. Hammond's object, he said, was not to debate the merits of the question, but to move, if it was in order to do so, the rejection of the petition" (27). Hammond explains why the petitioners must be silenced: "Still, he could not sit there, and allow petition after petition to pour in, until they became callous to the subject" (28). Hammond's pronoun reference makes it hard to determine just who might become callous (surely not the petitions, but Congress, slavers, or the general public?), but I assume he means Congress. If Congress were not outraged at the petitions, then they might take them seriously, and consider them on their merits. Hammond's concern is that people might have the wrong feelings on the topic.[3]

Hammond's argument assumes that the rights of "the South" are attacked by restricting slavery in the District. This begs the question, in technical terms, by assuming the very issue which is at stake. Other rhetors in this Congress said, but did not at the point argue, that Congress had no right to control slavery in the District of Columbia. Yet, no such assertion (let alone argument) arose in the discussion of congressional control of District banks, a logically analogous situation. The principle of congressional control was objectionable only when it might be used to do something the rhetor did not want.

Later in the session these rhetors would make arguments—especially that Virginia and Maryland would never have ceded the land had they thought slavery might be abolished, an example of the hypothetical triumphing over the historically demonstrable. That this line of argument was developed later suggests to me that proslavery rhetors initially had no *argument* as to why Congress could not abolish slavery in the District. Another line of argument that later arose was manifest in some of the state resolutions on the topic. The 1835 South Carolina "Report of the Joint Committee of Federal Relations" resolved "That we should consider the abolition of the slavery in the District of Columbia a violation of the rights of the citizens of that District [. . .] and [it] is an usurpation to be at once resisted as nothing more than the commencement of a scheme of much more extensive and flagrant injustice." The March 1835 Kentucky resolutions similarly resolve, "That any attempt by Congress to abolish domestic slavery within the District of Columbia, would be regarded by this Commonwealth as a breach of the implied faith of the nation, towards the citizens of that District, and as an usurpation of power, which, if acquiesced in by the slaveholding States, must end in the ultimate disregard, by that body, of the constitutional tenure by which they now hold their property." It is a violation of those citizens' rights, and a step down a slippery slope. Hammond's assertion of "rights" being violated by abolition of slavery within the District may assume a view of slave ownership that would become explicit in southern interpretations of the *Dred Scott* decision—that a slave owner has a "right" to own a slave regardless of where he takes that slave. By this argument, abolition anywhere is a violation of the slavers' "rights."[4]

One might wonder exactly why the most practical response was precluded, especially since scholars are agreed that this overreaction to the abolition petitions was the worst move proslavery rhetors could have made. The gag rule, like censorship of the mails and mob attacks on abolitionists, was intended to keep the topic of slavery out of the realm of public discourse, but it had the opposite effect, keeping slavery, and the power of slavery, on the national agenda. At the time of Hammond's motion, John Quincy Adams was deeply hostile to abolitionists, but he was even more opposed to the gag rule. By the time the gag rule was abolished, he had become one of the most effective antislavery rhetors, including winning the *Amistad* case. If historians like Michael Schudson, William Miller, and others are correct, Adams personified the reaction that many people had to policies like the gag rule—it made them abolitionist.

Ironically, the gag rule gave Adams the opportunity to make countless speeches about how the slavers were willing to sacrifice the rights of all men in order to protect and expand slavery; he thus helped rally people not behind abolition of slavery but in opposition to the expansion of slavery's power (both geographic and political). His strategy was to keep the gag rule and "the slave power" under constant discussion, and it was, as Leonard Richards says, "really quite simple. All it took was his superior talent in using and abusing parliamentary rules, so as to hold his own position and to put his enemies in the wrong, and a willingness to keep throwing out bait until hotheads like Alabama's Jacob Lawler or Virginia's

Henry Wise took the hook. At times it was child's play" (*Life and Times* 128). As Bennet Clark says, Adams "devised numerous methods of keeping the subject before the House [. . .] By such means, he contrived to take up a great deal more time and attract more attention than would have been necessary to receive his petitions" (367). Even Clark, who is highly sympathetic to slavers (see 356), says, "The South had made a tragic mistake in suppressing the reception of petitions. Adams's brilliant fight caught the attention of the North. As a result of his activities people who had never thought of being Abolitionists began to sign Abolition petitions" (375).

In December 1835, no one could know that Adams would take on this battle, but it was possible to predict a backlash that would benefit abolition, and that is exactly what several speakers predicted. Vanderpoel said, "It really appeared to him that we were aiding the efforts of the Abolitionists by shooting off upon a mere preliminary question into dissertations upon the evils and abominations wrought by northern Abolitionists" (32 first column). Adams, who spoke in favor of "silencing" the abolitionists, nevertheless pointed out that doing so by suppressing the right of petition would necessitate violating the right of free speech in the House, or, at least, the right of newspapers to report antislavery speeches made in the House, and then the right to free religion would be violated, as many of the abolitionists were inspired by religion. "What will be the consequence?" he asked. "You suppress the right of petition; you suppress the freedom of the press; you suppress the freedom of religion" (40). The result of the motion, several speakers pointed out, was that they were spending considerable time doing exactly what they all agreed should not happen: discussing abolition (see, for instance, Mercer's speech 27).

The question remains: why? Scholars have tended to puzzle over Hammond's motivations in moving to reject the petition. It has been suggested that Calhoun, ambitious to rally slave states behind him, directed Hammond to raise the petition controversy as a wedge issue that would weaken Van Buren. In his diary (written much later), Hammond maintained that his motion was spontaneous, an assertion accepted by his biographer, Faust. She argues that Hammond was too "innocent" of party maneuvering to have been Calhoun's lieutenant in the House (*James Henry Hammond* 171–72). I am more skeptical of Hammond's claim than is Faust (as well as hesitant to attribute the term "innocent" to Hammond's relation to parties). Given that the pro-Calhoun press had spent the previous spring trying to use anti-abolitionism as a wedge issue, it is reasonable to see the petition controversy as one more politically manufactured crisis.

Hammond and Calhoun may have agreed to look for a polarizing issue that would put Jackson (and Van Buren, especially) in a tight situation. Hammond's picking the petitions might have been spontaneous, but I do not think the strategy was; like Freehling, I think Hammond and Calhoun wanted "to force Southerners out of compromising national parties" (*Road* 310). It is also possible that, coming from South Carolina, he was accustomed to a politics of division and intimidation—much of state politics since the nullification controversy had consisted of trying to force the nationally successful side (the Unionists) to submit to the locally dominant side (the nullifiers), and silencing dissent was the major strategy. Given the alarmism and demands of loyalty (what Freehling aptly calls "loyalty politics") of South Carolina, it may be that Hammond was simply bringing state methods of politics to the national scene.

Leaving aside Hammond's motives, why did others go along with such an extreme response by a new member to a minor annoyance that was being handled in ways that had been satisfactory? When Calhoun took up the issue in the Senate, the same counter-arguments were made—that this response was overkill, and would extend discussion when silence was the best response (see especially Benton's speech). Coit grants the logical and practical problems of Calhoun's stance on the petition, and even that "deliberately he was forcing an issue which, it must be admitted, many of the more moderate slaveholding groups preferred not to force at all" (Coit 310). A contradiction of his states' rights philosophy, his stance on this issue was, Coit maintains, because his "feelings were too wrought up for any possibility of clear thinking" (311). He succeeded, she argues, because other members of the Senate were too intimidated by Calhoun's rhetorical skill to disagree.

Explaining Calhoun's actions as an irrational outburst, however, fits neither with Coit's presentation of him as relentlessly logical nor with the timing.[5] What is supposed to have made him so "wrought up"? The pamphlets had been mailed five months previous, and that's an awfully long time for someone as calculating as Calhoun to remain in a fit. If he was still in a state, why didn't he bring it up immediately in the Senate; why wait until after the issue had been raised in the House? One might try to explain the acquiescence of other members of the Senate as the consequence of their being intimidated by Calhoun, but that doesn't explain the prior acquiescence of the House to a marginal figure—Hammond—who was not famous for intimidating people with his logic or his rhetorical skill.

Lee Benson maintains that Hammond's action was spontaneous, but that the response to it was calculated. The gag rule controversy was

> consciously used to heighten sectional antagonism and Southern national consciousness. If a small group of Northern abolitionists had not existed, Southern nationalists, sectionalists, and provincials would have had to create them—as, in fact, they did. As long as abolitionists concentrated upon trying to arouse intensely racist Northerners to force Southerners to right the wrongs done to black slaves, they were doomed to remain a tiny sect, politically impotent, their lives literally endangered in the North. But the fight over the Gag Rule on petitions, deliberately initiated by a loose coalition of disaffected Southern elites as a tactical maneuver in the larger strategy of the presidential succession crisis, transformed the antislavery crusade. (in Stampp, 38)[6]

Freehling says, "In the early 1830s, Carolina radicals' warnings of a South in danger seemed destined to be ignored, unless some northern menace to slavery surfaced" (*Road to Disunion* 289). The gag rule was just such an opportunity to portray abolitionists as a menace: "Suddenly, in December of 1835, the apparently perfect issue descended into southern extremists' hands" (310). The extremists' proposal forced the hand of other, more moderate, proslavery politicians because "self-respecting Southerners could not ignore their fellow slaveholder's call to defy an attack on their honor" (311).

The problem is that, once an issue has been framed as a display of manliness, loyalty, and ingroup honor, it is extremely difficult for other rhetors to reframe the issue as one of governance or, in Habermas's terms, pragmatics. As Freehling says, in both the North and South, "mainstream politicians were damned however they responded to the lunatic fringe" (*Road to Disunion* 312). If southerners compromised, they looked "soft" on abolition; if they took a "hard" line, they increased sectionalism (which, as Freehling says, would make it hard for their party to win northern states—it may also have sincerely offended people who objected to the gag rule or sectionalism in principle). If northern politicians went along with a compromise gag rule, they still looked submissive to southern interests; if they took a "hard" line, they endangered party unity. Once Hammond threw down the gauntlet, it was all about who was manly and who was not, who was hard and who was soft.

William Cooper lists the response on the gag rule question as one of the many actions taken on the part of Democrats to present "a united front on what the southerners deemed essential" (92) in order to "reinforce their claim that their party remained a bulwark for the South" (91). In *Liberty and Slavery,* Cooper says that political parties had to engage in one-upmanship in regard to anti-abolitionism: "The institution of slavery itself, seemingly in jeopardy from outside assault, became the central issue of political discussion. Thus any political party hoping to prosper in the South had to ready all its weapons and close with the new, diabolical enemy of slavery. Any suggestion of trimming by a party or of less than all-out effort would cause terrible political damage because the party would find itself in the dock accused of violating its compact with the South, of failing to protect vigorously and at all costs southern interests" (*Liberty and Slavery* 183). The adverb is important—"seemingly" in jeopardy—and one might wonder who made it seem that way. In a previous chapter, I pointed out that anti-abolitionist political activity predated the pamphlet controversy, that anti-abolitionist newspapers gave more coverage to abolitionists than they could have gotten on their own steam, and that their activities were generally greatly exaggerated. Similarly, the discussion of the gag rule gave more attention to the abolitionist petitions than they could have mustered, and it did long-term harm to the proslavery cause. But, in the short term, it was politically useful. In the short term, it gave politicians an opportunity to demonstrate just how loyal they were to slavers, and just how far over they would bend. In other words, whatever Hammond's motivations, once anyone had called for a more extreme response to abolitionists, the honor code, the sense of criticism as submission, the electoral power of proslavery states, and the place of slavery in contemporary political rhetoric meant that other proslavery rhetors (from the North and South) were almost certain to submit. Otherwise, they would look soft, disloyal, and sympathetic to religious fanatics who were plotting terrorist insurrections.

That is not to say that the South Carolinians' alarmist rhetoric was entirely cynical, nor that they were not really worried about abolition. It is to say that, as with the anti-abolitionist alarmism of the newspapers, politicians' behavior in regard to the gag rule was motivated largely (but not exclusively) by faction. And, like the newspapers, the politicians continually denounced faction and denied its influence.

On December 18 (in other words, not the first day of debate over the petitions), Hammond defended the purity of his motives: "He did not make the motion with any reference to party politics. God forbid that he should make a motion of such a purport, to affect a miserable scramble for offices in this country. No! His object was a more sacred one: It was to protect the rights of his constituents and his own, and if they could not maintain them by the action of that House, they would maintain them by their own action" (31). Abijah Mann, a Jacksonian from New York, mentions Adams's suggested policy, and then says that Adams is welcome "to all the benefits which he can appropriate to himself in this, the next, or any other campaign" (44). Samuel Beardsley, another Jacksonian from New York, was the only one to mention what others might have been thinking—that the abolitionists were not the only extremists: "He would tell gentlemen there were fanatics and incendiaries at the South, as well as at the North, who hoped to profit by the agitation of this subject" (31). Of course, a Jacksonian accusing others of party politics may not have had much rhetorical force.

As historians have argued, this era was complicated by the simultaneous factional demands of party and region. In a sense, Freehling's argument is that competition among representatives to see who could take the most extreme response was a way to try to conflate party and region. Proslavery rhetors insisted that this issue was a test of northerners' loyalty: John Mercer Patton, for instance, acknowledges that some northern politicians may be unclear on the issue of whether the government has a right to abolish slavery in the District of Columbia, and says to such politicians: "Give us, then, a distinct, unequivocal, and unevasive vote upon the propriety of interfering with the subject of slavery in the District of Columbia. Satisfy us that the House is opposed to such interference upon the grounds of principle, permanent, abiding—which reach above and go beyond the transient and fleeting circumstances of the hour, and uninfluenced by the political contests of the day" (39). Patton does not say what the South will do in return for this deference on the part of the North, as proslavery politicians rarely did when they made such demands, but he is demanding satisfaction (that is, threatening a duel).[7] Eleazar Ripley's argument is similar: "If the gentlemen from the North were sincere in their friendship for their brethren in the South, and were desirous of breaking down the double wall of partition between these two sections of the country, they could give an earnest on the present occasion by voting promptly to reject this petition" (31). John Jones, of Virginia, said that "nothing but a direct vote would satisfy the members from the South" (45). Henry Wise invoked the scriptural passage so often used when rhetors want to polarize a situation; he said, "Gentlemen must show us they are either for or against us" (31).

The demands for submission on the part of the North were met with expressions of loyalty on the part of many representatives, northern and southern. James Bouldin, from Virginia, got himself into a verbal tangle when he said, "He had on another day expressed his willingness to meet the matter flatly, and that his constituents should know all he knew in relation to it; but in deference to his brethren from the South—a deference he had always felt, and would feel, and would act under, in some good degree, he had not insisted both sessions he had had the honor of a seat in that House, on coming directly to the question, and putting the South in possession of all that was contained in those petitions" (40). Ripley, Wise, Patton, and Bouldin are echoing the same language of the newspapers—all of which assume that "the South" (meaning the slave interests) has the right and power to tell the North what the North must do to demonstrate loyalty to southern interests and concern for southern feelings; the North must submit to the South.

As with the other proslavery rhetoric, and as indicated in Hammond's initial motion, the feelings of southerners are paramount. Ripley says that the problem with the fanatics was that they "do not understand the position and feeling of the South on this subject" (31). Franklin Pierce insists that the appropriate policy was the one that would "meet the approbation of all who are most sensitive upon this agitating question" (meaning the proslavery politicians, 33). John Mason asserts that they had "a sacred duty" to allay "those feelings of apprehension and excitement" felt by slavers (33).

Slavers' feelings are important because, if they feel bad enough, they will secede. Jones, of Virginia, says that abolitionists are willing "to endanger the perpetuity of the Union" (45). Francis Thomas poses the rhetorical question, "May not rash and misguided men, in one extreme of the Union, engender those suspicions and distrusts which will be necessarily destructive of all the ends for which this Government was established?" (30) It is not that slavers' extreme commitment to the institution of slavery endangers the Union, but abolitionists' criticism of that institution. Mason threatens that the House must "terminate those angry discussions, and allay those bitter, bitter feelings which scar, if they do not break, the pillars of the noble edifice of our Constitution and liberty" (33). Joel Sutherland says, "They were bound by all the ties that kept the Union together to meet this question freely and boldly, to throw aside every prejudice, and sacrifice it upon the altar for their country's good; and it did not become them to excite each other by any kind of language" (34).

The feelings of each southern speaker matter tremendously, especially his courage in this situation. Hammond, after saying that his constituents did not call upon the House for protection, described them: "They stood erect, self-confident, united, strong, and they asked no protection, but scorned assistance, and defied opposition" (31). In some obscure way, their manhood has been called into question, but they remain erect despite the women's petitions. Hammond, having raised the issue of the content of the petition, said he did not want a discussion of the topic, but "he would not shrink from it a hair's breadth" (27), a cliché Hammond repeated later that day when he tried to explain why he had made the motion: "His reason for making the motion was, not that he wished to enter into a discussion of this subject, though he did not fear it, and would never shrink from it" (28). He made a motion on a topic he did not want to discuss, but he wasn't afraid. Patton uses the same cliché, while similarly engaging in a discussion he was saying he did not want to have: "We do not desire discussion, and, for one, I will do nothing to provoke it, at the same time we will not, if we cannot—we dare not—shrink from it if it be forced upon us from other quarters" (39). Hammond and Patton seem anxious that their evading the discussion might be seen as impaired manhood, as "shrinking" when presented with abolitionist criticism.

The military metaphors—such as meeting the question—were repeated throughout the debate (for uses of "meeting" the question, for instance, see Mason of Virginia 32, 33; Hunt 34; Vanderpoel 31; Thomas 30; Bouldin 30, 40; Patton 39). Lacy Ford has discussed this perception of political debates as military engagements, arguing that they were particularly consequential in the admittedly "Pyrrhic victory" of the Kansas-Nebraska Act (343–45).

That antebellum rhetors would use battle metaphors for public discourse is not especially surprising; that practice goes back at least as far as Cicero, and remains a problem for teachers of argumentation. That it is a cliché should not, however, cause one to conclude that it is meaningless, or that it always means the same thing. After all, battles have been imagined in different ways; having noted that these rhetors thought of public discourse as a kind of battle, it's worth asking just what they thought of battle.

As mentioned previously, the history of American ways of fighting is actually toward increasing brutality, or, as a military historian says, "one of the American changes of emphasis [to European military strategy] was toward less restraint in the conduct of war" (Weigley 409). Historians of American military strategy emphasize the role that education at West Point played in American attitudes toward war. In the 1830s, such education was dominated by J. M. O'Connor's 1817 translation of S. F. Gay de Vernon's *Treatise on the Science of War and Fortifications* (see Weigley 413–14). Of particular significance was O'Connor's appendix, in which he claimed to distillize all the great theorists of strategy, especially the Baron Henri de Jomini.

O' Connor emphasizes de Vernon and de Jomini's concept of the general's coup d'oeil (mentioned three times on the first page of Vernon), decisiveness, and "uniting forces against a decisive point" (O'Connor 388). The last point is the one most frequently repeated in O'Connor's appendix, and the one O'Connor identifies as the "fundamental principle" (483). Or, as O'Connor concludes, "The General who, by the rapidity of his movements or skill of his maneuvers, puts in action at the same instant and at the principal point of attack, a greater number of men than the enemy, must necessarily be victorious" (466). The "first means" to achieve this end is "to assume the initiative of the movements. The General who has this advantage on his side, is master of his own movements, and can select his point of attack; while he who, on the contrary, awaits the enemy, is unable to form any combinations, because he subordinates his movements to those of his adversary" (483–84). One strategy is preferable to the other, not because it leads to a better outcome, but because it is mastery and the other subordinate. That subordinate position means that he is "beaten in one of his parts, even before being apprised of the attack" (484). This imposition of a master/subordinate frame is not in de Vernon's understanding, for whom neither the offensive nor defensive posture is inherently more advantageous. My point is that O'Connor frames the military strategy in the same terms as the proslavery political discourse—in terms of domination and subordination.

And this initial domination enables final domination; that is, it allows a general to "crush" the opposition. O'Connor, in his appendix summary of military theorists, identifies the ideal: "When arrived upon the decisive point, the troops must promptly make an impetuous command and simultaneous effort to crush the hostile forces" (389, see also 394). If the enemy is divided, "we must direct our attacks against the central points. By carrying against these the mass of our force, we will crush the isolated divisions that guard them" (484). The goal is a quick and decisive victory achieved through a united and superior force that demolishes the opposition.

As demonstrated by the successes of Frederick and Napoleon (the exemplars of great generals in de Jomini and de Vernon), this is a feasible *military* goal. A decisive military victory is possible in that the opposition might, and often does, surrender. Once they have surrendered, the opposing nation ceases to exist, or the disputed land becomes part of the victorious side's nation, or the victor can claim tribute. The war can be over. The same is not true if people have a sincere commitment to a political idea—under those circumstances, there is no such thing as a single decisive battle. Instead, there is the long, slow process of changing minds.

But, if people in antebellum America thought of the political realm as a battle, if they thought of battles in the ways described above, then the political and rhetorical goal of a united proslavery South going on the offensive to crush the North by crushing abolitionists (the weak point) might have seemed attractive. And, if it was not plausible, the rhetoric of doom would support this approach as more sentimental and nobler than a nonmilitary engagement with the problems raised, not by abolitionists, but by slavery. In fact, an endless military engagement would be the best possible outcome because an enemy who could never be met in battle could be used to demand an infinite number of demonstrations of submissive loyalty.

There were other significant clichés in the debate. Hammond says, "He could not sit there and submit" to the petitions being brought forward, and that "he could not sit there and see the rights of the southern people assaulted day after day by the ignorant fanatics" (27). Hammond says, "He could not sit there, and see the rights of the South assailed day after day by ignorant fanatics" (28). Bouldin "never could again, he trusted, sit patiently and hear abuse of his constituents" (40). The idea of sitting there (not here, but there) when such things are happening is, for some reason, particularly galling. Miller's interpretation of Calhoun's speech later that session seems to me applicable here. In that speech (January 7), Calhoun compared rejecting the petitions to knocking down someone who personally abused him. Miller says, "Just by proposing such a thing you insulted the *honor* of the South [. . .] And the appropriate response to that was the legislative equivalent of knocking the scoundrel down" (117). So, to remain seated while someone criticizes you is to be too afraid to duel.

Others made the same, somewhat puzzling, argument that they were not willing to discuss the issue that they had raised. Mason says "his constituents had instructed him not to engage in such a discussion" (32). Jones, of Virginia, having brought his speech around to the issue of slavery, says, "What it was the South desired? Was it to discuss the 'sublime merits of slavery?' That was a subject which Mr. J. could not discuss with that gentleman; and taunt them as he might with their slaves, whose condition they had no agency in producing, and no means of changing" (46). "That gentleman," is, presumably, Adams, whom Jones mentioned earlier in the speech. Adams had not raised the issue of the merits of slavery, and certainly had not taunted them with their slaves. Jones was, of course, doing exactly what he said he was not willing to do—discuss slavery—and he did so in a way that was conventional. That slavers had no agency in producing slavery was, as I have argued earlier, a crucial, if nonsensical, tenet in proslavery rhetoric. It, like the notion that they could not change the condition of slaves, was not true in the practical sense (a slave owner could free his or her slaves), but appealed to a sense of people trapped in a system for which they are blameless because they did not "start" it.[8]

The issue of blame, important in the other instances of proslavery rhetoric, also emerges in the petition controversy. Any reasonable narrative of events would say that Hammond started the debate by insisting on the petition being rejected. Owens, from Georgia, explicitly exempted the South from blame for the uproar: "It was useless to regret that this question had been a subject of discussion. The apple of discord had been thrown into the House. It had not been done by the South" (38). It is unclear to me whether this is cunning projection that he does not expect anyone to believe, or if he is appealing to the sense that the people who criticize dominant oppression are the ones who have caused "the" problem (so that critics of slavery, rather than slavers, are to blame for controversy over the issue), or if he is blaming the people who did not immediately go along with Hammond's motion for the ensuing debate. That is, Hammond's proposing something controversial is not the cause of the controversy; saying something is not necessarily raising the issue for discussion.

The goal is to have policy change without disagreement. The proslavery rhetor is announcing a position and demanding that others submit, but not raising the topic as something about which other points of view are welcome. This is especially clear in the speeches, like Vanderpoel's, that intersperse arguments for his point of view with condemnations of continuing the discussion. "Was it consistent with one of the cardinal doctrines of the friends of the South, that the subject was one so delicate in its nature, that the less that was said about it the better?" (32) he asks, less than halfway through a very long speech with much to say about it.

This move seems connected to what is often stated as the policy goal: a response to the petitions that will end the discussion forever. When Thomas describes the Sunday mail controversy, he concludes that the select committee wrote a report whose "arguments were unanswered, and unanswerable, and the petitioners were silenced. The oil was spread over the troubled waters, and the turbulent waters became still" (29).[9] Jones, in the course of demanding a show of loyalty from northerners, invoked the fantasy of ending "this subject": "It was for the gentlemen of the North to say whether we still rely upon their assurances by heartily cooperating with us in putting this subject to rest by a direct and decisive vote upon the question" (45). Several speakers mentioned the desire to "terminate" the discussion (see Mason 33), and the metaphor of "meeting" the question implies a final battle that will conquer the enemy.

It seems to me that there are several ways to understand these appeals to the fantasy of ending the discussion. First, it has to be pointed out that "this discussion" is extremely ambiguous. At moments, such as in Jones's speech, it is not clear whether he means the specific discussion in the House at that moment about that petition, or the larger cultural debate over slavery. When speakers talking about "allaying the fears" of slavers, they must be referring to that larger debate, as simply rejecting one petition could never have such a widespread effect. If we are to take those references to "the fears" of slavers seriously, then it is not a question of rejecting a petition, or even all petitions, but of trying to silence abolitionists generally. In that case, the response on the part of people like Adams, who saw Hammond's move as part of a large-scale attack, was prescient.

But, should we take them seriously?

That is, did they really believe that they could abolish criticism of slavery by rejecting petitions? Even if it was part of a larger political project to deny all rights to abolitionists, did they really think that could persuade people whom they characterized as fanatics? The anti-petition discourse, like anti-abolitionism generally, invokes a contradictory image of abolitionists. If they were irrational, fanatical, and beyond all reason, it is hard to see how tabling or rejecting their petitions would persuade them to stop sending petitions. As much as I have striven for taking proslavery ideology seriously, and for assuming that people held it sincerely, even I can't believe that they really thought that rejecting the petitions would have any impact on abolitionists' behavior. The petitions were the occasion, but not the object, of the argument.

It seems to me that Cooper and Freehling are correct—that the petition controversy was politically useful *because* it was so divisive. Earlier, I argued that nullifiers tried to use the issue of abolition to polarize the situation into their specific policy and abolition. Speakers on various sides of the petition controversy (that is, those arguing for rejecting and those arguing for tabling) behaved similarly. Samuel Vinton insisted "that all who voted against printing were decidedly opposed to the prayer of the petitioners" (32). Wise, George Owens, and Bouldin each made the same move in regard to their proposals—they tried to force a particular (and larger) interpretation on a single vote. In the passage previously mentioned (beginning with a scriptural reference), Wise sets up what he "would be willing to consider [. . .] as a test question. Those who are for laying the motion on the table he viewed as evading the question, and so would the South view them. Those who were for a direct vote on the motion of the gentlemen from South Carolina would be viewed as the friends of the South" (31).

Although there had been disagreement—other southern representatives had argued for tabling the petitions (Williams, of North Carolina, 28; Hunt, 34)—Wise dismisses that diversity in the self-essentializing move. Wise, like the others, is claiming to speak for the South, to be the most-manly champion of "the" South.

What, exactly, is the issue? For the most part, the goal of the discussion was as Hunt stated it: "silence the fanatics on the one hand, and satisfy our brethren of the South on the other" (34). This has the form of a balanced statement—on the other hand and the other—, so it looks as though Hunt is taking a centrist position, but the one and the other hand were the same. The goal was to satisfy the proslavery politicians by silencing the abolitionists (and engaging in name-calling at the same time). The extremism of the proslavery politicians' stances was obscured by the linguistic form of balanced concern.

For some proslavery speakers, the issue is who has the moral high-ground, and it is, of course, the South: "Did any man ever hear or know of a nation of people on any side of Mason and Dixon's line that stood higher for any of the cardinal virtues—honor, truth, justice, and charity, gentleness of heart, and honesty? Was it thought that we would suffer by a comparison with the petitioners?" (Bouldin 40). When George Briggs, a Whig from Massachusetts, explained that Bouldin was mistaken, that *this* petition did not have the kind of language Bouldin thought it did, Bouldin explained how it is that the petitioners' actual language, whether respectful or not, is irrelevant: "All these petitions took a swaggering stand over the South, and proposed a kind of guardianship over their morals, and were dreadfully afraid that holding negroes had made us vastly corrupt, and would make us more so. Let him that is without fault cast the first stone. We thank God that we are not as other men, whoremongers and adulterers. This was the language of these petitions, all of them" (40). This is a common response to criticism, and even commonly accompanied by that scriptural passage, but internally contradictory. If the abolitionists are wrong to criticize slavers because they are not free of sin, then Bouldin is wrong to criticize abolitionists unless he is free of sin. That is not the conclusion that Bouldin draws; his criticism of abolitionists is not swaggering. Given that Bouldin goes on to argue for the moral superiority of the South, it is not the taking of the moral high ground to which he objects; it is that *these people* would try to take that ground.

And, as with other proslavery discourse, Bouldin's argument moves the topic away from *this* petition to a generalization about antislavery petitions in the abstract. Owens, a Democrat from Georgia, explains why they should not argue about that specific petition and its language: "It was not to meet the question on this petition alone, but to meet the question, come in what shape it might. It was to operate upon all petitions that might come with the same tendency or object; nay, in one word, it was to grapple with the subject itself" (38). It was explicitly *not* to grapple with the subject—the point was to change policy without a debate.

As in the other proslavery rhetoric, the abolitionists' activity was associated with slave insurrection, albeit in even vaguer ways than either the newspapers or extended defenses. Bouldin, for instance, asserted that the petitions contained propositions "that would freeze the blood with horror to witness if put into execution, that could never be thought of without shuddering by any man who felt for his wife, his children, his friends, his neighbors, or his country" (40). The gradatio is poetical, but incoherent. The petition was read repeatedly, but the recorder did not write down the exact language. It was either one calling for the abolition of slavery in the District of Columbia or, as indicated in comments from Slade, calling for the abolition of the slave *trade* in the District of Columbia. Neither of those implies a policy that would freeze the blood with horror to witness. Various speakers brought up the issue of the language, and it was asserted that the language was respectful. People arguing for its rejection countered that other petitions had disrespectful language, or, more significantly, that this petition's language was disrespectful because it accused slavers of being man-stealers. By that latter argument, there was no such thing as a respectful attack on slavery; antislavery arguments could be dismissed as indecorous purely because they criticized a dominant institution.

In short, proslavery rhetoric was no different in the House of Representatives than it was in the newspapers, pamphlets, novels, or speeches. It depended upon the same topoi (e.g., the feelings of southerners are paramount), the same rhetorical moves (e.g., present one's own position as universally held, or condemn this petition for what other petitions might have done), and the same views of public discourse (i.e., that it alternates among epideictic, intimidation, and bargaining).

There is one topos present in the congressional controversy that was not so obvious in the other texts—the question of interest—to be discussed later. At this point, however, I want to pursue two other points: who engaged in proslavery rhetoric; how it compared to debate on other topics.

I use the term "proslavery" rhetoric rather than "southern" rhetoric because the rhetoric does not break down precisely on regional lines. Aaron Vanderpoel, for instance, was a Jacksonian representative from New York, which had abolished slavery in 1799. His speech on December 18 had many of the qualities of proslavery rhetoric (some of which have already been noted). The previous practice—tabling the petitions—had been characterized as "dodging" or "evading" the question, so Vanderpoel, like the southern speakers, "said that he was the last man on that floor to dodge or evade any direct point" (31). The superlative of "the last man" continued throughout this speech: wasn't his interpretation correct "according to all the known and legitimate deductions" (32); "Had gentlemen, before to-day, ever imagined or proposed a more summary and unequivocal mode of rejecting the prayer of a petition than was indicated by a refusal to print it, and an almost unanimous vote to lay in on the table?" (32); "He would always and forever, while he had a seat here, oppose any measure that might, directly or indirectly, favor, or forward, or countenance the views and objects expressed by such petitions" (31). The accumulation of "favor, or forward, or countenance" (31) was typical; he had "never had any doubts, or qualms, or scruples" (32) as to what was his duty; abolitionists were engaged in "evils and abominations" (32) with "exciting and diabolical" schemes (32).

Vanderpoel poses the rhetorical question, "Why not march directly to the point upon which all the true enemies of Abolitionists would agree?" (32) before explaining why rejecting the petition was the way to achieve this end. This single question has the military metaphors, polarizing, and universalizing typical of proslavery rhetoric. Beardsley, a Jacksonian from New York, took umbrage at the petitions, using a military metaphor and making honor central; the House could not change its previous position on the topic of slavery in the District "unless the House might be charged with abandoning the ground it had assumed upon this subject, a charge which was derogatory to its high character" (46).

There are some differences. Vanderpoel does not discuss southern feelings, and he does not assert a universal condemnation of abolition. Not only does he grant that some members of the House had voted in favor of printing a previous petition on this subject, but he is careful not to ascribe anti-abolitionist sentiment to the entire House, let alone the entire nation: "Many gentlemen doubtless voted in favor of printing from considerations of courtesy to the petitioner" and he referred to a "vast majority" of the House (32). Still and all, it would be a mistake to conclude that the authoritarian rhetoric that was so characteristic of proslavery discourse was unique to it.

And not all southern rhetors engaged in it, or, at least, not to the same degree. Thomas, in his praise of a committee's report on the Sunday mail issue, says it "was addressed to the understanding, not to the passions" (29). Mason, a Jacksonian from Virginia, also criticized emotionalism when he granted that the petitions raised a difficult subject: "He was aware of the extreme delicacy of the subject—of the deeply seated sensibility which it excited, and which it was impossible to allay—of the extreme difficulty of approaching it without excited feeling, but no practical good could result from strong denunciation or impassioned invective" (32). Whereas other speakers, and much proslavery rhetoric, assumed that the feelings of southerners are sacrosanct, Mason called for "a dispassionate and deliberate disposition" (32).[10] While asserting a false unanimity—"In the course of this debate he was happy to have heard every gentleman express a decided opposition to the prayer of the petition" (32)[11]—he did grant that there were "conflicting views as to the means by which this end is to be so attained" (32), and even that "an overwhelming majority" was opposed to the petition (33, thereby implicitly acknowledging that a minority might not be). He did insist that "the House should meet the question" (32, repeated at the end of his speech on 33) and that "it was necessary to adopt a more decisive mode" (32), but otherwise avoided military metaphors. Thomas Glascock, from Georgia, acknowledged that some of the representatives come from states that "might be favorable to the principles contained in the petition" and that there "was an honest difference of opinion" (34), thereby making himself one of the few speakers not to assert a false unanimity or demonize dissent. In the same speech, however, he said that discussing federal censorship of the mails (which Jackson had proposed) would enable "meeting the question fully, freely, and deliberately" when "they would have but one voice throughout that House [. . .] Then everything like disunion would be quieted; and, he trusted, forever" (34).

Perhaps more important, this kind of rhetoric was not unique to the petition debate. One would expect that a similar set of clichés and rhetorical moves would arise in the controversy over censorship of the mails (in the Senate during December), as that was also, explicitly, an argument about slavery, abolition, and the willingness of northern politicians to defer to the feelings of slavers. While the issues directly and explicitly related to slavery seem to demonstrate the largest number of the various qualities discussed, it would be a mistake to conclude that they were completely absent from other discussions. For instance, the question of blame and insult to honor came up in the House in regard to why the Committee on Ways and Means had taken so long the previous year to report (20) as well as the debate over seating the senators-elect from Michigan (42); the Senate engaged in a completely factionalized debate about referring an issue to a particular committee in which speakers continually disclaimed factional motivation;[12] Jackson's message to Congress was filled with discussion about feelings; Senator Benton threatened to try to reject a petition on the Bank issue (41; Bond made the same motion in the Senate, 69), in the course of which he said "he would not listen" to the arguments the petition made; Senator Tipton announced that "Indiana would never agree tamely to surrender" territory disputed with Michigan and emphasized the "ill feelings" produced by the admission of Michigan with the disputed territory (42); Hendricks, on the same topic, announced that "He had but one course to take," thereby invoking the same sense of imperious conditions so important to proslavery rhetoric (43); in the House, Hannegan moved to reject a petition from the Legislature of Michigan, which led to a fairly long dispute (85–87); Buchanon, on the topic of district judges, said, "Could he and his colleague then sit still?" (67).

One difference that does seem consistently regional among speakers in the House and Senate is the use of detailed historical precedent. With the exception of Andrew Jackson, whose "Communication" to Congress has considerable detail concerning the history of various negotiations with other countries, southerners tend toward abstractions and hypotheticals. Williams (of North Carolina) and Mercer (a Whig from Virginia) both spoke about a petition that had been rejected in the past, but it was very vague—from "a representative of some one of the South American revolutionary Governments" (28). Thomas referred to the Sunday mails petition (28), but most of his historical references were classical or hypothetical (the petitions were like the locusts of Egypt, what if someone petitioned asking for an end to representative government). Wise referred to the precedent of rejecting a petition regarding William Wilkins (31). In regard to the courtesy seating of the senators-elect from Michigan, Benton asked, "Had there been [. . .] a single instance since the formation of the Government, in which this courtesy had been refused to gentlemen coming from a new State?" (23). This was immediately after he had defended himself for not having looked into the precedents of such a courtesy; "he had not examined those precedents, for it did seem to him that on a question of mere courtesy it did not become the Senate of the United States to be following precedents, but to make them" (23). Benton does not try to redeem his assertion that such a thing has never happened, but instead refers to the specific case of Missouri, although, again, in hyperbole: "Was there one single Senator influenced in the vote he gave on that occasion by the fact, that seats had been assigned to the Missouri Senators?" (23). Of course, a *single* senator might have been, and, just as important, few of the senators present could know, as they had not been there. But, Benton is not referring to the history of documented events in which unanimity is rare, to a detailed history of complexity and nuance. He is referring, first and foremost, to his own experience, and speaking to an audience as though they have had and understood that experience exactly as he has. He is referring to an imagined history, that he assumes his audience shares, and which is untouched by actual examples.

It's possible that this was rhetorical backfilling—that he was trying to cover a hole in his argument with an elaborate screen of rhetorical questions—but that explanation doesn't take into account how uncommon it is in the congressional debate of 1835–36 to find people making extended arguments grounded in specific details. The few who do are all from free states. Adams, William Slade (Vermont), and Francis Granger (New York) engage in extended detailed arguments about historical precedent (Adams 40), the actual condition of slavery in the District (Slade, see especially 48), or what the petitions really say (Granger). Both Granger and Slade try to make distinctions among kinds of abolitionists, and even among different petitions. John Tipton and William Hendricks, both senators from Indiana, have detailed histories. I would suggest instead that there is, in the congressional debate, a disagreement about truth, much like the disagreement between Martineau and Simms. Benton appeals to an imagined history, just as proslavery rhetors appeal to an imagined Man, Woman, and Slave.

Appeals to such abstractions are what Van Eemeren and Grootendorst call "hermetic" wording. Through wording the assertion "in such a way that it is protected from any adequate assessment" (119), rhetors preserve the standpoint from attack. Their example is of such sentences as "The Frenchman is essentially intolerant" and "Women are, by nature, possessive" (119). As they say, "If an attempt is made to refute the standpoint that women are by nature possessive by citing one or more examples of women of whom there is nothing possessive, the opponent finds these examples irrelevant. [. . .] The women cited as examples to the contrary turn out not to be 'real' women or they make themselves out to be what they are not. All attempts at attack thus simply rebound from an armor of immunity" (119–20). Van Eemeren and Grootendorst categorize this fallacy as one way of "evading the burden of proof" (discussed 116–20). All parties' accepting the burden of proof, as they say, is absolutely necessary "to be able to resolve a dispute about a standpoint" (116). Yet, as I have argued, numerous strategies on the part of proslavery rhetors function, seem intended, to evade the burden of proof.

But it is not entirely clear that proslavery rhetors wanted the dispute resolved. As I have argued, it is not even clear what "the dispute" was. Hammond may have wanted the petition dispute resolved, but only insofar as he wanted abolitionists silenced. Others, if scholars like Freehling and Cooper are right, did not want the petition controversy resolved because it gave them a useful ground for fighting a political battle. If that is correct, then "the dispute" was not about slavery per se, as much as about which political party could best rouse, manipulate, and benefit by histrionics over abolitionists. As I keep emphasizing, that interpretation may be correct, but it does not mean that histrionics over slavery were not really about slavery. Hitler roused, manipulated, and benefited from histrionics about Jews, but he was genuinely anti-Semitic, and he really did kill them. Proslavery politicians engaged in fearmongering about abolition and freed slaves, but that fear was there for them to use, and their fearmongering was accompanied by very real policies designed to silence abolitionists, control free African Americans, and immunize the institution of slavery from criticism.

Van Eemeren and Grootendorst presume that the ideas of the interlocutors can be shaped by the argument. This was not the dominant assumption made by members of Congress during the session. At various moments, and in various ways, speakers would make comments about decision making itself, and what one gets if one adds them up is fairly close to what Wayne Booth calls one of the "modern dogma" about rhetoric. For instance, committee assignment came up in both the House and Senate on several topics: in the House concerning the northern boundary of Ohio, and a petition concerning the District of Columbia banks; and in the Senate concerning the censorship of the mails, and the admission of Michigan. The ostensible responsibility of a committee is to investigate the issue and reach a decision after having examined all the evidence. Yet, as anyone who has worked in an institution knows, the best way to get the decision one wants from a committee is to get the right committee to make the decision. This strategy is only effective when one can be fairly sure just how individuals will decide; the more that the committee members are open to persuasion during the investigation process, the less one can control the committee decision by pre-selection. The degree of jockeying in which participants in the Senate and House debates engaged suggests that they believed this to be a situation in which a high degree of control was possible, which suggests that they did not believe the committee itself would deliberate. Of course, no one explicitly says, "We need to put Jacksonians on this committee" or "This committee is filled with Jacksonians, so I know already I won't like their decision." Although an era of high party politics, it was also an era in which party politics were almost universally condemned. Instead, speakers argued about "interest," which was not demonized, and "prejudging," which was.

In the petition controversy, several speakers asserted that southerners "were more deeply interested than all others" (Jones 45), an assertion which not only invalidated the "interest" felt by abolitionists (northern or southern, slave or free), but which assumed that greater interest merits greater control. Vinton argued that the question of the admission of Michigan not be referred to the Committee on the Judiciary because so few of the members "came from a State west of the Ohio river" (51). Senator Silas Wright argued for delaying a decision about relief for the sufferers from a fire in New York until they could "consult the interests of those who had suffered" (52). Thomas defended his position on banking in the District of Columbia on the grounds that "his constituents were more interested in this matter than those of many gentlemen" (60). At the same time, several speakers condemned others for having "prejudged" the question (e.g., Adams, in regard to the boundary dispute between Ohio and Michigan). What this amounts to is that the rhetors appealed to two different views of the function of public discourse: to provide a place for the competition of interests; to allow interlocutors to transcend individual interest. When a speaker's precommitment was best supported by appealing to the first view, he appealed to it; and when it was best supported by appealing to the second, he did so. The fundamental question—is self-interest the end of discourse or a barrier to it—was neither asked nor answered.

There's a strange sense that one gets to a position through some process; one then uses discourse to try to get others to submit to that position; the people with the most power will necessarily win. I cannot say strongly enough that this is an abandonment of public discourse as the discovery of appropriate policies. This was the fatal error of proslavery rhetors, and a self-fulfilling prophecy. Their goal, and their success, was to keep the realm of public discourse from being a place in which dominant points of view could be criticized. They won that battle, and they proceeded to lose the expensive and unnecessary war that that first victory ensured.

Conclusion

"Any rational plan": The Responsibilities of Rhetoric

> The ordinary acceptation of words in their relation to things was changed as men thought fit. Reckless audacity came to be regarded as courageous loyalty to party, prudent hesitation as specious cowardice, moderation as a cloak for unmanly weakness.
>
> —Thucydides

In the late 1820s, Joseph Holt Ingraham, a native of Maine recently expelled from college, traveled to New Orleans, and then on to Natchez. He published his letters home in 1835 as *The South-West, by a Yankee.* In the first volume, he describes his initial visit to a plantation:

> An hour's drive, after clearing the suburbs, past a succession of isolated villas, encircled by slender columns and airy galleries, and surrounded by richly foliaged gardens, whose fences were bursting with the luxuriance which they could scarcely confine, brought us in front of a charming residence situated at the head of a broad, gravelled avenue, bordered by lemon and orange trees, forming in the heat of summer, by arching naturally overhead, a cool and shady promenade. We drew up at the massive gate-way and alighted. As we entered the avenue, three or four children were playing at its farther extremity, with noise enough for Christmas holidays; two of them were trundling hoops in a race, and a third sat astride of a non-locomotive wooden horse, waving a tin sword, and charging at half a dozen young slaves, who were testifying their bellicose feelings by dancing and shouting around him with the noisiest merriment. (I: 230)

He describes a "Hesperean" view of the elegant plantation house (I: 230), a sumptuous dinner "served by two or three young slaves, who were drilled to a glance of the eye" (I: 235), and a picturesque village of slave quarters. Yet, once he leaves the picturesque village, he comes across a villainous overseer: "A white man, with a very unpleasing physiognomy, carelessly leaned against one of the brick pillars, who raised his hat very respectfully as we passed, but did not change his position. This was the overseer. He held in his hand a short-handled whip, loaded in the butt, which had a lash four or five times the length of the staff. Without noticing us, except when addressed by his employer, he remained watching the motions of the toiling slaves, quickening the steps of a loiterer by a word, or threatening with his whip, those who, tempted by curiosity, turned to gaze after us, as we walked through the building" (I: 237). He comments later that, while sugar is being made, the slaves work from eighteen to twenty hours a day, and at other times, work twelve hours a day six days a week (I: 240, 241).

The coexistence of these two images of plantation life—the paternalistic side represented by the luxurious life of the master and picturesque life of the slaves, and the vicious side of that life represented by the overseer and long hours of work—is unremarked by Ingraham, who seems, instead, to believe both. He rides to a plantation with some slaves recently sold down the river from Virginia who "appear contented and happy," and concludes, "Say not that the slavery of the Louisiana negroes is a bitter draught" (I: 191). He uses such clichés as "the ignorant, careless-hearted slaves" (I: 103), the "careless slave" (I: 207), "the humble yet picturesque village or 'quarter' of the slaves, embowered in trees" (I: 242). In the first volume, he praises the recent Louisiana law prohibiting the intranational slave trade, remarks that such a law is under consideration in Mississippi, and says that Mississippi's passing such a law "certainly will be incalculably to her advantage" (I: 107).[1] When he visits the Louisiana Legislature, however, he discovers that they are in the process of repealing much of the law because, "The law occasioned greater inconvenience to the citizens of the state, than its framers had foreseen" (I: 181) with no comment, or revision, of his earlier praise of banning intranational trade. He notes the poor public education system (I: 235), the valorizing of idleness (see especially II: 85–87), the omnipresence of dueling (see especially page 218n10) and lynching (II: 186) with their consequent degradation of the law (II: 186), the necessity of the chain gang for habitual runaways (II: 189), and ever-present anxiety over slave assemblies (see especially II: 72 and 265).

He bemoans slavery, while carefully distancing him from "that wild Garrisonian theory" (II: 32), instead endorsing the view that the "interference" of northern abolitionists is "more injurious than beneficial" to the state of slaves and slavery (II: 265), claiming that the bonds of slavery must be extinguished by southerners "and thousands of southern gentleman are already extending their arms, ready to strike the blow" (II: 266). By "that wild Garrisonian theory" Ingraham appears to mean immediate and federally enforced emancipation, which is not what Garrison advocated. Ingraham hopes for voluntary emancipation, which is what Garrison advocated; so Ingraham rejects what he proceeds to advocate.

Ingraham's easy (and false) reference to Garrisonian abolition shows the extent to which repetition *is* persuasion. Like the equation of Noah's curse with the origin of slavery, or the assumption that Sodom was punished for what we call sodomy, a particular reading of a text is asserted so often that one reads it there. That this interpretation is achieved through interpolation, sometimes fairly elaborate, is pragmatically irrelevant; people think it is *in* the text. That people perceive the outgroup as interchangeable (so that people for whom abolitionists were an outgroup could substitute one person's words for another) worsens this sense of the transparency of the text of abolitionists. There were abolitionists who advocated federal imposition of emancipation on southern states, but they were few and far between (Mason calls them "exceptional souls" 132), and Garrison was not one of them. It surprises me, however, the extent to which this equation of Garrison and "radical" abolition continues, despite the fact that, as Stanley Harrold says, "In terms of aggressive action against the South, of an assertion of black manhood, and of endorsement of violent means, many non-Garrisonian abolitionists and most New York political abolitionists were more practically radical than the Garrisonians" (3). Garrison did not have the views attributed to him, and he was centrist. While calling for immediate emancipation without compensation and with full citizenship (thereby making him more "extreme" than others), he did not call for violent revolution or federally imposed emancipation.

Acknowledging the more extreme forms of abolitionism, accurately representing Garrison's position, and acknowledging how few and powerless were the advocates of the really radical abolitionism would have drawn attention to the inaccuracy of the "balance" metaphor. In every sphere, proslavery rhetors threatened that emancipation would result in their committing genocide; no abolitionist made the same threat. That was not a balance of extreme positions. Were one to put pro- and antislavery rhetors along a continuum of extremism, then Garrison would be far closer to the center than, for instance, Martin Van Buren (who worked for the open violation of the international agreement regarding the slave trade), yet Van Buren was not extreme enough for many slavers.

The pernicious absurdity of the "balance" metaphor becomes even more obvious if one considers the relative power of the "two" sides. For instance, one might match David Walker with John Calhoun (at least Calhoun's stance in the 1830s). Calhoun was at the center of political power:

a vice president of the United States, a U.S. senator, a candidate for president, with power over media outlets in several major cities; David Walker was a used clothing dealer who did not even have a vote.

This "balanced extremism of both sides" metaphor is pernicious because it assists in keeping the power on the side of the already powerful in bargaining situations. The "balance" metaphor, unless it acknowledges the relative power of the participants, virtually ensures a power imbalance. Ignoring the power and rhetorical *im*balance enabled people like Ingraham to present an extreme and actively fantastical position (that slavery will magically go away and will remain eternally) as a moderate one. Presenting abolitionists as fanatical distracts people from the fanaticism of slavers; cutting off a large chunk of what would be a balance enables bargainers to declare a position as the center which is actually far to one side. The "balance" metaphor was false and, more important, politically useful to slavers; that it was popular in its time simply shows the way that proslavery ideology dominated the political and rhetorical situation; there is no excuse for it now.

But, to return to Ingraham, as with other proslavery texts, the internal contradictions abound. Slaves are condemned for looking forward to not working, a characteristic noted without condemnation among whites who aspire to own slaves so that they may be idle. He has all the clichés about the animal-like nature of the African (see especially II: 123, 194) *and* several pages arguing that "when the negro, by the emancipation of his species, has opportunity for the culture of his own mind [. . .] a few generations will leave no traces of those mental shackles, which, like chains loaded upon the body, have so long borne him down to a level with the brute" (II: 200). He endorses the conventional view of the planter class as impractical *and* emphasizes their economic shrewdness (see especially II: 103); intrastate slave trade is necessary *and* abandoning it will bring great benefit to the slave states; the land will turn into wilderness given current practices (II: 87), but slavery cannot be abandoned because then the land will turn into wilderness (II: 91).

The vague hope that slavers would choose to free their slaves was impractical, as is shown in Ingraham's own description of the "mania" to own slaves (his term, see, for example, II: 84). Ingraham says that lawyers, doctors, even ministers all abandon their professions as soon as they have enough money to buy a plantation, "and this mania for planting will soon deprive the state of any benefit from it in a professional point of view" (II: 85). The mania, he predicts, will not pass away until "the lands become exhausted and wholly unfit for farther cultivation" (II: 86), a "waste, barren, and wild" (II: 87), something he sees happening quickly, given the tendency to "constant culture" (II: 86, unless a Yankee patents some method that will save the land). Early in the second volume, the same one that ends with the claim that southerners had already begun to abandon slavery willingly, Ingraham argues that the end of slavery would mean economic ruin to the South because whites will not labor in the southern climate; without slaves, he says, "Mississippi would be a wilderness, and revert to the aboriginal possessors. Annihilate [slaves] tomorrow, and this state and every southern state might be bought for a song" (II: 91, the same argument—and contradiction—present in proslavery rhetoric as early as 1819). His own argument, in other words, demonstrates his own argument to be hopeless. As did his own life—Ingraham went on to own, and not free, slaves.

This espousal of a vague hope contradicted by the actual conditions he saw (and chose to live) was far from uncommon. A perfect description of the colonization fantasy, it was shared by famous critics of slavery like Jefferson, Clay, and, at least for a time, Lincoln. It was also shared by a merchant in Lexington, Missouri. In 1835, the Philadelphia firm of Siter Price and Company wrote to James and R. Aull explaining that, while Siter and Price had obliged the Aulls in a recent transaction, they would not in the future assist in the handling of money exchanges involved in the slave traffic. James Aull wrote back promptly, explaining that they were not involved in the slave trade. He owned slaves, certainly, as did everyone in the state because "in this state as well as other slave holding states you must either have slaves for servants or yourself and family do your own work." The transaction in question arose out of their obliging a friend, and he and his brother chose not to profit from it. This decision shows the ideological importance of an excessively nice distinction between profiting from owning slaves in the role of slave owner (who thought of him- or herself as working them, but often profited from leasing them out or trading them), and in the role of a slave trader (who did not pretend to do anything other than lease or trade them). In Aull's case, it was a very nice distinction as, although he did not charge interest, he did benefit financially from his "obliging" the slave trader: according to Lewis Atherton, the Aulls purchased most of their goods from the East, and "the transferring of sufficient credit to the East to meet the bills for these goods was a problem which consumed much of James Aull's time" (24). What the trader had done for the Aulls was "made it both easier and safer to make remittances East, a problem of no small proportion" (23).

Aull claimed to be opposed to slavery, but was forced by circumstances into participating in the practice: "It would gratify me exceedingly to have all our negroes removed from us." His use of passive agency signifies the passive stance slavers took in regard to slavery, as though they had no agency in its continuing. He will not, he says, live where there are freed slaves, of course ("to free them and suffer them to remain with us, I for one would never concent [*sic*] to"), which makes the notion of abolishing slavery somewhat problematic. He hopes the legislature will take up the issue of "*gradual*" (his emphasis) abolition in the next session: "I have no doubt but we will have a convention and I have as little doubt that such steps will be taken as will free all our slaves in a limited number of years." That was a common perception (Elijah Lovejoy, an advocate of gradual abolition, also hoped for a convention that year), but it did not happen. This fantasy of slavery somehow magically taking care of itself gradually was very comforting. It enabled slavers like Calhoun and Aull to profit from slavery, while evading thinking carefully about just what it was and how it could be ended pragmatically. It also enabled them to own slaves and to feel good about feeling bad about it.

Thus far, I have argued that proslavery rhetors posited a consistently inconsistent philosophy of government, human nature, history, human rights, truth, and public discourse: the purpose of government is to compel obedience to the existing hierarchy; the secular and the sacred are conflated, not only in the sense that God endorses one political party and condemns the other, but that one holds political beliefs with the same degree and kind of conviction as tenets of religious faith. People are motivated to obey laws only through fear or thoughtless obedience. There was once more rigid order and obedience, but a period of flaccid indulgence has led to a degree of immorality and disorder that leaves us on the brink of chaos. The political realm is made up of good people, who are trying to maintain the order (from which they happen to benefit), and the malevolent, who are secretly plotting to bring about chaos (from which they hope to benefit).[2] Although the hierarchy benefits the privileged, and they are, openly, more privileged, they are also embattled, besieged, and martyred, albeit in obscure ways, by the system. At the same time, however, they *are* the system, so that anything that injures them (economically, socially, or emotionally) is an attack on the entire culture. There are no universal human rights, but socially constructed privileges that are distributed unevenly along the social hierarchy. Truth is what those highest in the hierarchy say it is. Disagreement not only fosters disorder, insofar as it complicates the thoughtlessness presumed necessary for obedience, but disloyalty, if it contradicts what the privileged say, as criticism or dishonors the privileged and hurts their feelings. The function of public discourse is to announce truth, rouse the public to a sense of its danger, and exhort them to take action against the malevolent plotters. Freedom of speech is the freedom to agree with the dominant way of thinking; because dissent is disloyalty and fosters disorder, it is appropriate for individuals or the government to respond to it with violence. Discussion alternates among epideictic, threats, and bargaining. Finally, the ends justify the means.

Above are the ways the philosophy is consistent. But, its very nature means that it is also deeply *in*consistent. That there are privileges rather than rights means that standards of behavior are inconsistent—good behavior in a white male planter is bad behavior in a free African American male; good behavior in a slave is sinful behavior in a slaver. Because truth is constructed by the privileged, what is true at one moment is untrue at another, and "true" statements are not logically consistent in themselves or taken together. So, what are we to make of the contradictions that run throughout proslavery rhetoric?

In 432 BCE, war was declared between Sparta and Greece, the beginning of what would later be called the Peloponnesian War. According to Thucydides, there was an appalling decline in Athenian culture—a degree of savagery in wars not known before, and a passion for party politics previously unimagined. Donald Kagan, a more recent historian, draws the same conclusion: "Anger, frustration, and the desire for vengeance increased as the war dragged on, and they gave rise to a progression of atrocities rarely or not at all known before that time" (488). Everything fell before faction—family, honor, oaths, even language itself. Thucydides remarked on the degradation of language: "The ordinary acceptation of words in their relation to things was changed as men thought fit. Reckless audacity came to be regarded as courageous loyalty to party, prudent hesitation as specious cowardice, moderation as a cloak for unmanly weakness" (Thucydides 3.82.4). Just as language was separated from meaning, so was action separated from thought: "Frantic impulsiveness was accounted a true man's part, but caution in deliberation a specious pretext for shrinking" (3.82.4). Words were used to mean whatever enabled a faction to triumph, loyalty to faction mattered more than keeping one's word, and using words deliberately, or even deliberating at all, was dismissed. "The cause of all these evils," Thucydides tells us, "was the desire to rule which greed and ambition inspire, and also, springing from them, that party-spirit which belongs to men who once have become engaged in factious rivalry" (3.82.8).

Hannah Arendt, watching the trial of Adolf Eichmann, was fascinated by the ways that the Third Reich had managed to get a rather dim, very boring, failed salesman to work as efficiently and effectively as he could toward genocide. An important strategy was a set of language rules that "proved of enormous help in the maintenance of order and sanity in the various widely diversified services" cooperating in the Holocaust (*Eichmann* 85). People did not refer to murder, killing, or even deportation: "The net effect of this language system was to keep these people from equating it with their old, 'normal' knowledge of murder and lies" (86). Eichmann knew what was happening; he saw the preparations for a gas chamber, he watched a mobile gassing van in action, and he witnessed two shooting massacres. At his trial he claimed to have been horrified by such atrocities, and many observers believe that he was, but only in those brief moments when he was forced to think about them. The language rules enabled him not to think, so that he could go away from a sight that horrified him in order to work hard to ensure that such atrocities would continue. He knew, at the same time that he could keep himself from knowing, exactly what he was doing.

Victor Klemperer's *The Language of the Third Reich* similarly emphasizes how effective Nazi propaganda was at blocking critical thought. Hitler's "golden rule" for party propagandists "is always: don't let your listeners engage in critical thought" (Klemperer 176). Klemperer, a German Jew who only barely escaped the Holocaust because of his non-Jewish wife, described the effect of the relentless mendacity of Nazi language rules: "If someone replaces the words 'heroic' and 'virtuous' with 'fanatical' for long enough, he will come to believe that a fanatic is really a virtuous hero, and that no one can be a hero without fanaticism. The Third Reich did not invent the words 'fanatical' and 'fanaticism', it just changed their value" (Klemperer 16). The four points again connected: political party, violence, savagery, and a language that makes thinking impossible.

Arendt noted that Heinrich Himmler was the master of coining slogans, many of which were intended to minimize the human tendency to feel compassion for others. He praised concentration guards, who were engaged in activities that required no bravery whatsoever, for how hard it is to be a concentration camp guard (see, for instance, "Speech of Reichsfuhrer SS Heinrich Himmler" 370). Arendt describes the effect of this use of language: "So that instead of saying: What horrible things I did to people!, the murderers would be able to say, What horrible things I had to watch in the pursuance of my duties, how heavily the task weighed upon my shoulders!" (*Eichmann* 106). One reverses the language in order to reverse the roles—the guards become the victims of the Jews, just as Fisk claimed the slavers were the victims of slaves, and Hammond claimed to be the victim of abolitionists. Whether the guards *really* believed they were the victims is difficult to know and remains a scholarly controversy. What is most likely is that they sincerely did. And they didn't.

This is the process of thought which George Orwell famously called "doublethink": "*Doublethink* means the power of holding two contradictory beliefs in one's mind simultaneously, and accepting both of them" (*1984* 176). In *1984*, the totalitarian regime of Oceania and its central party, Ingsoc, depend upon doublethink: "*Doublethink* lies at the very heart of Ingsoc, since the essential act of the Party is to use conscious deception while retaining the firmness of purpose that goes with complete honesty. To tell deliberate lies while genuinely believing in them, to forget any fact that has become inconvenient, and then, when it becomes necessary again, to draw it back from oblivion for just so long as it is needed, to deny the existence of objective reality and all the while to take account of the reality which one denies—all this is indispensably necessary" (177). The primary goal of doublethink is simply to maintain the power of the party. It is, more specifically, to maintain the social hierarchy from which Ingsoc benefits in the face of the natural human demand for equality. As the book that Winston finds explains, the demand for human equality is tremendously threatening to hierarchy; it creates what theorists like Arendt or Habermas would call a "legitimation crisis." That was, of course, precisely the situation of slavers, who wanted to maintain a rigid economic and racial hierarchy while claiming to believe in a political theory of democracy and religious system of reciprocity. The ideology of chivalry emphasized protecting the helpless; the economics of slavery depended on exploiting them.

The structure of Oceanic society "rests ultimately on the belief that Big Brother is omnipotent and that the Party is infallible. But since in reality Big Brother is not omnipotent and the Party is not infallible, there is need for unwearying, moment-to-moment flexibility in the treatment of facts" (175). It is the loyalty to party, not the behavior, that is good, as is demonstrated by one's willingness to condemn the same behavior in one's opponents that one praises in one's allies. *Blackwhite,* and doublethink generally, is about loyalty to the ingroup. Hence, the educational system emphasizes loyalty and respect for authority. In an authoritarian system, education is first and foremost the inculcation of respect for authority, with all information (textbooks, teaching strategies, even assessment methods) assessed on the basis of whether or not it honors the current system. Critical thinking, with its emphasis on noting contradictions, is abjured in favor of an openly conservative educational agenda that is intended to strengthen conformity and ingroup loyalty. The book that Winston is given explains that Oceania's educational system emphasizes the facilities of "not grasping analogies, of failing to perceive logical errors, of misunderstanding the simplest arguments if they are inimical to Ingsoc, and of being bored or repelled by any train of thought which is capable of leading in a heretical direction" (175). The anti-intellectualism is politically motivated and politically consequential.

War is not necessary for doublespeak, but "loyal willingness" to party is, and a state of war (whether real or imagined) is assisted by war. I've noticed that people often overlook that there really is a war in *1984;* it is not entirely manufactured. The need for the war (resources in one region) and the needs created by the war (for security, surveillance, and sacrifice) are exaggerated because of the political, rhetorical, and psychological power created by the war. There really were abolitionists, and there really was resistance to the expansion of slavery, and slaves really did resist in sometimes violent ways. But, those conditions could be exaggerated and distorted for political purposes, and any attempt to deliberate concerning them was demonized.

There is a mutually reinforcing cycle; fanatical commitment to a system is created and recreated through conditions that are themselves justified by a fanatical terror of social change. Thinking is dangerous because it fosters dissent, and because it threatens to expose the various contradictions, resulting in what Klemperer called "the fear of the thinking man and the hatred of the intellect" (3). I am not quoting Klemperer because I want to raise, let alone endorse, the argument that slavers were essentially Nazis, but because I want to raise the issue of language and critical thinking in an authoritarian culture.

Throughout this book, I have criticized proslavery rhetors' generalizations, but that is not to say that generalizations are inappropriate. On the contrary, they're necessary for public deliberation: public policy is always about categories of people or behavior, so it's inevitable that the debate over public policy involves discursively constructed perceptions of those categories. That the generalizations do not apply equally accurately to every individual in the category is simply a fact of generalizations. What makes proslavery rhetors' generalizations so irresponsible is that they were impervious to disproof. To challenge their abstract characterization of abolitionists was to challenge the construction of ingroups and outgroups, hence an act of disloyalty to the ingroup. Since authoritarian public debate is always premised on maintaining the honor of the ingroup, any criticism of the ingroup was similarly prohibited, so that accuracy was less important than maintaining honor.

Doublethink functions in two mutually reinforcing ways at the same time. First, it puts loyalty above truth (that is, loyalty to group *is* truth). For authoritarians, accuracy is irrelevant, and truth is already attained by ingroup ideology, so that one ignores any brute facts that might invite disloyalty, and one can enforce truth through violently enforcing group loyalty. It is because of this particular hierarchy of loyalty and linguistic accuracy that authoritarians are so drawn to loyalty oaths. Such oaths never uncover spies, plotters of insurrection, or terrorists, as such people will quite cheerfully sign them. But, exposing genuine traitors is not the goal. The oaths are often mildly incoherent (what, exactly, does allegiance to a *flag* mean?) but that is necessary to achieve the goal. The logical and linguistic incoherence of loyalty oaths function to expose people who think carefully about language, who take their own words seriously, and who believe that language is best when accurate. In other words, they are not intended to expose traitors, but critical thinkers who would place accuracy above group loyalty.

It is in this light that I would argue one should understand proslavery hyperbole. The rhetor engaged in hyperbole is demonstrating his (or her) loyalty to the group through willingness to make public assertions that are patently absurd, but that they both do and do not mean. As argued before, my criticism is not that they were vehement, nor even that they engaged in hyperbole. The problem is that they excused themselves from responsibility for their own actions and rhetoric.

This isn't to say that authoritarians are oblivious to brute facts; they knew that there were slave insurrections, that African Americans were talented and intelligent, that slaves did love their children, and that slave "owners" did trade slaves, hence the contradictions in proslavery rhetoric. Loyalty is not demonstrated through something easy to do, so loyalty in thought is demonstrated through the rather difficult task of believing what is obviously absurd.[3]

The second way that doublethink functions is through a kind of verbal scapegoating, or cunning projection. One takes the major and most damning criticism of one's own position and simply asserts that it is true of the opposition (what Goebbels called the "Stop! Thief!" method). If repeated often enough, as in the characterization of abolitionists as inciting insurrection (or, for that matter, as fanatical), the characterization is accepted (as in Ingraham's assuming that Garrison believed the federal government should force abolition on slave states). This strategy shifts the stasis from slavery to abolitionists, thereby, at the very least, confusing the issue for many observers (as happened with Nixon's famous use of praeteritio in the "Checkers" speech). If it's very effective, this strategy actually serves to persuade people that the name-calling group must be innocent of the charge, as they condemn it with such vehemence. Whether effective with observers, rhetorical displacement has a noted emotional cleansing, as in the ritual killing of one's opponent for committing sins one has projected on to them.

Social psychologists have argued that scapegoating of groups results from "*shared attributions and appraisals*" (Glick, in *On the Nature of Prejudice* 250, emphasis in original) that were themselves created by group-level "heightened frustration, needs, and anxieties" (Glick 252). These "difficult life conditions [. . .] lead to a *collective* search for explanations and solutions" (Glick 253, emphasis added). That is, individuals who feel they are alone in their troubles will attribute blame to other individuals, but, if there is a collective sense of anxiety and frustration, then groups are drawn to blaming other groups. In the 1830s, the roller-coaster economy coupled with the privileging of risk taking frustrated any ability to achieve security in either economic or social esteem. As Glick says, "Scapegoat movements address frustrated needs for esteem, belonging, and transcendence by reasserting the ingroup's superiority and offering membership in a wider social movement that promises symbolic immortality" (255). Or, in the words of the Texas Declaration of secession, slavery "had existed from the first settlement of her wilderness by the white race, and which her people intended should exist in all future time." Since slavery would exist forever, being a slaver meant being part of an immortal system.

The likelihood of scapegoating has little to do with whether or not the scapegoated group bears any real responsibility for the situation and far more to do with the rhetorical and psychological needs of those engaged in the act: "Complex explanations involving largely uncontrollable, impersonal forces are difficult to fathom and may fail to suggest a clear solution, rendering them unattractive (because they do not fulfill heightened psychological needs for control and optimism). Scapegoat movements attract followers by offering simpler, culturally plausible explanations and solutions for shared negative events" (Glick 253). In the 1830s, many slavers faced a plethora of threats and negative events: their economic and political vulnerability, especially manifest in the successful imposition of tariffs; threats to their control, economic uncertainty (because of fluctuations in cotton prices), cultural uncertainty (due to exhaustion of the soil), threats to political power, anxiety regarding safety (due to real and imagined insurrection plots), and, quite possibly most important, a legitimation crisis created by the shift in world opinion toward slavery. People dependent upon, or enamored with, the slave/cotton economy could either try to understand the complicated and uncontrollable forces that threatened them, or they could find a scapegoat. Proslavery rhetors found several.

The British were scapegoated for "causing" slavery, as though it was not actually caused by a person buying and then holding ownership of another person. The "Meeting of the Southern Gentlemen in New York" resolved,

> No one will deny that slavery is an evil, but it is one which these States found entailed upon them by Britain, and which, since their independence, has been of such magnitude, as to set at defiance the schemes of the most sagacious for its immediate abolition [. . .] they [slave owners] have found them [slaves?] as they are, and have had no agency in creating their peculiar relationship to the whites. They contemplate their condition with regret, and would be the first to embrace any rational plan to ameliorate their condition, which would promise security to the master, freedom and happiness to the slave. ("The Meeting Called by Gentlemen from the South," *U.S. Telegraph* July 27, 1835)

Kenneth Burke identified something similar as Empson's "prim irony"—when, he says, a southern intellectual bemoans a racist institution he claims he is powerless to change, but from which he benefits. A rhetor, simultaneously, takes the moral high ground from the abolitionists (for being just as concerned with the morals of slavery) *and* excuses himself from action, while evading political and rhetorical responsibility for his stance. Scapegoating the abolitionists for slaves' unhappiness enabled everyone—both northerners and southerners, all of whom were deeply implicated in slavery—to ignore the institutional injustices and fall into a simple solution (eradicate or silence abolitionists). To describe slavery as caused by the act of owning slaves, however, would make every slaveholder responsible for the institution in every minute of every day.

By scapegoating overseers, Wiethoff argues (although he does not use the term "scapegoat"), slavers created an abusive system from which they profited while they could place responsibility for the abuse on the shoulders of the overseers. It was conventional for the "slave trader" to be looked on with disgust, excluded from polite society, and generally condemned (see Tadman 5). Alexander Sims says that the domestic slave trade "which is carried on by speculators as a constant employment for gain, we consider abusive of the right of dominion over slaves. As generally conducted, it is productive of bad consequences; and those engaged in it are reputed to be, and generally are, men of corrupt morals and little feeling" (28). Slave owners were represented as reluctant to sell slaves, only breaking up families when absolutely necessary. In contrast to this image, close attention to bills of sale and exportation rates show that "the great majority of sales to the trader were not involuntary or reluctant" (Tadman 117). If slave "owners" sold their slaves only when economically necessary, then sales to traders should be inversely correlated to the southern economy, but the reverse is true: "Sales were most numerous [. . .] in exactly those periods when returns from agriculture were especially favorable and there was least economic necessity to sell" (Tadman 129). People sold slaves when the price for them was high; slave sales corresponded to profit, not need.

The demonizing of slave traders is very convenient; it suggests a resistance to the practice of selling slaves that, in fact, slavers did not practice. There was a consistently brisk trade in slaves; Tadman calculates that "at least" 69.3 percent of the 154,000 interregional exportations in the 1820s were sales (with the rest of the slaves taken along with immigrating planters; Tadman 246). Unless those 106,722 slaves were all unmarried orphans, slave "owners" broke up a lot of families. Tadman estimates that the interregional slave trade broke up families in 51 percent of cases (150); this trade would have led to the termination of one out of every five marriages in the Upper South; one out of three children under the age of fourteen would have been sold away from parents. Local sales, Tadman says "would have raised this proportion to about one in two" (211–12).

Abolitionists were scapegoated for the problems inherent to slavery, such as insurrection, repressive laws, mutual suspicion; they were also scapegoated in that they were accused of and condemned for precisely the actions in which proslavery rhetors engaged: aggression, fanaticism, factionalism, and a politically cunning alarmism. One of the most important of these accusations was aggression, as it was a false accusation that stuck. Proslavery aggressions (in Mason's term) fueled antislavery rhetoric on the part of people who were trying to resist the expansion of slavery. As Holt says, "Most historians of the war's causation now agree that the issue that most aggravated sectional conflict during the fifteen years prior to 1861 was slavery's extension beyond the existing slave states, not demands for its abolition within them" (*The Fate of Their Country* 4). By focusing on the abolitionists as the major opponents of proslavery policies, we follow a sleight of the hand that proslavery rhetors made in the antebellum era: that the largest amount of antislavery rhetoric in the 1820s and 1830s was from anti-expansionists.

Slavers' acknowledging the complexity of the situation would also necessitate acknowledging their own role in it both politically (that their problems were caused by insisting upon expanding slavery) and personally (that they owned slaves). James Aull and John Calhoun (and, eventually, James Ingraham) would all have to acknowledge not that slavery was imposed on them by some vague group, but that it was an option they chose on a daily basis. Social psychologists who have studied the process of "defensive projection" have shown that "trying to suppress negative thoughts about their group indirectly caused these individuals to overperceive that very trait in other groups" (Newman and Caldwell, in *On the Nature of Prejudice,* 385). Scapegoating was rhetorically and politically powerful because it enabled proslavery politicians specifically, and slavers generally, to feel better.

The internal contradictions are inherent to proslavery discourse, because, I would suggest, at the very heart of the proslavery position was a contradiction. Proslavery rhetors expressed the vague hope that slavery would somehow go away *and* the equally vague hope that it was eternal. The hopes were not vague in the sense of being indecisive or of being held without deep conviction—on the contrary, these hopes were often expressed with great vehemence—but in the sense of just how, exactly, slavery would disappear or continue (let alone do both). The vagueness of these contradictory hopes, like the cunning projection, was like a curtain that was useful for keeping people from thinking practically about the long-term possibilities of slavery.

Proslavery rhetors were tied to slavery. As in the case of Ingraham, it was not that they were economically tied to slavery—as his travels go on, he expresses increasing admiration for slavery, yet still has no economic ties to it (although he would soon develop them). And, indeed, his description of the slave-owning mania emphasizes that it was not an economic decision—not that slave owning was a necessary consequence of the economic desire to profit through cotton-growing, but the reverse. When describing the planter class, Ingraham insists that their primary motivation was to own slaves and that cotton was the most effective means to that end. The goal, Ingraham says, is not to buy slaves in order to grow cotton, but "to sell cotton in order to buy negroes—to make more cotton to buy more negroes, 'ad infinitum,' is the aim and direct tendency of all the operations of the thorough-going cotton planter; his whole soul is wrapped up in the pursuit" (II: 91). To succeed in the South was to own slaves; to be a southern man was to be a slave owner. Southern white manhood depended upon having slaves to dominate: "In a slave society the white man's zeal for personal independence and his fear of dependence and consequent degradation often developed some peculiar manifestations. The ideal of independence requires individual autonomy but also prized mastery over others considered unfit for citizenship" (Ford 361). Even those who did not own slaves could force their submission—the laws regarding insolence did not specify insolence to the owner or overseer, but to *any* white.

Abolitionists were accused of trying to overthrow the entire system of the south, and, to the degree that Ingraham's observations were correct, the accusation was accurate. Henry de Saussure describes the horror that might occur were African Americans freed from slavery:

> They might not only be cultivators of the earth, day-labourers, artizans, and manufacturers, but merchants, and professional men. They might according to law, glide into our families as physicians in the perfect confidence of that delicate relation; they might vindicate or violate our rights as advocates; sit in judgment upon our lives and property as jurors and judges; and instruct and guide our consciences as pastors. They might vote and control the popular elections; be themselves elected to state legislatures, and to congress; command our armies and navies; preside over our councils, as Presidents and Ministers of state; and represent the dignity and the interests of the nation as ambassadors to foreign countries. We might hear a white member of congress from Massachusetts, or Connecticut allude to the argument or compliment the speech, of his honorable black friend from Pennsylvania or Virginia; of his yellow friend from Maryland or South Carolina; of the tawney gentleman from Georgia or Tennessee; or of the spotted or brindled gentleman from Louisiana or Arkansaw. (15)[4]

His point was that African Americans might be in positions of authority, positions not all whites can achieve, so that some whites might have to defer to African Americans. To the extent that "the south" was a slave-based racial hierarchy in which manhood was constituted by a white man owning slaves, the abolitionists wanted to take away the very thing that constituted white southern manhood.

It did not matter how nicely they said it. Proslavery rhetors, it should be remembered, did not object to the *way* that people criticized slavery; they objected to the criticism. Proslavery rhetors and politicians began insisting on the silencing of debate over slavery long before Garrison broke with colonization; during the 1820 debate on the Missouri Compromise, proslavery rhetors seemed to want federal policy toward slavery significantly shifted without any discussion of the merits of slavery. The March 1836 Kentucky resolutions argued that free speech and freedom of the press did not apply to criticisms of slavery: "It cannot be that the right of discussion at the north, carries with it the right to excite a portion of the population to rapine and murder" (4). Proslavery rhetors in the gag rule controversy refused to distinguish among the petitions on the basis of rhetoric; it was accepted that congressional debate over the expansion of slavery had led to the Vesey rebellion; *Human Rights* (the pamphlet that was mailed) did not call for insurrection; polite abolitionism like Channing's and Child's were just as hostilely received as Garrison's (in fact, they were generally conflated).[5] Austin's hostile response to Channing does not, it should be emphasized, condemn him for his rhetoric, and it does not suggest that abolitionists make their arguments in a different way; Austin says, "What is to be done? I answer NOTHING" (43).

One problem with public discourse generally, but that I've found especially vexing in proslavery rhetoric, is the issue of sincerity. What does one make of a culture that harps on a particular theme? Are people who continually describe themselves as honest really honest? If they were honest, why would they protest so much? Proslavery rhetors talked constantly about honor, and they loved books and stories about chivalry, which (in the words of G. R. James) meant "'*To speak the truth, to succour the helpful and oppressed, and never to turn back from an enemy*'" (28), and scholars like Genovese conclude that they were, therefore, sincerely motivated by chivalry. Proslavery rhetors claimed *and* denied that slavery was profitable. They said that owning slaves cost them more money than employing laborers, but they also said that emancipation would have been too costly. Whether the first proposition is true is unclear, but the second points to something that proslavery rhetors tried very hard to keep obscure: slavery was profitable because of the market value of slaves, a fact which made all slave owners incipient slave traders. The economic value, and even physical control, of a slave "owner" came from the possibility that he or she might, at any moment, sell a slave. Without slave traders, slave "owners" had no control and slaves had no value.

Fogel and Engerman, and, more recently, Huston, have concluded that close analysis demonstrates that slavery was extremely profitable, with it becoming increasingly profitable as time went on: "If we treat the North and South as separate nations and rank them among the countries of the world, the South would stand as the fourth most prosperous nation of the world in 1860" (Fogel 63). These numbers calculate the "wealth" of the South, and the economic viability of slavery, by including the economic value of the slaves themselves. Huston makes this clear in an aside when he defines net value: "the net value of slaves—that is, the wealth of slaveholders" (99). That value is market value.

Things, or people, only have "market" value if you are willing to sell them. Thus, the profitability and economic viability of slavery depended on the slave trade. In that case, slave trading was not a peripheral quality, but the very center of the slave economy, something also suggested by Tadman's analysis of the frequency and pattern of slave trading—that slavers held their slaves when prices were low and traded when they were high. If so, slavery was economically viable only as long as new slave territory was continually being opened up. I think this makes sense of the dilemma of self-styled slave "owners." They knew slavery had to expand because they knew their economy depended heavily on the interregional sale of slaves. That meant they knew, at some level, that they were *all* slave speculators; breaking up families and selling people down river was the essence, not the accident, of their wealth. That was an unacceptable, almost literally unthinkable, contradiction of their self-image as chivalrous people who succoured the oppressed. The economics of slavery meant that they *were* the oppressors.

Had the United States policy toward slavery been debated openly, the centrality of the slave trade to slave "owners'" well-being would have had to come out. While slave owners were obsessed with the price of slaves, and constantly traded slaves, they could deny the importance of slave trading in their economic lives through finding some group that did it more (slavers) and then condemning them. This is the projection (we don't trade slaves—they do) that marks the first step in scapegoating; by making some group synecdochic for behavior that is actually systemic, people can fantasize that controlling that group's behavior (or exterminating them) will end the problem. Hence, in periodic fits of conscience or terror of insurrection, state legislatures would pass laws restricting slave trading, but their own dependence on the practice necessarily meant that they backed down. Slave "owners" were slavers.[6]

This is the consequence of valuing honor, then: proslavery rhetors valued it so much they couldn't think about whether they were honorable. And it seems to me very clear that they continually emphasized their disdain for money-making because, in fact, it was so important to their national policy. They could not have open deliberation of the expansion of slavery without their dependence on slave trading coming up, something that would put the lie to their sense of group identity. So they did everything they could to make sure the debate was not open.

In March 1961, a group of students marched peacefully from the Zion Baptist Church in Columbia, South Carolina, to the state house grounds in order to protest segregation. They were met, initially, by thirty or more police officers, and an increasing number of pro-segregationist protestors (possibly as many as two or three hundred). According to Justice Stewart's 1963 U.S. Supreme Court decision (*Edwards v. South Carolina),* the trial evidence was clear that the protesters (of both sides) were orderly and were not blocking traffic (a reading of the evidence not shared by the South Carolina state supreme court). The police ordered only the anti-segregationist protestors—those dissenting from consensus—to disperse, on the grounds that vehicular and pedestrian traffic was being blocked by both sides (239 S.C., 123 S. E. 2d p. 249). To apportion responsibility this way, and to arrest only the antisegregationist protestors, the police invoked the notion of a "breach of the peace," a vague concept the South Carolina Supreme Court decision supporting the arrest of the civil rights protestors (and not the counter-protesters) tried to clarify. A "breach of the peace," that court declared "may consist of an act of violence or an act likely to produce violence. It is not necessary that the peace be actually broken to lay the foundation for a prosecution for this offense [. . .] By 'peace,' as used in this connection, is meant the tranquility enjoyed by citizens of a municipality or community where good order reigns among its members, which is the natural right of all persons in political society" (239 S.C. 339, 123 S. E. 2d 247; qtd. in *Edwards et al. v. South Carolina*). The protestors committed a breach of the peace because they engaged in behavior that upset the previously tranquil community. It was not violent in and of itself, but it was violent insofar as that behavior might cause others to engage in violence. Like the slaves responsible for the violence of the slavers, like the abolitionists responsible for the intransigence of proslavery rhetors, the protestors were responsible for the feelings and consequent actions of segregationists, who themselves were not responsible for what they did.

Being irresponsible, they might lose control, and then the protestors were responsible for not having sufficiently placated them. This is, I've argued, the masculine position in narratives of abusive men who must (and in some vague way can) be inspired to stop engaging in the abuse through sufficient nice-ness on the part of the oppressed. Yet, the gendered roles are considerably complicated, as indicated in my characterizing proslavery rhetoric as histrionic. The notion that women's uteruses cause us to argue badly is both old and new; that women are more emotional and less rational in public discourse is a point of consensus shared by a surprising array of people. It is also, I hope to have shown, empirically false.

Proslavery rhetors were obsessed with feelings. A recurrent complaint about abolitionists was that they hurt slavers' feelings. Proslavery rhetors emphasized how angry they were made, with implicit and explict threats of consequent violence, but also how sensitive they were. They felt good about being kind to their slaves, and they felt bad about whipping them or leaving their care to overseers, they were sorry that there were bad slave owners, but they felt pride in slavery as a whole, or they felt that slavery should go away, but they weren't doing anything to end it personally.[7] Part of the function, I would argue, of Ingraham's emphasizing his feelings about slavery, or Aull saying he didn't like slavery, was showing that their hearts were in the right place. They had the right sentiments, which meant that they were good people. Because they were good people, their actions were immune from scrutiny. This, too, is a form of stasis-shifting: the stasis shifts from their actions (or, if politicians, their policies) to their feelings, which are presumed to be indicative of their identities. This is the "I feel your pain" approach to politics.

Abolitionist rhetors were no more emotional than proslavery ones, and they were far more rational. Emotionalism and rationality are not at opposite ends of a spectrum; they are only tangentially related (unless one has the circular, and useless, definition of each as the absence of the other). William Lloyd Garrison, whose writing style I personally find irritating, engaged in rational argumentation insofar as he accurately represented his oppositions' arguments and engaged them. He strove for internal consistency, his paper presented multiple sides of various arguments, he published arguments with which he disagreed. Harriet Beecher Stowe, another author often condemned for polemicism, demonstrates deep knowledge of proslavery rhetoric in *Uncle Tom's Cabin.* Passionate, sentimental, committed, and assertive, these authors still managed to represent proslavery arguments clearly and accurately. Abolitionists were not more histrionic than proslavery rhetors, but they did have more uteruses among them, and I would suggest that the extremely sexist tendency to perceive women as more emotional, coupled with a desire to shift the stasis away from slavery, facilitated the creation of a political, and then scholarly, consensus about the fanaticism of abolitionists. Women were excluded from public discourse because they would be emotional and irrational; they would, in other words, behave the same way proslavery rhetors already did. Whether we are to understand histrionic outbursts as a point of white male privilege, or to see proslavery rhetors' condemning abolitionists for doing what they themselves do as yet another instance of cunning projection, is unclear to me. But it is clear they did it.

A famous exponent of an extreme version of this tendency is Frank Owsley, who blamed "egocentric sectionalism" for the war, a flaw practiced more by the North than the South: "The people in one section failed in their language and conduct to respect the dignity and self-respect of the people in the other section" (Stampp, *Causes* 56). It is striking the extent to which this echoes proslavery rhetoric. By "the people" of the South Frank Owsley means slavers—if anything, abolitionists had far more respect for the dignity and self-respect of slaves and African Americans than did slavers—and the war was caused by not respecting *their* feelings. Owsley does not condemn the South for failing to respect the feelings of the North; this is not, despite his concluding sentence (that unity is in danger when "one section fails to respect the self-respect of the people of another section" 58), an image of mutual respect.[8] Less extreme versions of this explanation arise in Larry Tise and Drew Guilpin Faust, both of whom still accept that there was something provoking in abolitionists' rhetoric. What one wonders is just what Owsley, Tise, and Faust think abolitionists should have done instead—there was, as made clear in the gag rule, no way to criticize slavery that was not provocative; slavers took any criticism as a personal attack.

To blame abolitionists for incivility is to preclude abolition. My grievance is not with the notion that public discourse ought to have certain standards and that billingsgate should be avoided—I hope it's been clear that I consider proslavery rhetors' reliance on smear tactics as juvenile, hypocritical, and destructive. The problem is that conventional notions of civility, which tend to emphasize whether the audience is offended, inevitably put an impossible burden on dissenters. While calls for social change might themselves call for more or less violence, they always necessarily involve criticism, and no one likes to be criticized. To prohibit anything other than "civil" political discourse, as long as "civil" is defined as discourse that does not upset anyone, is to prohibit social change.

Finally, it should be emphasized that this blaming of abolitionists for provoking slavers is not supported by the historical evidence. Earlier, I pointed out that the causal narrative has two steps—the AAS flooded the South; proslavery rhetors responded. The first step never happened. The evidence supports the AAS contention that they mailed pamphlets only to Charleston, South Carolina. Leonard Richards, in *"Gentlemen of Property and Standing,"* says that the correspondence of Samuel Gouverneur, postmaster of New York, shows that he chose not to forward along the pamphlets in question and thereby "he stymied the postal campaign at its point of origin" (74). The letter from Huger, the Charleston postmaster, was forwarded to Gouverneur by Calhoun, and that is the only letter from a southern postmaster claiming to have received any large number of pamphlets from the AAS. In other words, while the AAS may have hoped or tried to flood the southland, an assertion for which I've found no evidence, they did not.

The narrative that makes the AAS pamphlets the catalyst is wrong in its attribution of causation, not in its description of the situation. It is hyperbolic, but not entirely wrong, to describe the Southland as flooded with pamphlets, but it is wrong to attribute all references to "pamphlets" as references to those mailed by the AAS. The meeting of "southern gentlemen" that passed various resolutions about abolitionist pamphlets was July 20, nine days before the AAS pamphlets were delivered. There were pamphlets that terrified slavers, but they weren't the AAS ones. Like Simms's refuting Martineau's claims about the AAS pamphlets with evidence about different pamphlets sent by a different group to a different place via a different method, this claim about the AAS pamphlets relies on substitution.

Abolitionists of various kinds did manage to distribute pamphlets through the South, with the successful distribution of David Walker's *Appeal* the most terrifying to racists. But, to describe the situation as it was—a fairly large number of individuals, some of them African Americans, were sending antislavery material in various ways to the slave states, sometimes to people who had requested and agreed with that material—suggests a widespread and disparate antislavery sentiment, rather than a single, marginalized group that can be usefully characterized as fanatic, and who can be imagined to impose abolition upon people who do not want it.

The latter narrative is much more comforting to proslavery ideology, in that it facilitates the equation of "southern" and "proslavery" (thereby erasing southerners who were opposed to slavery). It maintains the illusion of African American passivity, whereas the successful writing and distribution of pamphlets by African Americans proves that fantasy was false. In addition, a fanatic group can be "met" in battle, but a widespread phenomenon that results from the system of slavery itself cannot. If antislavery was pervasive in the South, then something about slavery itself made antislavery arise. If, however, it existed only when this fanatic and nefarious group had contact with southerners, slavery could be maintained through killing that group. All one has to do is maintain a body count.

If, furthermore, anti-abolitionism was a unification strategy, then the accuracy of its characterization of abolitionists was less important than the effectiveness of its alarmism. A single enemy, a specific individual, is more conducive to alarmism than an amorphous political phenomenon because it can be associated with a specific image. The abstract fact of various people who are various degrees of abolitionist for various reasons and in various ways can be reduced to a single individual, almost in the way a metaphor or model is literalized. This single individual embodies the movement(s), thereby promising the possibility of killing the movement(s) through the death of a single individual. Just as Orlando Patterson has argued that lynching performs the symbolic act of community cleansing through ritual blood sacrifice of someone who can be made to embody the multiple and amorphous sins of the community, so I am arguing that embodying antislavery sentiment in a single person enabled a kind of community cleansing through rhetorical ritual killing. This was the rhetorical power that anti-Jacksonians, in a certain sense, unleashed in the 1830s—the power of going on the offensive against abolitionists.

Going on the offensive does have considerable rhetorical and political rewards. Immediately, it raises the costs of participation, thereby making more attractive the option of acquiescence. The increased stridency (rhetorical and physical) of proslavery forces did successfully silence southern antislavery; in that sense, the bellicosity of proslavery rhetors was not merely rhetoric, so to speak. It was tremendously effective. As I've suggested, that silencing may not have been in their long-term best interest, but consideration of long-term best interest is precisely what falls away in authoritarian public discourse, because it is unmanly to think carefully and deliberate cautiously (especially about worst-case scenarios).

The internal irrationality, bellicosity, and hyperbole of proslavery rhetoric were mirrored (or perhaps acted out) in policy, and these qualities were ultimately self-destructive. To equate criticizing slavery with being an abolitionist in favor of violent rebellion was hyperbole, but to call for lynching or jailing all "abolitionists," particularly in light of the previous definition, was politically impractical and ultimately self-destructive (and it was murder when it was done). Northerners, even those notorious for doing the bidding of slavers, would (and did) balk at jailing abolitionists. Even less extreme policies, such as the gag rule, were too extreme for many people, who were thereby made anti-slave power, if not antislavery. But, southern politicians were infamous for Pyrrhic victories. Ford discusses this issue in regard to the Kansas-Nebraska Act, quoting South Carolina representative William Porcher Miles, who regretted, even at the time, making the issue a "war to the knife" (qtd. in Ford 344) when everyone admitted that Kansas did not have a climate hospitable to slavery. In an authoritarian culture, the discourse is all about the manliness of the rhetors. Once the issue has become, not the efficacy of policies, but the manliness of political figures, which is demonstrated through their ability to demand submission and enact punitive policies, then one is necessarily starting a race toward extremism. In communities concerned with deliberation and governance, one "wins" by proposing a more effective solution; in *mano a mano* posturing, one wins by taking a more hyperbolic stance. The pointlessness, expense, and even self-destructivenss of the policy does not matter; what matters is some vague sense about the "principle" of the thing (with the operating principle the redemption of impaired masculinity).

What also matters is maintaining control while evading responsibility. Proslavery rhetors, like authoritarians generally, wanted things their way, without acknowledging the criticisms, flaws, or consequences of that way or how they got it. England was responsible for the institution of slavery, abolitionists were responsible for slave insurrection, slaves were responsible for their own punishment, overseers were responsible for the cruelty, slave traders were responsible for breaking up families, and anyone who resisted them was responsible for slavers' violent response. Authoritarians are in control of everyone but themselves, and they control others through their being on the edge of losing self-control.

The mailing of pamphlets did not rock a previously stable boat, but was simply one more (and not even the biggest) crisis in an era of crisis-driven politics, fear-mongering media, and bellicose resolutions passed by factionalized self-appointed committees (who denounced faction). It was not antislavery rhetoric that became more strident that year, but anti-abolitionist. This is not to say that I think slavery was "an ersatz issue demogogically agitated by calculating politicians," Grimsted's justifiably dismissive way of characterizing scholarship that does not take abolitionism seriously (13). What, then, is the relation between rhetoric and reality? Or, more accurately, between discourse and slavery? It was an economic, political, lived, and, eventually, military fact. But, each way in which it was a fact was, ultimately, understood discursively, and, in many ways, constructed discursively. Those ways were not always the same—I am not saying that slavery was purely a discursive construct. In fact, I think that one problem with much scholarship on slavery and the slavery debate is that it tends to treat the slavery debate as a consequence of economics *or* politics. James Huston, in his impressively argued book, says that, had slaves been worth less than they were, slavers would not have been "so hypersensitive to attacks" (65): "At the root of the controversy over slavery was the wealth invested in slavery. Remove the wealth, and the controversy, like a Cheshire cat, fades away with a knowing grin" (66). But, what this ignores is that the economics of slavery were ideologically unacceptable. Slavery was dependent on expansion because the wealth of slavers depended upon the slave trade. Had slavery been a purely economic issue—had slavers not been ideologically determined to obscure their financial dependence on the slave trade—then proslavery rhetors could have debated slavery and its consequences without feeling their self-image threatened. Had it been purely an imaginative construct, then expansion—the source of proslavery rhetors' greatest political problems—would not have been necessary. The political and rhetorical log-jam into which proslavery rhetors put themselves was created by the ways that the economics, ideology, and rhetoric were interwoven. As Mark Longaker elegantly puts it (although about another aspect of antebellum culture entirely), the "emphasis on cultural and political institutions should not lead us to imagine economic variables as similar or subordinate to elements like religion, education, or rhetorical practice. Rather, economic institutions—though identifiably removed and though developing somewhat independently of cultural institutions—get articulated in interesting and productive ways to and in discursive formations" (xvi). Slavery was a discursive and ideological construct, as in the often capitalized hypotheticals that people pro- and antislavery rhetoric—the Happy Slave, the Woman, the Slave owner, the sneering overseer, the cunning abolitionist. The relation between this discourse and reality is very hard to describe. There may have been happy slaves, cunning abolitionists (John Brown comes to mind),[9] some overseer may have sneered, and there were women and people who "owned" slaves. In the case of the cunning abolitionist, the rhetoric may have created the reality; in the case of the others, the rhetoric and reality were disconnected (or only randomly connected). In some situations, the rhetoric did correspond to reality, but the wrong one. What I mean is that proslavery rhetors like Duff Green accused others of doing what he was doing (such as engaging in alarmist sectionalism, being fanatical); these accusations were not true of the people whom he accused, but they were true. Proslavery rhetors regularly (and quite successfully) projected their actions onto their opponents.

In some ways, then, the rhetoric was the opposite of reality, but the assertions (that abolition was impossible without race war, for instance) were repeated so often that they came to construct a kind of reality. Inaccurate as a description (or prediction) of history, they were, however, of profound significance, serving as the premise for actions that constituted brute (and sometimes brutal) facts. In other words, like Ayers, Cooper, Freehling, Ratner, Stampp, and others, I am arguing that the Civil War was not economically, militarily, or even politically inevitable, but was the consequence of rhetoric. Rhetoric, instead of opening up options, served to shut them down. Unlike some of these historians, however, I am not arguing that "both sides" were at fault. This was not a case of evenly matched irrationality, or two sides making a fight, or paralleled fanaticism. As in various other cases, the tendency to muddle "fairness" with blaming both parties misleads us. While I think the most useful ways of describing the conflict involve multiple valances (such as the distinction between those who were opposed to slavery in the slave states versus those who were opposed to its spreading), one must, at least, describe three sides in this debate: the oppressors, the resisters, and the compromisers. To hold the resisters responsible for the behavior of the oppressors is to rationalize the oppression. Whether, or how much, the compromisers should be held responsible is something I still don't know.

I would argue that Ayers's formulation of the relationship is accurate: "The Civil War was caused neither by the mere existence of slavery nor by the twists and turns of politics, however, but rather by catalysts that emerged in the two or three decades before the war began" (238). Proslavery rhetoric scapegoated abolitionists, and that scapegoating was politically useful, but it was also tragically consequential. Proslavery rhetors succeeded in creating certain consensual understandings of slaves, slavery, race, and abolition. Abolitionists did not promote race war or call for insurrection, and they certainly engaged in rhetoric less personally insulting and irrational than the proslavery rhetors, yet a consensus was created that they behaved badly, thereby provoking slavers who had to defend themselves. The vague hope that a nicer abolitionism would have prevented war is part and parcel of the long tradition of demonizing open conflict, putting the responsibility for conflict on the dissenters who call attention to the injustice, rather than on the people who protect and promote the unjust system. As long as the oppression is grounded in consensus, the conflict will seem to arise the moment someone complains. That the consensus itself was entrenched in conflict is hidden by the curtain of vague hopes about civil social change. The consensus that was achieved by proslavery rhetors was not just about slavery, nor even just about race. It was about manhood, and authority, and education, and political action. It was about authoritarianism, about an authoritarian political and legal structure, and a public discourse of epideictic and war. The extent to which proslavery rhetors succeeded at generating a consensus that the slavery debate was an issue of southern manhood and ingroup loyalty is the extent to which they, and not abolitionists, made war inevitable.

Notes

Introduction

1. The metaphor of "flood" is also used by Peterson (257), Niven (206), Miller (102), and Wyatt-Brown ("The Abolitionists' Postal Campaign" [227]).

2. Somewhat confusingly, Faust also notes that proslavery writings predate Garrisonian abolitionism (see *Ideology of Slavery* 2–3). Similarly, Snay, just two paragraphs after the above quote, notes that "among Southern clergymen and denominational groups, proslavery emerged far earlier than the 1830s" (20). Similarly, Tise's own evidence complicates this narrative: he also says that the proslavery literature began appearing in late 1834 (309); i.e., one year before the pamphlet controversy. I would suggest that scholars invoke the "abolitionists provoked defenses of slavery" story even when their own evidence disproves it because the narrative (cultural conflict is caused by inadequate civility on the part of dissenters) is so deep as to be an almost dead metaphor: people don't necessarily realize that we are using metaphors that imply a causal argument (such as "provoke").

3. The other narrative, that David Blight has traced so elegantly, is one that buries the racial and slavery conflict altogether. That version, especially popular in the first half of the twentieth century, describes the Civil War as the inevitable conflict of "cavalier" versus "roundhead" cultures, or of economic cultures. It is striking to me that the implicit metaphor for North-South relations in the 1830s was spousal (with much posturing over who had to play the submissive wife) whereas the material that Blight discusses emphasizes a brotherly relation.

4. A topic I have not been able to pursue in this project is the notion of a shift in abolitionist rhetoric. It is a myth; there was no shift. Garrison's rhetoric was no more strident than eighteenth-century abolitionist tracts had been, nor was his rhetoric any more fervent than that of colonizationists or temperance advocates. Throughout his lifetime, he was not the most radical abolitionist (see Harrold). He was certainly no more hyperbolic or vehement than Calhoun or Jackson or the majority of antebellum rhetors. (As I will argue, it was an age of high hyperbole.) His abandonment of colo-

nization was a change, as was his call for immediate emancipation and full citizenship for African Americans. So, he shifted from a kind of "abolition" that preserved white supremacy to one that threatened it; his rhetoric didn't change, but his policies did.

5. For this discussion of separately published proslavery texts, it should always be understood as having a caveat that I have included what I have been able to find. My intention is to indicate trends, so, although I give numbers, I would not want to be understood as implicitly claiming to have made a thorough quantitative study of proslavery publications from 1800 to 1840. I have relied heavily on Larry Tise, the Samuel May Anti-Slavery Collection at the Cornell Library, the microfiche series produced by the Negro Universities Press, and OCLC WorldCat. I have restricted the search to texts published on their own (as opposed to magazine or newspaper articles). But, I should be clear that Tise mentions several texts that I was unable to locate (such as Thomas Cooper's *Crisis,* about which there appears to be some confusion regarding the title), so I have not included them. I have also restricted the discussion to texts that actively defend slavery: if the question is whether abolitionists provoked slavers, then it seems to me that things like catechisms for slaves are not relevant texts, as none of the ones I've read defended slavery. As Janet Cornelius argues, "The content of the catechisms emphasized salvation, not subordination, though most did include lengthy sections on duties of slaves to masters" (47).

6. The vehemence and alarmism prevalent in 1830s public discourse means that rhetors relied heavily on italics, capitalization, and other forms of emphasis. It's so common that I've not noted when the emphasis is in original in the quotes, only when I've added emphasis.

7. Although false, and obviously false, this notion that African Americans were not harmed by working in the swamps was the premise for many proslavery arguments. Daniel Kilbride has argued that it was one of two premises for Thomas Cooper's utilitarian proslavery defense (479).

8. I have struggled with this term. In my attempt to persuade scholars of the antebellum era that rhetoricians have much to offer this conversation, I have tried to avoid Greek terms. But, two terms in particular are unavoidable: topoi (or topos) and stasis. By topoi (the plural of topos) I mean nothing more sophisticated than what Aristotle was describing in *Rhetoric:* the recurrent ways that people tend to argue on a subject (such as that we must go to war in self-defense). Because they are so recurrent, argumentative cliché is also an apt term, but that term implies a criticism not intended; sometimes a way of argument becomes a cliché because it is so sensible (as in the self-defense argument); sometimes because it is repeated so often that people mistakenly think it has been proven (as in the connection between insurrection and exposure to abolitionist rhetoric). The term "stasis" is sometimes used by rhetoricians in fairly complicated ways; I simply mean the hinge of an argument—the place that two (or more) positions disagree. When rhetors succeed in shifting the stasis, it can be helpful. For instance, if two people disagree about policy toward Iraq *because* they disagree about why Vietnam ended as it did, shifting the stasis from Iraq to Vietnam could be helpful. But, if the stasis shifted because one person wanted to get it away from their

weak ground, then it is what a dear friend used to call rhetorical hand-waving—much like a magician distracts the viewer from the hand performing the trick by calling attention to the other hand.

9. Tise characterizes Dwight's work as defending slavery (45), but Dwight's descriptions of the slave ships in Liverpool and slave whipping in British colonies are clearly antislavery. Similarly, Tise says that James Kirke Paulding's *Letters from the South* (1817) is a "two-volume defense of slavery and the South" (46). While the latter is accurate, the former is not. The book has several very positive passages about slavery—he describes happy slaves ("they dance with a glee to which the vivacity of French peasants is nothing" 119, see also 23–26), but he makes the odd comment that he hopes that slaves are happy, "for then I should be relieved from certain doubts about the equal distributions of Providence, that confound me not a little" (119). Paulding himself was (or would soon become) vehemently proslavery, but *Letters from the South* is not.

10. While Kingsley's text defends slavery, it is extremely critical of southern U.S. practices, and argues that such practices are *not* patriarchal; free African Americans are treated badly (12–13), there is too much reliance on fear (9), and manumission is too restricted (12). Kingsley does not blame insurrection on criticism of slavery, but on "influential preachers of the gospel" (13). In 1828, Benjamin Palmer's *A Plain and Easy Catechism, Designed Chiefly for the Benefit of Coloured Persons* was published in Charleston; while I suspect that Palmer was personally proslavery, like other catechisms, the text is neither a defense of slavery nor an attack on abolitionists. Thomas Bacon's *Sermons Addressed to Masters and Servants* (originally published in Maryland in the mid-eighteenth century, and republished by William Meade in Virginia in 1813), Benjamin Palmer's *A Plain and Easy Catechism* (1828), Thomas Colcock's *Religious Instruction of Negroes* (1832), Thomas Clay's *Detail of a Plan for the Moral Improvement of Negroes on a Plantation* (1832), and Nathaniel Bowen's *A Pastoral Letter* (1835) were, in effect, supportive of slavery, but their main point is that masters should ensure that their slaves are Christian, and hence are not defenses of slavery. It is interesting that, even while openly supportive of slavery, they were not necessarily supportive enough for some people—Seabrook calls Clay's plan "Tappanist" (*Essay* 24).

11. Another newspaper series, S. Pye's *Essay on Negro Emancipation,* was published as a book in 1832 by A. Spooner. While actually antislavery—he says, in fact, that emancipation and enfranchisement of African Americans is "laudable" (3), and that "there can be no doubt that the Ethiopian slaves in the United States of America, black though they are, are as well entitled to their liberty as the Caucasion slaves at Algiers" (23)—it is an example of the kind of pseudoscientific racialism that would later become central to proslavery rhetoric (see especially his argument that the shape of Africans' heads signifies weak mental abilities, 11–22). Colfax uses the same science (and some of the same sources) to argue for slavery.

12. Tise mentions William Meade, who wrote *Pastoral Letter* (1834), which was proslavery in effect, but not a defense of slavery; like his earlier framing and reprinting of Bacon's sermons, it was intended to persuade masters to evangelize slaves. Tise also discusses David Reese, author of *A Brief Review of the First Annual Meeting* (1834) and

Letters to the Honorable (1835) as proslavery, but both were antislavery. The confusion arises because they were also both vehemently anti-abolitionist (Reese defended colonization). In the course of attacking abolitionists, he used the same topoi as proslavery rhetors in many cases—they are fanatics, they will do more harm than good, they instigate violence.

13. Miller was primarily a regional publisher; his best-known journals were *Southern Agriculturist, The Southern Review* (it operated for four years, and was not related to the one begun in 1935), and *The Gospel Messenger* (later *The Charleston Gospel Messenger*).

14. It seems to me that there is a shift in emphasis. The amalgamation slur (that abolitionists advocate and practice amalgamation) is not always mentioned in the earlier texts (but is ubiquitous in later texts) and there is more reliance on the "necessary evil" (slavery is awful but there is nothing we can do about it) while less reliance on the "positive good" (slaves, slavers, and the U.S. actively benefit from slavery) in the earlier texts more than in later ones.

Chapter 1

1. That is not to say that the relation between rhetoric and slavery has been ignored. There have been studies concerning the rhetorical practice on both sides of the slavery argument (e.g., Ericson), on the abolitionist rhetors (e.g., Bacon, Browne, Darsey, Hinks, Kraditor, Mayer) and on proslavery (e.g., Faust, Finkelman, Tise). In addition, books not specifically about the rhetoric of slavery and antislavery, but about antebellum southern culture in general, often discuss at length southern attitudes toward rhetoric (Braden, Cash, Greenberg, Tate). And several histories of the era or specific controversies have a rhetorical emphasis (e.g., Cooper, Dew, W. L. Miller). Instead, my position is that slavery has not been sufficiently studied in terms of what it means for the theories of public discourse that implicitly or explicitly call for a return to a more agonistic and neoclassical rhetoric (Arendt, especially *The Human Condition;* Booth, Burke, Clark and Halloran, Kastely, Mouffe, Roberts-Miller, Sloane, Walzer).

This issue is of particular importance because so many histories of rhetoric (both as a pedagogy and public practice) idolize the antebellum era. Advocates of civic-republican models of democracy (such as Gordon Wood), of neoclassical writing pedagogy (such as Thomas Miller), and of agonistic public discourse (such as Kenneth Cmiel) describe the early part of the nineteenth century as a high point from which we have fallen. Mark Longaker has aptly called such narratives "Edenic": "Typically this golden age precedes a fall, sometimes into belletrism, sometimes into liberal individualism, sometimes into formalism" (xii). Longaker's book elegantly argues that the histories we tell in such narratives are inaccurate because they are oversimplified (see especially his conclusion); therefore, simply reinstituting a more civically oriented pedagogy in rhetoric classes will not magically transport us back to more active civic rhetoric.

2. Merril Christophersen describes the typical speech education for boys of the South Carolina planter class: "From the outset [. . .] speech training was a natural part

of family life. It continued in the elementary schools, with the student reciting aloud, first in English, and then [. . .] at about the age of nine, in Latin, and later in Greek, the well-known speeches of the great orators, past and present [. . .] Speaking, writing, and criticism, therefore, were complementary elements of the education which developed men well able to express themselves by the time of maturity. As they matured the young gentlemen became eloquent, better able to argue public questions persuasively" (74–75, see also Cash 51–52, Bruce 179–80).

3. Fehrenbacher has recently argued that this narrative is wrong, and that the actual record shows little or no bargaining over the slavery issue. He says that the main issue was taxation, not whether slaves counted, and that framers of the Constitution simply followed the practice already set out in the Articles of Confederation. While he disagrees with the origins of the clause, he does not dispute the power it gave slave states.

4. In *The Slave Power Conspiracy and the Paranoid Style,* David Brion Davis used this faith in a "slave power" as evidence of the widespread conspiracy thinking in the antebellum era. I partially agree with Davis's argument. People did misperceive the "slave power" insofar as they imagined it as a conspiracy with secret meetings and whispered agreements, but the perception was accurate in that there was a concatenation of behaviors that served to strengthen the political and economic power of slavers.

5. Michael Johnson has argued that the entire rebellion plot was fabricated. See the debate in *William and Mary Quarterly,* "The Making of a Slave Conspiracy, Part I" (3rd Ser., Vol. 58, No. 4, Oct., 2001, pages 913–76) and Part II (Vol. 59, No. 1, Jan., 2002, pages 135–202). For more discussion of the topos that abolitionists cause slave insurrection, see Mason 30; Greenberg *Masters and Statesmen* 99; W. L. Miller 67–68; David Lindsey 235; Dillon 49–50.

6. Hofstadter has said that anti-Catholicism has always been the pornography of the Puritan, and it seems to me that black men marrying white women has always been the pornography of the racists (see especially Drayton 156). Equally pornographic are the fantasies of servile insurrection that emphasize the humiliation of white men and the raping of white women (Drayton has an especially strange description of a slave auction of white women that is supposed to have happened in Saint Dominque, see all of chapter 21). These descriptions of what *would* happen to white men and women are descriptions of what *did* happen to African American men and women under slavery—rape, slave auctions, the men being forced to watch their wives and children beaten, and so on. I'm not sure whether these descriptions should be understood purely and simply as defensive projection or as a kind of hypothetical rationalization of that behavior (slave auctions and so on are justified as preemptive revenge for what the African Americans would do if they had the chance).

7. But, since Walker advocated more resistance than was considered acceptable to white supremacists, and since he did advocate self-defense, he could (like Malcolm X one hundred years later) be characterized as advocating violence. This line of argument—black men have the right to self-defense—is always taken as advocating violence. This is, therefore, a good example of a position that cannot be perceived as

"civil" by people whose sense of identity is tied to denying identity to an outgroup: there was (and in many communities, still is) no "civil" way to advocate African American self-defense.

8. The Nullification Crisis arose out of conflict over the protective tariffs of the 1820s and especially 1828. "Nullifiers" or "State Rights" (sometimes "States' Rights") party members argued that a state has the right to nullify federal laws the state deems unconstitutional. William Freehling (*Prelude*) has persuasively argued that nullification was primarily an issue because of anxiety about federal emancipation schemes. I am not here referring to Yeadon's use of the term, as he was not a nullifier; that is, he was not a member of the State Rights Party, and was editor of the Unionist *Charleston Courier.*

9. Charles Farley says, "Circumstances alter cases—and the thing which to-day is sin, becomes at some future time virtue. Slavery might be a sin in the sixteenth century in this country, and its existence a moral obligation in the 19th" (10).

10. See also his discussion of the "vehement" style: "This always implies strength. [. . .] It has a peculiar ardour; it is a glowing style; the language of a man, whose imagination and passions are heated, and strongly affected by what he writes; who is therefore negligent of lesser graces, but pours himself forth with a rapidity and fullness of a torrent. It belongs to the higher kinds of oratory" (159), especially Demosthenes.

Chapter 2

1. Scott scholars generally insist that Scott was critical of the Romantic ideology (see, for instance, Andrew Hook's introduction to the 1985 Penguin edition), but that was not how he was most commonly read in the United States. What may have made his form of romanticism so attractive to southerners is that, "Where romanticism is liberal, forward-looking, politically progressive, Scott is by nature and conviction deeply conservative" (Hook 13).

2. Yet another terminological struggle involves what to call the non-African Americans. "White" did not have quite the same meaning then as it does now, as it meant primarily Protestants of Anglo-Saxon descent; Orlando Patterson's "Euro American" is more accurate, but distinctly clunky, so I have settled for "white." I have tried to use "Amerindian" when I mean actual Native Americans, but "Indians" when referring to the imaginative construct in authors like Bird.

3. Both of them, it should be noted, explain the fatalism in terms of forces external to southerners, and do not acknowledge the role that slavery had in creating those supposedly external forces; Faust might have, but does not, mention that the soil was depleted by agricultural practices.

4. When Hammond was exposed for having molested his teenage nieces, his diary entry blamed the girls for being seductive (*Secret and Sacred* 173).

5. Fisk's quote raises an issue I have not been able to explore as fully as I would have liked: the role that anti-Catholicism played in anti-abolitionism. As early as the eighteenth century, slavers expressed anxiety about African American churches, and

not without reason: they were often expressions and sources of African American autonomy and resistance. To acknowledge that they were legitimate churches, or that the sermons were grounded in scripture, would have implied acknowledging that Protestant Christianity was not necessarily proslavery—an impossible admission. Hence, proslavery rhetors tossed out accusations of Catholicism, voodooism, or both.

6. For more on this contradiction in regard to breaking up families, see Freehling, *Road to Disunion* 70–73; Young 234. For Genovese's more recent stand on the issue of profitability, see *Mind of the Master Class,* especially 97–98 and 110.

7. Many scholars of southern history emphasize the importance of the mythic identification of the South with the Cavaliers, and the North with the Roundheads (see especially Genovese and Fox-Genovese 92–95). It is in that light that I think one should read Simms's portrayal of the Puritan in *Yemassee,* not, as Tate argues, as a condemnation of rigidity in religion. The adjectives applied to the Puritan minister, and Puritans generally, which Tate quotes, are all terms connoting abolitionists: bigot, fanatic, hypocrite (205–8).

8. The syntax makes the quote somewhat confusing. He is saying that he, personally, rarely punishes slaves, but instead makes his driver do it. His reason is that he does not want his slaves to think he enjoys punishing them, an idea to which slaves are prone.

9. Francis Philpot argues that accusations of slave owner brutality comes from northerners' witnessing an overseer punishing a slave (in "nine cases out of ten," Philpot says, the owner doesn't know that they are being punished). The owner of slaves, however, should not try to improve his knowledge of the actual punishment of slaves by listening to slaves, "otherwise he would be eternally run down with news of ill-treatment" (22).

10. That slaves (and Africans generally) were inherently lazy was a cliché in proslavery rhetoric. Because of their laziness, they had to be punished, they could not handle freedom, and so on. Yet, proslavery rhetors sometimes mentioned that slaves routinely worked their own crops past their "daily labour" (that is, what the master required they do, see Seabrook, *Essay,* especially 11, and Drayton's previously quoted argument that slaves were allowed to keep their own property), without noticing that this behavior contradicted their supposedly lazy natures. Such contradictions happened in the same texts, as when Seabrook, having said one of the best punishments is preventing slaves from having time to do their own labor, says that "the black man will not voluntarily labor" (28).

Chapter 3

1. One could put this kind of rhetoric even earlier: Greenberg (*Masters and Statesmen*) discusses the use of the "they are making slaves of us" rhetoric in the Revolution; he refers to the anti-British "hysteria" in which southern Federalists and Republicans engaged in 1807 (when the *Chesapeake* was boarded). The cliché of kissing the rod was used by Thomas Jefferson in a November 29, 1775, letter to John Randolph, in which

he says, the colonists must "drub [the British] soundly before the sceptered tyrant will know we are not mere brutes, to crouch under his hand and kiss the rod with which he deigns to scourge us."

2. This threat, it seems to me, was most likely to come from South Carolina rhetors, but was not limited to them (even as early as the 1830s). Mason quotes from a Georgia slaver's 1819 letter to the *National Intelligencer* that threatens "fierce and bloody strife" over congressional support of the American Colonization Society (124).

3. I have been unable to find any explanation as to why they were asked to report on that issue; this was before the AAS was founded, and the major abolitionist organizations did not advocate federal intervention in the conditions of slaves (or free African Americans) in the slave states until the 1840s.

4. *Workingman's Advocate* was antislavery, and introduced the selection from the *Wilmington Reporter* by referring to the "alleged attempted insurrection" and advising that executions without trial will "make men submit to being enslaved, and men who receive no mercy from their enemies will show none when they get the upper hand."

5. This emphasis on feelings was not peculiar to the slavery debate. The second sentence of Thomas Cooper's essay defending nullification is: "My mind has been harassed with anxious thoughts relating to the present situation of our State" ("Preface"). Cooper says that South Carolina has protested against tariffs "with exemplary patience, under anxious hopes of the return of just feelings" (12).

6. I am not endorsing the rational-irrational split (in fact, I think the tendency to think in terms of that split is precisely what encourages people to conflate the feeling of certainty with the assertion about which they have that feeling). It is, of course, the logic behind dueling. Dueling does not settle whether a statement is an accurate description of reality, but it does prove that a person has considerable conviction about the statement. A duelist "proves" the assertion by being willing to die for it.

7. I think this is why Fabian reverses the chronology of events—many sources from the era did so.

8. Stone felt his remarks had been misrepresented, in that he had been made to seem abolitionist, and the *Telegraph* published his clarification on January 28.

9. It's interesting that this strategy of his, attempting to please all sides, simply enabled both sides to find points on which he could be attacked. Essentially, Van Buren fell victim to the process that Chaim Perelman describes regarding orienting rhetoric to "particular" audiences.

10. The accusation of northern sectionalism was used to rationalize the open advocacy of southern sectionalism on April 25 in "For the Presidency—Hugh L. White, of Tennessee."

11. The article does reprint a passage from an un-named "Collar" paper that says that Van Buren was among those who voted for striking the word "white" from the voter qualifications. There is no mention (in that article or the *Telegraph*) of a Van Buren move to disenfranchise African Americans *de facto* through a poll tax. This same issue of the *Telegraph* has an article, "Mr. Van Buren and the Roman Catholics," which condemns Van Buren for using the Catholics for political purposes.

12. I like this passage, as it is similar to the situation Wayne Booth describes in *Modern Dogma and the Rhetoric of Assent,* when opponents had so little common ground they simply reprinted one another's statements as obviously wrong. It seems to me that the sentiment Green is rejecting is a reasonable one, and turned out to be true: slave states destroyed the Union when they seceded. The point is that abolitionists were damned regardless of what they did: if they "provoked" the South into seceding, they were at fault; if they advocated secession from the South, they were at fault.

13. That last sentence has a significant slip: a free negro is, by definition, a free man. The author does not say, "a free negro is put on an equality with a free white man." The distinction the author assumes demonstrates the racial basis of citizenship for many Americans.

14. Coit defends Calhoun's use of slavery to promote southern sectionalism as forced on him by the North (see especially 306).

15. Mark M. Smith has elegantly argued for the importance of senses in the construction of race. The fantasy that blacks inherently smelled worse than whites, Smith shows, is as old as the colonial era, important throughout the slavery debate, and still maintained considerable power in defenses of segregation (*How Race Is Made: Slavery, Segregation, and the Senses*). Similarly, the amalgamation charge (although generally in the context of African American men and white women) was, according to Jane Dailey, crucial in twentieth-century churches' arguments over segregation.

16. My inference is that this call for anti-abolitionist meetings was, like earlier and unsuccessful calls for nullifying conventions, intended to provide a platform for various nullifier and pro-Calhoun rhetors to advocate unification under their banner. What appears to have happened with this meeting is that, aware of the strategy, Jacksonians attended and highjacked it.

17. As Greenberg has argued, this condemnation of slavery runs throughout slave state rhetoric, which he takes to be "another form of their fear of power" (87). He argues that southerners faced a logical and philosophical dilemma: sincerely committed to liberty (which was abhorrence of unchecked power) and slavery (which necessarily involved unchecked power), "they denied that their own institution was really slavery" (90). This may be a later development in proslavery thought; although some of the 1830s proslavery rhetoric made the argument that northern workers were enslaved, that topos seems to me to become more common in the 1840s and 1850s. In the 1830s, slavery was defended *qua* slavery. I would suggest that the later development was not necessarily indicative of southern constructions of liberty, but a handy argument with which to swat away the cognitive dissonance created by oppressors praising freedom. On the whole, I think proslavery rhetors demonstrate "social dominance orientation" (discussed later) which is used to describe people who consistently support policies that enhance hierarchy; they are outraged at changes to the hierarchy, especially ones that threaten their ability to attain (or maintain) a place at the top.

18. According to Faust, the same accusation was made by Hammond and Simms (*Sacred Circle* 126–27). The article goes on to accuse Calhounites of being the authors of the petitions to abolish slavery in the District of Columbia, purely in order to rouse

southerners. This rhetoric is, of course, exactly the same as the paranoid style of the anti-abolitionists: while one's opponents are motivated by vicious ambition and love of faction to engage in a devilish conspiracy, one's own party, motivated by love of country and truth, is sternly blocking their efforts.

Chapter 4

1. Davis is here describing how the paranoid style was used by abolitionists in the 1850s, at which point they had the possibility of unifying a diverse group of antislavery views. I haven't found abolitionists using it in the 1830s, perhaps because the immediate abolitionists were not as diverse as later antislavery forces were. Paranoia is necessary for rousing diverse groups that might not otherwise identify with one another; in the 1830s, abolitionism wasn't trying to be a unified group. The 1850s was also a point when antislavery had become politically powerful as a unification device, something that had not been true previously (although Mason argues that the Federalists tried to use it in the 1810s).

2. The *Charleston Mercury* editor liked the "syren song" metaphor: "The syren song of the Enquirer, that they are in a minority at the North, should not deceive the South. A minority can stir up sedition as well as a majority" (reprinted from *The Whig* August 5, 1835).

3. Were this a political history of slave states, I would need to be more precise in what were parties and what were factions. But, since the line was often blurred, especially in South Carolina, I use the terms interchangeably. Ford argues that the South Carolinian objection to faction was not grounded in philosophical principle, but was largely a consequence of the Nullification Crisis (339). Factions had been so destructive to the state that South Carolinians would forgo them; the problem is that they tried to do so by making everyone members of the same faction. Granted, that is typical of how "united we stand" rhetoric runs—it's commonly a call for unification behind one's own group.

4. Another letter on the same topic accuses the opposition of being "confederated to destroy our noblest Institution, or subject it to *sectarian Domination*" and ends with the exhortation, "Will true christians countenance this sort of thing? But enough!" (*Charleston Mercury,* August 1, 1835).

5. The article is somewhat vague concerning what it is condemning, but I infer that it refers to the North Carolina legislature's "instructing" a senator to vote a particular (pro-Jackson) way. Considering that the *Charleston Mercury* supported the practice of the test oath—which required all South Carolina elected officials to swear to be nullifiers—this is yet another example of predicting catastrophe when other parties engage in one's own political practices. Notice also that the article refers to "the mad career" of the opposition—a cliché in the anti-abolitionist rhetoric.

6. I would say that my argument is that the war was irrepressible because anti-Jacksonian rhetors tried to unify the South via anti-abolitionism. As part of that proj-

ect, they framed the slavery issue (and every other one, for that matter) as manly domination or girly submission.

7. For an example of Hammond's use of the "submission" frame for secession, see his diary entry for November 21, 1851, in which he refers to those opposed to secession as "Submissionist."

8. I want to emphasize that to say this view is particularly southern is not to say that it is peculiarly so. As will be seen in the discussion of the congressional debate, many northerners operated with the same set of options.

9. I've used the term "naïve realism," rather than a foundationalism (the term frequently used in rhetoric) because I think it is more helpful. If one presses hard enough, all political theories, perhaps all theories, have a foundation—that is, a set of beliefs upon which the others rest, and beyond which the inhabitants are not interested in digging (so calling some foundationalist and other anti-foundationalist is misleading). In proslavery ideology, slavery itself was the foundation.

10. Just as one hundred years later, racists would explain the civil rights movements by the myth of the "outside agitator" who made previously happy African Americans unhappy with their good situation.

Chapter 5

1. I should be clear, Drayton does not argue "in the alternative"—he does not say, "and if they didn't stay south, but moved north." Instead, each alternative is presented as *the* consequence of abolition.

2. Simms ends this paragraph, "But let us turn from this unpleasant subject" (40), which, I assume, means prostitution and sexual abuse of slave women, but it may mean the idea of racial mixing.

3. She is talking about "modern masses," which would suggest that historians like Ayers, who insist upon the "modernity" of the slave South, are correct.

4. Unionists, it seems to me, often advocated the nullification theory of state to federal relation. It seems to me that the distinction between nullifiers and unionists was not their theory of government, but their attitude toward secession.

5. Drayton was writing this text *because* slavery did not exist everywhere—the institution was under attack because an increasing number of countries were finding themselves able to do without it. Drayton's later arguments, in which he contrasts slave with free societies, logically depends upon acknowledging that slavery is not universal. So, Drayton, at some level, knew that his assertion was not true.

6. Genovese and Fox-Genovese's reference to and endorsement of Mark Noll's argument that "a stronger hermeneutic [. . . could] have provided the resources to establish the abolitionist case on traditional Christian grounds" (527) seems to me wishful thinking at best, as though a really good hermeneutic would have caused slavers to abandon slavery. Hermeneutics was neither the source of the problem nor its solution.

7. This was where the abolitionists applied a different hermeneutic. It is often forgotten that many, if not all, the early white abolitionists had been in the temperance movement, and the argument for temperance (meaning abstinence) assumes the same method of interpretation. Scripture has people drinking wine, and it condemns drunkenness, yet temperance advocates took the latter as forbidding the former. Their argument—generally conveyed narratively—was that all drinking is drunkenness (or leads to it), that the only temperance of which humans are capable is abstinence. Similarly, abolitionists took condemnations of cruelty to slaves as a condemnation of slave owning (although there are slave owners in the scripture) because it necessarily leads to abuse.

8. Of course, the race argument operated against them, unless referring to the claimed racial descent from the Jews. Dalcho has argued that the stories of Sodom and Gomorrah, the Arabic version of Genesis, and the Muslim historian Abulfaragi show that descendants of Ham were racially bound to the race of Jews, then mentions that the Jews, as a nation, were dispersed. He says that the curse of servitude was never lifted, but never shows why it was transferred (19).

9. Mississippi governor and senator Theodore Bilbo, in his 1948 book arguing for transporting African Americans "back" to Africa, simply refers to scripture telling us there are three races—almost certainly a reference to Genesis 9, and I remember "Noah's curse" was frequently cited during the civil rights movement to justify segregation. Haynes's point, in fact, is that the passage became even more important after emancipation than it had been before.

10. Nor is this the only way to read scripture. Some methods of reading privilege New over Old Testament (that is, if Old and New Testament texts conflict, the latter is understood to supersede the former); some privilege Gospel texts over all; some privilege what is seen as the message of the Gospel (which, for Friends, was to love thy God and neighbor), interpreting texts in terms of how they further explicate that basic message.

11. Paulding's use of the Garden of Eden metaphor is surely unreflected. Not only is the notion that slavery is Edenic more than a little troubling, the analogy works against him—in Christian theology, it is presumed that the tree of knowledge provided true knowledge, and that eating of it was predestined by God, so that humans could rise to greater glory. So, were we to take the metaphor seriously, abolitionists provide the true knowledge to slaves of their state, and that knowledge, while it has its costs, will lead to salvation. I doubt that's what Paulding wanted his readers to infer.

12. Research in social psychology emphasizes that everyone possesses this tendency to some extent—we always see ourselves as more complicated, nuanced, and harder to understand than others. But, people in positions of privilege are more prone to it than others (for a particularly interesting study of this phenomenon, see Galinsky et al.).

13. Greenberg aptly describes southern defenses of what he calls virtual versus actual representation (*Masters and Statesmen,* chapter 4). I would suggest it has to do with their greater faith in their asymmetric insight.

14. In at least one instance, a proslavery rhetor was right in his prediction of the consequence of emancipation. Harper says, the next thing abolitionists will be asking for is equality of women (83–84), and, in fact, it was.

15. I've tried very hard to take proslavery ideology seriously as a philosophy, but here I am stumped. This only makes sense if one sees it as a step removed from the Jeremiad tradition. In that tradition, a prophet warns the people that we have been God's people up until now, and he has protected us until now, but our current waywardness is threatening that status with God—he may stop protecting us. This notion of history, however, is slightly different, and at least mildly Manichean—not in the sense of being divided among good and evil, but in the sense of seeing God as no more powerful than the Devil (a heresy in Christian theology).

I think there is a possibility of taking proslavery ideology too seriously as a philosophy and ignoring the economics of the situation. Thus, when Tate argues that "southern conservatives simply tried to preserve a measure of tradition within a liberal state" (3), he is ignoring that the tradition, and the only tradition, they were trying to maintain was slavery. When the institution of slavery came into conflict with any other system or ideology (free speech, property rights, states' rights, scriptural literalism), it was the other system or ideology that gave. Or, in the words of Whitemarsh Seabrook, "As slavery exists in South Carolina, the actions of the citizen should rigidly conform to that state of things" (*Essay* 6).

16. Genovese and Fox-Genovese say that southerners "turned to history as well as religion for moral guidance for nations and for individuals" (125), but I would suggest they turned to it for justification, not guidance.

17. In addition, as Jacqueline Bacon has discussed at length, abolitionist rhetors actively avoided philosophizing. She has argued, persuasively, that this evasion was the result of a social sense that women and minorities did not have the right to engage in abstract argumentation. I am suggesting that, in addition, Garrison's preference for the specific represented a different epistemology.

18. Mason notes that the race war argument came up as early as during the congressional debate over banning the slave trade (18).

19. Laurie Green's *Battling the Plantation Mentality* emphasizes the importance that manhood and womanhood had in twentieth-century civil rights movements; she says of the Memphis sanitation workers (whose motto was "I AM A MAN") and their supporters, "In rejecting the 'plantation mentality,' they staked a claim to equal humanity—to manhood and womanhood" (293).

20. Drayton's sneers about northern hierarchy are not condemnation of hierarchy, but of the kind of hierarchy—one of money—while, one infers, he imagines (or his audience is willing to imagine) southern hierarchy is based on some other quality. This may be one of the instances, noted in the earlier chapter, of southerners priding themselves on not caring about money. In that case, though, Drayton's careful and detailed economic argument concerning the costs of abolition are one more indication of the ways that southerners could be very practical, while eschewing a practical ethos.

21. The Alabama memorial regarding the abolitionists passed by the General Assembly on January 9, 1836, says, "We were born in a land of domestic slavery;—like our liberties it descended from our fathers: we were innocent of its introduction."

Chapter 6

1. Mason comments that slavery came up in regard to almost every issue on a national level as well. He interprets its omnipresence as a sign of its rhetorical utility rather than political relevance, but utility and relevance aren't mutually exclusive. It may be that slave politicians genuinely perceived slavery as constantly at stake, and it may be that it was rhetorically useful because it was involved in every issue. When I began this project, I had the naïve idea that I would compare 1835 congressional deliberation over a slavery-related issue to deliberation over an issue not related to slavery; after reading through the 1835–36 *Globe,* I gave up because I couldn't find an example of the latter.

2. William Wiethoff, in *Crafting the Overseer's Image,* describes in some detail the legal ambivalence and ambiguity concerning slave literacy, access to weapons and liquor, and assembly (see especially 38–50).

3. Another striking instance of this move was the condemnation of abolitionists like Garrison and Thompson for not having traveled to the South (see, for instance, Sullivan 11–12) coupled with statements that they would be killed if they did so. Proslavery rhetors thereby set up a condition of disproof that cannot be met—the claim is that such abolitionists would change their minds if they saw what slavery was really like, coupled with threats that prevent them from doing so.

4. The 1836 Kentucky resolutions threaten to resist "any attempt on the part of the federal government to interfere with [slavery in Kentucky] in any manner" (*Communication from the Governor, Transmitting Resolutions from the Legislature of Kentucky on the Subject of Abolition Societies* 5, the same point made in the fifth resolution of the 1835 South Carolina legislative resolutions). This is the implication of the first of the Virginia resolutions (that there was a move afoot to get federally imposed emancipation). This set of resolutions twice asserts that Congress has no right to ban slavery from the territories, showing that position had some adherents as early as 1836.

5. Morris's point is that southerners were willing to permit considerable tampering with "property" rights by the state, despite their accusing abolitionists of interfering with private property (see also Wiethoff, *The Insolent Slave,* especially 37). I would suggest that accusation be seen as defensive projection—they made the accusation *because* they themselves did not respect property rights. Of course, the laws were not consistently enforced, but the inconsistent enforcement permitted terroristic control (Wiethoff has some interesting examples of this, especially regarding literacy and insubordination, in *Constructing the Image of the Overseer* and *The Insolent Slave*).

6. It is interesting that while the first part is a concept shared by positive and natural law, the second is not—that there might be limits to one's rights does not necessarily mean that they are connected to duties. This point complicates David Eric-

son's argument that proslavery and antislavery rhetors both appealed to liberal ideas. He defines liberal ideas as "a general set of ideas that appeal to personal freedom, equal worth, government by consent, and private ownership of property as core human values" (14). In addition to arguing that these ideas were not particularly important in proslavery rhetoric, I take issue with the basic definition. Ericson has left out three crucial pieces in most definitions of liberal philosophy: equality before the law, universal human rights, and rational public discourse (see Roberts-Miller, *Deliberate Conflict* 18–24). On the contrary, I am saying that proslavery rhetors did not see these as core *human* values, but as privileges which white men possessed to a greater degree than others. Thus, while Ericson is correct that proslavery rhetors often argued from consequences, the negative consequences which they predicted almost exclusively involved the breaking down of social hierarchy. That breakdown necessarily constituted a breakdown of social order only because it threatened to displace *their* position in the hierarchy.

7. David March attributes the 1837 law to that perception, and the abolition scare in St. Louis (822); the same explanation given by Benjamin Merkel (246). I think this explanation is more plausible than Savage's, but I also think that the role of the Murrell "conspiracy" shouldn't be underestimated.

8. Stealing is in quotes because the whole idea of slaves' "stealing" is problematic. In a system which depends on stealing—slavery is the theft of people and their labor—it seems odd to characterize the victims of that more substantial theft as stealing anything.

9. The same kind of law was passed for Augusta on December 22, 1829. This was part of the 1799 Mississippi law, North Carolina's 1794 "An Act to prevent the owners of slaves from hiring to them their time to take compensation," and South Carolina's 1822 "An Act for the better regulation and government of free negroes and persons of colour, and for other purposes."

10. The *Niles' Weekly Register* article refers to the *Raleigh Register* of December 9, 1830, but that paper does not mention the secret session, nor any of the other contextual information.

11. The governor's comment that "it is fruitless to complain," like Judge Ruffin's comment in *State v. Mann* that "it is useless, however, to complain of things inherent in our political state," typifies how the rhetoric of doom was applied to the institution of slavery.

12. Ashe's history was published in the early part of the twentieth century. It is striking to me that more recent histories don't discuss these laws, nor do they mention the various panics. To find secondary material on them, I had to rely on fairly old histories. Samuel Ashe and Guion Griffis Johnson are racist and defensive of slavery; this short passage from Ashe, for instance, demonstrates the Anglophobia that Greenberg has argued was so important in antebellum southern culture, as well as a muddled history that shifts the blame from slavery. Yet, they did talk about slave laws and insurrection. More recent histories demonstrate the problem that Loewen discusses in popular textbooks' treatment of slavery and the Civil War. While not as openly racist and pro-

slavery as textbooks used to be, there is instead a troubling kind of evasion that fails to confront the Lost Cause myth still prevalent in southern states.

13. If so, then there is an interesting double standard. For whites like Meares, that they have been pushed into action by "imperious" circumstances is an excuse; African Americans are not granted the same excuse. When slave owners have legislated their own group into certain behavior, their lack of choice is a reason to excuse and forgive them; when the same happens to the outgroup, it is even more reason to condemn them. Evasion of responsibility is a white privilege.

14. In e-mail, Mark E. Dixon informed me that the judge in *Contentnea v. Dickinson,* decided in 1826 by the Wayne County (N.C.) Superior Court and sustained in 1827 by the state supreme court, opined that Quakers should not be allowed to own slaves. Mr. Dixon cites *Toward Freedom for All* by Hiram Hilty (Richmond, Ind.: Friends United Press, 1984).

15. It seems to me that this perception of government is behind the argument that it doesn't really matter that many victims of the death penalty are innocent of the crime. When I've talked to death penalty advocates, I've been surprised by the number of people who say, "They may not have done that crime, but they weren't innocent." That the penalty is randomly applied (so that the person who actually did the killing may not get the death penalty, while the person who drove the car does), that it is disproportionately applied to poor minorities, that people may not have even committed the crime in question, does not bother such advocates because they are more concerned with getting the poor minorities to internalize coercion, and they think a more or less randomly applied death penalty is the most effective means for that end.

16. I have been struck that some people assume that government can only be grounded in coercion or blind faith. When I try to talk with such people about the power of legitimacy, I am reminded of the discussion in Abbot's *Flatland,* of someone aware of three dimensions trying to describe something to people in a two-dimensional world (or the times that people have tried to explain various musical concepts to a tone-deaf person like me). It isn't a question of stupidity, as these are not necessarily stupid people, but of attempting to appeal to experiences someone has just never had.

Chapter 7

1. This chapter and the previous consider the question: if proslavery rhetoric is epideictic, how does it function in an explicitly deliberative setting? Elsewhere, I have argued for thinking of discursive communities on a matrix. On one axis, the agonistic-irenic is the extent to which the community allows discursive conflict; on the other, the deliberative-expressive is the extent to which the community is trying to make a joint decision. The behavior of proslavery rhetors in deliberative settings—the state legislatures of the previous chapter, or the House of Representatives, as will be discussed in this chapter—suggests serious problems with that matrix, specifically my formulation of the agonist-irenic axis. Proslavery rhetors were very comfortable with conflict, perhaps too much so, yet deeply averse to settling the conflict discursively—they

were, by my previous definitions, neither irenic nor agonistic. This problem suggests that the irenic-agonistic axis needs to be imagined as the extent to which a community acknowledges *and* resolves conflict discursively, or that there should be a third axis, violence-discourse.

2. It was accepted by proslavery rhetors at the time, and seems to be accepted by many scholars today, that this was a "thin edge of the wedge" strategy on the part of many abolitionist groups. If they could get slavery abolished there, this would be the thin edge that would enable them to abolish slavery in actual states. The presumption is that the petitions were all organized by the major abolitionist organizations like the AAS. Given what various speakers say about the petitions, however, I'm skeptical. From congressional representative Slade's comments, it appears that at least some petitions explicitly distanced themselves both from abolitionists and from abolition of slavery within slave states. It seems to me quite plausible that a large number of petitioners were sincere in their statements that they thought slavery was inappropriate in the nation's capitol. It also seems to me that this was threatening to slavers, not because it was a "thin end of the wedge," but because it meant that they would have to do without slaves for whatever period of time they were in Washington; since owning slaves was their identity, going without slaves for an extended period of time would have had a very strange impact on their sense of manhood.

3. Hammond seems to be saying that a rhetor's goal, at least in regard to abolition, is to keep the idea outrageous—to keep people outraged. Whether for political purposes, or some other reason, it means a more or less conscious decision to engage in fear-mongering on the subject.

4. This would become an increasingly important point of view, crucial to the secession movement, and one of many ways that the proslavery position became more extreme as time went on.

5. Coit's rationalization of Calhoun's behavior is a good example of the kind of external attribution that enables people to rationalize embarrassing behavior on the part of members of the ingroup. Calhoun's articulation of the States' Rights philosophies contradicted his political actions in that Coit describes the first as essential and inherent, and the latter as externally necessitated (or as incidental). Coit dismisses examples of Calhoun's profound racism and full support of slavery as incidental to his essence. I would suggest, on the contrary, that the fact that he always supported racism and slavery when it conflicted with his stated philosophy implies that slavery and racism were more important to him than the philosophy.

6. But, if Benson's other (and more central to his argument) point is correct, then the gag rule was much like the anti-abolitionist newspaper controversy—abolitionists were useful as scapegoats, but the proslavery rhetors' use of them actually aided abolitionists.

7. In fact, the willingness of northern politicians to do slavers' bidding was fast becoming notorious—while there were numerous times in which southerners would demand shows of loyalty and deference, I've never run across a similar demand made by the North of the South.

8. The recorder begins this passage with the unusual editorial comment, "At length, lashing himself up to a state of high excitement, he asked" (46).

9. Actually, agitation over the Sunday mail continued until it was abolished in 1912, so this example is not a very helpful one (see Fuller).

10. Hamer, a Democrat from Ohio, also criticized emotionalism: "he did not believe that such a debate was well calculated to a calm, dispassionate, and deliberate consideration of the question" (33).

11. Then he must not have been listening when Slade spoke in favor the petition.

12. The argument concerned the post office, a topic over which Calhoun and Jackson had tangled much of the previous year. A proposal to permit federal censorship of the mail reopened that argument. Calhoun and other anti-Jacksonians did not want the topic referred to the Jacksonian-dominated Committee on the Post Office; Jacksonians did. It seems to me that they were wrangling over who would get the credit for solving the problem of abolitionists using the mail to criticize slavery.

Conclusion

1. He is almost certainly talking about the wave of laws passed after the Nat Turner rebellion that were intended to prevent slaves from that area from coming to other states and carrying news of a violent rebellion (see Dillon 84–88), yet he indicates no awareness of the motives for the law.

2. That they would benefit is one of the reasons to dismiss their plans as self-interested and evil; that the privileged do benefit, however, is not a reason to characterize them as self-interested or evil.

3. Thus, whereas Genovese and Fox-Genovese try to describe the mutual contradictions as a "balancing act," I would suggest that they were not extremes between which a person tried to balance, but instances of doublethink.

4. James Henry Hammond, in his rambling two-hour speech February 1, 1836, ostensibly on the abolition petitions has a similar argument—abolition would mean that there might be a black congressman.

5. Larry Tise points out that the characterization of abolitionists as "*visionary, fanatical, enthusiastical, ignorant, distempered,* and *designing*" goes back at least as far as 1773 (his emphasis, 29). Edwin Holland's 1822 proslavery piece blames missionaries "bearing tracts that 'excited among our Negroes such a spirit of dissatisfaction and revolt, as has, in the end, brought down upon them the vengeance of offended humanity'" (from Tise 59; he doesn't give the page number he's quoting from).

6. That antebellum rhetors, especially proslavery ones, would maintain this meaningless distinction, makes perfect sense, but it is important to notice that the distinction—the only function of which is to make slavers feel better about themselves—is still made in current scholarship. This deference to the feelings of people who feel implicated in slavery runs throughout material on slavery. Dew has noted that the citizenship question permits people to answer that the Civil War was caused by conflict over states' rights; some private schools in the South have taken to showing "both sides"

of slavery by assigning a book called *Southern Slavery as It Was* that describes slaves as happy and slavery as kindness; James Loewen has shown the degree to which textbooks evade controversies about slavery and the Civil War in order not to offend textbook adoption committees in southern states. We are still excessively worried about making defenders of slavery feel bad.

7. It seems to me that this unfortunate tendency is reflected in scholarship over slave punishment, in which scholars try to determine how much punishment there was by looking at what proslavery rhetors recommended about punishment. Since they often condemned severe punishment, they must not have done it. But, quotes from slavers about how they *feel* is not evidence as to what they *did;* I'm not even convinced it's evidence as to how they felt—it's just something they said.

8. It is also interesting that Owsley asserts that "the language of insult which the so-called fire-eaters employed, however, was not usually coarse or obscene in comparison with the abolitionists; it was urbane and restrained in a degree—but insulting" (58). This is simply not the case.

9. With Brown, the issue of rhetoric and reality is especially interesting. Evan Carton has argued that Brown's plot was largely the result of his believing proslavery rhetoric, that the slaves were a tinderbox that a cunning abolitionist might light. If so, proslavery rhetors' alarmist rant created the reality about which they were so alarmed: an abolitionist trying to start a slave rebellion.

Works Cited

Adams, Henry, Lester W. Wright Jr., and Bethany A. Lohr. "Is Homophobia Associated with Homosexual Arousal?" *Journal of Abnormal Psychology* 105, no. 3 (August 1996): 440–45.

Adams, John Quincy. *Lectures on Rhetoric and Oratory, Delivered to the Classes of Senior and Junior Sophisters in Harvard University.* 2 Vols. Cambridge: Hilliard and Metcalf, 1810.

Adelman, Janet. *The Common Liar: An Essay on Antony and Cleopatra.* New Haven: Yale University Press, 1973.

Adorno, Theodore, et al. *The Authoritarian Personality.* New York: Harper, 1950.

Altemeyer, Bob. *Right Wing Authoritarianism.* Winnipeg: University of Manitoba Press, 1981.

"An American." *Letter to the Edinburgh Reviewers; First Published in the "National Intelligencer," of November 16, 1819.* s.n., 1819.

Anonymous. *Bigotry Exposed, or A Calm Discussion of the Abolition Question. By a Constitutionalist.* New York: s.n., 1835.

Anonymous. *Negro Plot: An Account of the Late Intended Insurrection among a Portion of the Blacks of the City of Charleston, South Carolina: Published by the Authority of the Corporation of Charleston.* Boston: Joseph Ingraham, 1822.

Anonymous. *Remarks on "Slavery by William E. Channing."* Boston: J. H. Eastburn, 1836.

"Appomattox." *The Letter of Appomatox [!] to the People of Virginia: Exhibiting a Connected View of the Recent Proceedings in the House of Delegates, on the Subject of the Abolition of Slavery; and a Succinct Account of the Doctrines Broached by the Friends of Abolition, in Debate: and the Mischevious [sic] Tendency of Those Proceedings and Doctrines.* Richmond: T. W. White, 1832.

Aptheker, Herbert. *American Negro Slave Revolts.* New York: International Publishers, 1963.

Arendt, Hannah. *Eichmann in Jerusalem: A Report on the Banality of Evil.* Rev. and enl. ed. New York: Penguin Books, 1977.

———. *The Origins of Totalitarianism.* New York: Harcourt Brace Jovanovich, 1973.

Aristotle. *Rhetoric.* Trans. W. Rhys Roberts. New York: Modern Library, 1954.

Ashe, Samuel A. *History of North Carolina.* Greensboro: C. L. Van Noppen, 1908–25.

Ashworth, John. *Slavery, Capitalism, and Politics in the Antebellum Republic, Commerce and Compromise.* Vol. 1. Cambridge: Cambridge University Press, 1995.

Atherton, Lewis E. "James and Robert Aull—A Frontier Missouri Mercantile Firm." *Missouri Historical Review* 30 (1935): 3–27.

Aull, James. *Letters of James and Robert Aull.* Ed. Ralph P. Berber. Columbia: n.p., 1928. 285–86. Reprinted from the Collections of the Missouri Historical Society, 5, no. 3 (1928): 267–310.

Austin, James Trecothick. *Remarks on Dr. Channing's Slavery.* Boston: Russell, Shattuck & Co.: J. H. Eastburn, 1835.

Ayers, Edward. *What Caused the Civil War?: Reflections on the South and Southern History.* New York: W. W. Norton, 2005.

Bacon, Jacqueline. *The Humblest May Stand Forth: Rhetoric, Empowerment, and Abolition.* Columbia: University of South Carolina Press, 2002.

Bales, Kevin. *Disposable People: New Slavery in the Global Economy.* Berkeley and Los Angeles: University of California Press, 2004.

Bellinger, Edmund. *Speech on the Subject of Slavery Delivered 7th Sept'r. 1835 at a Public Meeting of the Citizens of Barnwell District, South-Carolina.* Charleston, S.C.: Dan J. Dowling, 1835.

Benson, Lee. "Secession and the 'Southern Revolutionary Nationalist Party.'" *The Causes of the Civil War.* 3rd rev. ed. New York: Simon & Schuster, 1991.

Beringer, Richard, Herman Hattaway, Archer Jones, and William Still Jr. *Elements of Confederate Defeat: Nationalism, War Aims, and Religion.* Athens: University of Georgia Press, 1988.

Berlet, Chip, and Matthew N. Lyons. *Right-Wing Populism in America: Too Close for Comfort.* New York: Guildford Press, 2000.

Bird, James Montgomery. *Nick of the Woods; A Story of the Early Settlers of Kentucky.* New York: A. L. Burton Company, n.d (1837).

Blair, Hugh. *Lectures on Rhetoric and Belles-Lettres.* Ed. Harold F. Harding. Carbondale: Southern Illinois University Press, 1965.

Bleser, Carol, ed. *Secret and Sacred: The Diaries of James Henry Hammond, a Southern Slaveholder.* Columbia: University of South Carolina Press, 1997.

Blight, David. *Race and Reunion: The Civil War in American Memory.* Cambridge, Mass.: Belknap Press of Harvard University Press, 2001.

Bohman, James. *Public Deliberation: Pluralism, Complexity, and Democracy.* Cambridge: MIT Press, 1996.

Booth, Wayne. *Modern Dogma and the Rhetoric of Assent.* Indiana: University of Notre Dame Press, 1974.

———. *The Rhetoric of Rhetoric: The Quest for Effective Communication.* Malden, Mass.: Blackwell, 2004.

Braden, Waldo. *The Oral Tradition in the South.* Baton Rouge: Louisiana State University Press, 1983.

Breedon, James. *Advice among Masters: The Ideal in Slave Management in the Old South.* Westport, CT: Greenwood Press, 1980.

Brogan, Hugh. *The Pelican History of the United States of America.* Harmondsworth, N.Y.: Penguin Books, 1986.

Browne, Stephen H. *Angelina Grimke: Rhetoric, Identity, and the Radical Imagination.* East Lansing: Michigan State University Press, 1999.

Bruce, Dickson D., Jr. *Violence and Culture in the Antebellum South.* Austin: University of Texas Press, 1979.

Burke, Kenneth. *The Philosophy of Literary Form: Studies in Symbolic Action.* 3rd ed. Berkeley and Los Angeles: University of California Press, 1973.

———. *A Rhetoric of Motives.* New York: Prentice-Hall, 1950.

Capers, Gerald M. *John C. Calhoun, Opportunist; a Reappraisal.* Gainesville: University of Florida Press, 1960.

Carmichael, Stokely. "What We Want." *New York Review of Books.* New York: New York Publishing, September 22, 1966.

Carton, Evan. *Patriotic Treason: John Brown and the Soul of America.* New York: Free Press, 2006.

Cash, W[ilbur] J. *The Mind of the South.* New York: A. A. Knopf, 1941.

Cauthen, Kenneth. *I Don't Care What the Bible Says: An Interpretation of the South.* Macon, Ga.: Mercer University Press, 2003.

Channing, William Ellery. *Slavery and Emancipation.* 3rd rev. ed. New York: Negro Universities Press, 1968.

Christophersen, Merril. "The Anti-Nullifiers." *Oratory in the Old South, 1828–1860.* Ed. Waldo W. Braden. Baton Rouge: Louisiana State University Press, 1975. 74–75.

Clark, Bennet Champ. *John Quincy Adams: "Old Man Eloquent."* Boston: Little, Brown, 1932.

Clark, Gregory, and S. Michael Halloran. *Oratorical Culture in Nineteenth-Century America: Transformations in the Theory and Practice of Rhetoric.* Evanston: Southern Illinois University Press, 1993.

Clayton, Bruce. "No Ordinary History: W. J. Cash's 'The Mind of the South.'" *The Mind of the South: Fifty Years Later.* Ed. Charles W. Eagles. Jackson: University Press of Mississippi, 1992.

Clough, Simon. *A Candid Appeal to the Citizens of the United States.* New York: A. K. Bertron, 1834.

Cmiel, Kenneth. *Democratic Eloquence: The Fight over Popular Speech in Nineteenth-Century America.* New York: Morrow, 1990.

Cobb, James. *Away down South: A History of Southern Identity.* New York: Oxford University Press, 2005.

Coit, Margaret L. *John C. Calhoun: American Portrait.* Boston: Houghton Mifflin, 1950.

Colfax, Richard. *Evidence against the Views of the Abolitionists: Consisting of Physical and Moral Proofs, of the Natural Inferiority of the Negroes.* New York: James T. Bleakley, 1833.

Cooper, Thomas. *Hints, Suggestions, and Contributions toward the Labours of a Convention.* Columbia [S.C.], 1832.

———. *Two Essays: On the Foundation of Civil Government; On the Constitution of the United States.* Columbia, S.C.: n.p., 1826.

Cooper, William J. *Liberty and Slavery: Southern Politics to 1860.* New York: A. A. Knopf, 1983.

———. *The South and the Politics of Slavery, 1828–1856.* Baton Rouge: Louisiana State University Press, 1978.

Cornelius, Janet Duisman. *"When I can read my title clear": Literacy, Slavery, and Religion in the Antebellum South.* Columbia: University of South Carolina Press, 1991.

Dailey, Jane. "Sex, Segregation, and the Sacred after *Brown.*" *Journal of American History* 91, no. 1 (June 2004).

Dalcho, Frederick. *Practical Considerations Founded on the Scriptures.* Charleston, S.C.: A. E. Miller, 1823.

Darsey, James. *The Prophetic Tradition and Radical Rhetoric in America.* New York: New York University Press, 1997.

Davenport, J. *A Chapter in the History of Abolitionism at Syracuse Together with a Glance at the Principles of Abolitionism, as Connected with Religion and Morality.* Syracuse: s.n., 1839.

Davis, David Brion. *The Slave Power Conspiracy and the Paranoid Style.* Baton Rouge: Louisiana State University Press, 1969.

Davis, William. *Look Away!: A History of the Confederate States of America.* New York: Free Press, 2002.

Degler, Carl. *The Other South: Southern Dissenters in the Nineteenth Century.* Gainesville: University Press of Florida, 2000.

de Saussure, Henry. *A Series of Numbers Addressed to the Public, on the Subject of the Slaves and Free People of Colour First Published in the South-Carolina State Gazette, in the Months of September and October, 1822.* Columbia [S.C.]: State Gazette Office, 1822.

Dew, Charles B. *Apostles of Disunion: Southern Secession Commissioners and the Causes of the Civil War.* Charlottesville: University Press of Virginia, 2001.

Dew, Thomas R. *Review of the Debate (on the Abolition of Slavery) in the Virginia Legislature, 1831–'32.* (Extract from The *Political Register,* v.2, no. 25, October 16, 1833.) Washington, D.C., 1833.

Dillon, Merton. *Slavery Attacked: Southern Slaves and Their Allies, 1619–1865.* Baton Rouge: Louisiana State University Press, 1990.

Dippie, Brian. *The Vanishing American: White Attitudes and U.S. Indian Policy.* Middletown, Conn.: Wesleyan University Press, 1982.

Doggett, Simeon. *Two Discourses on the Subject of Slavery.* Boston: Printed by M. Pratt, 1835.

Douglas, Mary. *Purity and Danger: An Analysis of the Concepts of Pollution and Taboo.* London: Ark Paperbacks-Routledge, 1989.

Douglass, Frederick. "Letter to an Abolitionist Associate." 1849. *Organizing for Social Change: A Manual for Activists in the 1990s.* Washington, D.C.: Seven Locks Press, 1991.

Drayton, John. *A View of South Carolina.* Charleston, S.C.: W. P. Young, 1802.

Drayton, William. *The South Vindicated from the Treason and Fanaticism of the Northern Abolitionists.* Philadelphia: H. Manly, 1836. New York: Negro Universities Press, 1969.

Dwight, Timothy. *Remarks on the Review.* Boston: Samuel T. Armstrong, 1815.

Ellis, Richard, and Aaron Wildavsky. "A Cultural Analysis of the Role of Abolitionists in the Coming of the Civil War." *Comparative Studies in Society and History* 32, no. 1 (January 1990): 89–116.

Ericson, David F. *The Debate over Slavery: Antislavery and Proslavery Liberalism in Antebellum America.* New York: New York University Press, 2000.

Fabian, Ann. *Card Sharps, Dream Books, and Bucket Shops: Gambling in Nineteenth-Century America.* Ithaca, N.Y.: Cornell University Press, 1990.

Faust, Drew Gilpin. *The Ideology of Slavery: Proslavery Thought in the Antebellum South, 1830–1860.* Baton Rouge: Louisiana State University Press, 1981.

———. *James Henry Hammond and the Old South: A Design for Mastery.* Baton Rouge: Louisiana State University Press, 1982.

———. *A Sacred Circle: The Dilemma of the Intellectual in the Old South, 1840–1860.* Baltimore: Johns Hopkins University Press, 1977.

Fehrenbacher, Don E. *The Slaveholding Republic: An Account of the United States Government's Relations to Slavery.* Ed. Ward M. McAfee. Oxford: Oxford University Press, 2001.

Finkelman. Paul. *Defending Slavery: Proslavery Thought in the Old South: A Brief History with Documents.* Boston: Bedford/St. Martin's Press, 2003.

———. "The Statute Laws of the Slave South, 1789–1865." Preface. *State Slavery Statutes: Guide to the Microfiche Collection.* By Paul Finkelman. Frederick, Md.: University Publications of America, 1989.

Fisk, Theophilus. *The Bulwark of Freedom. An Oration Delivered at the Universalist Church, in the City of Charleston, S.C., June 28, 1836, on the Anniversary of the Glorious Victory at Fort Moultrie, June 28, 1776.* Charleston, S.C.: Printed for the publishers at the office of the Southern Evangelist, 1836.

Fogel, Robert. *Slavery Debates, 1952–1990: A Retrospective.* Baton Rouge: Louisiana State University Press, 2003.

Fogel, Robert William, and Stanley L. Engerman. *Time on the Cross: The Economics of American Negro Slavery.* New York: Norton, 1989.

Foner, Eric, and Olivia Mahoney. *A House Divided: America in the Age of Lincoln.* New York: Norton, 1990.

Ford, Lacy K. *Origins of Southern Radicalism: The South Carolina Upcountry.* New York: Oxford University Press, 1988.

Fraser, Nancy. "Rethinking the Public Sphere: Contribution to the Critique of Actually Existing Democracy." *The Phantom Public Sphere.* Ed. Bruce Robbins. Minneapolis: University of Minnesota Press, 1993. 1–32.

Freehling, William W. *Prelude to Civil War: The Nullification Controversy in South Carolina.* New York: Harper, 1966.

———. *The Road to Disunion: Secessionists at Bay, 1776–1854.* Vol. 1. New York: Oxford University Press, 1990.

———. *The South vs. the South: How the Anti-Confederate Southerners Shaped the Course of the Civil War.* Oxford: Oxford University Press, 2001.

Freeman, George W. *The Rights and Duties of Slaveholders. Two Discourses Delivered on Sunday, November 27, 1836. In Christ Church, Raleigh, North Carolina.* Raleigh, N.C.: J. Gales, 1836. 5–14.

Fuller, J. F. C. *A Military History of the Western World. Volume II. From the Defeat of the Spanish Armada to the Battle of Waterloo.* New York: De Capo Press, 1955.

Fuller, Wayne Edison. *Morality and the Mail in Nineteenth-Century America.* Urbana: University of Illinois Press, 2003. 39–40.

Furman, Richard. *Rev. Dr. Richard Furman's Exposition of the Views of the Baptists.* Charleston, S.C.: A. E. Miller, 1823.

Gallagher, Gary W. "Introduction." *The Myth of the Lost Cause and Civil War History.* Ed. Gary W. Gallagher and Alan T. Nolan. Bloomington and Indianapolis: Indiana University Press, 2000. 1–10.

Gallinsky, Adam, Joe C. Magee, M. Ena Inesi, and Deborah H Gruenfeld. "Power and Perspectives Not Taken." *Psychological Science* 17, no. 12 (December 2006): 1068–74.

Genovese, Eugene D. *The Political Economy of Slavery: Studies in the Economy and Society of the Slave South.* Middletown, Conn.: Wesleyan University Press, 1989.

Genovese, Eugene D., and Elizabeth Fox-Genovese. *The Mind of the Master Class: History and Faith in the Southern Slaveholders' Worldview.* Cambridge: Cambridge University Press, 2005.

Glatthaar, Joseph T. "Black Glory." *Why the Confederacy Lost.* Ed. Gabor S. Boritt. New York: Oxford University Press, 1992. 145.

Glick, Peter. "Choice of Scapegoats." *On the Nature of Prejudice: Fifty Years after Allport.* Ed. John F. Dovidio, Peter Glick, and Laurie A. Rudman. Malden, Mass.; Oxford: Blackwell, 2005. 244–61.

Goldin, Claudia. "The Economics of Emancipation." *Journal of Economic History* 33 (March 1973): 66–85.

Goldin, Claudia, and Frank Lewis. "The Economic Cost of the American Civil War: Estimates and Implications." *Journal of Economic History* 35 (June 1975): 299–326.

Green, Laurie. *Battling the Plantation Mentality: Memphis and the Black Freedom Struggle.* Chapel Hill: University of North Carolina Press, 2007.

Greenberg, Kenneth S. *Honor and Slavery: Lies, Duels, Noses, Masks, Dressing as a Woman, Gifts, Strangers, Humanitarianism, Death, Slave Rebellions, the Proslavery Argument, Baseball, Hunting, and Gambling in the Old South.* Princeton: Princeton University Press, 1996.

———. *Masters and Statesmen: The Political Culture of American Slavery.* Baltimore: Johns Hopkins University Press, 1985.

Greene, Sally. "Committed upon the body of one negro slave Lydia": Gleanings from the Edenton Trial of *State v. Mann.* Unpublished paper delivered at the symposium "The Perils of Public Homage: *State v. Mann* and Thomas Ruffin in History and Memory," University of North Carolina-Chapel Hill, November 16, 2007.

Grimsted, David. *American Mobbing, 1828–1861: Toward Civil War.* New York: Oxford University Press, 1998.

Guenebalt, J. H., Julien Joseph Virey, and Samuel Thomas von Soemmering, eds. *Natural History of the Negro Race.* Charleston, S.C.: D. J. Dowling, 1837.

Habermas, Jürgen. "A Genealogical Analysis of the Cognitive Content of Morality." *The Inclusion of the Other: Studies of Political Theory.* Cambridge, Mass.: MIT Press, 1998. 3–48.

Hadden, Sally E. *Slave Patrols: Law and Violence in Virginia and the Carolinas.* Cambridge: Harvard University Press, 2001.

Harper, William. *Anniversary Oration.* Washington, D.C.: Duff Green, 1836.

———. *Memoir on Slavery, Read before the Society for the Advancement of Learning, of South Carolina, at Its Annual Meeting at Columbia, 1837.* Charleston, S.C.: J. S. Burges, 1838.

Harrold, Stanley. *The Rise of Aggressive Abolition: Addresses to the Slaves.* Lexington: University Press of Kentucky, 2004.

Hart, James D[avid]. "Nick of the Woods." *The Oxford Companion to American Literature.* 3rd ed. New York: Oxford University Press, 1956.

Haslam, S. Alexander, John Turner, Penelope Oakes, Katherine Reynolds, and Bertjan Doosje. "From Personal Pictures in the Head to Collective Tools in the World: How Shared Stereotypes Allow Groups to Represent and Change Social Reality." *Stereotypes as Explanations: The Formation of Meaningful Beliefs about Social Groups.* Ed. Craig McGarty, Vincent Yzerbyt, and Russell Spears. New York: Cambridge University Press, 2002. 157–85.

[Hayden, Thomas]. *An Appeal to the People of the United States Shewing the Conditions of the Slaves of the South, Contrasted with the Poor Laborers of Europe and America.* Charleston, S.C.: Thos. A. Hayden, 1835.

Haynes, Stephen. *Noah's Curse: The Biblical Justification of American Slavery.* New York: Oxford University Press, 2002.

Held, David. *Models of Democracy.* 2nd ed. Stanford: Stanford University Press, 1996.

Hinks, Peter. *To Awaken My Afflicted Brethren: David Walker and the Problem of Antebellum Slave Resistance.* University Park: Pennsylvania State University Press, 1997.

Hobby, William. *Remarks upon Slavery, Occasioned by Attempts Made to Circulate Improper Publications in the Southern States.* Augusta: Printed at the S. R. Sentinel Office, 1835.

Hodge, Charles. *View of the Subject of Slavery Contained in the Biblical Repertory for April, 1836 in Which the Scriptural Argument, It Is Believed, Is Very Clearly and Justly Exhibited.* Pittsburgh: [A. Jaynes], 1836.

Hofstadter, Richard. *The Paranoid Style in American Politics and Other Essays.* New York: Vintage Books, 1967.

Holland, Edwin. *A Refutation of the Calumnies Circulated against the Southern & Western States, Respecting the Institution and Existence of Slavery among Them. To Which Is Added, a Minute and Particular Account of the Actual State and Condition of Their Negro Population. Together with Historical Notices of All the Insurrections That Have Taken Place since the Settlement of the Country.* Charleston, S.C.: A. E. Miller, 1822.

Holt, Michael. *The Fate of Their Country: Politicians, Slavery Extension, and the Coming of the Civil War.* New York: Hill and Wang, 2004.

———. *The Rise and Fall of the American Whig Party: Jacksonian Politics and the Onset of the Civil War.* New York: Oxford University Press, 1999.

Hook, Andrew. "Introduction." *Waverly.* New York: Viking Press, 1981.

Huston, James L. *Calculating the Value of the Union: Slavery, Property Rights, and the Economic Origins of the Civil War.* Chapel Hill: University of North Carolina Press, 2003.

Ingersoll, Charles. *Inchiquin, the Jesuit's Letters, during a Late Residence in the United States of America: Being a Fragment of a Private Correspondence, Accidentally Discovered in Europe: Containing a Favourable View of the Manners, Literature, and State of Society, of the United States, and a Refutation of Many of the Aspersions Cast upon This Country, by Former Residents and Tourists.* New York: I. Riley, 1810.

Ingraham, Joseph Holt. *The South-West. By a Yankee.* 1835. Vols. 1 & 2. New York: Harper & Brothers, 1835.

James, G. R. *History of Chivalry and the Crusades.* New York: J&J Harper, 1831.

Jenkins, Jeffrey, and Charles Stewart. "Out in the Open: The Emergence of Viva Voce Voting in House Speakership Elections." *Legislative Studies Quarterly* 28 (2003): 481–508.

Johnson, Guion Griffis. *Ante-bellum North Carolina: A Social History.* Chapel Hill: University of North Carolina Press, 1937.

Johnson, Michael. "Denmark Vesey and His Co-Conspirators (in Forum: The Making of a Slave Conspiracy, Part I." *William and Mary Quarterly,* 3rd Ser., 58, no. 4 (October 2001): 915–76.

Johnson, Nan. *Nineteenth-Century Rhetoric in North America.* Carbondale: Southern Illinois University Press, 1991.

Jones, Charles Colcock. *The Religious Instruction of the Negroes. A Sermon, Delivered before Associations of Planters in Liberty and M'Intosh Counties, Georgia.* Princeton, N.J.: Printed by D'Hart & Connolly, 1832.

Jones, Norrece T., Jr. *Born a Child of Freedom, Yet a Slave: Mechanisms of Control and Strategies of Resistance in Antebellum South Carolina.* Hanover: Wesleyan University Press, 1990.

Jones, Thomas. *An Address on the Progress of Manufactures and Internal Improvement, in the United States; and Particulary, on the Advantages to Be Derived from the Employment of Slaves in the Manufacturing of Cotton and Other Goods. Delivered in the Hall of the Franklin Institute, November 6, 1827.* Philadelphia: Published by Judah Dodson; Jesper Harding, 1827.

Julius, Kevin C. *The Abolitionist Decade, 1829-1838: A Year-by-Year History of Early Events in the Antislavery Movement.* Jefferson, N.C.: McFarland & Co., 2004.

Kagan, Donald. *The Peloponnesian War.* New York: Viking, 2003.

Kastely, James. *Rethinking the Rhetorical Tradition: From Plato to Postmodernism.* New Haven: Yale University Press, 1997.

Kilbride, Daniel. "Slavery and Utilitarianism: Thomas Cooper and the Mind of the Old South." *Journal of Southern History* 59, no. 3 (August 1993): 469–86.

Kimmel, Michael. *Manhood in America: A Cultural History.* New York: Free Press, 1996.

Kingsley, Zephaniah. *A Treatise on the Patriarchal, or Co-operative System of Society as It Exists in Some Governments, and Colonies in America, and in the United States, Under the Name of Slavery, with Its Necessity and Advantages.* S.n., 1829.

Kitzhaber, Albert. *Rhetoric in American Colleges, 1850–1900.* Southern Methodist University Press, 1990.

Klemperer, Victor. *The Language of the Third Reich: LTI—Lingua Tertii Imperii: A Philologist's Notebook.* Tr. Martin Brady. New York: Continuum, 2002 (1957).

Kolchin, Peter. *American Slavery: 1619–1877.* New York: Hill and Wang, 1993.

Kraditor, Aileen. *Means and Ends in American Abolitionism: Garrison and His Critics on Strategy and Tactics 1834–1850.* New York: Pantheon Books, 1969.

Lakoff, George. *Don't Think of an Elephant!: Know Your Values and Frame the Debate: The Essential Guide for Progressives.* White River Junction, VT: Chelsea Green Pub., 2004.

Landes, Richard. "Scapegoating." *Encyclopedia of Social History.* Ed. Peter N. Stearns. Vol. 780. Garland Reference Library of Social Science. New York: Garland, 1994.

Laurens, Edward. *A Letter to the Honorable Whitemarsh B. Seabrook.* Charleston, S.C.: A. E. Miller, 1835.

Leckie, Robert. *George Washington's War: The Saga of the American Revolution.* New York: HarperCollins, 1992.

Lewis, James E., Jr. *John Quincy Adams: Policymaker for the Union.* Wilmington, Del.: Scholarly Resources, 2001.

Lewis, Seth. *Abolition Reviewed, Being a Further Exposure of the False, and Most Dangerous and Mischevious Doctrines and Proceedings of the Abolitionists.* New Orleans: Executive Committee of the Conservative Association of Citizens of Louisiana, 1830.

———. *A Review of Abolitionism, or, The Question of Slavery, as It Exists in the United States.* New Orleans: Conservative Society of Citizens of Louisiana, 1830.

Longaker, Mark Garrett. *Rhetoric and the Republic: Politics, Civic Discourse, and Education in Early America.* Tuscaloosa: The University of Alabama Press, 2007.

Lowance, Mason I., Jr. *A House Divided: The Antebellum Slavery Debates, 1776–1854.* Princeton: Princeton University Press, 2003.

Maas, A., D. Salvi, L. Arcuri, and G. Semin. "Language Use in Intergroup Contexts:

The Linguistic Intergroup Bias." *Journal of Personality and Social Psychology* 57, no. 6 (1989): 981–93.

Man, Thomas. *A Picture of Woonsocket, or, The Truth in Its Nudity: To Which Are Added Translations from the Best French, Spanish and Italian Writers.* N.p. printed for the author, 1835.

March, David. *History of Missouri.* New York: Lewis Historical Pub. Co., 1967.

Martineau, Harriet. *Society in America.* London: Saunders and Otley, 1837.

Mason, Matthew. *Slavery and Politics in the Early American Republic.* Chapel Hill: University of North Carolina Press, 2006.

Mayer, Henry. *All on Fire: William Lloyd Garrison and the Abolition of Slavery.* New York: St. Martin's Press, 1998.

McDuffie, George. *The Communication from His Excellency, Governor McDuffie, Inclosing a Report of the Joint Committee on Federal Relations of the State of South Carolina to the Governor of Maryland, Relative to Incendiary Abolitionists.* Annapolis: Wm. M'Nier, 1836.

McPherson, James. *Battle Cry of Freedom: The Civil War Era.* New York: Oxford University Press, 1988.

Merkel, Benjamin. "The Abolition Aspects of Missouri's Antislavery Controversy, 1819-1865." *Missouri Historical Review* 44, no. 3 (April 1950): 232–53.

Meyers, Marvin. *The Jacksonian Persuasion; Politics and Belief.* New York: Vintage Books, 1960.

Miles, Edwin A. "Andrew Jackson and Senator George Poindexter." *Journal of Southern History* 24, no. 1 (February 1958): 51–66.

Miller, Thomas. *The Formation of College English: Rhetoric and Belles-Lettres in the British Cultural Provinces.* Pittsburgh: University of Pittsburgh Press, 1997.

Miller, William Lee. *Arguing about Slavery: The Great Battle in the United States Congress.* New York: A. A. Knopf, 1996.

Mississippi Legislature. *Communication from the Governor, Transmitting a Preamble and Resolutions Adopted by the Legislature of Mississippi, Relative to the Persons, Denominated Abolitionists.* Albany, N.Y.: s.n., 1836.

Mitchell, Reid. "The Perseverance of the Soldiers." *Why the Confederacy Lost.* Ed. Gabor S. Boritt. New York: Oxford University Press, 1992. 109–32.

Monk, Maria. *Awful Disclosures of Maria Monk, as Exhibited in a Narrative of Her Sufferings during a Residence of Five Years as a Novice, and Two Years as a Black Nun, in the Hotel Dieu Nunnery at Montreal.* New York: Howe & Bates, 1836.

Morris, Thomas. *Southern Slavery and the Law, 1619–1860.* Chapel Hill: University of North Carolina Press, 1996.

Morse, John. *John Quincy Adams.* Boston: Houghton, Mifflin, 1898.

Morse, Samuel. *Foreign Conspiracy against the Liberties of the United States; the Numbers of Brutus, Originally Published in the New York Observer, Revised and Corrected with Notes, by the Author.* New York: Leavitt, Lord, & Co., G. C. Carvill & Co.; Boston: Crocker & Brewster, 1835.

Mouffe, Chantal. *The Return of the Political.* London: Verso, 1993.

Nagel, Paul C. *John Quincy Adams: A Public Life, a Private Life.* Cambridge: Harvard University Press, 2000.

Nelson, Todd. *Psychology of Prejudice.* 2nd ed. New York: Allyn & Bacon, 2005.

Nisbett, Richard E., and Dov Cohen. *Culture of Honor: The Psychology of Violence in the South.* Boulder, Colo.: Westview Press, 1996.

Newman, Leonard, and Tracy Caldwell. "Allport's 'Living Inkblots': The Role of Defensive Projection in Stereotyping and Prejudice." *On the Nature of Prejudice: Fifty Years after Allport.* Ed. John F. Dovidio, Peter Glick, and Laurie A. Rudman. Malden, Mass., and Oxford: Blackwell, 2005. 377–92.

Niven, John. *John C. Calhoun and the Price of Union.* Baton Rouge: Louisiana State University Press, 1988.

———. *Martin Van Buren: The Romantic Age of American Politics.* New York: Oxford University Press, 1983.

Nolan, Alan T. "The Anatomy of the Myth." *The Myth of the Lost Cause and Civil War History.* Gary W. Gallagher and Alan T. Nolan, eds. Bloomington and Indianapolis: Indiana University Press, 2000. 11–34.

Nolan, Alan T., and Gary W. Gallagher. *The Myth of the Lost Cause and Civil War History.* Bloomington: Indiana University Press, 2000.

Ober, Benjamin. *Slavery a Lecture Delivered before the Lyceum in Attleborough, Jan. 4th 1838.* Pawtucket, R.I.: R. Sherman, 1838.

O'Connor, John Michael. *A Treatise on the Science of War and Fortification: Composed for the Use of the Imperial Polytechnick School . . . and Translated for the War Department, for the Use of the Military Academy of the United States. To Which Is Added, A Summary of the Principles and Maxims of Grand Tactics and Operations.* New York: Printed by J. Seymour, 1817.

Olsen, Christopher. *Political Culture and Secession in Mississippi: Masculinity, Honor, and the Antiparty Tradition, 1830–1860.* New York: Oxford University Press, 2000.

Orwell, George. *1984.* New York: New American Library of World Literature, 1961 (1949).

Owsley, Frank L. "Egocentric Sectionalism." *The Causes of the Civil War.* 3rd rev. ed. New York: Simon & Schuster, 1991. 56–58.

Parsons, Lynn H. *John Quincy Adams.* Madison, Wisc.: Madison House, 1998.

Patterson, Orlando. *Rituals of Blood: Consequences of Slavery in Two American Centuries.* Washington, D.C.: Civitas/CounterPoint, 1998.

Paulding, James Kirke. *Letters from the South.* Vols. I & II. New York: AMS Press, (1817) 1973.

———. *Slavery in the United States.* New York: Harper & Brothers, 1836.

Phillips, Kevin. *The Cousins' Wars: Religion, Politics, and the Triumph of Anglo-America.* New York: Basic Books, 1999.

Philpot, Francis. *Facts for White Americans with a Plain Hint for Dupes, and a Bone to Pick for White Nigger Demagogues and Amalgamation Abolitionists, including the Parentage, Brief Career, and Execution, of Amalgamation Abolitionism, Whose Fu-*

neral Sermon Was Preached at Washington on the 7th of February, 1839. Philadelphia: s.n., 1839.

Pinckney, Charles Cotesworth. *An Address Delivered in Charleston, before the Agricultural Society of South Carolina, on Tuesday, the 18th of August, 1829.* Charleston, S.C.: A. E. Miller, 1829.

Pinckney, Henry Laurens. *An Address to the Electors of Charleston District.* Charleston, S.C.: Burges & Honour, 1836.

———. *An Oration, Delivered in the Independent, or Congregational Church, Charleston: before the State Rights & Free Trade Party, the State Society of Cincinnati, the Revolution Society, the '76 Association, and the State Volunteers: on the 4th of July, 1833, Being the 57th Anniversary of American Independence.* Charleston, S.C.: A. E. Miller, 1833.

———. *Remarks of the Hon. H. L. Pinckney, of South Carolina, on the Resolution Offered by Him Relative to the Abolition of Slavery: Delivered in the House of Representatives, Monday, February 8, 1836.* Washington, D.C.: Printed by Galles and Seaton, 1836.

Pinckney, Thomas. *Reflections Occasioned by the Late Disturbances in Charleston.* Charleston, S.C.: A. E. Miller, 1822.

Pratto, Felicia, Jim Sidanius, Lisa Stallworth, and Bertram Malle. "Social Dominance Orientation: A Personality Variable Predicting Social and Political Attitudes." *Stereotypes and Prejudice: Essential Readings.* Ed. Charles Stangor. Philadelphia: Taylor & Francis, 2000. 259–88.

Pronin, Emily, Justin Kruger, and Kenneth Savtisky. "You Don't Know Me, but I Know You: The Illusion of Asymmetric Insight." *Journal of Personality and Social Psychology* 81, no. 4 (October 2001): 639–56.

Ransom, Roger. *Conflict and Compromise: The Political Economy of Slavery, Emancipation, and the American Civil War.* New York: Cambridge University Press, 1989.

Ratner, Lorman A., and Dwight L. Teeter Jr. *Fanatics and Fire Eaters: Newspapers and the Coming of the Civil War.* Urbana: University of Illinois Press, 2003.

Reed, Rebecca. *Six Months in a Convent, or, the Narrative of Rebecca Theresa Reed Who Was under the Influence of the Roman Catholics about Two Years, and an Inmate of the Ursuline Convent on Mount Benedict, Charlestown, Mass., Nearly Six Months, in the Years 1831–2.* Boston: Russell, Odiorne & Metcalf; New York: Leavitt, Lord, 1835.

Reisigl, Martin, and Ruth Wodak. *Discourse and Discrimination: Rhetorics of Racism and Antisemitism.* London: Routledge, 2001.

Rhett, Barnwell. *Address to the People of Beaufort and Colleton Districts upon the Subject of Abolition.* Washington, D.C.: s.n., 1838.

Richards, Leonard L. *The California Gold Rush and the Coming of the Civil War.* New York: Alfred A. Knopf, 2007.

———. *Gentlemen of Property and Standing: Anti-Abolition Mobs in Jacksonian America.* London: Oxford University Press, 1971.

———. *The Life and Times of Congressman John Quincy Adams.* New York: Oxford University Press, 1986.

———. *Slave Power: The Free North and Southern Domination, 1780–1860.* Baton Rouge: Louisiana State University Press, 2000.

Roberts-Miller, Patricia. *Deliberate Conflict: Argument, Political Theory, and Composition Classes.* Carbondale: Southern Illinois University Press, 2004.

———. "Agonism, Wrangling, and John Quincy Adams." *Rhetoric Review* 25, no. 2 (2006): 141–61.

———. "John Quincy Adams' Amistad Argument: The Problem of Outrage; Or, the Constraints of Decorum." *Rhetoric Society Quarterly* 32, no. 2 (2002): 5–26.

———. "Robert Montgomery Bird and the Rhetoric of the Improbable Cause." *Rhetoric Society Quarterly* 35, no. 1 (winter 2005): 73–90.

Rubin, Louis D. "Foreword." *Secret and Sacred: The Diaries of James Henry Hammond, a Southern Slaveholder.* Ed. Carol Bleser. Columbia: University of South Carolina Press, 1997.

Rucker, Derek D., and Anthony R. Pratkanis. "Projection as an Interpersonal Influence Tactic: The Effects of the Pot Calling the Kettle Black." *Personality and Social Psychology Bulletin* 27, no. 11 (November 2001): 1494–1507.

Russell, Greg. *John Quincy Adams and the Public Virtues of Democracy.* Columbia: University of Missouri Press, 1995.

Savage, W. Sherman. "The Contest over Slavery between Illinois and Missouri." *Journal of Negro History* 28, no. 3 (July 1943): 311–25.

Scarborough, William. *Masters of the Big House: Elite Slaveholders of the Mid-Nineteenth-Century South.* Baton Rouge: Louisiana State University Press, 2006.

[Schley, William]. *Communication from the Governor of Georgia, Relative to the Abolitionists of the South.* Annapolis: Wm. M'Neir, 1836.

Schudson, Michael. *The Good Citizen: A History of American Civic Life.* New York: Free Press, 1998.

Scott, Walter. *Waverley.* Andrew Hook, ed. New York: Viking Press, 1981.

Seabrook, Whitemarsh. *An Appeal to the People of the Northern and Eastern States, on the Subject of Negro Slavery in South Carolina.* S.n., 1834.

———. *A Concise View of the Critical Situation, and Future Prospects of the Slave-holding States.* Charleston, S.C.: A. E. Miller, 1825.

———. *An Essay on the Management of Slaves and Especially, on Their Religious Instruction: Read before the Agricultucal [sic] Society of St. John's Colleton.* Charleston, S.C.: A. E. Miller, 1834.

Sidanius, Jim, Felicia Pratto, and Colette van Laar. "Social Dominance Theory: Its Agenda and Method." *Political Psychology* 25, no. 6 (December 2004): 845–80.

Simms, William Gilmore. *Slavery in America: Being a Brief Review of Miss Martineau on that Subject.* Richmond: T. W. White, 1838.

Sims, Alexander Dromgole. *A View of Slavery, Moral and Political.* Charleston, S.C.: A. E. Miller, 1834.

Sinha, Manisha. *The Counterrevolution of Slavery: Politics and Ideology in Antebellum South Carolina.* Chapel Hill: University of North Carolina Press, 2000.

Sloane, Thomas. *On the Contrary: The Protocol of Traditional Rhetoric.* Washington, D.C.: Catholic University Press, 1997.

Slotkin, Richard. *Regeneration through Violence: The Mythology of the American Frontier, 1600–1860.* Middletown, Conn.: Wesleyan University Press, 1973.

Smith, Henry Nash. *Virgin Land: The American West as Symbol and Myth.* Cambridge, Mass.: Harvard University Press, 1950.

Smith, Mark. *Debating Slavery: Economy and Society in the Antebellum American South.* Cambridge, Mass.: Cambridge University Press, 1998.

Smith, Mark M. *How Race Is Made: Slavery, Segregation, and the Senses.* Chapel Hill: University of North Carolina Press, 2006.

Smylie, James. *A Review of a Letter from the Presbytery of Chillicothe to the Presbytery of Mississippi on the Subject of Slavery.* Woodville, Miss.: Wm. A. Norris, 1836.

Snay, Mitchell. *Gospel of Disunion: Religion and Separatism in the Antebellum South.* New York: Cambridge University Press, 1993.

Sperber, Hans, and James Tidwell. "Words and Phrases in American Politics." *American Speech* 25, no. 2 (May 1950): 91–100.

Stampp, Kenneth Milton, ed. *The Causes of the Civil War.* New York: Touchstone, 1991.

———. *The Imperiled Union.* New York: Oxford University Press, 1980.

Steele, John. *The Substance of an Address.* Washington, Guernsey Co., Ohio: Hamilton Robb, 1830.

Sullivan, T. R. *Letters against the Immediate Abolition of Slavery, Addressed to the Free Blacks of the Non-Slave-Holding States.* Boston: Hilliard, Gray and Co., 1835.

Symonds, Craig L. "Rank and Rancour in the Confederate Navy." *Military History Quarterly* 14, no. 2 (winter 2002): 14–19.

Tadman, Michael. *Speculators and Slaves: Masters, Traders, and Slaves in the Old South.* Madison: University of Wisconsin Press, 1989.

Tate, Adam L. *Conservatism and Southern Intellectuals, 1789–1861.* University of Missouri Press, 2005.

Taylor, William R. *Cavalier and Yankee: The Old South and American National Character.* Cambridge: Harvard University Press, 1979.

Thomas, William. *The Enemies of the Constitution Discovered.* New York: Leavitt, Lord, & Co., 1835.

Thucydides. *The History of the Peloponnesian War.* New York: Penguin Classics, 1954.

Tise, Larry. *Proslavery: A History of the Defense of Slavery in America, 1701–1840.* Athens: University of Georgia Press, 1987.

Tsesis, Alexander. *Destructive Messages: How Hate Speech Paves the Way for Harmful Social Movements.* New York: New York University Press, 2002.

Tucker, St. George. *Blackstone's Commentaries.* South Hackensack, N.J.: Rothman Reprints; New York: Augustus M. Kelley, Publishers, 1969 (1803).

Tushnet, Mark. *Slave Law in the American South: State v. Mann in History and Literature.* Lawrence: University of Kansas Press, 2003.

Van Buren, Martin. *Opinions of Martin Van Buren, Vice President of the United States,*

Upon the Powers and Duties of Congress in Reference to the Abolition of Slavery Either in the Slaveholing States or in the District of Columbia. Washington, D.C.: Blair & Rives, Printers, 1836.

Van Eemeren, Frans, and Rob Grootendorst. *Argumentation, Communication, and Fallacies: A Pragma-dialectical Perspective.* New York: LEA, 1992.

Vaughan, John. *Negro Slavery.* Philadelphia: s.n., 1833.

"Vindex." *Vindex on the Liability of the Abolitionists to Criminal Punishment, and on the Duty of Non-slave-holding States to Suppress Their Efforts.* Charleston, S.C.: A. E. Miller, 1835.

Walker, David. *David Walker's Appeal to the Coloured Citizens of the World.* Ed. Peter Hinks. University Park: Pennsylvania State University Press, 2000.

Walsh, Robert. *An Appeal from the Judgments of Great Britain.* Mitchell, Ames, and White; William Brown, printer, 1819. New York: Negro Universities Press, 1969, reprint.

———. *Free Remarks on the Spirit of the Federal Constitution, the Practice of the Federal Government, and the Obligations of the Union, Respecting the Exclusion of Slavery from the Territories and New States.* Philadelphia: A. Finley, 1819.

Walton, Augustus. *A History of the Detection, Conviction, Life and Designs of John A. Murel, The Great Western Land Pirate; Together with His Scheme of Villainy, and Plan of Exciting a Negro Rebellion. Also a Catalogue of the Names of Four Hundred and Fifty-five of His Mystic Clan Fellows and Followers, and a Statement of Their Efforts for the Destruction of Virgil A. Stewart, the Young Man Who Detected Him.* Cincinnati: Augustus Q. Walton, 1836.

Walzer, Arthur. "Aristotle's Rhetoric, Dialogism, and Contemporary Research in Composition." *Rhetoric Review* 16 (1997): 45–58.

Weigley, Russell F. "American Strategy from Its Beginnings through the First World War." *Makers of Modern Strategy from Machiavelli to the Nuclear Age.* Ed. Peter Paret. Princeton, N.J.: Princeton University Press: 1986. 408–43.

Westbrook, B. Evelyn. "Debating Both Sides: What Nineteenth-Century College Literary Societies Can Teach Us about Critical Pedagogies." *Rhetoric Review* 21, no. 4 (2002): 339–56.

Whitaker, Daniel Kimball. *Reflections on Domestic Slavery, Elicited by Judge Harper's Anniversary Oration.* Charleston, S.C.: n.p., 1836.

Widmer, Ted. *American Presidents: Martin Van Buren.* New York: Times Books, Henry Holt and Company, 2004.

Wiecek, William M. *The Sources of Anti-Slavery Constitutionalism in America, 1760–1848.* Ithaca: Cornell University Press, 1977.

Wiethoff, William. *Crafting the Overseer's Image.* Columbia: University of South Carolina Press, 2006.

———. *The Insolent Slave.* Columbia: University of South Carolina Press, 2002.

Williams, Joseph. *An oration delivered before the citizens of the town of New-Bedford Fourth of July, 1835.* New Bedford, Mass.: J. G. W. Pope, 1835.

Wilson, Michael T. "'Saturnalia of Blood': Masculine Self-Control and American Indians in the Frontier Novel." *Studies in American Fiction* 33, no. 2 (autumn 2005): 131–46.

Winston, Robert P. "Bird's Bloody Romance: Nick of the Woods." *Southern Studies: An Interdisciplinary Journal of the South.* 23, no. 1 (spring 1984): 71–90.

Wood, Gordon. *Radicalism of the American Revolution.* New York: Vintage Books, 1993.

Wyatt-Brown, Bertram. "The Abolitionists' Postal Campaign." *Journal of Negro History* 50 (October 1965): 227–30.

———. *The Shaping of Southern Culture: Honor, Grace, and War, 1760s–1880s.* Chapel Hill: University of North Carolina Press, 2001.

Wyly-Jones, Susan. "The 1835 Anti-Abolition Meetings in the South: A New Look at the Controversy over the Abolition Postal Campaign." *Civil War History* 47 no. 4 (December 2001).

Yeadon, Richard. *The Amenability of Northern Incendiaries, as Well to Southern as to Northern Laws, without Prejudice to the Right of Free Discussion; to Which Is Added an Inquiry into the Lawfulness of Slavery, under the Jewish and Christian Dispensations, Together with Other Views of the Same Subject, Being a Series of Essays, Originally Published in the Charleston Courier, by Richard Yeadon, One of the Editors.* Charleston, S.C.: T. A. Hayden, 1835.

Young, Jeffrey Robert. *Domesticating Slavery: The Master Class in Georgia and South Carolina, 1670–1837.* Chapel Hill: University of North Carolina Press, 1999.

———. "Ideology and Death on a Savannah River Rice Plantation, 1833–1867: Paternalism Amidst 'a Good Supply of Disease and Pain.'" *Journal of Southern History* 59, no. 4 (November 1993): 673–706.

Index